KT-226-567

View across the Danube from the quayside at Pest. On the far side of the river, the Royal Palace ● *70* ▲ *190* can be seen as it was before its restoration in the late 19th century; below it are the arcades enclosing the palace gardens ▲ *182*.

At the end of the 19th century the Drechsler House ▲ *144* (opposite the State Opera House on Andrássy út) had a popular café on the ground floor. It is currently being converted into a luxury hotel.

Leopold Boulevard (Lipót körút) – now St Stephen's Boulevard (Szent István körút) ▲ *164* – as it was in the late 19th century. Houses were just beginning to be built on Rózsadomb (Rose Hill) ▲ *211*, which can be seen in the distance.

This photograph of a courtyard in the Belváros district ▲ *116* was taken toward the end of the 19th century. One of the twin towers of the Inner City Parish Church ▲ *120* is just visible above the rooftops.

HUNGARY

BUDAPEST

EVERYMAN GUIDES

Published in collaboration with the Hungarian Tourist Office (Paris)
and the Budapest Tourist Office

ABOUT THE AUTHORS

Mohammed Bansar
Art historian and journalist, graduate of Lóránd Eötvös University. Author of the Architecture section, and the pages on Parliament and the Király Baths.
Beatrix Básics
Author of the pages on the Hungarian National Museum.
Sándor Bodó
Director of the Budapest History Museum and author of the pages on the museum.
Péter Buza (1)
Journalist and lecturer. He has published around twenty books on Hungary, mainly on Budapest. Author of the Buda itineraries.
Livia Fuchs (2)
Dance historian, senior lecturer at the Hungarian Academy of Dance, dance critic for the daily newspaper *Hungarian News*. Author of the spread on Hungarian dance.
Mariann Gergely and Árpád Mikó
Authors of the pages on the Hungarian National Gallery.
Annamaria Keller
(3) Author of the texts on the Academy of Music, where she is head of international relations.
Sophie Képès
Writer, translator (from Hungarian) and literary critic. Author of the pages on the Hungarian language.
Anthony Krause (4)
Graduate in history from the École Normale Supérieure in Paris, currently teaching at INALCO (National Institute of Oriental Languages and Civilisations). Head of the book section in the cultural department of the French Embassy in Budapest (1992-4). Author of the Pest itineraries, 'The baths of Budapest' and 'Budapest, capital of the Hungarian cinema'.
Florence La Bruyère (5)
Graduate of the Institute of Political Sciences (Paris) and the University of Cambridge (England), Hungarian correspondent for the French ublications *La Croix* and *Libération,* and Radio France. Responsible for reading and updating the guide.
Anna Lakos
Involved in theater- and dance-related projects at the French Institute. Author of the spreads on 'Hungarian theater' and 'Opera in Budapest'.
Guilhem Lesaffre
Naturalist and co-author of the Nature section.
Katalin Madas (6)
Forestry engineer and PhD who worked for twenty years in the field of nature conservation in the Budapest region. She is currently involved in forestry management and planning in the Hungarian Forest Service. Member of the 'Joventry' committee of the Hungarian Academy of Sciences. Co-author of the Nature section.
Marcel Marnat (7)
After studying sciences, Marcel Marnat made a name for himself writing articles on painting, cinema, fringe literature and especially records and music. He also broadcasts on radio and has published books on Mussorgsky, Stravinsky, Beethoven and Ravel. Between 1978 and 1992 he produced programs for France Musique. Author of the spread on 'Hungarian music'.
Miklós Mátyássy
(8) Born (1959) in Budapest, he has lived in Paris since 1981. Journalist and translator. Since 1994, he has edited the Central- and Eastern-European column of the French weekly, *Courrier international*. Author of the texts on 'Hungarian photographers', 'The Danube: banks and bridges' and 'Around Budapest'.
Judit Pataki (9)
Curator of the Museum of Applied Arts, she has written several publications or the museum, including a CD-ROM on 'Applied arts and crafts'. Author of the pages on the Museum of Applied Arts.
Yannick Penagos (10)
Multimedia writer-reporter.
He collaborated on the writing of the Practical Information section.
Krisztina Rády (11)
Graduate of the universities of Budapest and Lisbon (Faculty of Arts), and the Institute of European Studies in Paris. Former head of artistic activities at the French Institute in Budapest and the Hungarian Institute in Paris. Author of the 'Specialties' spread.
Gilles Sensini
Graduate of the schools of Architecture and Fine Arts in Versailles. Member of the Paris urban-development unit. Author of 'From houses to apartment blocks'.
Vilmos Tátrai (12)
Born (1946) in Budapest. Graduate in art history and classical philology from the Eötvös Lóránd University Arts Faculty, and assistant director of the Museum of Fine Arts in Budapest. He edited the museum's general catalogue on Italian, French, Spanish and Greek paintings. Author of the pages on the Museum of Fine Arts.
András Török (13)
Author, lecturer, minister for culture. Former dissident who became assistant minister for culture and president of the national-heritage department. He has founded a national photographic center, and an institute of modern art in Budapest of which he is also the president. Author of *Budapest: A Critical Guide.* Author of 'Profile of Budapest' and 'The café tradition'.
Annamária Vígh (14)
Historian specializing in heraldry, head curator of the Budapest History Museum and director of the Kiscell Museum. Author of the History section, and the pages on Heroes' Square and the Kiscell Museum.
József Vinkó (15)
Journalist, playwright, translator, editor, producer. Author of the Óbuda itineraries.
Paula Zsidi
Graduate in art history and archaeology from the Budapest University Faculty of Arts. Director of archaeological excavations within the context of the project for the development of Roman Budapest. Director of the Aquincum Museum since 1989, and author of the pages on the museum.

Everyman Guides are published by Alfred A. Knopf, New York

Completely revised and updated in 2006

Series editors
Clémence Jacquinet and Shelley Wanger

Translated by
Wendy Allatson

Typeset and production by
Adrian McLaughlin

Edited by
Peter Leek

Printed and bound in Italy by
Editoriale Lloyd

Update material translated and edited by
Clive Unger-Hamilton and Sandra Pisano

Everyman Guides
Northburgh house
10 Northburgh Street
London EC1V 0AT
guides@everyman.uk.com

ORIGINAL FRENCH EDITORIAL TEAM
Architecture: Bruno Lenormand
Nature: Frédéric Bony
Photography: Patrick Léger
Editor: Patrick Jézéquel
Layout: Carole Gaborit
Consultant: Yannick Penagos
Production: Catherine Bourrabier

ILLUSTRATIONS
Nature : Jean Chevallier, François Desbordes, Claire Felloni, Catherine Lachaux, Alban Larousse, Pascal Robin
Architecture : Philippe Biard, Philippe Candé, Jean-Marc Lanusse, Maurice Pommier, Claude Quiec, Jean-François Péneau, Christian Rivière, Jean-Sylvain Roveri, Amato Soro
Itineraries: Philippe Biard (Parliament, background illustrations), Jean-Marc Lanusse ('The Danube: banks and bridges'), Amato Soro ('Király Baths')

TRANSLATION
Beata Huber, Anna Kárász, Sophie Képès, Bernadette Nozarian, Krisztina Rády

MAPS
Édigraphie

We would like to thank:
Krisztina Rády, Odile George, Annamária Vígh, Florence La Bruyère, Sophie Képès, Frédérique Hugot, Thierry Hugot, Ferenc Aczél, Réka Győrfi and János-Pál Hárricz for their patience and very precious help.
And we would also like to thank Lajos Menyhart, Agnès Vatin, György Ifju, Attila Laszlo, Katalin Madas, Zsuzsa Medgyes, András Török and Emmanuelle Sacchet.

All information contained in this guide has been approved by the many specialists who have contributed to its production.

CONTENTS

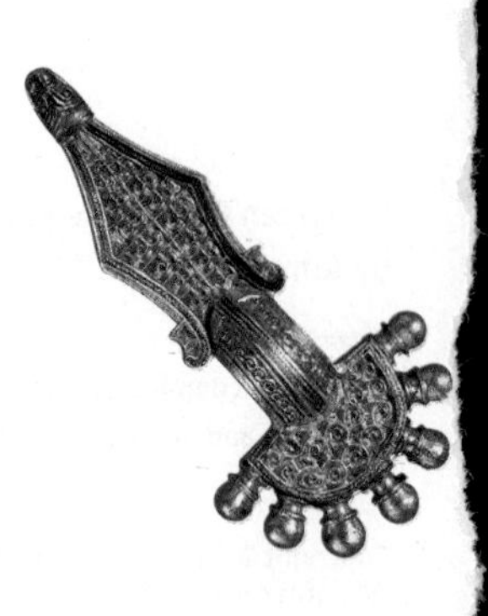

CONTENTS

BELVÁROS

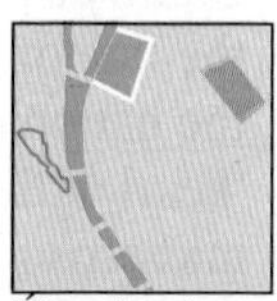

ÚJLIPÓTVÁROS

TERÉZVÁROS

VÁROSLIGET

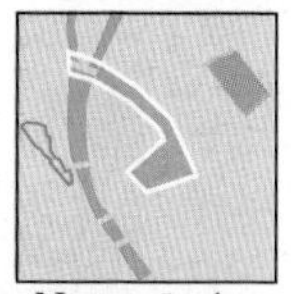

NAGYKÖRÚT

NAGYKÖRÚT

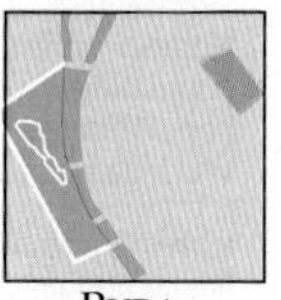

BUDA

ÓBUDA

Budapest's size and imposing character are due to the fact that it was conceived as the capital of a country much larger than present-day Hungary. Today around 20 percent of the country's population live in the capital, where the rate of unemployment is well below the national average. The 'Pearl of the Danube' is a microcosm of the country's geography. On the left bank of the Danube the lower town of Pest stretches to the edge of the Great Plain (Nagyalföld), while on the right bank the steep hills of the upper town of Buda are the last bastions of the mountains of Transdanubia (Dunántúl).

FACTS AND FIGURES

Year of foundation: 1873 (following the unification of the towns of Óbuda, Buda and Pest ● 29)
Surface area: 203 square miles
Number of districts (*kerület*): 23
Population: 1,695,000 (and declining)
Population density: 9,189 inhabitants / sq mile
Working population: approx. 690,000

INDUSTRY Smoke from the factories of Csepel Island no longer drifts across the city. With their closure in 1989, Budapest's role in Hungarian industry was considerably reduced; shopping centers have been built on some of the abandoned industrial sites. The city now has a fast-developing service sector (especially information technology).

THE TWO FACES OF BUDAPEST
Although destined to become a major banking and financial center in the 21st century, the Hungarian capital has nevertheless managed to retain a certain provincial charm. Only a stone's throw from the city center you can go skiing or gather wild lilac.

'Budapest is the loveliest city on the Danube. It has a crafty way of being its own stage-set, like Vienna, but also has a robust substance and a vitality unknown to its Austrian rival.'

Claudio Magris

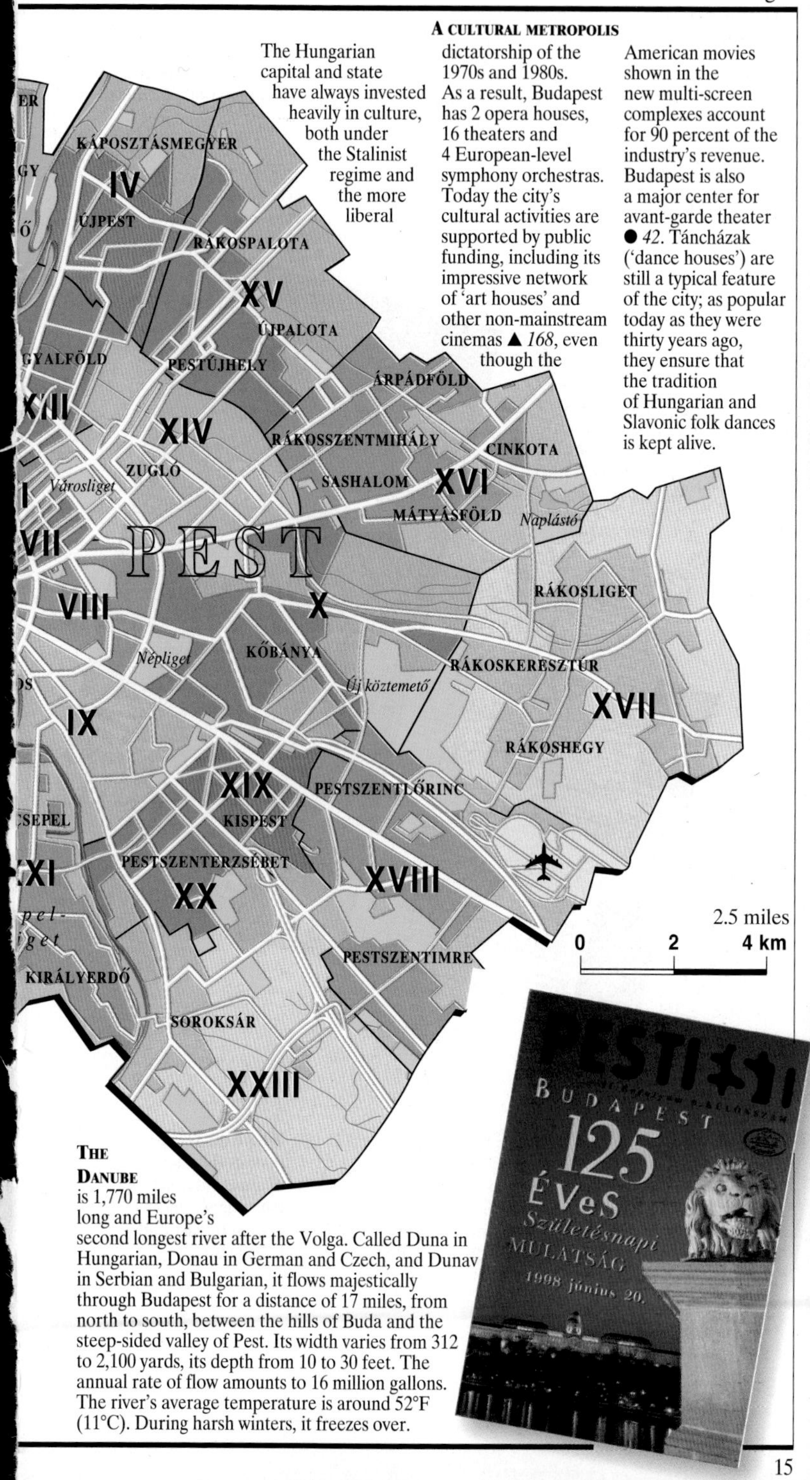

A cultural metropolis

The Hungarian capital and state have always invested heavily in culture, both under the Stalinist regime and the more liberal dictatorship of the 1970s and 1980s. As a result, Budapest has 2 opera houses, 16 theaters and 4 European-level symphony orchestras. Today the city's cultural activities are supported by public funding, including its impressive network of 'art houses' and other non-mainstream cinemas ▲ *168*, even though the American movies shown in the new multi-screen complexes account for 90 percent of the industry's revenue. Budapest is also a major center for avant-garde theater ● *42*. Táncházak ('dance houses') are still a typical feature of the city; as popular today as they were thirty years ago, they ensure that the tradition of Hungarian and Slavonic folk dances is kept alive.

The Danube

is 1,770 miles long and Europe's second longest river after the Volga. Called Duna in Hungarian, Donau in German and Czech, and Dunav in Serbian and Bulgarian, it flows majestically through Budapest for a distance of 17 miles, from north to south, between the hills of Buda and the steep-sided valley of Pest. Its width varies from 312 to 2,100 yards, its depth from 10 to 30 feet. The annual rate of flow amounts to 16 million gallons. The river's average temperature is around 52°F (11°C). During harsh winters, it freezes over.

HOW TO USE THIS GUIDE

The symbols at the top of each page refer to the different parts of the guide.

■ NATURE SECTION

● ENCYCLOPEDIC SECTION

▲ ITINERARIES

◆ PRACTICAL INFORMATION

The mini-map locates the particular itinerary within the wider area covered by the guide.

The itinerary map shows main points of interest along the way and is intended to help you find your bearings.

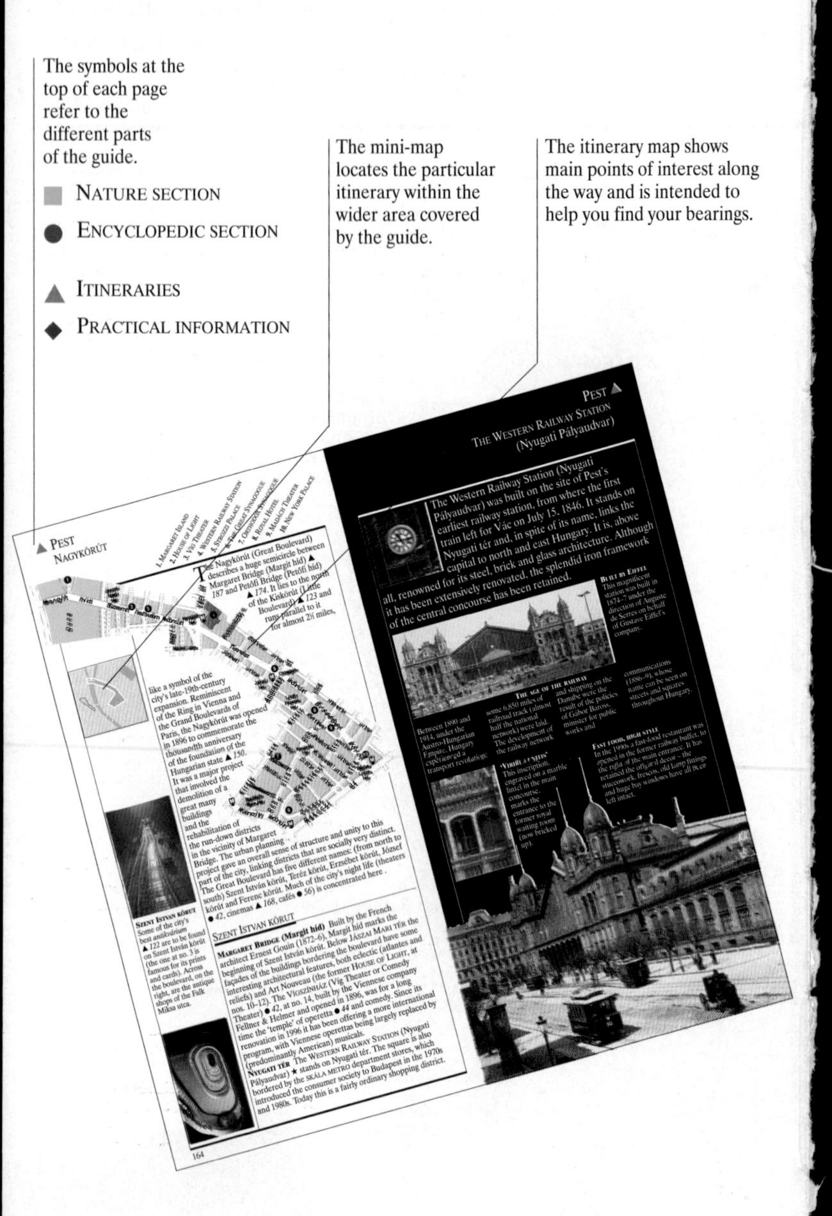

●▲■◆ The symbols alongside a title or within the text itself provide cross-references to a theme or place dealt with elsewhere in the guide.

★ The star symbol signifies that a particular area has been singled out by the publishers for its special beauty, atmosphere or cultural interest.

Where the layout permits the names of museums, squares, monuments etc. are in both English and Hungarian.

NATURE

Katalin Madas, Guilhem Lesaffre

On leaving Austria, the Danube enters a narrow pass at Esztergom, before describing a huge meander and flowing south to Budapest. Here, despite its urban surroundings, it creates an attractive environment for wildlife – especially for birds, which vary according to the season. In particular, the river valley attracts the migratory birds that spend fall and spring on the eastern fringes of Europe, en route for their Mediterranean overwintering sites. During the winter months, when the region's lakes are frozen over, the Danube welcomes aquatic species; the broader stretches of the river, in places as much as 655 yards across, make an ideal habitat for waterfowl and divers.

COOT
Coots dive to find food on the riverbed. They "run" across the surface when taking off.

GRAY WAGTAIL
In winter this elegant and fairly tame member of the wagtail family frequents quays and embankments.

TUFTED DUCK
This small diver, with its characteristic two-tone plumage, is a winter visitor.

POCHARD
In winter these divers live in small groups on the river. They often remain submerged for half a minute or longer.

BLACK-HEADED GULL
In winter, when the Danube rings with its cries, this gull no longer has a black head, as it does during the mating season.

KINGFISHER
Kingfishers are most widely seen during the fall.

BREAM
In the evening bream can be seen feeding near the river banks.

CARP
The females lay their eggs on the underwater plants along the river banks.

CATFISH
Older specimens can reach lengths of over 6 feet.

The five islands of Budapest have retained some of their original appearance. You can explore them on foot, or take a boat trip round them. The best preserved of the five is Háros, although due to the partial silting of the Danube in the early 20th century, it is now a peninsula rather than an island. Its flood forest of willows and poplars is a designated nature reserve. Csepel, the largest of the islands, has several nature reserves; other interesting features include its 'floating marsh' – a thick raft of aquatic plants, in a bay on the 'Little Danube' – and the Tamariska dunes, with their rare plants.

Gray heron
When they are not fishing, herons perch in the trees along the river bank.

Little bittern
This unobtrusive migratory heron hides in the reed beds.

Mute swan
During the nesting season the male is extremely aggressive toward intruders.

BLACK POPLAR
Wet river valleys provide the ideal environment for this tree.

COMMON ASH
The ash can withstand floods and high water. It produces bunches of long winged seeds, or 'keys'.

WHITE WILLOW
This tree is named after the silvery white hairs that cover the new leaves.

GREAT CRESTED GREBE
This skillful diver lives mainly on fish.

MOORHEN
Its long toes prevent it from sinking into the mud along the river banks.

GOLDEN ORIOLE
This bird's piping song is heard from April onward. It lives mainly in poplar forests.

YELLOW WAGTAIL
The yellow wagtail feeds on insects found in the short grass.

SPARROWHAWK
The sparrowhawk's short wings enable it to fly through forests and among trees.

NIGHTINGALE
Its ringing song can be heard in the damp thickets that are its favorite haunt.

The seven large wooded parks and dozens of public gardens spared by the city's urban development cover a total area of several hundred acres. City Park (Városliget) ▲ *160*, where planting began in 1751, is one of the largest and is reputed to be the world's finest public park. Its green spaces harbor a wide variety of exotic and native trees, which attract many of the hundred or so bird species recorded in Budapest, especially woodland birds.

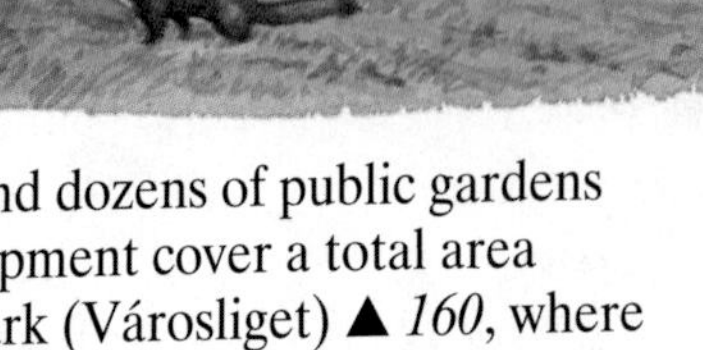

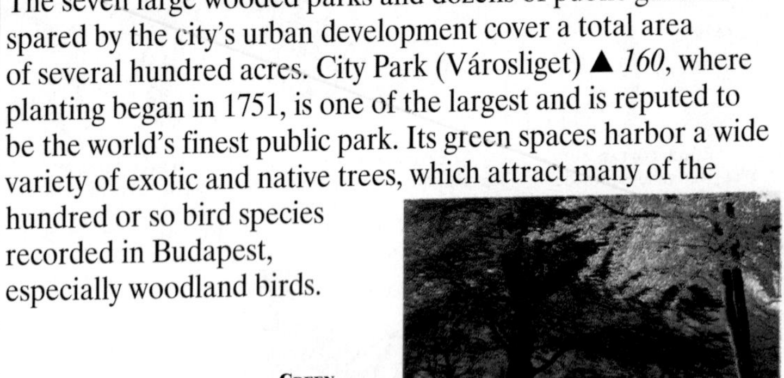

Syrian woodpecker
The area of distribution of this Central European bird is currently extending westward.

Green woodpecker
The green woodpecker is often seen on lawns, searching for ants, which form its staple diet.

Grosbeak
Even the hardest seeds are no match for this bird's powerful beak.

Fieldfare
This bird is seen mainly in winter. It eats the berries of ornamental bushes.

FIELD MAPLE
The field maple's smallish five-lobed leaves turn amber-yellow in the fall.

PEDUNCULATE OAK
This oak has long-stemmed (pedunculate) acorns and short-stemmed leaves.

BEECH
Beechnuts are one of the favorite foods of the red squirrel.

Female

Male

WHITE-COLLARED FLYCATCHER
These birds take over nesting holes abandoned by woodpeckers.

SERIN
The male's song is rapid and shrill. Its mating display takes the form of a slow circular flight.

SHORT-TOED TREE CREEPER
This little bird picks out insects and spiders from the tree trunks to which it clings.

TITMOUSE
The black-capped titmouse looks for food on leaves by hanging from twigs and small branches.

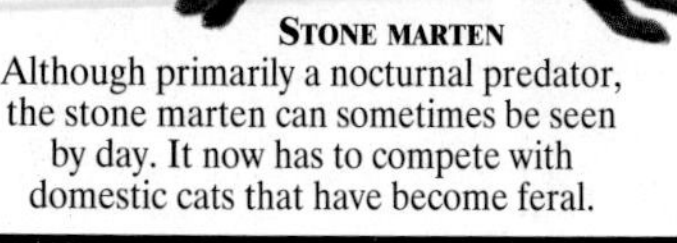

STONE MARTEN
Although primarily a nocturnal predator, the stone marten can sometimes be seen by day. It now has to compete with domestic cats that have become feral.

RED SQUIRREL
The parks of Budapest provide these little acrobats with all the food they need throughout the year. Although they mainly eats seeds, they sometimes take fledglings from birds' nests.

These exquisite natural aragonite crystal formations are extremely fragile.

The rock underlying the Buda Hills is riddled with some 160 caves. Their galleries extend for a total distance of 12 miles or more. Although most of them are closed to the public, parts of the caves of Pálvölgy, Szemlő-hegy and Mátyás-hegy are open to visitors. Pálvölgy boasts the largest cavern in the world (about 4½ miles long); Szemlő-hegy's features include 'cauliflower' reliefs, bands of calcite and pisolite ('peastone') formations; and Mátyás-hegy has a lake that lies 300 feet below its entrance. The huge cave of József-hegy is interesting on two counts: as well as being rich in crystals, it contains the largest known underground cavern formed by thermal waters, approximately 230 feet long by 50 feet wide.

RECENT DISCOVERIES
For a long time the substratum of Buda's hills was literally *terra incognita*. The cave of Pálvölgy was discovered in 1904, Szemlő-hegy in 1930, and József-hegy in 1984.

Stalagmites (above and far right).

Stalactites on top of the 'great column' in the cave of Pálvölgy (top right).

Pisolite looks like lots of tiny marbles (bottom right).

HISTORY

Annamária Vígh

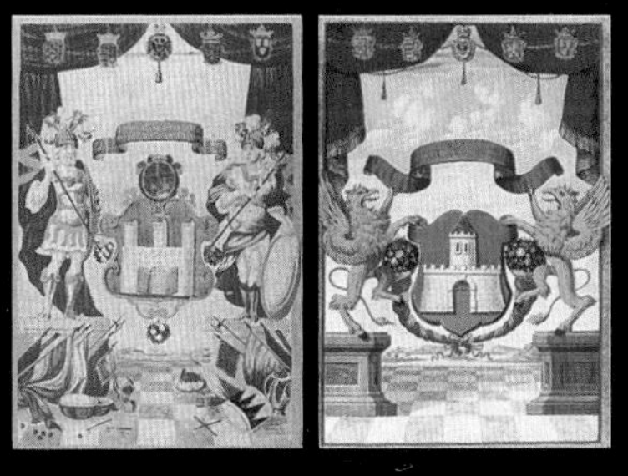

4th-3rd MILLENNIUM BC	2nd MILLENNIUM BC	10 BC	AD 90	106
Neolithic settlements on the hills bordering the Danube	Bronze Age communities	Romans occupy Eraviscan (Celtic) settlements at Buda	Romans build military camp at Óbuda	The province of Pannonia is divided in two, with Aquincum as capital of Pannonia Inferior

THE SITE OF BUDAPEST BEFORE THE ROMANS

Objects found during archeological excavations indicate that the site of modern Budapest has been inhabited continuously from the 4th millennium BC. Traces of Iron Age communities date from c. 900 BC, and *columbaria* – sepulchral buildings, rather like dovecotes, with dozens of small niches containing cinerary urns – have been unearthed at Békásmegyer and Pünkösdfürdő. Eraviscan (Celtic) settlements have been discovered dating from the late Iron Age (4th century BC). The *oppidum* (citadel) of the Celtic tribes was situated on what is now Gellért Hill ▲ *215*. While the citadel was being built on the higher ground, settlements were also being established on the plain, on the right bank of the Danube.

THE ROMAN OCCUPATION (1ST CENTURY BC–5TH CENTURY AD)

In c. 10 BC the Eraviscan settlements came under Roman control, and in c. AD 90 a legionary camp was established at Óbuda. In 106 Aquincum (the Roman forebear of Budapest) became the capital of Pannonia Inferior, the eastern part of the Roman province of Pannonia, which lay on the route of continual Barbarian attacks and formed part of the line of defense that ran parallel to the border (*limes*). Hadrian was the first of several governors of Pannonia who went on to become Roman emperors. He had a palace built on Óbuda Island ▲ *226*, and in 124 made Aquincum a municipium, an autonomous town under the jurisdiction of a praetor (senior magistrate). The legionary camp lay to the south of the Aquincum, its center occupying what is now Flórián tér (Flórián Square). The population of the military town that developed around the *castrum* (camp) must have been in the region of 20,000. Beyond the main residential districts, laid out on a grid of streets at right angles, there were groups of villas, and farms dotted here and there along the major roads. Along the banks of the Danube stood a series of watchtowers punctuated by two forts: Trans-Aquincum – on what is now Dagály út (Dagály Street) – and Contra-Aquincum, on the east side of Március 15 tér ▲ *120* in Pest. These two forts protected the crossing points on the Danube: a permanent bridge built on piles near the modern Árpád Bridge, and a pontoon probably situated where the Elizabeth Bridge (Erzsébet híd) stands today. In 409 Aquincum fell to the Huns.

Left: *Mithras slaying the cosmic bull (now in the Aquincum Museum* ▲ *228*).

260-70	465-6	896-906	1001-38	1242
Barbarian tribes burn Aquincum	The territory of Buda falls under the control of the eastern Goths	Magyar tribes conquer the Carpathian Basin and settle in Buda and on Csepel Island	Reign of Stephen I	Mongols devastate Hungary

The Magyar conquest

Following the establishment of the seven victorious Hungarian tribes in AD 896, the two chieftains Árpád (below) and Kurszán decided to settle on the site of what is now Budapest. Árpád's summer residence was on Csepel Island, while Kurszán's castle stood in the geographical center of the region, modern Óbuda.

The Kings of the Árpádian dynasty (1000–1301)

In the 10th century the center of power was moved to Esztergom ▲ 238, and neither Buda nor Pest featured among the *comitats* (counties) and archdioceses created by King Stephen I (István I) (1000–38), founder of the Christian state ▲ 203. Buda, the name of present-day Óbuda until the 13th century, established itself as the geographical and administrative center of the country. This process was interrupted by the Mongol invasion of 1242, when the unfortified town fell and most of its houses were burned to the ground. The commercial town of Pest suffered the same fate. The construction of fortified towns and fortresses began during the reign of Béla IV (1235–70), who ordered the population living at the foot of the hill of Buda (1243) and in Pest (1247) to move to what is now Castle Hill (Várhegy) ▲ *190*, probably uninhabited until then. This population consisted of two ethnic groups. The Germans from Pest settled around their church, Boldogasszony ('Our Lady'), now Matthias Church ▲ 202, while the Hungarians from the foot of the hill of Buda settled around their own church, of which the sole remnant is the Mary Magdalene Tower in Kapisztrán tér ▲ *205*. The construction of the fortified town and the royal palace could now begin. In spite of developing later than Buda, 13th-century Pest – rebuilt along the lines of the old town – became an important thoroughfare and market town. Its development was boosted by the king's decision to hold meetings of the Diet (the legislative assembly) in the fields alongside a nearby stream, the Rákos.

1308-82	1385	1418	1458-90	1526	1541
The House of Anjou rules Hungary	Sigismund of Luxembourg marries Maria, daughter of King Louis I of Hungary and Poland, in Buda	Sigismund of Luxembourg orders a new royal palace to be built in Buda	Reign of Matthias Corvinus	The Hungarian army is defeated by the Turks at the Battle of Mohács	The Turks occupy Buda

THE HOUSES OF ANJOU AND LUXEMBOURG (14TH CENTURY)

The House of Árpád came to an end in 1301, when András III died without leaving an heir. The ensuing conflicts of succession ended with the accession of Charles Robert of Anjou who, as Charles I (1308–42), wanted to move the royal court from Visegrád ▲ 235 to Buda. For five years the inhabitants refused to let him enter the town. He finally gained access by subterfuge and, after executing the officials, had himself crowned king. He made Buda a 'place of call', which meant that, no matter where they came from, merchants had to stop there to sell their merchandise. A walled castle was built for the king and his court, and until the 14th century the royal residence remained within the city walls. The ramparts surrounding the new castle ran down to the Danube, which greatly facilitated water supply, the mooring of boats and the operation of the water mills. At this time the Danube played a key role in the town's economy, so the castle and fortifications formed a cohesive system of defense.

The castle did not, however, satisfy the imperial requirements of Sigismund of Luxembourg (1387–1437 below). Gothic extensions were added at his instigation, then the royal archives and a treasury and treasurer's residence. Buda became the country's new capital. In 1406 Pest was granted the status of 'free town', and it soon became the country's second largest city. An enclosure wall punctuated by three gates was erected on what is now the Kiskörút (Little Boulevard) ▲ *123*, and round bastions were built on the banks of the Danube. In 1355 Louis the Great of Anjou (1342–82) ▲ *199* made Óbuda the permanent possession of the queens of Hungary. It was given the status of market town, with lesser freedoms and rights than Buda and Pest. During the 14th century, which witnessed the founding of many universities in Central Europe, Hungary's second largest university (after that of Pécs) was founded at Óbuda, in 1395. King Matthias Corvinus (1458–90) ● *32* reaffirmed central power and established the seat of his government in Buda, which soon became famous throughout Europe.

- **1686** The united Christian armies deliver Buda from Ottoman occupation
- **1703** Leopold I confirms the legal status of Buda and Pest by royal charter
- **1703-11** War of Independence against the Habsburgs, led by Ferenc Rákóczi
- **1795** Execution of the 'Hungarian Jacobins' at Vérmező
- **1848-9** First legislative assembly, first representative government. War of Independence against the Habsburgs
- **1867** The Compromise: Austria-Hungary ruled by two governments

The Ottoman presence: Buda, a Turkish town (1541–1686)

On August 29, 1526 a 25,000-strong Hungarian army was annihilated by the Turks at the Battle of Mohács. The queen was in Buda when she learned of the defeat. She immediately abandoned the castle and fled to Pozsony (Pressburg, now Bratislava) with her entourage. Suleiman the Magnificent (1494/5–1566), Sultan of the Ottoman Empire (1520–66), entered Buda, where he had the royal treasure loaded into 7,000 leather trunks and transported to Istanbul. Then he crossed the Danube and plundered and burned the town of Pest. Although Buda did not fall into Turkish hands until 1541, the battle marked a turning point in the history of this hitherto flourishing town, which entered a long period of external attacks and internal conflict. Most of the population fled, and for almost 150 years Buda was a Turkish city, while Pozsony became the capital of the part of the country that remained under Hungarian rule. Apart from religious and military buildings, the Turks mainly built baths, to which the town's natural resources were ideally suited ● *62*, ▲ *208*. Buda was linked to Pest by a pontoon, and a toll was collected by the deputy of Buda's principal judge.

The unification of Buda, Pest and Óbuda (1703–1873)

On September 2, 1686 Buda, which had been the stronghold of Turkish power in Hungary, fell to the Austrians. The former seat of the kings of Hungary was devastated; on the other side of the Danube, Pest was depopulated, too. When the fighting was over, Buda was rebuilt on its old foundations and repopulated by moving people there from other areas. In the early 19th century, Pest became the region's second largest market town after Vienna. The walls and gates of the city, which impeded expansion, were demolished between 1788 and 1808. After the extensive changes of the Age of Reform ● *34*, Pest became the intellectual center of the 1848 uprising. The loss of the War of Independence merely postponed the unification of Buda, Pest and Óbuda, and their joint accession to capital status, by a few years. The Compromise (*Ausgleich*) of 1867 removed political obstacles, and the unification of the three towns was completed in 1873, with the creation of Budapest.

1868 – Nationalities Law paves way for introduction of Hungarian as the official language ● 38

1872 – Law instituting the unification of Buda, Pest and Óbuda to create Budapest

1887 – Introduction of trams on the Nagykörút (Great Boulevard)

1896 – Opening of the Földalatti (Underground Railway ▲ 117, 145). Celebration of the thousandth anniversary of the Magyar conquest

1914-18 – Hungary fights alongside Austria in World War One

1918 – Hungary declares independence, as a Republic, with Mihály Károlyi as president

BUDAPEST DURING THE AUSTRO-HUNGARIAN MONARCHY

During the last thirty years of the 19th century Budapest, together with Vienna and Prague, became one of the great economic and cultural centers of central Europe. Its urban planning was developed by the Council of Public Works, which was inspired by other European models. Boulevards were built, and extensive investments made in the urban infra-structure. The city's traffic increased greatly and Margit híd (Margaret Bridge) was built, followed by the first Erzsébet híd (Elizabeth Bridge) ▲ *181* begun in 1897. In the course of its construction most of the old city center was demolished, including Pest's town hall, hitherto regarded as the symbol of the town. By 1900 the reformist dream had come true: Budapest had become the modern heart of Hungary. The 1000th anniversary of the foundation of the Hungarian state – the Millennium ▲ *150* – was commemorated by extensive celebrations in which the major event was the depositing of the royal crown in the Parliament building, still under construction, on June 8, 1896. The outbreak of World War One put an end to the long period of peace enjoyed by Hungary and its capital. As the nerve center of unoccupied Hungary, Budapest had to assume the heavy responsibilities of feeding its people and caring for the wounded.

Count Andrássy ▲ *140.*

Queen Elizabeth ▲ *182, 240.*

AN EXPANDING CAPITAL IN A DIMINISHED COUNTRY (1918–44)

The military defeat of 1918 led to the collapse of the Austro-Hungarian monarchy. Hungary, whose territory was reduced by two-thirds, became an independent state and retained Budapest as its capital. During the ensuing period, under a succession of revolutionary and counter-revolutionary governments, the city was inundated by thousands of refugees from the ceded territories, plus around 100,000 demobilized soldiers returning from prisoner-of-war camps. The fact that in the 1920s less than 12 percent of the country's population lived in Budapest indicates the sharp rise in the number of inhabitants. The so-called 'Capital Law' of 1930, which created thirteen administrative districts (*kerületke*), adapted the structure of the city to the new demands being made upon it. During the interwar period Budapest became a major industrial city, and the suburbs and outlying districts developed accordingly. In the second half of the 1930s, even though the city's administration was heavily influenced by Nazi and Fascist ideology, Budapest's Jewish community – which represented 20 percent of the city's population – was not forced to live in ghettos. However, in November 1944 a decree issued by the 'leader of the nation,' Ferenc Szálasi, a Nazi puppet and founder of the Fascist Arrow Cross Party, set up a ghetto (bounded by Dohány útca, Király útca and Károly körút), and concerted efforts were made to exterminate its inhabitants.

FEGYVERBE!
FEGYVERBE!

- **1919** Hungarian Soviet Republic. On August 1 Romanian troops occupy Budapest
- **1920** Admiral Miklós Horthy becomes regent of Hungary. Treaty of Trianon: Hungary loses two-thirds of its territory
- **1941** Hungary enters World War Two alongside Germany
- **1944** Budapest is occupied by German troops
- **1956** Hungarian (anti-Stalinist) national uprising
- **1989** The Republic of Hungary is proclaimed
- **200** Hungary become member of th European Unio

BUDAPEST: 1945–89

Like Berlin and Warsaw, Budapest was almost completely destroyed by World War Two. In a pitched battle between Russian and German troops that lasted several months, 25,000 civilians died, all the bridges over the Danube were demolished, and three-quarters of the buildings were either destroyed or badly damaged. Immediately after the cessation of hostilities, the inhabitants and municipal authorities set about clearing and rebuilding their ruined city. After the elections in May 1949, a law for the creation of a 'Greater Budapest' was adopted, which officially incorporated 7 towns and 16 villages into the capital. At a stroke, the geographical area of the city was more than doubled and its population increased to 1.6 million. To meet political objectives, this development was subject to compulsory industrialization. In 1956 Budapest was once again under siege, this time by the tanks of the Soviet army ● *36*. After the uprising of 1956 had been crushed, the city's political masters adopted a more pragmatic approach to theoretical problems, and the centralization of the municipal authorities under János Kádár had the effect of greatly limiting the autonomous decision-making powers of the district councils. In accordance with the model of Socialist urban planning, apartment blocks were constructed and the older residential districts were allowed to decline. In 1989 the years of the so-called 'soft dictatorship' came to an end, when Budapest was once again the focus of political change. The first free legislative elections were followed by municipal elections, and the new multi-party city council initiated an extensive program of urban development on a truly European scale.

The People's Republic of Hungary lasted from August 1, 1947 until October 23, 1989, when the Republic of Hungary was proclaimed. Below: the funeral ceremony, in 1989, for those who died during the 1956 uprising.

Stove tile showing King Matthias on his throne, holding the royal orb and scepter.

In 1458 Mátyás (Matthias) 'Corvinus' Hunyadi, son of János Hunyadi, became king of Hungary at the age of fifteen. His foreign policy consisted of waging a defensive war against the Turks, on one hand, and attempting to annex Austria and Bohemia, on the other. His domestic policy was inspired by the Italian model (in 1476 he married Beatrice of Naples), and he made his court one of the cultural centers of Europe.

'BIBLIOTHECA CORVINIANA'

The library was housed in a wing of the palace overlooking the Danube, in two square vaulted rooms with astronomical frescos. The vault of one of the rooms was decorated with the king's 'birth sky'. Bookcases embellished with marquetry stood against the wall, their shelves protected from the dust and light by gold veils.

'MATYAS REX MANU PROPRIA'

(signature of King Matthias)

The library housed between 1,000 and 1,500 volumes containing some 3,000 contemporary scientific and literary works.

BUDA AND THE ROYAL PALACE AT THE END OF THE MIDDLE AGES

Brought up in the Humanist tradition, Matthias invited scholars, architects, artists and miniaturists from Italy and Dalmatia to transform the Royal Palace ▲ *190* in accordance with his tastes. In addition, he employed famous artists such as Botticelli, Mantegna and Filippo Lippi to work on his behalf in Italy.

King Matthias and Queen Beatrice (manuscript from the Bibliotheca Corviniana)

After Italy, Hungary was the next European country to embrace the Renaissance and Humanist movements. Buda's close links with Italy had already been forged during the Angevin dynasty. Matthias' accession to the throne made the Bibliotheca Corviniana – and Buda – the center of Humanism in Hungary.

Matthias' arms carved in red marble
Matthias was given the name 'Corvinus' by the Humanists because of the raven in the family coat of arms and a legendary Roman ascendancy.

Majolica tiles (opposite)
From the Royal Palace, Buda.

'There was a King who governed his affairs as wisely in times of peace as in times of war. Toward the end of his life, and seeing himself without enemies, he became an extremely pretentious and triumphant King in his house and gathered together a huge treasure of beautiful furniture and rings and services to decorate his house.'
Philippe de Commynes

Matthias the educationalist
In 1467, with the help of Hungarian and foreign Humanists, Matthias founded the University of Pressburg (now Bratislava). It was closed a few years later.

Between 1831 and 1848 what had previously been a group of feudal states was transformed into a nation-state. But major changes had been taking place in Budapest since the 1780s, when Joseph II (1780–90) transferred the most important administrative departments and law courts from Pozsony (now Bratislava) to Buda and Pest. To accommodate the vast body of employees, he distributed land and simultaneously levied a property tax. He was succeeded by Archduke Sándor Lipót who, as Leopold II (1790–2), moved into the castle in Buda, which had become the governor's seat.

PALATINE ARCHDUKE JOSEPH OF HABSBURG ▲ *199*
The 'urban embellishment' committee set up in 1808 by Archduke Joseph (1776–1847), son of Leopold II, became the driving force behind Pest's development. Neoclassical palaces and public buildings, built according to the plans of the young architects József Hild and Mihály Pollack, reflected the aspirations of the city's new commercial classes: traders, industrialists and bankers. The Újváros ('New City') district – now Lipótváros – was the first fruit of this coordinated urban planning and became the economic heart of Pest.

Pest's neoclassical quay in 1834.

István Széchenyi
In 1831 Count István Széchenyi (1791–1860) ▲ *185* suggested linking Buda and Pest to form the city of Budapest. The construction of the Széchenyi Lánchíd (Chain Bridge ● *74,* ▲ *184*) – the first permanent structure across the Danube – began in 1841. Designed by the English engineer William Tierney Clark, it was built under the direction of the Scottish engineer Adam Clark ▲ *183*. The count also promoted the construction of a tunnel ▲ *184*, and in 1845 he became president of the newly formed 'tunnel society'. The tunnel was built between 1853 and 1857.

Lajos Kossuth
Hungary's economic crisis during the 1840s exacerbated social and national conflicts. Moderate opposition to the Conservatives focused on Széchenyi, more radical opposition on Lajos Kossuth.
Below: *Kossuth's electoral rally in front of the National Museum.*

At 9.30pm on October 23, 1956 the statue of Stalin on Dózsa György út was overturned by the crowd.

Since 1945 Hungary has been shaken by a series of major revolutions. The Yalta agreements in 1945 placed Hungary within the sphere of Soviet influence. In 1947 the process of nationalization began in the fields of property, production and education. A policy of ultracentralized economic planning favored the development of heavy industry, of which the Soviet Union was the main beneficiary. Declining living standards and the development of a repressive police regime by the one-party government kindled widespread anger. On October 23, 1956 around 200,000 people took to the streets of Budapest.

THE BEGINNINGS OF THE UPRISING
After Stalin's death, in 1953, two main streams formed within the Hungarian Communist Party: the hardline Communists led by Mátyás Rákosi and the reformists led by Imre Nagy ▲ *151*, former Minister of Agriculture. Nagy became prime minister in 1953, but was accused of 'deviationism' and removed from office, before being reinstated in 1956. It was the members of the Petőfi Circle ▲ *119* – a group of intellectuals and students – who began to demand radical reforms.

Left to right: Zoltán Tildy, Imre Nagy and Pál Maléter in the Hungarian Parliament.

IMRE NAGY, THE VOICE OF REFORM
In a radio broadcast on November 1, 1956 the prime minister, surrounded by representatives of the former coalition parties, announced Hungary's neutrality and secession from the Warsaw Pact.

'...for an independent, free and democratic Hungary.'

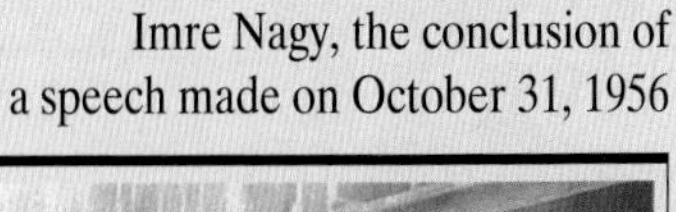

Imre Nagy, the conclusion of a speech made on October 31, 1956

JÁNOS KÁDÁR

János Kádár, first secretary (1956–88) of Hungary's Communist Party, left Budapest and formed a new government under Soviet auspices.

THE FIRST RUSSIAN INTERVENTION
After forming a military committee, the Communist Party leaders called upon the commanders of the Soviet troops stationed in Hungary, in accordance with the Warsaw Pact, to reestablish order. On the night of October 24 Russian tanks entered Budapest. They were attacked by several thousand people: young workers, students and even schoolchildren, the 'urchins of Pest'.

THE REVOLUTION BETRAYED
During the subsequent street fighting and demonstrations, the opposition demanded political and economic reforms under an enlightened Socialist regime and the withdrawal of Soviet troops. The latter reoccupied Budapest at the request of the shadow government formed by János Kádár.

EXILE, IMPRISONMENT AND EXECUTIONS
200,000 Hungarians left the country at the end of December to escape the repression. Nagy was arrested and executed in 1958. Cardinal Mindszenty sought refuge in the United States Embassy... until 1971.

● History of the Hungarian language

Left: King Stephen I, with his son Imre (Emeric). Illustration from the *Gesta Hungarorum* (12th century), the first source of Hungarian historiography, written in Latin by the anonymous notary known as 'P. dictus magister' or 'Master P.'.

Most of the legends surrounding the origins of the Magyar people existed as an oral tradition only and have now been lost. When Stephen I (Saint Stephen) was crowned king in 1000, he forced the Magyar people to convert to Christianity. The earliest texts written in Hungarian, dating from the end of the 12th century, were translations of religious texts. With the development of the feudal system, 'Master P.' – alias 'Anonymus' (sic) – translated the most popular French chivalric novels. Then Latin was reinstated as the official language throughout the Gothic period.

Manuscript mixing Latin, German and Hungarian

The first Hungarian grammar

The first Hungarian printing press was founded in Buda in 1472, during the reign of Matthias Corvinus ● *32*, who introduced Humanism and other Renaissance ideas into his court. But it was the disciples of Erasmus who were responsible for the development of the Hungarian language. János Sylvester translated the New Testament, and wrote a Latin-Hungarian primer and the first Hungarian grammar (1539). 'If we do not hesitate to use our mother tongue,' he said, 'this treasure that has remained hidden from us until now but which we have just discovered, then from the poor people we once were we will soon become rich indeed.'

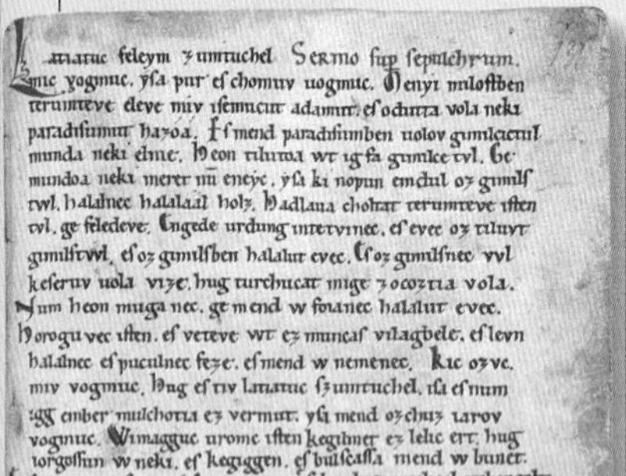

The first Hungarian Bible

During the Reformation the use of Hungarian became widespread, since Martin Luther (1483–1546) wanted the Gospel to be preached in the language of the people. Gáspár Károlyi produced the first Hungarian translation of the entire Bible in 1590. Religious writers used the language for their treatises, hymns and history books to spread new ideas and denounce the feudal lords who oppressed the people. This period also witnessed the birth of Hungarian theater ● *42*.
Although a native German speaker, at the age of thirty-six the minister Gáspár Heltai (1500–74) began to write in Hungarian.
Péter Bornemisza (1535–84) applied his talent to all types of prose: 'It is already a number of years since people began writing in Hungarian, and it falls to us to follow the example of Cicero and every civilized nation – to cultivate and enrich our own language.'
Bálint Balassi (1551–94), the first great Hungarian poet, wrote about love and religion, and abandoned melody as a concomitant of poetry to reinvent versification.
Left: *one of the earliest Hungarian manuscripts.*

> 'The fact that my mother tongue is Hungarian and that I speak, think and write in Hungarian is the most important event in my life, unique of its kind.'
>
> Dezső Kosztolányi

Hungarian literature in the 17th century

During the Baroque period the Puritan János Tolnai, inspired by the English model, demanded that Hungarian be used in public education. In 1655 János Apáczai compiled a Hungarian encyclopedia. The amount of literature written in Hungarian increased: Miklós Zrínyi (1620–64) created a politico-military genre, and Kelemen Mikes (1690–1761) adapted the style of literary correspondence developed in France by the Marquise de Sévigné. The exiled Ferenc II Rákóczi (1676–1735), on the other hand, had little choice but to write his memoirs in French. But Hungarian was then replaced by the 'popular Latin' used by Jesuit authors.

The linguistic reform of the Enlightenment

Toward the end of the 18th century Hungarian proponents of the Enlightenment launched a linguistic reform. György Bessenyei (1747–1811) noted: 'So far, no nation has been able to become cultivated other than through its own language. The first duty of any nation that wants to spread knowledge among its people, so as to contribute to their greater happiness, is to elevate its mother tongue to the level of perfection.' Because the language of the time had been the vehicle for religious and feudal ideology, the reformers felt it was unsuited to this mission. They therefore wanted to enrich it and make it more fitting for their vision of social progress and national identity, and were even prepared to impose it on the country's non-Magyar minorities. One leading writer of the day, Ferenc Kazinczy (1759–1831, right), translated many European classics into Hungarian and devoted his life to the movement. However, it encountered resistance from the Conservative nobility, and by insisting on German for official purposes Joseph II

provoked an energetic campaign of reform. This included launching twenty-three periodicals, creating lending libraries and a chair of Hungarian at the University of Pest (1791), and teaching the rural population to read and write. A colorful 'army' traveled the length and breadth of the country, delivering the message of nationalism and linguistic reform. Finally linguists developed the theory of the Finno-Ugric origins of the Hungarian language, which received recognition thanks to *Demonstratio. Idioma Ungarorum et Lapponum idem esse*, published by János Sajnovics in 1770. Left: *Certificate of trading written in Hungarian (18th c.).*

Nationalism and Romanticism

The Hungarian language had become by 1825 a homogenous tool, purged of dialects and enriched with neologisms. The reforms ● *34* inaugurated by the Diet (legislative assembly) of 1825–7 favored using Hungarian as the official language. Then during the Diet of 1843–4 the Conservatives accepted a 'language law' advocating the introduction of Hungarian as the national language – thus arousing the hostility of the country's ethnic minorities, who demanded equal rights and linguistic autonomy. Finally on March 17, 1848 Ferdinand I, spurred on by the revolutionary momentum, appointed Lajos Batthyány head of the 'responsible independent Hungarian Ministry', and ratified the laws introduced by the Diet.

The Hungarian (or Magyar) language belongs to the group of Finno-Ugric languages, which form part of the larger family of Altaic-Uralic languages. Unlike the languages of its neighbors, Hungarian is therefore not of Indo-European origin but is related, if only distantly, to Finnish, Estonian and Lapp. It is the official language of the Hungarian Republic.

The alphabet contains the following vowels:
a – 'o' as in hot
á – 'a' as in father
e – 'ai' as in air
é – 'a' as in day
i – 'i'
í – 'ee' as in feet
o – 'o'
ó – long, closed 'o'
ö – 'ur' as in pleasure
ő – like ö but longer
u – 'oo' as in pool
ú – long 'oo'
ü – 'u' as in tube
ü – long 'u'

The length and degree of openness of the vowels are extremely important, as they often make it possible to distinguish between certain words and phrases – for example, *örülök* (I am happy) and *őrülök* (I am going mad)!

The consonants are pronounced as follows:
b – 'b'
c – 'ts' as in roots
cs – 'ch' as in such
d – 'd'
f – 'f'
g – 'gu' as in go
gy – 'd' as in dew
h – aspirate 'h'
j – 'y', 'aïe'
k – 'k'
l – 'l'
ly – 'y' as in yellow
m – 'm'
n – 'n'
ny – 'n' as in new
p – 'p'
r – rolled 'r'
s – 'sh' as in wash
sz – 's' as in sat
t – 't'
ty – 't' as in tube
v – 'v'
z – 'z'
zs – 's' as in casual

The very marked tonic accent is placed on the first syllable of the word. The Hungarian language can sound rather monotonous because of the vowel system, which only uses front (i, í, e, é, ő, ö, ű, ü) or back (a, á, o, ó, u, ú) vowels in a word. Although disconcerting, its structure has very regular forms. An agglutinative language, it adds 'affixes' to a usually monosyllabic root and uses 'post positions' rather than prepositions – so the literal meaning of *ház-am-ban* is 'house-my-in'.
Also, in Hungarian:
◆ The verb 'to be' lacks a third person singular – so 'the boy is tall' is rendered as *a fiú magas* ('the boy tall').
◆ There is no gender. On the other hand, there are nine local suffixes. Two conjugations (objective and subjective) are used, depending on the nature of the complement of the direct object.
◆ Word order, which is extremely flexible, can be utilized to convey subtle shades of meaning.
◆ Given its aptitude for coining neologisms, the vocabulary is virtually unlimited.

There are about 11 million Hungarian speakers in Hungary, plus those who live in neighboring countries and other parts of the world. Not surprisingly, they are immensely proud of their language, which, despite a national history marked by oppression, has successfully resisted dilution by the Germanic, Slavic, Turkish and Latin languages.
Top: *'Eight o'clock? Relax!' (from an advertising poster).*

ART AND TRADITIONS

Considered 'unperformable', Imre Madách's *The Tragedy of Man* (1861) was staged for the first time, by Ede Paulay, on September 21, 1883.

One of the most memorable events in the history of Hungarian theater was the famous Budapest tour of the László Kelemen theater company in October 1790. In a manner of speaking, it marked the birth of professional Hungarian-language theater. Kelemen's performances had all the value of a political event, since they represented a decisive stage in the fight for national and linguistic independence. Between 1880 and 1905 many theaters were opened in Budapest, as its population rose from 400,000 to 1 million. In 1949 theaters were nationalized, as the new (Communist) government took control of all aspects of Hungarian culture. Hungarian theater eventually managed to free itself from its ideological shackles – partially during the early 1960s, and completely since 1989.

THE HUNGARIAN NATIONAL THEATER (NEMZETI SZÍNHÁZ)

In September 1935 the authorities of the comitat (county) of Pest gave Mátyás Zitterbach the task of building a national theater. The new building was inaugurated on August 22, 1837 with a play by Mihály Vörösmarty (1800–55 ▲ 116). The theater's aim was to present classics plays by Hungarian and foreign playwrights. Such works as *Csongor and Tünde* by Mihály Vörösmarty and *The Tragedy of Man* (*Az ember tragediája*) by Imre Madách (1823–64) featured regularly on the bill. Below: scene from István Örkény's *Catsplay.* The new National Theater, located on the banks of the Danube in the IXth district, opened its doors for the first time in 2001.

VÍGSZÍNHÁZ

The Vígszínház (Comedy Theater) opened in 1896 and became the theater of the new bourgeoisie that was developing along with the city. Initially it was devoted to French comedy, but subsequent directors also staged works by contemporary Hungarian playwrights such as Sándor Bródy, Ferenc Molnár and Zsigmond Móricz.

Ferenc Molnár
(1878-1952)

KATONA JÓZSEF SZÍNHÁZ ▲ *121*

Between 1951 and 1982 the Katona József Theater occupied the small auditorium of the Hungarian National Theater. However, thirty or so actors gave up the privilege of performing in the National Theater to work under the directorship of Gábor Székely and Gábor Zsámbéki, who wanted to work outside the official program. The new Katona József Színház acquired an international reputation for its performances of Chekhov, Bulgakov, Gogol, Shakespeare, Molière, Jarry and György Spiró. Below: poster for a production of György Spiró's *Csirkefej*.

Ferenc Molnár was one of the leading playwrights of the Vígszínház in the 1920s. His career reached its peak in 1910 with *Liliom*. Although he had refused Puccini permission to turn *Liliom* into an opera, it was later made into the famous musical *Carousel* by Rodgers and Hammerstein. In 1962 Zoltán Várkonyi took over the directorship of the theater and, as well as his own plays, staged the works of other contemporary Hungarian writers, including Gábor Thurzó, Gyula Illyés, Károly Szakonyi and Tibor Gyurkovics. István Örkény (1918–79) was extremely popular at the Vígszínház in the 1970s.

TRAFÓ ▲ *174*

On October 5, 1998 the opening of the Trafó (Contemporary Arts) Theater in a power station built at the turn of the century was a first for Budapest. The theater does not have a permanent company, as its aim is to promote experimental theater.

During the first half of the 19th century the Hungarian National Theater gradually opened its doors to a new genre: operetta. The German Theater in Pest acquired the rights to perform the operettas of Offenbach and the genre became so popular that the Municipal Operetta Theater was opened in Pest in 1875. It performed the works of Johan Strauss, Franz von Suppé, Offenbach and József Konti, the master of Hungarian operetta.

FRANZ (FERENC) LEHÁR (1870–1948) was born in Komáron, into a family of French origin (his great-grandfather's name was Le Harde). He studied at the conservatory of Prague before joining his father in Vienna.

JACQUES OFFENBACH (1819–80)
At the turn of the century, when the literary and musical life of Budapest was in a state of flux, a great many theaters were opened. In 1903 the Király Színház (Royal Theater), the temple of Hungarian operetta, opened on Király út with a performance of the *Golden Flower* by Jenő Huszka (1875–1960).

IMRE KÁLMÁN (1882–1953)
After studying under János Koessler at the Academy of Music ▲ *146*, Kálmán became music critic for Pesti Napló and, between 1904 and 1908, held the post of *répétiteur* at the Vígszínház ● *42*. In 1908 he had his first major success with the operetta *Tatárjárás* (*The Gay Hussars*). From 1910 onward most of his works were performed abroad.

Róbert Rátonyi
After World War Two, the Municipal Operetta Theater of Budapest continued to promote this highly distinctive genre. The individual style and charismatic performances of such great operatic stars as Hanna Honthy, Kálmán Latabár, Kamill Feleki and Robert Rátonyi ensured the success of the theater's productions.

Hanna Honthy in 'The Merry Widow'
Franz Lehár became a violinist in the military orchestra conducted by his father. From 1890 he led the military orchestras of several Austro-Hungarian towns (Losonc, Trieste, Budapest and Vienna).
In November 1906 his famous operetta *The Merry Widow* was performed at the Magyar Színház; in March 1907 it celebrated its 100th performance.

Rátonyi (Ákos) and the merry widows.

During the period of Socialist Realism the performances and personality of stars like Rátonyi and Honthy evoked a bourgeois era that had vanished.

Hanna Honthy
(1893-1978)
Hanna Honthy began her singing career in 1912 at the municipal Operetta Theater and by 1916 was one of the young stars of operetta. In the 1930s she played the leading role in many major operettas and was idolized by her fans. She had her greatest success after World War Two, in Kálmán's *The Csárdás Princess.*

TRADITIONAL HUNGARIAN MUSIC
FOLK, RELIGIOUS AND COURTLY MUSIC

Bagpiper.

The Hungarian musical tradition originated among the Finno-Ugric and Altaic tribes, and was inspired by pentatonic (five-note) scales. In this respect it was essentially different from the Italo-Germanic music that dominated the rest of Europe. Over the centuries this oriental characteristic – apparent in all aspects of a flourishing popular tradition, from children's nursery rhymes to battle songs and funeral dirges – has remained untainted by foreign influences, even surviving the conversion to Christianity. Only the clergy and nobility were affected by Western influences. Thus, at the end of the 19th century János Erdélyi, Gábor Mátray and István Bartalus (1821–99) were able to compile remarkable collections of unpublished traditional music.

ETHNO-MUSICOLOGISTS
The early transcriptions of Hungarian folk music, which had inspired many researchers, were soon challenged by Béla Vikár, who replaced the romantic approach of his predecessors with more scientific methods. In 1905 Zoltán Kodály ● *50* started to compile an authoritative record of this corpus of traditional music, using a phonograph, and in 1906 he was joined by Béla Bartók.

Page from a late-15th-century antiphonary.

Violin and *gardon* players.

RELIGIOUS MUSIC
In addition to Hungary's very fertile folk tradition, more cosmopolitan forms of music developed in more formal environments. The Church was the prime example of this 'westernization', since in spreading the Gregorian tradition it ignored national boundaries and local traditions. The older monasteries (Esztergom ▲ *238*, Vác ▲ *235*) disseminated a plainchant tinged with popular influences (*Antiphonary of Graz*), whereas the Hungarian people did not adapt their music to meet the needs of religion until the *Codex of Nádor* (1508).

The shadow of the Reformation

Paradoxically the Reformation, which revitalized music in the rest of Europe, was disastrous for Hungarian music. Wars, invasions, divisions and secessions divided a country that had hitherto been united, especially by its language. Right: fragment from a 15th-century stove.

The *Chronicle* of András Farkas, which included Hussite (Bohemian Reformation) and Franco-Flemish polyphonic songs, gives some idea of this heterogeneity, whilst the *Chronicle* of Sebestyén Tineodi (mid 16th century) tried to provide a synthesis of the heroic genre, folk music and biblical psalmody.

Courtly music

The nobility resolutely copied Western customs, and in the 15th century Matthias Corvinus ● *32* filled his court with troubadours, minnesingers and other poet-musicians from France, Italy and Germany. From this point on, institutionalized Hungarian music disdained local tradition and aspired to cosmopolitanism.

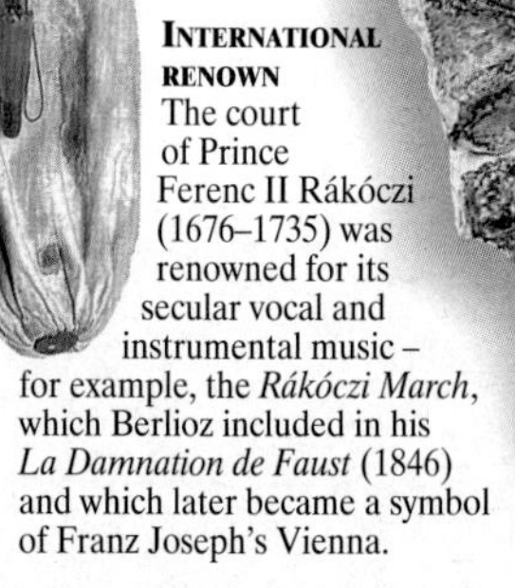

Pipe and bagpipes.

International renown

The court of Prince Ferenc II Rákóczi (1676–1735) was renowned for its secular vocal and instrumental music – for example, the *Rákóczi March*, which Berlioz included in his *La Damnation de Faust* (1846) and which later became a symbol of Franz Joseph's Vienna.

Revival under the Counter-Reformation

The Counter-Reformation saw an increase in religious music (*Cantus catholici*), written both by anonymous composers and by masters such as Ferenc Szegedy, Iván Nagy and János Kusser. Poets were often musicians and vice versa – for example, Bálint Balassi and Péter Bornemissa or, a century later, Prince Pál (Paul) Esterházy (1635–1713), who wrote *Harmonia coelestis*, a collection of 55 short cantatas covering the religious year. This courtly art also produced an increasing number of famous musicians, such as the lutenist Bálint Bakfark and the organist János Kajoni.

COSMOPOLITANISM AND NATIONALISM

Hungary's best-known composers are Joseph Haydn (1732–1809) and Franz Liszt (1811–86). Haydn was born in Hungary and spent most of his working life in Eisenstadt, the home of the descendants of Prince Pál Esterházy. Liszt, who was born near Sopron – not far from Eisenstadt – was, by contrast, much more cosmopolitan. He led an itinerant existence, drawing on the elements of Italian and French music that inspired the more flamboyant music of such German composers as Robert Schumann and Richard Wagner. Faced with this increasingly varied input, the wave of nationalism that followed the Napoleonic wars gave rise to the vogue for a specifically Hungarian genre, the *verbunkos*. This rousing 'recruitment music' was exploited by wealthy families to recruit their militias.

THE 'VERBUNKOS' formed a diptych of dances, initially slow (*lassu*) and becoming very fast (*friss*). It was originally vocal, but soon used instruments (violins) and even reinstated traditional instruments such as the dulcimer (a tuned percussion instrument comprising a set of strings of graduated length stretched over a sounding board and struck with two hammers). The *verbunkos* was quickly adopted by the Hungarian gypsies (right) and even inspired Liszt's famous *Hungarian Rhapsodies*.

'ALLA HUNGARESE' The *verbunkos*, which appeared at the end of the 18th century, inspired the phrase *alla hungarese* used by Haydn, Schubert and, until the late 19th century, Liszt, Wagner, Brahms and Dvorák. For a century the international acclaim given to the *verbunkos* eclipsed all other forms of traditional Hungarian folk music.

Military musicians

‘But the murderer of pianos [Liszt] infected his compatriots with a national fever, for this Parisian from Italy had the idea of glorifying Hungarian gypsy music. He ended his first concert with a transposition of the *Rákóczi March* that held his audience spellbound.’

Guy de Pourtalès

Ferenc Erkel (1810–93)
The operas of Ferenc Erkel are still popular in Hungary, despite the dated political content of some of the librettos; musically speaking, they are elegant syntheses of various genres. *Bátori Mária* (1840), *Hunyadi László* (1844) – a veritable anti-Austrian manifesto – and *Bánk Bán* (1852–61) ▲ *142* were crowned by such historical works as *István Király* (*King Stephen*, 1885). Erkel’s contribution to Hungarian music is immense: not only did he compose the Hungarian national anthem, but he also founded the Budapest Philharmonic Society, in 1853. Under his direction, the city’s new bourgeoisie was introduced to the latest trends in European music. One of his sons, László, taught Béla Bartók.

The Baryton Geographically isolated near Eisenstadt and making little use of traditional sources, Joseph Haydn (1732–1809) was only able to become the initiator of the extremely cosmopolitan Viennese classical style thanks to his own genius and the prestige of his music teachers. Haydn composed a total of 175 pieces for the baryton, a now obsolete cello-like instrument.

Franz (Ferenc) Liszt
Having reached the pinnacle of his art, Liszt set about illustrating the most outstanding aspects of his country’s music. He did not hesitate to combine classical Hungarian and gypsy music, *verbunkos* and folk music. However, his use of strange harmonies in his later works, such as *Cszardas macabre* (1882), detracted from his immediate influence to the extent that, under Habsburg pressure (left, Liszt playing in front of the imperial couple), late-19th-century Hungarian music became increasingly subject to German influence. This was mainly transmitted by the Hungarian Academy of Music and its teachers, who were among the best instrumentalists of the period ▲ *146*.

In the early 20th century the dominant esthetic influences in Budapest were those of the German composers Richard Wagner and Richard Strauss and, in a wider sense, of the Western symbolists. However, from 1905 the two great masters of the new Hungarian school, Kodály and Bartók, followed in the footsteps of Béla Vikar and began to explore the roots of traditional Hungarian music. The eloquence of the material they discovered significantly revitalized the work of both composers.

TWO BRILLIANT ETHNO-MUSICOLOGISTS: KODÁLY (1882–1967) BARTÓK (1881–1945)

For thirty years this brilliant duo overcame many difficulties and pursued work that was probably unique in the field of ethno-musicology.
From 1925 Bartók published 350 popular Hungarian melodies according to an entirely new method of classification.
The years 1936, 1951 and 1958–70 saw the complete publication of a huge body of work, which was pursued by teams of ethnological composers trained in the methods of their predecessors László Lajtha and Bence Szabolcsi.
Under the postwar leadership of Kodály, the popular foundations of Hungarian music were taught from primary school onward, to a nation that already had a highly developed love of music.

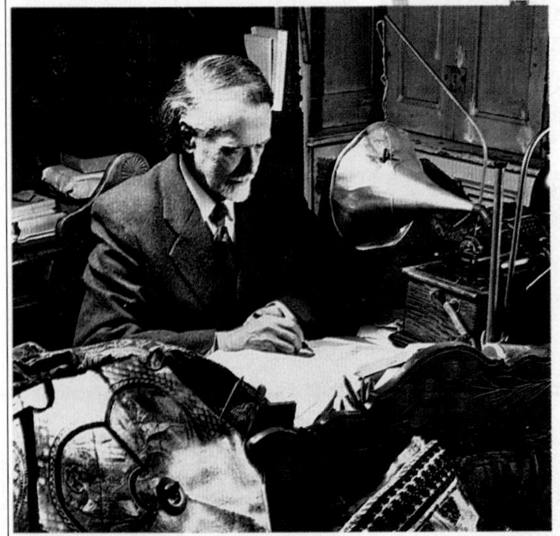

ZOLTÁN KODÁLY
● *46*, ▲ *148*
Kodály based many of his compositions on folk music – initially rediscovered in a series of enchanting pieces of chamber music (such as his *Sonata for Cello solo*, 1915), then further developed in a number of lively orchestral works (*Dances of Marosszêk*, 1927–30; *Dances of Galánta*, 1933; *Variations on a Hungarian Folksong, The Peacock*, 1939). He also produced a great many vocal and choral works.

'Bartók presented an austere, forbidding front to the world, and even in those years, when he was still in his mid-forties, his reputation was daunting. [...] We music students knew exactly how important he was, and we revered him. We were fully aware that there was an authentic genius teaching at our academy.'

Sir Georg Solti

'The Székely Spinning-Room' (1932) In his choral works Kodály treated the popular origins of Hungarian music extremely elaborately – for example, in *Psalmus Hungaricus* (1923) and in various religious pieces (1930–40). His comic opera *Háry János* (1926) is also deliberately rustic.

Béla Bartók ▲ *146* Bartók was first noted for works inspired by a fascinating blend of Straussian esthetics and French symbolism – such as his two *Pictures* (for orchestra, 1910), his magnificent one-act opera *Duke Bluebeard's Castle* (1911) ▲ *143*, his first string quartet (1909) and his extremely expressionist ballet *The Miraculous Mandarin* (1918–19, below). When Hungary gained independence from Austria after World War One, Western influences – especially the neoclassical dogmas illustrated by Stravinsky – led Bartók to combine the strictness of form inherited from Haydn ● *48* with a series of themes that, although not used directly, were inspired by central European folk music. The use of this 'fictionalized folklore' dominated most of his work up to his death. He died in exile, in New York, at the end of World War Two.

The various political upheavals since the 1930s resulted in periodic 'diasporas' of Hungarian artists (writers, film directors and especially musicians), who emigrated to other parts of Europe or, more frequently, to the United States. Furthermore, the ascendancy of serial (twelve-note) music during the postwar period favored the international revival of Hungarian music. Thus, while such composers as György Kurtág (b. 1926) and György Ligeti (b. 1923) were heavily influenced by Bartók in their early careers, they subsequently evolved a personal style based on the post-Webernian mold.

MUSIC ON THE AIR
Radio, which has always been more important than television in Eastern European countries, is the principal broadcasting medium for the Hungarian Radio Orchestra. 'Bartók', one of the few national channels to broadcast on FM, plays mainly classical music, jazz and traditional music.

THE BENEFITS OF COLLECTIVISM
One of the benefits of the Communist regime was the *carte blanche* given to Kodály to organize the theoretical and practical teaching of music from nursery school onward. Another was that a number of state-owned recording companies (such as Hungaroton, bought back by a consortium of artists in the 1990s) were able, in the absence of commercial competition and with the help of technically first-class recordings, to build up a catalog of Hungarian music that constituted a vast system of artistic reference. Hungary was also one of the few countries in Central Europe to have a musical publisher – EMB (Editio Musica Budapest) – with an extensive catalog.

MÁRTA AND GYÖRGY KURTÁG
György Kurtág studied under Sándor Veress in Budapest, and under Darius Milhaud and Olivier Messiaen in Paris. Although his references to Hungarian folk music are indirect, Kurtág has – with pieces such as *The Sayings of Péter Bornemissa* (for voice and piano, 1963–8) – established himself as one of Hungary's leading modern composers. He teaches composition in Budapest.

'The technique of Ockeghem – in vogue in the late 15th century – uses varietas: although there are rules, they do not observe a strict form. It is a magnificent example of ordered disorder.'

György Ligeti

Some celebrated musical émigrés
It is important to remember the Hungarian origins of such soloists as the pianists György Cziffra (above) and György Sebők, the cellist János Starker, the violinists Joseph Szigeti and Ede Zathurecsky, and conductors such as Fritz Reiner, Antál Doráti, George Szell, Eugene Ormandy and Georg Solti (right). Solti, a pupil of Kodály, is buried between his former teacher and Bartók in the Farkasréti Temető ▲ *217* in Buda.

György Ligeti
Ligeti became an expatriate in early 1956, after teaching at the Franz Liszt Musical Academy ▲ *146*. He appears to have welcomed the changes of the period, and his music – multidimensional and unpredictable – is a skillful combination of extreme musical sophistication and openly aggressive experimentation. The 'nationalist' works written for choir and piano (1946–55) were followed by two string quartets (1954–68), *Atmosphères* (1961), *Aventures and Nouvelles Aventures* (1962–5), *Requiem* (1963–5), *Lontano* (1967), *Continuum* (for harpsichord, 1968), *Horn Trio* (1982), *Viola Sonata* (1994) and *Études* (for piano, 1985–95).

Costume design for
The Wooden Prince.

The Opera House is still the 'mecca' of classical dance in Budapest. Its 100-strong *corps de ballet* has an international reputation, acquired primarily through the productions of the choreographers Gyula Harangozó and László Seregi. Modern dance made its debut in Budapest in the 1930s, when a group of dancers founded the first modern-dance dance schools and independent dance troupes based on the German model. At the same time there was a renewed interest in the origins of traditional Hungarian dance, as a result of the collection of historical documentation – especially films of peasant dances.

INNOVATIONS IN DANCE
In the 1980s talented young dancers developed a new form of dramatic expression and experimented with a new body language. This in turn gave rise to a new form of minimalist choreography that combined innovation with elements of traditional folklore. This modern trend produced the choreographer Joseph Nadj and the soloist and innovative post-modern artist Yvette Bozsik (below).

CLASSICAL DANCE
In the 1930s Gyula Harangozó's spirited ballets raised the status of the Budapest Opera troupe to that of a national ballet company. From the 1960s Hungarian ballet acquired another innovative choreographer, László Seregi, who made his debut with *Spartacus* (1968). He reached the pinnacle of his career with three ballets inspired by Shakespearean plays: *Romeo and Juliet, The Taming of the Shrew* (above) and *A Midsummer Night's Dream.*

Gyula Harangozó's
interpretation of
The Miraculous Mandarin.

In the 1950s Russian-style professional folk groups used ethno-musicological research to enhance the authenticity of their productions.

FOLK DANCING

The revival of authentic traditional Hungarian dancing dates from the 1970s. Previously it had mainly been presented on stage, whereas it now began to form the basis of folk evenings and was restored to its natural function. Today the *táncházak* ('dance houses') still help to promote a sense of national identity among the young, while making a valuable contribution to traditional festivals.

Every week in Budapest dancers aged from seven to seventy-seven take part in Hungarian, Greek, Irish, Jewish and Transylvanian *táncház* evenings.

CONTEMPORARY DANCE

The expressive power of Hungarian folk dancing has provided a source of inspiration for contemporary dance. In particular, a number of young Hungarian choreographers have drawn upon the rich national heritage. The most representative creations of this new wave are those of Gerzson Péter Kovács and Csaba Horváth.

The first coffee shops in Budapest were opened by the Turks and reserved exclusively for Turkish customers. Cafés made their debut in Pest in 1714, and soon after in Buda. One hundred years later they had become a favorite meeting place for students and intellectuals. The golden age of Hungarian cafés was between 1890 and World War One, as evidenced by the words of Dezső Kosztolányi: 'After its Turkish baths, the Hungarian café is the most oriental feature [of Budapest]. It is where we spend our lives' (1914).

'AT THE CAFÉ'
(January 1940)

CAFÉ GERBEAUD
▲ *117*
The Café Gerbeaud, which has been in business since 1884, is a fine example of the 'tearoom' tradition. It comprises several buildings (with a single entrance, on Vörösmarty tér), and each of the rooms is different. Today the Gerbeaud is a popular tourist venue.

MEETING AT THE CAFÉ PILVAX IN 1848
The original Café Pilvax, the focus of the 1848 uprising ▲ *119*, has disappeared. Its modern namesake stands about 100 yards from the original site.

Table decorated with portraits of its 'regulars'.

That cafés became a social phenomenon was partly due to inadequate living conditions, which prevented 'bohemians' and even members of the bourgeoisie from inviting friends into their homes. As a result, the café became a sort of forum or universal meeting place.

Literary revival
Attempts are being made to keep alive the tradition of literary cafés such as the Spinoza or Eckermann (next to the Goethe Institute), which now offer free Internet connections in the afternoon, or to revive it with the reopening of cafés such as the Central.

Café New York ● *77* ▲ *167*
In the late 1940s cafés were converted into sports shops, libraries, post offices or self-service restaurants. When the New York reopened in 1954, a popular actor is said to have exclaimed: 'Waiter, bring me a pair of tennis shoes!'
Evocative menus (right).

Among today's most fashionable cafés are the Vian, the Incognito, the Paris Texas, the Greco and the Szimpla cafés. The latter are, in summer, set up in the courtyards and gardens of premises which are being renovated.

'Nyugat' reader on the terrace of the New York (1917)
Opened in 1894, the Café New York rapidly became the refuge of Hungary's new young literary movement. It was here that the legendary periodical *Nyugat* ('The West') ● 97 was launched in 1908. In the 1910s, as well as the local and international newspapers, some 400 Hungarian periodicals were among the reading matter devoured at the café.

Why Hungary should have produced so many 'classic' photographers, both in the early days of photography and later, is still a mystery. But the fact remains that Daguerre and Niepce soon found a following, with the result that the face of the poet Sándor Petőfi ▲ *119* was immortalized in 1848 shortly before his glorious death. In the following decades, at the Universal Exhibitions held in Paris Hungarians won awards for their technical inventions. In the early 20th century photography was regarded as a 'good career' in Hungary, and Budapest had over 300 photographic studios, plus numerous amateur clubs.

André Kertész, Paul Almásy, Brassaï, Robert Capa, Emeric Fehér, Lucien Hervé, László Moholy-Nagy, Martin Munkácsi, Rosie Ney, Rogie André... All these photographers had their own individual style, and one thing in common: they were born in Hungary. So were Rudolf Balogh, Károly Escher, Iván Vidarény, Kata Kálmán and József Pécsi, but the latter chose to remain in Hungary and are less well known in other countries.

From the end of the 19th century until 1920 the main photographic trend was 'pictorialism': a style of photography that imitated fin-de-siècle academic painting. It used such techniques as placing gauze over the lens, soft focusing, touching up, and printing on grainy paper.

1. Rudolf Balogh : *Snow in Budapest*, c. 1920.
2. Károly Escher : *Hail in Budapest*, 1928.
3. Iván Vydarény : *The Tabán District*.
4. János Reismann : *Buda Hill*, 1970s.
5. André Kertész : *Spring Shower*, 1920.

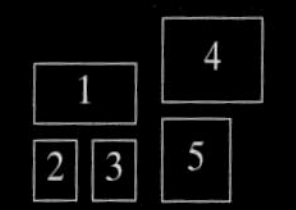

In the 1920s photography became a means of expression in its own right and assumed different forms, from reportage and sociological studies to avant-garde art. 'Hungarian' photography was very much in vogue in the interwar period, when many Hungarian artists such as Brassaï and Robert Capa (whose real names were Gyula Halász and Endre Ernö Friedmann) pursued their careers abroad.

1 2	3 4 5	6

Once established, the new discipline was constantly being regenerated, both in the field of 'reporting' (Tamás Féner, György Lőrinczy, Péter Korniss), in the broadest sense, and in its purely artistic and experimental form (Tibor Hajas, Tamás Baranyai, János Vető, Lenke Szilágyi, Ágnes Eperjesi, Tibor Várnagy). To these names should be added those of Nora Dumas (Nóra Kelenföldi Telkes), Árpád Szélpál and Lucien Hervé (László Elkán) – the Hungarian founders of the Keystone, Dephot and Rapho agencies – and Andor Krazna-Krausz, founder of Focal Press publications. The Hungarian Museum of Photography in Kecskemét contains a wealth of historical and modern documentation, and exhibits the work of contemporary photographers. In 1995 a gallery named after Manó Mai, the photographer of the imperial court, was opened next to the museum. The gallery (Mai Manó ház) is located at 20 Nagymező utca ▲ *144*.

1. Robert Capa: *Váci út*, 1940.
2. Károly Hemző: *Holy Trinity Square*, 1990.
3. Miklós Rév: *Aerial View of Parliament*, 1970.
4. Zoltán Zajky: *On Gellért Hill*, 1950s.
5. József Pécsi : *Ruins in Budapest*, 1945.
6. Miklós Rév : *Elizabeth Bridge at Night*, 1970.

The Rác Baths in the late 19th century.

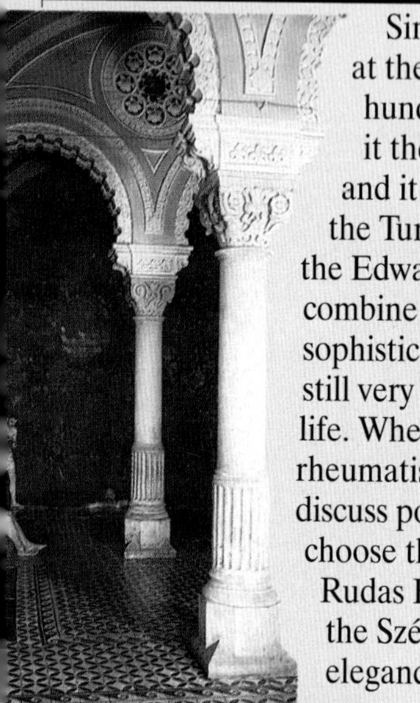

Since the Romans built their *thermae* at the foot of the Buda Hills, Budapest's hundred or so hot springs have made it the most beautiful spa town in Europe; and it may bc the last. Rediscovered by the Turks in the 16th century, and later by the Edwardian bourgeoisie, the baths combine sumptuous architecture with a sophisticated use of light. Today they are still very much a part of the city's everyday life. Whether you want a treatment for rheumatism, a massage, to play chess or discuss politics, or simply to relax, you can choose the more muted ambience of the Rudas Baths, the neo-Baroque radiance of the Széchenyi Baths, or the Art Nouveau elegance of the Gellért Baths.

RUDAS GYÓGYFÜRDŐ ÉS USZODA
Many of the city's public baths were built by the Turks, to observe the rituals of the Muslim religion and cure certain ailments. The Rudas Baths, built in 1566 by the pasha of Buda, are among the most beautiful. A magnificent interior vault inlaid with shards of colored glass (as in the Király Baths) filters and tints the light above an octagonal central pool fed by three springs.

Chess players at the Széchenyi Baths.

The dome of the Király Baths.

‘At Királyfürdő, a 16th-century bath built by a padishah of uncertain memory, the light falls from a dome of multicolored glass, producing an effect worthy of *The Arabian Nights*.’

Julien Green

Gellért Gyógyfürdő ▲ *216*

The Hotel Gellért, with its beautiful Art Nouveau façade, was built in 1914. In 1934 an indoor pool was installed in the old conservatory, beneath the magnificent metal-and-glass dome, which was retained. The central pool is surrounded by Rococo cabled columns, a mosaic floor, and flower-filled balconies below the glass roof. The outdoor ‘wave pool’, with its rocky setting, is a favorite with children in summer.

Széchenyi Gyógyfürdő ▲ *160*

(Left) These are incontestably the largest baths in Europe. In summer sunshine or winter snow, Hungarians come to the vast open-air pool with its grandiose neo-Baroque setting, to play chess or relax in water temperatures of around 100°F.

Lukács Gyógyfürdő és Uszoda ▲ *210*

These beautiful 19th-century baths are situated more or less on the boundary of Óbuda. This is the capital’s most restrained but also its most comprehensive baths complex: as well as three warm springs and twenty-three hot springs, with temperatures varying between 60°F and 120°F (17°C and 50°C), it offers massages and mud baths. In the 1970s and 1980s it was a favorite meeting place for they city’s dissident intellectuals.

AZ ÉG ÁLDÁSÁT KÉREM
E NAGYSZERŰ HATÁSU FÜRDŐRE,
MELYBEN SULYOS BAJOMTÓL
GYORSAN SZABADULTAM MEG.
1902 AUGUSZTUS 5.
REISMANN JOZEFA
TASNÁD.

Left: votive plaque.

CHICKEN PAPRIKA AND 'GALUSKA'

Chicken paprika *(paprikás csirke)* is one of Hungary's most popular dishes. It is prepared like a stew *(pörkölt)*, with a sauce that should be neither too thick nor too thin. The only difference between this dish and an ordinary *pörkölt* is the addition of fresh sour cream. *Galuska* (pronounced 'galooshka') are small dumplings rather like gnocchi.

INGREDIENTS FOR THE CHICKEN

- 1 chicken cut into small pieces
- 2 small onions
- 1 green pepper
- 2 tomatoes
- 1 tbsp mild paprika
- ⅓ cup lard or pork fat (or olive oil)
- 10 fl oz fresh sour cream
- salt

INGREDIENTS FOR THE 'GALUSKA'

- 3 cups flour
- 5 eggs
- salt

(CHICKEN) 1. Slice the tomatoes and pepper, and chop the onions.

2. Lightly brown the onions in the fat.

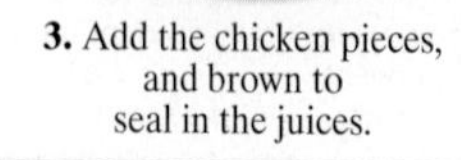

3. Add the chicken pieces, and brown to seal in the juices.

4. Sprinkle the chicken pieces with paprika, and lightly brown. Stir.

5. Add the sliced tomatoes and pepper. Add a little water, so that the chicken cooks in a very thick sauce. Season, cover, and leave to simmer gently.

6. Stir in the sour cream, to obtain a thick creamy sauce.

'GALUSKA' I. Put the eggs and flour into a mixing bowl. Mix together using a wooden spoon, adding enough warm water to form a dough.

II. When the mixture has a dough-like consistency, use a wooden spatula to press it slowly through a large-holed sieve (the Hungarians have a special utensil for this). Drop the pieces of dough into boiling water.

III. Alternatively, roll the dough out onto a pastry board and chop it into small pieces (about the size of a teaspoon), then drop them into boiling water. Don't make too many galuska at a time.

IV. Remove the pieces immediately with a slotted spoon. Rinse, drain, and reheat in butter or lard. Season to taste before serving.

Chicken paprika is traditionally accompanied by *galuska*, but can be served with steamed or boiled potatoes. A green salad goes well with it.

● Specialties

Herend porcelain and Zsolnay vase ● *69*.
These are the jewels in the crown of Hungarian craftsmanship. They are sold in a number of shops and at the Museum of Applied Arts ▲ *172*.

Pimento garlands
In rural areas, the red pimentos are hung up to dry on the fronts of houses.

'Foie gras'
Hungarian *foie gras* is spread on bread, salted and eaten with sweet onions.

Ribbons
The markets sell embroidery at very reasonable prices. Avoid buying it in city-center shops.

Wines
Bull's Blood of Eger *(Egri bikavér)* is so called because of its color and strength. *Tokaji aszú* is made from very sweet grapes harvested in October, when almost dried, in baskets known as *puttony*.

The more *puttonyos* (specified on the label of a bottle of *Tokaji aszú*), the sweeter the wine.

CDs ● *52*
Hungaroton's catalog offers a wide range of musical styles. In Hungary, its CDs are reasonably priced.

The Gerbeaud Patisserie was opened at the end of the 19th century by a master Swiss chocolate maker. It is renowned both for its patisserie ▲ *117* and for its morello cherries in brandy *(konyakos meggy)*.

Dried paprika
The Great Plain is the favored home of the red pimento. Szeged is the town for paprika.

Salami
Hungarian salami is traditionally eaten at breakfast and tea time. The best salami is the *pick téliszalámi*, made from well-seasoned pork and pieces of bacon.

ARCHITECTURE

Mohamed Bansar, Iván Bojár

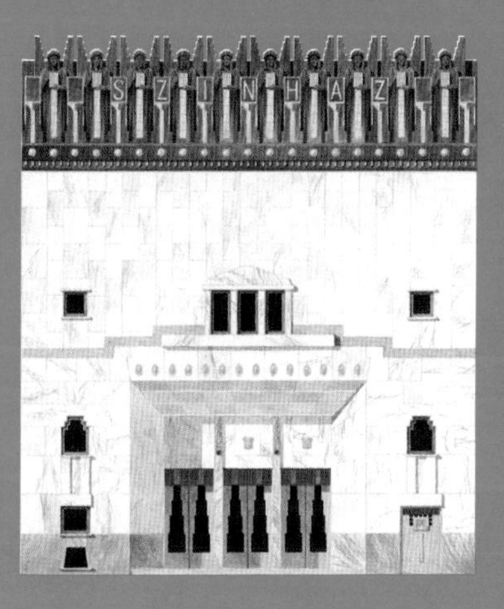

The rich colors of Budapest reflect the diverse influences that have shaped the city's development. And yet these vibrant colors combine to create an impression of harmony in which their individual brightness is softened by the overall effect. For this reason, all that the eye retains of the extravagance of detail and the bold use of contrasting colors is the impression of a dominant color that varies from district to district: the ocher tones of Baroque Buda, the white and green-ocher of neoclassical Pest, the multicolored Art Nouveau style of the newly unified Budapest...

BAROQUE BUDA
The buildings of Baroque Buda are mostly built of brick and the rather crumbly limestone (*méskő*) quarried in the Buda Hills. The originally white or yellow-ocher façades are today decorated in a much richer range of colors (1). Doors and windows are highlighted with hard gray or beige stone (2, 3) or a plain white band that creates a trompe-l'œil effect (6). Window lintels of Hungarian marble (*süttő*), from the Esztergom region, are decorated with the sculpted heads (4) characteristic of the *copf* style (a variation of Rococo) ▲ *231*. The pure, simple lines of the façades are embellished by outlines, set-backs and square corbeled balconies that catch the light and create the typically Baroque chiaroscuro effect (5).

PEST: NEOCLASSICISM AND ROMANTICISM
Between the early 1800s and 1867 the architecture in the center of Pest evolved from neoclassicism to historicism. Its public buildings were built of stone, and the white façades of the brick apartment blocks were highlighted by stone

2
5
4
6
7
8
9

details (7). The vast inner courtyards were paved with pink *süttő* marble. Today white has been largely replaced by greens and ochers (8, 9).

PEST: ECLECTICISM AND ART NOUVEAU
From 1867, with the rise of the bourgeoisie, stone and colored façades were the order of the day at a time when decoration was deemed more important than the quality of the materials (12). There was an increase in richly decorated architectural features – domes (13), spires (14), towers (11, 15) and turrets – and façades were stuccoed (17, 18), painted and decorated with mosaics.
Around 1880 the Zsolnay ● *66*, ▲ *136, 172* manufactory developed a range of glazed ceramic tiles that the best Hungarian architects – Ödön Lechner, Miklós Ybl and Imre Steindl – used for polychrome roofs (10) and the decoration of façades (20).

MODERN BUDAPEST
After 1918 the development of materials and the appearance of concrete resulted in simple monochrome decoration, highlighted by the geometric effects of light and shade (21, 22). Today the use of brick (23, 24) marks a return to natural materials.

AN EYE FOR DETAIL
Whatever the style, Budapest has always had a remarkable eye for detail that makes close examination well worthwhile.

Baroque architecture appeared in Hungary around 1620. It became very popular from the end of the 17th century, and reached its peak in the 18th century. The Turks, driven from Hungary in 1686, left nothing but ruins in their wake. The establishment of the Austrian Habsburg dynasty in Hungary and the extensive Jesuit influence gave rise to intense architectural activity, especially in Buda and Pest. Although initially religious in nature, it was soon emulated by the nobility, impressed by the examples of Italian Baroque architecture introduced into Hungary via Austria.

ST ANNE'S CHURCH ▲ *207* (1740–62, Kristóf Hamon and Mátyás Nepauer) The Baroque façade of St Anne's Church (Szent Anna templom) is marked by an interplay of vertical and horizontal lines. Its two slender towers seem to rise from ground level, giving the structure a vertical dynamic – tempered by the horizontal lines, which divide the building into three equal sections and reestablish its equilibrium. The God's-eye motif dominate the composition of the tympanum.

GOD'S-EYE MOTIF The triangular God's-eye motif (above) represents the Holy Trinity. This Baroque motif was widely used in the 18th century.

THE ROYAL PALACE OF BUDA ▲ *190* (1753, Pacassi; 1765, Hillebrandt). The construction of the Baroque palace on the ruins of its Gothic predecessor had a symbolic and moral significance. After the departure of the Turks and Hungary's incorporation into the Holy Roman Empire, it was important to reaffirm the status of a site that was, ironically, unsuitable. Situated on a rocky spur, it would be impossible for it to fulfill the traditional function of royal palace and residence. The new U-shaped building had a central dome dominated by a watchtower, a feature inspired by northern Italian architecture.

'THE 100-YEAR-OLD RESTAURANT' (Százéves Étterem, 2 Pesti Barnabás utca) (1755, Mayerhoffer) The projecting central section is all that remains of this two-story building, which originally had two wings, forming a U-shape. Built for János Péterffy, it is a fine example of secular Baroque architecture.

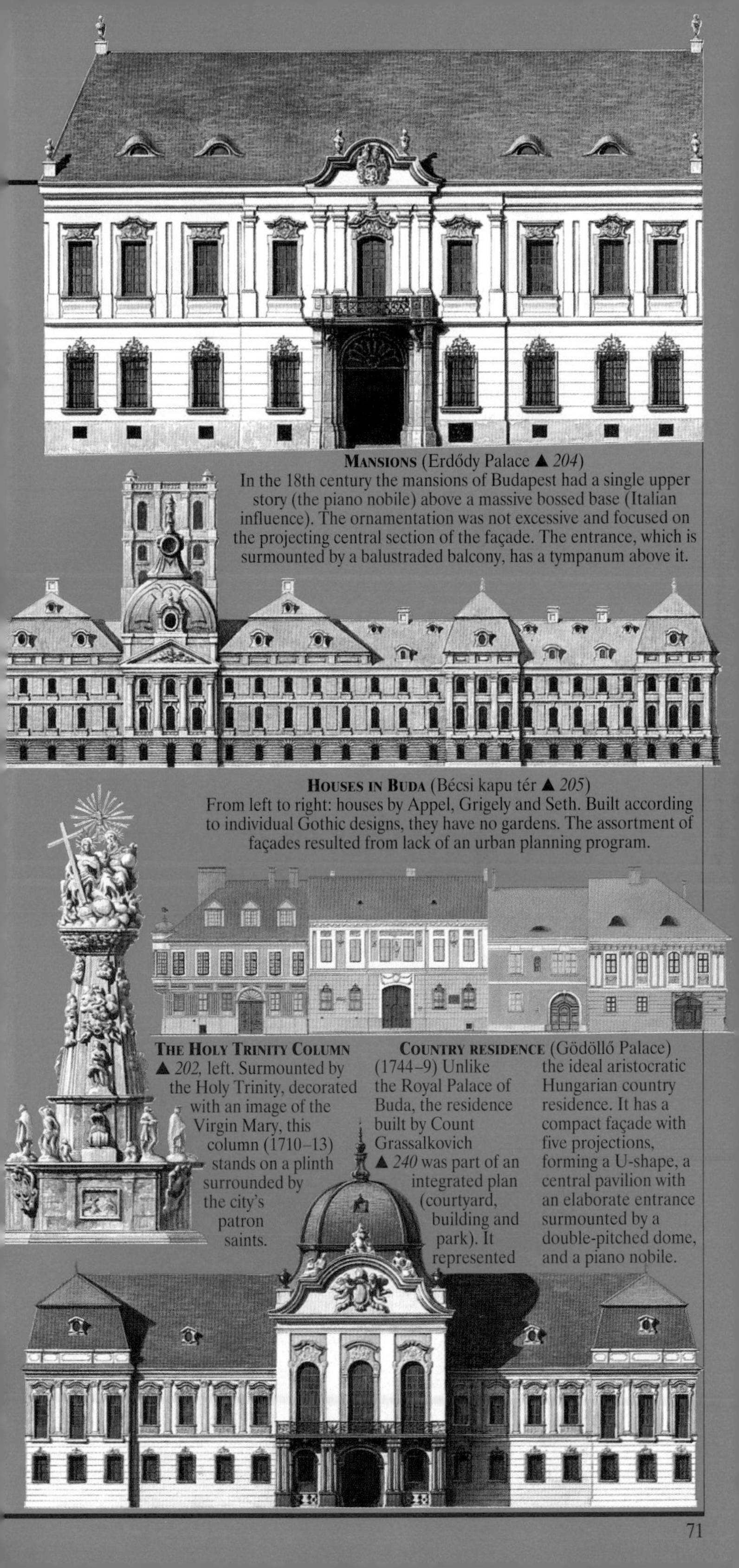

MANSIONS (Erdődy Palace ▲ *204*)
In the 18th century the mansions of Budapest had a single upper story (the piano nobile) above a massive bossed base (Italian influence). The ornamentation was not excessive and focused on the projecting central section of the façade. The entrance, which is surmounted by a balustraded balcony, has a tympanum above it.

HOUSES IN BUDA (Bécsi kapu tér ▲ *205*)
From left to right: houses by Appel, Grigely and Seth. Built according to individual Gothic designs, they have no gardens. The assortment of façades resulted from lack of an urban planning program.

THE HOLY TRINITY COLUMN ▲ *202,* left. Surmounted by the Holy Trinity, decorated with an image of the Virgin Mary, this column (1710–13) stands on a plinth surrounded by the city's patron saints.

COUNTRY RESIDENCE (Gödöllő Palace) (1744–9) Unlike the Royal Palace of Buda, the residence built by Count Grassalkovich ▲ *240* was part of an integrated plan (courtyard, building and park). It represented the ideal aristocratic Hungarian country residence. It has a compact façade with five projections, forming a U-shape, a central pavilion with an elaborate entrance surmounted by a double-pitched dome, and a piano nobile.

From houses to apartment blocks

Variations on a theme

Recessed seat in the entrance passage at 2, Országház utca ▲ *204*, in Buda.

One of the main features of Budapest's apartment blocks is that they are arranged around a central courtyard, a characteristic inherited from rural architecture. In the farms of the Danube plains living accommodation and outbuildings are arranged around an open central courtyard. The more compact urban version, rationalized and developed over three centuries, is still based on the same layout.

The Gothic town

Because Budapest was so often devastated by war, there are not many courtyards that offer a glimpse of the Gothic town. The houses had an overhanging upper story pierced by two (often double) windows, a façade that did not face the street, and an arched entrance passage large enough to accommodate horse-drawn vehicles.

Farm on the Danube plain

Traditional layout of the farms of the central plains

'...the houses are all equidistant from and back onto the outer wall...the windows are set in a single arcaded façade. Thus, each house has its own courtyard and enjoys perfect privacy.'
Le Corbusier

Buda, 2, Országház utca

A stone street façade

Gothic urban housing echoed the farm layout. However, the building was unified by the addition of a stone street façade. An arched entrance passage, with a recessed seat in the middle of the wall, gave access to the courtyard.

A Baroque 'veneer'

The façade, refurbished in the Baroque style (with bosses, capitals, and pilasters framing the windows), conceals the typical Gothic structure of the building.

RATIONALIZATION OF THE COURTYARD AREA
Baroque buildings rationalized the courtyard and service area. From the entrance a flight of steps led to landings that gave access to the buildings at the rear. The reception rooms of the piano nobile overlooked the street.

BUDA, 11, ORSZÁGHÁZ UTCA

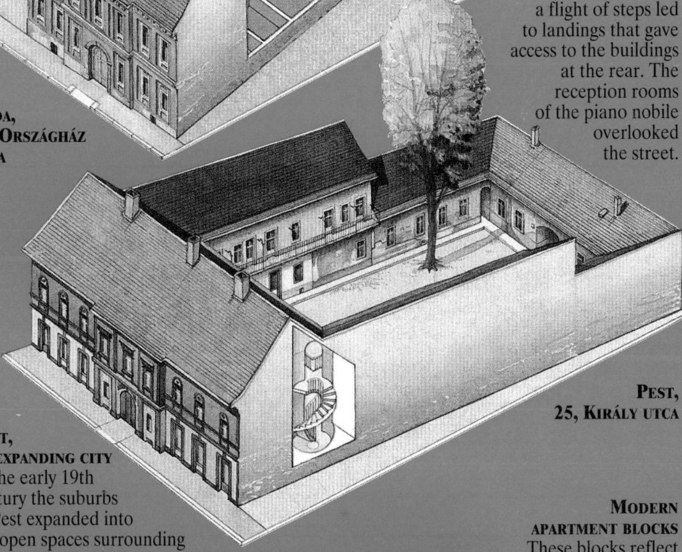

PEST, 25, KIRÁLY UTCA

PEST, AN EXPANDING CITY
In the early 19th century the suburbs of Pest expanded into the open spaces surrounding the city. Neoclassical architecture retained the traditional two-story building; the larger plots of land made more spacious, planted courtyards feasible.

MODERN APARTMENT BLOCKS
These blocks reflect the rapid expansion of Budapest. Although they stand on a geometrical grid of streets and have three to six floors, they have retained the traditional layout around a central courtyard .

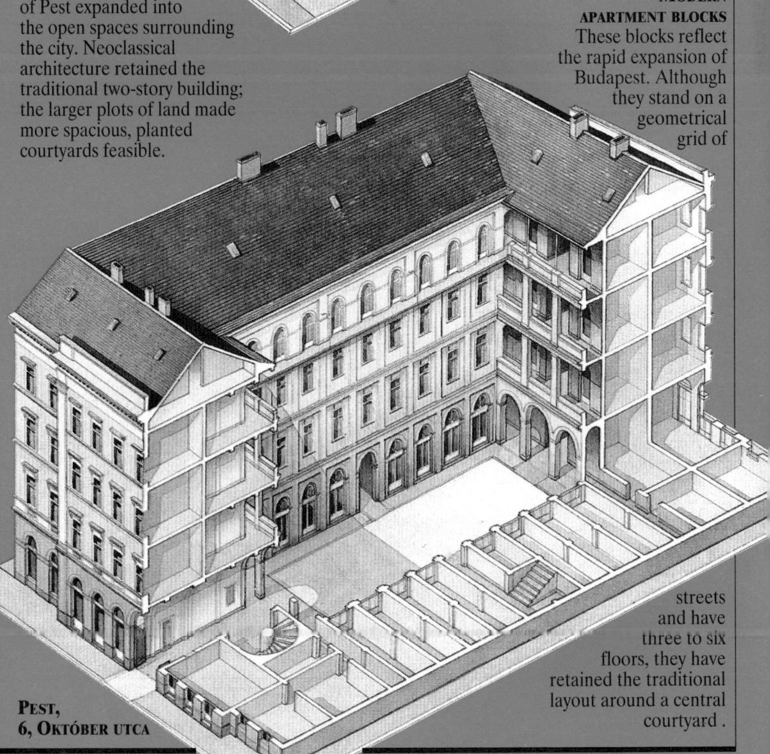

PEST, 6, OKTÓBER UTCA

Detail from an entrance porch on Apáczai Csere János utca.

From the 1820s onward Hungary experienced a period of prosperity known as the Age of Reform ● *34*. It was during this period that Pest began to acquire public and cultural buildings (museums, baths, theaters, hotels). Characterized by a style that is both rigorous and majestic, these buildings reflect the aspirations of a new bourgeoisie that wanted an architecturally homogeneous city. Baroque was abandoned in favor of neoclassicism, and official monuments and apartment blocks alike were built in neoclassical style. Despite differences of form and function, they all shared the same clean, harmonious lines and carefully balanced symmetry.

THE HUNGARIAN NATIONAL MUSEUM ▲ *123, 124* ◆ *265*
(1837–44, Mihály Pollack) This is one of the best examples of neoclassical Hungarian architecture in the early 19th century. The long rectangular building has a sculpted tympanum, a central portico, derived from the Erechtheion in Athens, with eight Corinthian columns, and a base supporting two rows of symmetrical windows. The epitome of gravitas and restraint.

PLAN OF THE NATIONAL MUSEUM

Mihály Pollack adapted the plan for the ideal museum described by J.N.L. Durand in 1801. He divided the building in two to create twin courtyards and placed his rotunda near the entrance, instead of in the center.

THE CHAIN BRIDGE
(1839–49, Adam Clark and William Tierney Clark ● 35, ▲ *183, 184*) The first stone bridge built across the Danube, the Chain Bridge is symbolic of the city's development. Previously Buda and Pest had been linked by two wooden bridges that suffered damage every winter. The chains that give the bridge its strength are suspended from two piles, each with its base resting on the river bed and an upper section resembling a miniature triumphal arch. The bridgeheads are guarded by apotropaic

CHURCHES
Religious architecture was also influenced by the dominant architectural style. The Lutheran Church (1799–1809, plans by János Krausz) on Deák Ferenc tér ▲ *123* was completed by Mihály Pollack, the great 'planner' of neoclassical Pest. The façade overlooking the square has a portico with four Doric columns supporting an architrave decorated with a simple frieze.

THE FORMER GYÜRKI MANSION
(1814–15 and 1855, plans by József Hofrichter) Placed under the protection of the gods of Olympus – the head of Zeus is sculpted above the entrance – this four-story building (at 5, Apáczai Csere János utca) is a model of neoclassical symmetry.

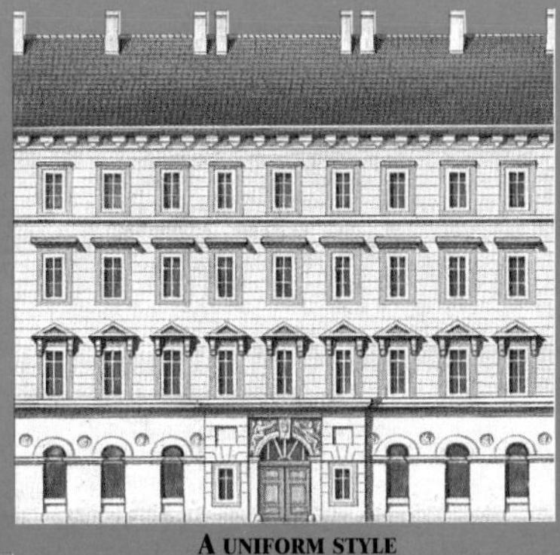

DECORATION OF THE GYÜRKI MANSION
The stone arcature decorating the ground floor of the mansion is surmounted by medallions featuring heads inspired by figures from Greco-Roman mythology.

A UNIFORM STYLE
Apartment blocks and official buildings received identical treatment. The neoclassical façade of the Tänzer apartment block (left), dating from 1836, has a central six-columned balcony supporting a tympanum. The same 'truncated portico' is found at the center of the façade (below) of Pest County Hall (Pest Megyei Őnkormányzat, ▲ *121*), built between 1838 and 1841.

HISTORICISM AND ECLECTICISM

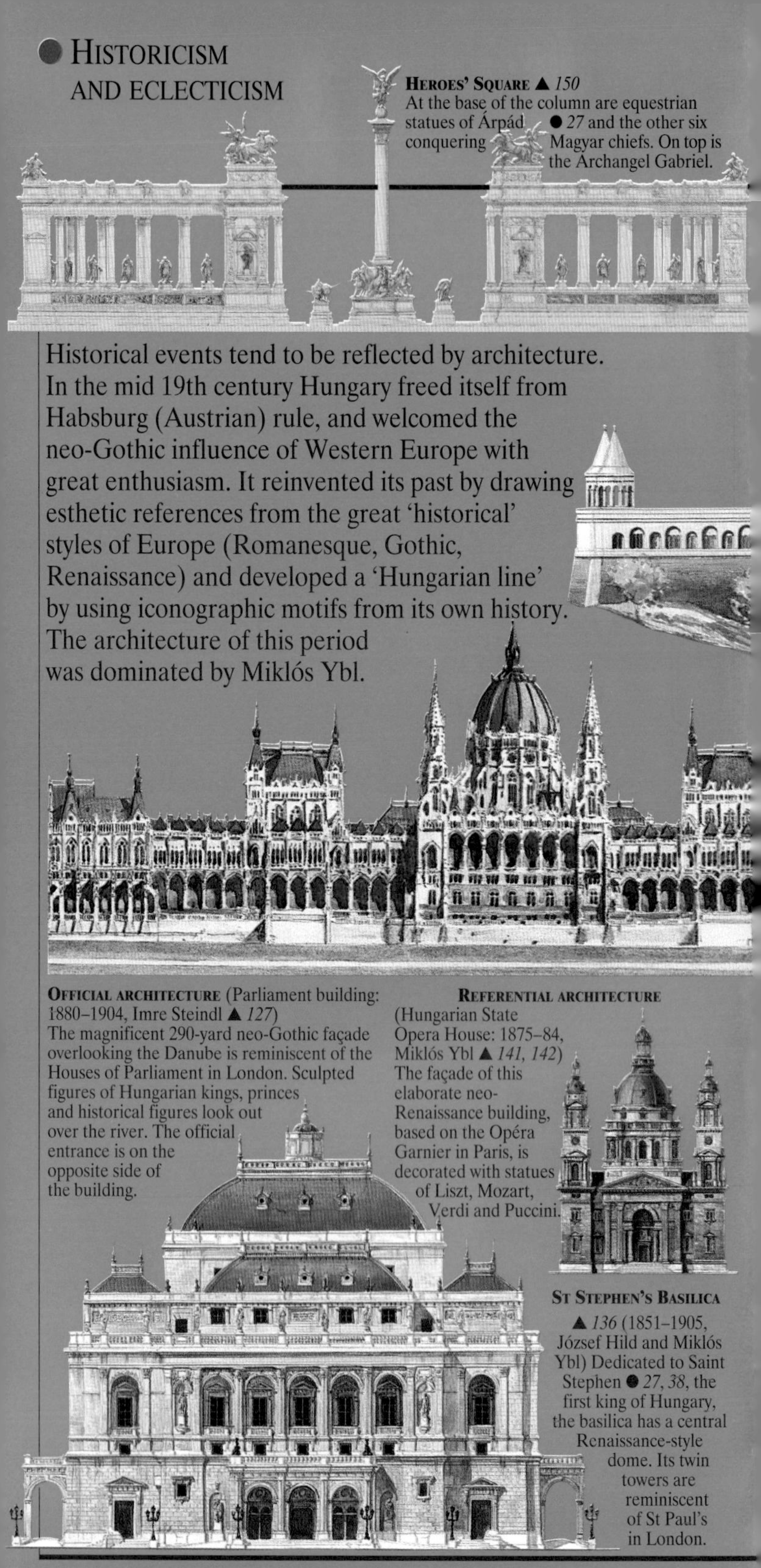

HEROES' SQUARE ▲ *150*
At the base of the column are equestrian statues of Árpád ● *27* and the other six conquering Magyar chiefs. On top is the Archangel Gabriel.

Historical events tend to be reflected by architecture. In the mid 19th century Hungary freed itself from Habsburg (Austrian) rule, and welcomed the neo-Gothic influence of Western Europe with great enthusiasm. It reinvented its past by drawing esthetic references from the great 'historical' styles of Europe (Romanesque, Gothic, Renaissance) and developed a 'Hungarian line' by using iconographic motifs from its own history. The architecture of this period was dominated by Miklós Ybl.

OFFICIAL ARCHITECTURE (Parliament building: 1880–1904, Imre Steindl ▲ *127*)
The magnificent 290-yard neo-Gothic façade overlooking the Danube is reminiscent of the Houses of Parliament in London. Sculpted figures of Hungarian kings, princes and historical figures look out over the river. The official entrance is on the opposite side of the building.

REFERENTIAL ARCHITECTURE
(Hungarian State Opera House: 1875–84, Miklós Ybl ▲ *141, 142*)
The façade of this elaborate neo-Renaissance building, based on the Opéra Garnier in Paris, is decorated with statues of Liszt, Mozart, Verdi and Puccini.

ST STEPHEN'S BASILICA
▲ *136* (1851–1905, József Hild and Miklós Ybl) Dedicated to Saint Stephen ● *27, 38*, the first king of Hungary, the basilica has a central Renaissance-style dome. Its twin towers are reminiscent of St Paul's in London.

Details of the Fishermen's Bastion (Magyar soldiers) ▲ *203*.

Millennial architecture

The Fishermen's Bastion (right), the Matthias Church (left) and Heroes' Square (top left) were the architectural *tours de force* of the town-planning project that commemorated the thousandth anniversary of the founding of the Arpadian dynasty. The neo-Romanesque Fishermen's Bastion (1899–1905) was built on the city's medieval ramparts. A little further on, the Matthias Church, founded in the 13th century by Béla IV, was extended and refurbished as part of the same project. In Pest, Heroes' Square marked the limit of the new urban development to the east.

Symbolic image

This statue of the architect Imre Steindl, dressed in medieval costume and holding the plans of the Parliament building, is highly symbolic. When Pest freed itself from Habsburg rule, it invented a past that gave its Parliament a precedence free from Austrian influence.

Eclectic architecture

(New York Palace: 1891–5, plans by Alajos Hauszmann ▲ *167*) This five-story building combines neo-Renaissance and neo-Baroque architectural elements to produce a truly eclectic style. The façade is decorated with towers, spires, corner domes, a great many windows, balustraded balconies, Ionic columns and statues. On the ground floor, the Café New York ● *56* has frescos signed by Lotz, Eisnhut and Magyar-Mannheimer.

In the 1860s, while still under Habsburg (Austrian) rule, Budapest was seeking to establish its identity. It preferred Romanticism to the neoclassical style that was still very much in vogue, since it offered greater creative freedom. Architects sought to develop a specifically Hungarian style, that would be distinct from other 'historical' styles, by infusing them with Hungarian symbolism and idealism.

THE GREAT SYNAGOGUE (Zsinagóga) ▲ *166* (1854–9: plans by Ludwig Förster, elevation by Ignác Wechselmann) Hungary's growing Jewish population led to the construction of many synagogues throughout the country. Although ostensibly eastern, the Great Synagogue, in Pest, reflects other architectural styles: the two minaret-like towers surmounted by onion-shaped domes are certainly reminiscent of the columns of the Temple of Solomon in Jerusalem, but they also echo the twin towers of Western European churches. The multicolored glazed bricks of the façade were an innovation. The synagogue's remarkable longitudinal plan, supported by a metal frame, is reminiscent of Christian churches – hence its nickname, the 'Jewish cathedral'.

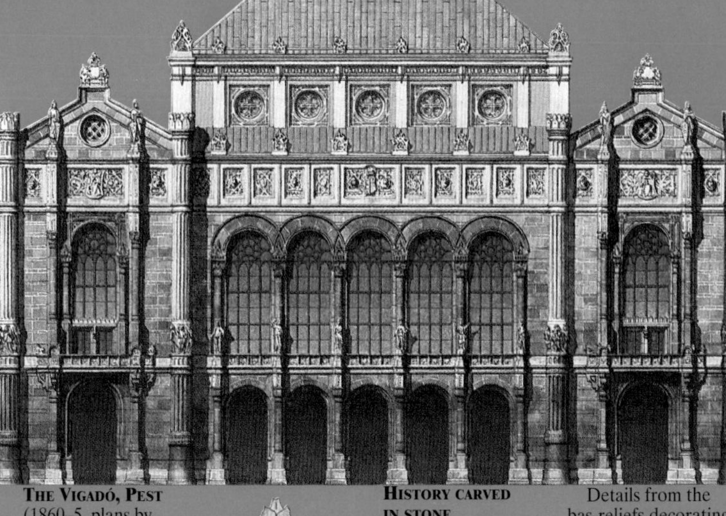

The Vigadó, Pest
(1860–5, plans by Frigyes Feszl ▲ *118*)
Built as a ballroom and concert hall, the Vigadó is one of the supreme achievements of the Hungarian Romantic movement. In this instance, the 'Hungarian style' asserts itself via a Moorish theme – with high arcades, inspired by Venetian Orientalism, and Islamic-style geometric friezes referring to the eastern origins of the Hungarian people.

History carved in stone
The statues of great Hungarian leaders, such as kings Matthias Corvinus and Béla IV, that grace the Vigadó's façade proudly recall Hungarian history. In addition, allegories of dance and music allude to the building's function.

Details from the bas-reliefs decorating the façade of the Vigadó.

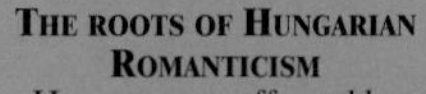

The roots of Hungarian Romanticism
Hungary was affected by the revolutionary fervor that swept across Europe in the 1840s. But the uprising of 1848 was suppressed by the Habsburgs, and the Emperor Franz Joseph incorporated Hungary into a unified empire. The Hungarians opposed this enforced integration with a cultural resistance in which architects played a major role, investing their monuments with the spirit of Hungarian nationalism.

The Pékary house
(1847–8, Ferenc Brein)
This mansion (5, Király utca) is a fine example of the stylistic amalgam favored by Hungarian Romanticism. In niches on either side of the central balcony, two Magyar warriors recall the ancient origins of the Hungarian nation. The stylized lines of the doors (left) were later echoed by the architectural Cubism of Prague (1910–20).

HUNGARIAN ART NOUVEAU...

Finial from the former Post Office Savings Bank (1899–1901, Ödön Lechner ▲ *136*) in Pest. The finials of the towers framing the main façade have winged serpents, symbolizing renewal.

On the eve of the 20th century the revival of Hungarian nationalism found expression in the unprecedented use of forms and techniques manifested by the 'explosion' of Hungarian Art Nouveau. Ödön Lechner, the uncontested master of this innovative period, defined the archetypes of a 'language of national forms' that successfully combined oriental references and images of Hungarian folklore to produce a strongly individualistic style.

MUSEUM OF APPLIED ARTS (1893–6, Ödön Lechner and Gyula Pártos ▲ *171, 172*) It was designed to demonstrate the extraordinary richness of Hungarian decorative and applied arts. Inside, oriental elements and folkloric motifs are incorporated into the fabric of the building. When it was opened, some people derisively referred to it as the 'gypsy palace'.

THE VOGUE FOR POLYCHROME TILES The façade and roofs of the Museum of Applied Arts are entirely covered with plant motifs painted on polychrome tiles – an inexpensive and waterproof material – from the Zsolnay manufactory. Above: the central lantern.

FROM HOUSES AND VILLAS... (Villa Egger: 1902, Emil Vidor ▲ *149*) Initially the new stylistic freedom found expression in the design of private houses. This villa was the first to be built entirely in Art Nouveau style.

...TO GRANDIOSE OFFICE BLOCKS (Gresham Palace: 1905–7, Zsigmond Quittner and the Vágó brothers ▲ *138*) This lavish building, originally the offices of the London-based Gresham insurance company, is typical of the Hungarian Secessionist style. At first the authorities disapproved of this type of Art Nouveau, and refused to finance Ödön Lechner's work because they regarded his style as Secessionist. Nevertheless, Lechner's ideas soon triumphed and greatly influenced the architecture of Budapest.

HYBRID STYLE
(Entrance of the Sonnenberg Mansion: 1904, Albert Körössy ▲ *148*) An example of a hybrid style: Art Nouveau (wavy lines) and Baroque (chiaroscuro effects).

HISTORICISM AND ART NOUVEAU
(Former Turkish Bank: 1906, Ármin Hegedűs, Henrik Böhm ▲ *121*) This is a fine blend of the Hungarian Art Nouveau and historicism that coexisted until 1914. The glass and steel façade are surmounted by a wavy-edged tympanum decorated with a large mosaic of Hungaria, the symbolic representation of Hungary.

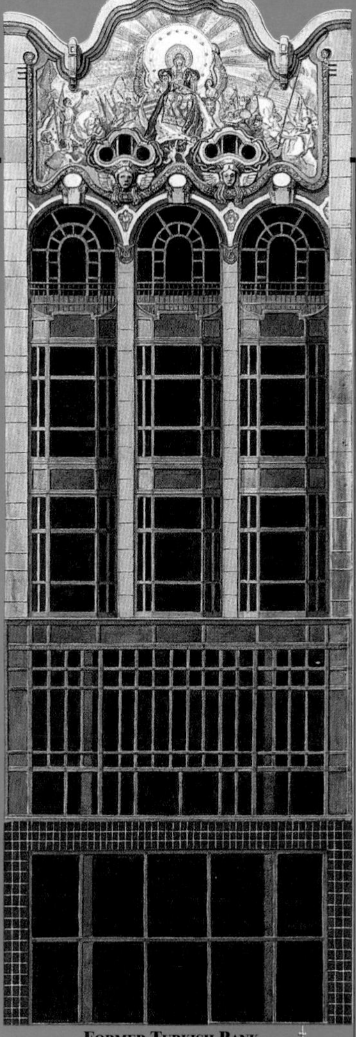

FORMER TURKISH BANK

THE ART OF DETAIL
The key materials of Hungarian Art Nouveau were tiles and wrought iron. Above, the polychrome ceramic tiles with stylized motifs used on the façade of the Gresham Palace, and the wrought-iron gates decorated with a peacock design. Four years of delicate restoration work have restored the building to its former splendor.

GRESHAM PALACE

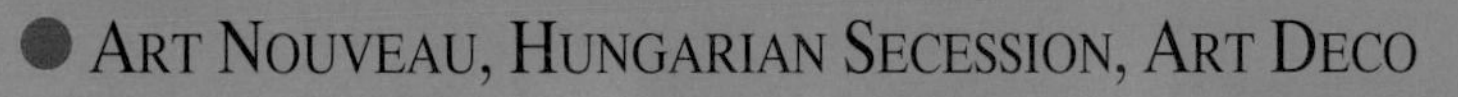

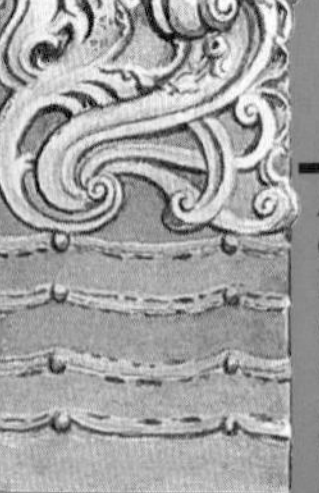

ART NOUVEAU CAPITALS
From left to right: Gresham Palace ▲ *138*, Hotel Gellért and the apartment block at 18, Szent Gellért Rakpart (St Gellért Quay).

TOWARD GEOMETRIC STYLIZATION
(Institute for the Blind: 1905–7, Béla Lajta ▲ *113*) The building is amazingly avant-garde and "European" in style. A sober façade of dark-red brick attests to a Scandinavian influence. The only 'decorative' feature is the parabolic arch of the entrance porch and, on a reduced scale, over some of the windows. Folkloric motifs, combined with biblical scenes, reaffirm the national identity.

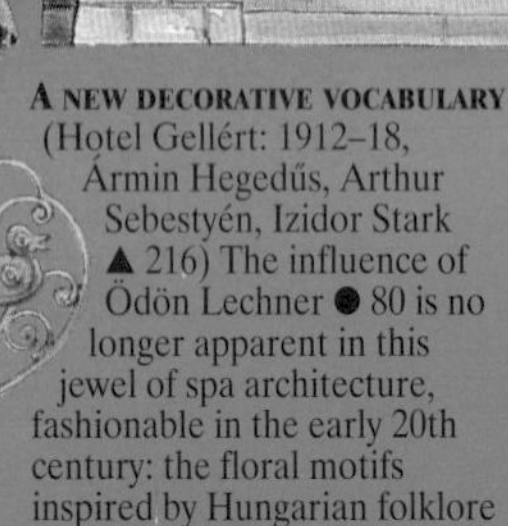

A NEW DECORATIVE VOCABULARY
(Hotel Gellért: 1912–18, Ármin Hegedűs, Arthur Sebestyén, Izidor Stark ▲ 216) The influence of Ödön Lechner ● 80 is no longer apparent in this jewel of spa architecture, fashionable in the early 20th century: the floral motifs inspired by Hungarian folklore that embellish the building have become geometric, while the richly detailed decoration, typical of late Art Nouveau, is combined with a neo-Baroque style (evident in the domes). There is also an underlying reference to Roman baths.

Symbolic form
(Porch of the Hospital of Neurosurgery: 1908–11, Béla Lajta) The parabolic form of this porch, decorated with Hebraic motifs and scenes from the Old Testament, was favored by Béla Lajta, for whom it symbolized Hungary's architectural heritage.

Jozsef Rippl-Ronái
A member of the French Nabis group, this artist created the stained-glass window on the staircase of the Ernst Múzeum (8, Nagymező utca).

Toward Art Deco
(Porch of Calvinist Church and details: 1911–13, Aladár Árkay ▲ 112)
The massive porch of the Calvinist Church (at 5–7, Városligeti fasor) is an amazing example of late Art Nouveau. It is decorated with magnificent ceramic tiles in subdued colors (ochers, golds and blacks) and uses geometric rather than figurative motifs.

Modernism did not become firmly established or conquer the public domain until a few years before World War Two, despite the fact that the character of certain early 20th-century architectural works (the forerunners of Art Deco) had fore-shadowed functionalism. In the early 1920s an attachment to traditional values placed the emphasis on historicism and neo-Baroque, postponing the development of Modernism until the 1930s.

TOWARD MODERNISM
(Új Színház: 1909; Béla Lajta ▲ 144) This committedly Art Nouveau theater building foreshadows the Modernism that came into vogue twenty years later. The Art Nouveau angels contrast with the stark grayish-white marble façade.

STRUCTURE EXPOSED TO VIEW
(Rózsavölgyi building: 1911–12, Béla Lajta) The dual purpose (public and private) of this building is immediately apparent: the glass façade of the lower floors marks the office area, while the residential upper floors are characterized by judiciously positioned traditional windows. The structure of the building is visible on the ground floor.

Villa no. 2 of the Napraforgó utca housing estate: 1931, Gyula Wälder. Based on the principle of a square within a square. The function creates the form.

MODERNISM AND FUNCTIONALISM
Modernism, with its intellectual, avant-garde connotations, proved unsuccessful within the context of the grave economic and moral crisis that followed World War One. However, a small group of architects provided fresh impetus to innovation by creating the Napraforgó utca housing estate (1931), applying the functional concepts of Modernism inspired by the Bauhaus. These principles (economy and clarity of form, linear precision, simplicity of interior spaces) are also evident in the Villa Zenta (above, 1933).

Geometrization
(Rózsavölgyi building) Modernism abandoned decoration to highlight structure. Nevertheless, the Hungarian love of decoration has survived in this building, where the horizontal strata of the façade are emphasized by ornamental friezes , with geometrized motifs (above) foreshadowing Art Deco.

Minimalist decor
(Átrium Cinema: 1935, Lajos Kozma) The emphasis on structure is immediately apparent in Budapest's first Modernist building. Color, the ultimate decorative medium, is employed to highlight function and use of materials: white for walls, black for fixed metal frames, and red for mobile frames.

Constructivism
A constructivist composition (1923), signed by the architect, features on the wall of the entrance hall of this residential building (1937) in Trombitás utca. Farkas Molnár, one of the first Hungarian architects to apply Bauhaus concepts to architecture, was the leader of the Hungarian Modernist movement.

Italian monumentalism
(Városmajor Church: 1932–3, Aladár & Bertalan Árkay) The travertine cladding used for the exterior of this church softens the complex interplay of space. Bertalan Árkay had just returned from Italy, and the design reflects the influence of Northern Italian rationalism; it is in effect a contemporary adaptation of a basilica.

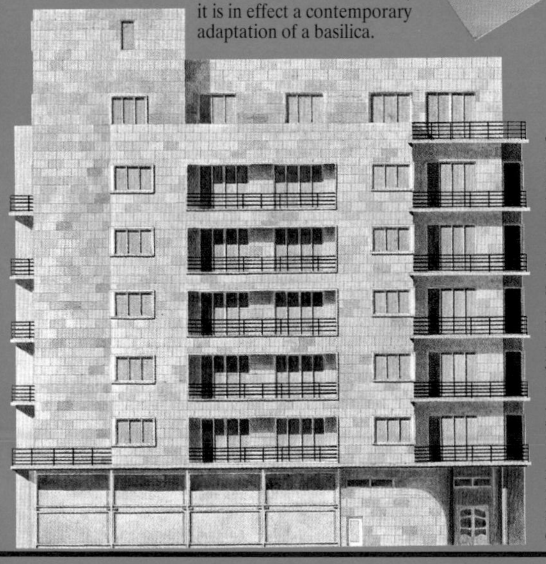

The war years
(Apartment block in Szent István Park: Béla Hofstätter and Ferenc Domány, 1941 ▲ *139*) Modernism, for a long time criticized for its starkness by the authorities and the bourgeoisie, was perfectly suited to the war years and the great urban development project for the left bank of the Danube. Its lack of decoration, rationalism and use of inexpensive materials made quick, efficient construction possible.

The Yalta agreements placed Hungary within the Eastern bloc, under the aegis of the Soviet Union. Nevertheless, this rebellious country, brought sharply to heel in 1956 and ostensibly subjected to the Stalinist architectural model, succeeded in expressing its determination, often very subtly, to create an authentically national architectural style. It was this spirit of nationalism that sometimes managed to modify the unprepossessing appearance of Communist architecture.

POSTWAR RATIONALISM (LEFT)
(Apartment block on Lakóház út: 1948, MATI)
In the period immediately after World War Two priority was given to reconstruction and local authority housing projects, which as a logical consequence of Modernism still observed the principles of functionalism.

MODERNIST CONTINUITY (RIGHT)
(Deák Ferenc tér: 1949, István Nyíril ▲*123*)
In the early years of Communism Modernism accommodated Socialist ideology, and the great Modernist architects continued to express themselves via public buildings such as this dynamic, functional bus station.

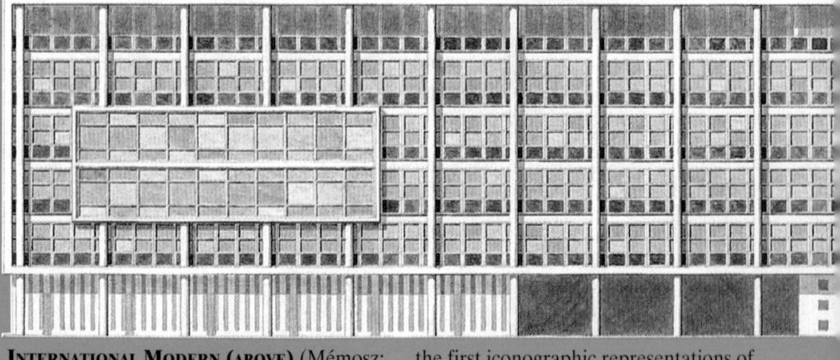

INTERNATIONAL MODERN (ABOVE) (Mémosz: 1947–50, MATI). Born of Modernism, the International Modern style enjoyed widespread success. An example is this trade-union building – although it also contained the first iconographic representations of Socialist Realism, in the form of sculptures of manual workers in the assembly hall. The façade (above) displays a kinship with ones designed by Le Corbusier.

Details of bas-reliefs, Budapest Technical University.

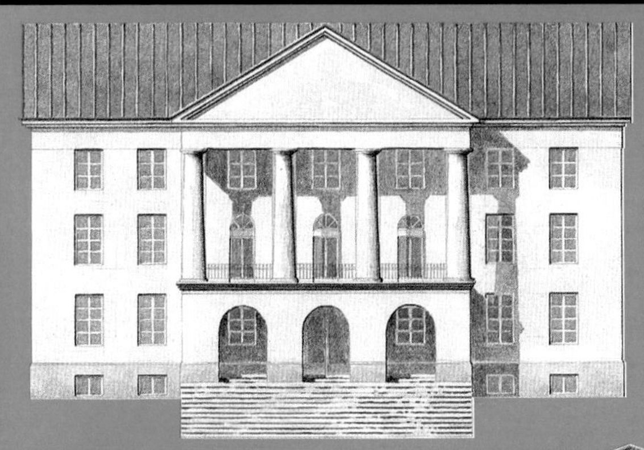

Implicit protest (School of Applied Arts: 1935, Zoltán Farkasdy) The return to neoclassicism under the Soviet regime had a symbolic, 'anti-propagandist' significance – since classical elements such as the portico and tympanum were associated with Athens and democracy.

Edifying architecture (right) (Entrance to the Technical University; 1955; Gyula Rimanóczy) The pure Socialist Realism of this building (right) constitutes a celebration of manual labor. The images of manual workers in the bas-reliefs (left and top right) on either side of the entrance have a nobility reminiscent of classical sculpture. The classical reference is also reflected in the form of the tympanum and its decorative frieze of Greek motifs.

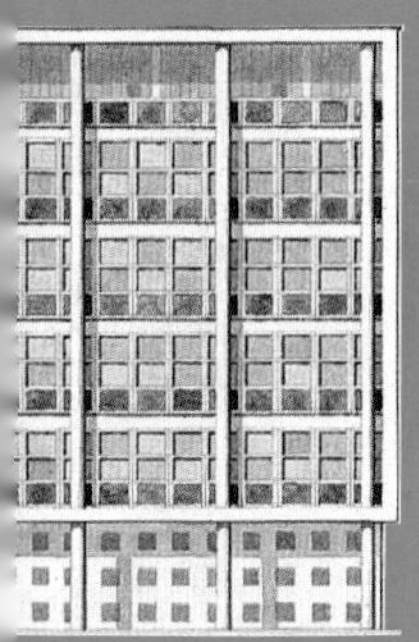

The return to neoclassicism (left) (Town Hall of the District II) The Communist dictatorship, which condemned Modernism as an embodiment of Western bourgeois decadence, demanded a break with the immediate past and imposed neoclassicism as the expression of Hungarian national style.

Socialist Realism Hungarian-style (below) (OTP Bank: 1963, Zoltán Gulyás) The post-Stalinist era of the 1960s reestablished links with Modernism, a concept that incorporated Western influences – in this instance, those of New York – and, with its emphasis on essentials and people's needs, aspired to a more 'human' scale. Here the spaces are clearly defined: the ground floor is opened up by a central patio, while the two towers are devoted to offices.

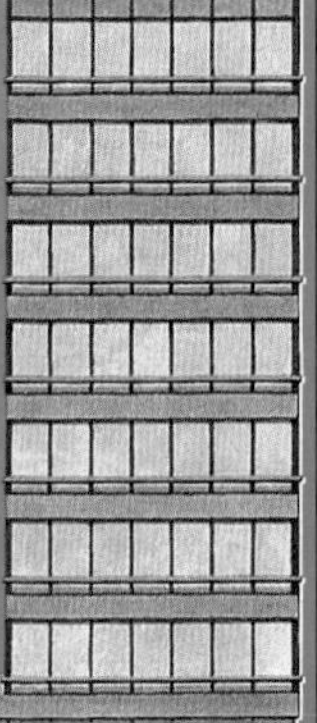

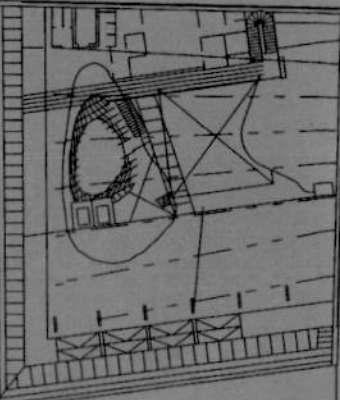

Plan for the renovation of the ING Bank, 1994.

Certain aspects of Budapest's modern architecture can be ascribed to the ecological considerations being taken into account throughout Europe. In addition, as well as respecting the urban landscape and the environment, it aims to preserve the city's rich monumental heritage. When it is not an amalgam of materials and references, it tends toward an organic style that reflects the individuality found throughout Budapest's architectural history.

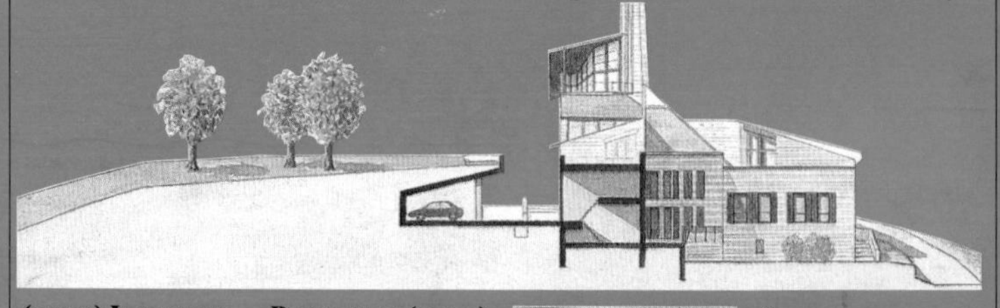

(ABOVE) INTEGRATED ARCHITECTURE
(Ferenc Ctágoly and Richárd Hönich 1993) The apartments of this architectural complex on the western slope of Gellért Hill ▲ *215* are, literally, incorporated into the hillside. Instead of interrupting the natural contours of the hill, the S-shaped complex blends into them and complements them with its roof gardens.

RENOVATION (RIGHT)
(ING Bank: 1994, Erick Van Egeraat) A historical façade, dating from 1883, conceals the very modern offices of the ING Bank. The glass roof above the courtyard incorporates a highly original caterpillar-like conference room.

SEARCH FOR IDENTITY (BELOW) (Church of the Hungarian Saints: 1996, Ferenc Török and Mihály Balázs) This building sets out to create a sense of identity. It combines a wide range of materials (copper, glass, wood, granite, brick) and a variety of features that refer to the past: the dome provides a reference to Budapest's Turkish baths, while the central plan is inspired by Baroque.

ORGANIC ARCHITECTURE (BELOW)
Organic architecture is not so much a collection of architectural principles as a way of perceiving architecture. It aims to codify the spatial relationship between human beings and nature according to criteria that focus on people within an environment, rather than on stylistic considerations.

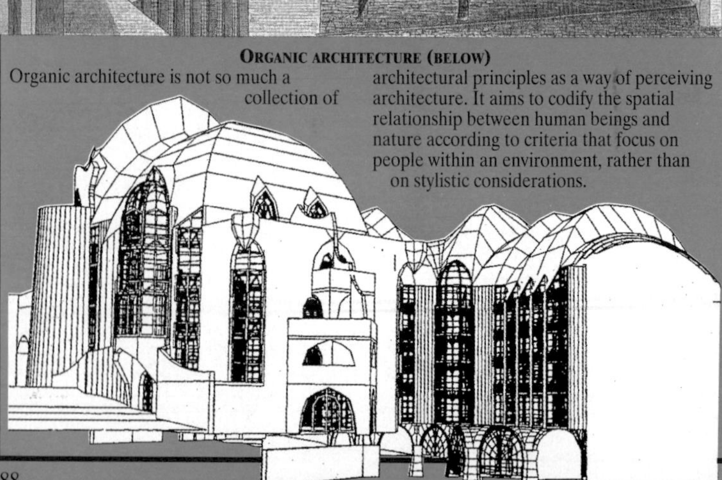

BUDAPEST AS SEEN BY PAINTERS

'From there, I crossed the Danube and entered Buda, the most beautiful town in Hungary. There is a large and magnificent palace... And I was told the Emperor Sigismund began it.'

Bertrandon de La Brocquière

Under Matthias Corvinus ● *32,* the Royal Palace had become the symbol of Buda throughout Europe. During the Turkish occupation artists continued to paint its awesome battlements, as can be seen from the painting [1] by an anonymous Hungarian artist (c. 1664). However, the citadel – very much in the background – merely serves to identify the figure in the foreground: the Hun chieftain Buda. The reconquest of 1686 gave military engineers the opportunity to record the battles, with a view to informing the general public of the most decisive events. Their drawings inspired a number of artists, including the Flemish painter Frans Geffels, whose *Siege of Buda* (1686) [3] was probably commissioned by the Duke of Mantua. After the duke was exiled, his collection was dispersed and a few works found their way to Budapest. As well as being highly evocative, its topographical detail is extremely accurate: Óbuda, Castle Hill, Gellért Hill, Margaret Island and the small town of Pest are all clearly recognizable. It is easy to understand how, after such a formidable siege, Buda was completely devastated and took over a century to become a capital once again. A painting by Charles Herbel (c. 1659–1702) inspired Heinrich Faust's *Triumph of the Duke of Lorraine on the West Slope of the Castle of Buda* (1694) [2]. This unrealistic Roman-style victory, with Castle Hill relegated to the distance, is in effect an allegorical celebration of the glory of Charles, Duke of Lorraine, whose victory over the Turks enabled the Hungarians to turn once more toward Europe after a century and a half of Turkish rule.

1	2
	3

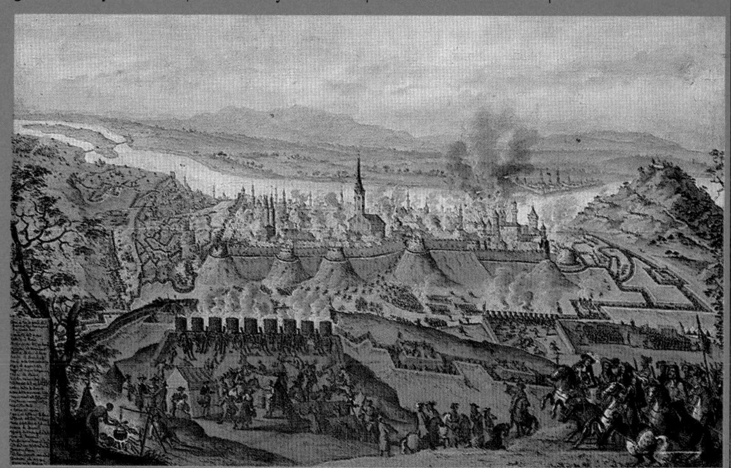

Work carried out to regulate the Danube in the late 19th century had major repercussions for the city's development. Public buildings and private mansions were built in an eclectic style on the reclaimed land, masking the traditional houses that stood near the river. These buildings on the riverfront of Pest were closely monitored by a committee formed under the aegis of the Palatine Archduke, Joseph of Habsburg (1776–1847) ● *34*, to ensure that they presented an overall architectural unity. Visitors were captivated by the majestic image of Pest and wanted to immortalize their impressions. This period of urban development and prosperity corresponded to the golden age of *vedute* (topographically accurate landscape paintings). The most talented of the *vedutisti* was the Transylvanian artist Miklós Barabás (1810–98) ▲ *212*, who painted *Quay on the Danube at Pest, from the North* [1] in 1843 and *Quay on the Danube at Pest, from the South* [2] in 1842. Although Antal Ligeti (1823–90) did not paint many views of Budapest, scenes such as *Budapest from József-hegy* (1884) [3] were among his most accomplished works.

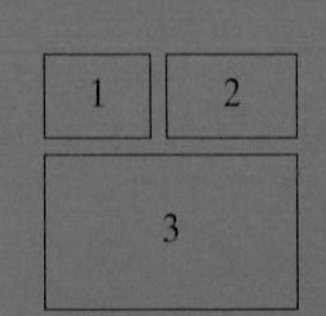

‘The hotel entrances were on Mária-Valéria út, while their terraces stretched beneath the awnings of the Duna korzó, the promenade overlooking the loading platforms of the Danube.’

John Lukacs

‘My Hungarians took great pride in their appearance. They were veritable dandies in this respect, and dressed carefully in outdated English style; but they were not in the least offended by the coarseness of my apparel.’

Patrick Leigh Fermor

This aquatint [3] of the Franciscans’ Square (Ferenciek tere) in the 1840s was the work of two artists: Josef Kuwasseg 1799–1859) did the ink drawing, and Frederick Martens (c. 1809–75) did the painting. The formality of the buildings is offset by the relatively naïve depiction of everyday scenes. In 1884 the city of Budapest organized a competition to revive the genre of *veduta*, which had fallen into disuse. It was won by two architects: Róbert Nádler and Albert Schickedanz (1846–1915) ▲ *148*, 150. The authorities also saw this as a way of compiling an artistic record of the city’s monuments. The painting [2] by Albert Schickedanz (1884) shows Holy Trinity Square (Szentháromság tér ▲ *202*, formerly Market Square) before the restoration of the Matthias Church. It includes the Holy Trinity Column ● *71*, and the old town hall of Buda (on the right). The competition judges awarded third place to József Molnár (1821–99) for his study of Calvin Square (Kálvin tér). Molnár was then commissioned to produce an oil painting on the same theme: *Kálvin tér, Pest* [1]. It shows the Pest Savings Bank on the right and the National Museum ▲ *124* in the center. (The Danubius Fountain was resculpted and placed in Elizabeth Square (Erzsébet tér) in 1959, after being badly damaged in World War Two.) The competition attracted a number of artists. However, in the end the municipal committee for the arts decided to promote photography, and the photographer György Klösz (1844–1913) was commissioned to create a photographic record of Budapest’s principal monuments.

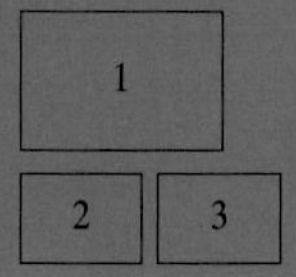

A HISTORIC SCENE

Painting by József Rippl-Rónai (1861–1927) ● *83*, ▲ *176* of the coronation of the last Habsburg emperor, Charles I (Károly IV), on December 30, 1916, in the Matthias Church ● *77*, ▲ *202*.

BUDAPEST AS SEEN BY WRITERS

Attila József (1905–37) was born in Budapest, and became one of the greatest Hungarian poets of the 20th century. Central themes in József's poems are poverty, loneliness and suffering, and although often melancholic, they also express the author's faith in life's essential beauty and harmony.

I sat there on the quayside by the landing,
a melon rind was drifting on the flow.
I delved into my fate, just understanding:
the surface chatters, while it's calm below.
As if my heart had been its very source,
troubled, wise was the Danube, mighty force.

Like muscles at work, when lifting the axe,
harvesting, welding, or digging a grave,
so did the water surge, tighten, relax
with every current, every breezy wave.
Like Mother, dandled, told a tale, caressed,
laundered the dirt of all Budapest.

A drizzle started, moistening the morning
but didn't care much, so it stopped again.
And yet, like someone who under an awning
watches the rain – I gazed into the plain:
as twilight that may infinitely last,
so grey was all that used to shine, the past.

The Danube flowed, and like a tiny child
plays on his musing, lively mother's knee,
so cradled and embraced and gently smiled
each playful wave, waving hallo to me.
They shuddered on the flood of past events
like tombstones, tumbling graveyard monuments.

ATTILA JÓZSEF, *BY THE DANUBE* (excerpt), translated by Peter Zollman, in *In Quest of the 'Miracle Stag': The Poetry of Hungary*, Adam Makkai (ed.), Atlantis-Centaur Inc., Chicago; M. Szivarvany, Budapest; Corvina, Budapest, 1996

Hungarian-born author and journalist Arthur Koestler (1905–83), is the best known political refugee and prisoner of his time. His experiences as a political correspondent, Communist party member and prisoner of war are described in Scum of the Earth (1941), *and they provide the background for his first novel in English,* Arrival and Departure (1943). *In the following excerpt, taken from his autobiography,* Arrow in the Blue, *Arthur Koestler discusses the life and work of his poet friend, Attila József.*

[...] Though in his native Hungary Attila József is posthumously regarded as the greatest poet the nation has produced, his name is still virtually unknown in the West. This may justify the pages that follow – quite apart from my personal feelings for a dead friend.

Attila József committed suicide at the age of 32; both his work and his personal fate were a terrifying symbol of our time. He was a contemporary Villon, whose life and poetry revolved around the two treacherous poles of this age, Marx and Freud, and who died a victim of both.

Attila was born in 1905, the son of a day-labourer and of a charwoman. His father disappeared when he was three, and until his seventh year Attila was brought up in an orphanage. He earned his living while at school as a movie-usher, newsboy and night-waiter; and at college as a railway porter, Danube sailor, dock-worker, office-cleaner and private tutor.

His first poems were published in the leading Hungarian literary magazine, *Nyugat* ('Occident') when he was sixteen. One year later, in 1922, *Nyugat* printed his poem 'Innocent Song' which caused a nation-wide scandal, and his expulsion from the University of Szeged. 'Innocent Song' was acclaimed as a kind of manifesto of the Central European post-war generation.

Innocent Song

I have no God, I have no King,
my mother never wore a ring,
I have no crib or funeral cover,
I give no kiss, I take no lover.

For three days I have chewed my thumb
for want of either crust or crumb.
Though I am twenty, strong and hale –
my twenty years are up for sale.

Should there be none who wish to buy
The Devil's free to have a try;
then shall I use my commonsense
and rob and kill in innocence.

Till, on a rope, they hang me high,
and in the blessed earth I lie –
and lush and poisoned grasses start
rank from my pure and simple heart.

[...] When I met Attila in 1933, we were both twenty-seven. He was of pure-bred Magyar, rural stock: of medium height, lean, sparse, sinewy, he carried his body like a regimental sergeant-major. He had a narrow face with a high forehead, calm brown eyes, and calm, regular features to which a certain dash and enterprise was added by a trim moustache with pointed ends. It was a handsome and manly, but quite unremarkable face that could have been a ladies' hairdresser's; nothing in its unruffled appearance suggested that its owner had spent several months in a mental hospital, suffering from delusions, and was heading for the final break-up.

[...] At the time of our friendship, however, Attila was an extremely amiable and amusing, though somewhat exhausting, companion. He had his moments of exuberance and would write drinking songs – 'O wine, milk of virile men..'– though he drank rarely. He also wrote a congratulatory poem to his own birthday – the thirty-second and last:

Thirty-two and very wise –
this poem shall be a surprise
    and so pret-
    ty-pretty.

A gift that shall the spirits rouse
of the lonely guest in the coffee-house:
        my-
        self.

Thirty-two, what an event,
and never enough to pay the rent,
    and always hungry
    in Hung'ry...

He had moments of a classical and festive mood: his poem of welcome to Thomas Mann, on the occasion of Mann's visit to Budapest, has the beautiful closing lines:

> ... We shall listen to you and some
> will just gaze at you in joy, for it delights
> us to have you here: a European among the Whites.

ARTHUR KOESTLER, *ARROW IN THE BLUE*
First published by Collins with Hamish Hamilton Ltd, 1954

The following excerpts are taken from Paul Hoffman's book The Man Who Loved Only Numbers – *the story of the Hungarian mathematical prodigy, Paul Erdős (1913–96). The details of Erdős's life are related against the historical and cultural backdrop of his native Budapest.*

The Budapest of Erdős's birth was a sophisticated modern city, home of the largest stock exchange in Europe and the most grandiose parliament building in the world. Budapest rivaled Paris and Vienna in first-class hotels, garden restaurants and late-night cafés, which were hothouses of "illicit trading, adultery, puns, gossip and poetry, the meeting places for the intellectuals and those opposed to oppression." It was also an Old World city, its women praised for their beauty and its men for their chivalry. Budapest "has never been an agreeable town. But desirable, yes: like a racy, full-blooded young married woman about whose flirtations everyone knows and yet gentlemen are glad to bend down and kiss her hand," wrote Gyula Krúdy, an acclaimed writer of Magyar prose, who moved from the Hungarian provinces to Budapest, in 1896, the year the city's subway system opened, the first in Europe. Krúdy's enthusiasm for Budapest was irrepressible:

> Here the dancing in the theaters is the best, here everyone in a crowd may think that he is a gentleman even if he had left jail the day before; the physicians' cures are wonderful, the lawyers are world-famous, even the renter of the smallest rooms has his bath, the shopkeepers are inventive, the policemen guard the public peace, the gentlefolk are agreeable, the streetlights burn till the morning, the janitors will not allow a single ghost inside, the tramcars will carry you to the farthest places within an hour, the city clerks look down on the state employees, the women are well-read from their theater magazines, the porters greet you humbly on the street corners, the innkeeper inquires of your appetite with his hat in hand, the coach drivers wait for you solemnly during an entire day, the salesgirls swear that your wife is the most beautiful of women, other girls in the nightclubs and orpheums hear out your political opinions politely, you find yourself praised in the morning newspaper after you had witnessed an accident, well-known men use the spittoons in the café gardens, you are being helped into your overcoat, and the undertaker shows his thirty-two gold teeth when you take your leave from this city forever.

[...] Death and tragedy have long been part of the Hungarian character. According to the historian John Lukacs, on All Soul's Day in Erdős's youth, "thousands of people streamed toward the cemeteries of Budapest, with flowers in their hands, on that holy day which is perhaps taken more seriously in Hungary than anywhere else because of the national temperament. *Temetni tudunk* – a terse Magyar phrase whose translation requires as many as ten English words to give its proper (and even then, not wholly exact) sense: 'How to bury people – that is one thing we know.'" The phrase was coined long before Hungary had experienced the devastation of the two world wars, whose carnage would come disproportionately from within its borders.

Few countries have had as violent a history as Hungary. In the ninth century, nomadic Magyar warriors from the steppes of Eastern Europe crossed the Carpathian Mountains and, renouncing their peripatetic way of life, settled in the middle Danube basin at the heart of what is now Hungary. The Magyars, also known as the On-Ogurs ("people of the ten arrows"), were skilled archers and javelin throwers who raided their neighbors, plundering Germany from Bavaria to Saxony. Recent converts to Christianity, the Magyars had to defend their own territory against a series of invaders. They held their own until 1241, when several hundred thousand Mongol horsemen from Genghis Khan's empire slaughtered half the Magyar population and enslaved much of the rest, a bloodbath from which the country barely recovered. "The problem with Hungary," Erdős once joked, reflecting on his country's history, "is that in every war we chose the wrong side."

PAUL HOFFMAN, *THE MAN WHO LOVED ONLY NUMBERS*
Published by Fourth Estate, 1998

Acclaimed travel writer Jan Morris (b. 1926) is an honorary D. Litt. of the universities of Wales and Glamorgan and a Fellow of the Royal Society of Literature. In one of her many volumes of collected travel essays, she offers her own observations of the city of Budapest.

[...] the Hungarian Rising was the most tragically heroic event of the entire Cold War between capitalism and Communism [and] Budapest was just the place for it.

It does not seem to me a very lovely city, as the tourist brochures claim, but it is made for glory. On the right bank of the Danube is piled the old capital of Buda, with its royal castle and cathedral resplendent at the top; on the left bank extends the mass of Pest, all grand boulevards, parks and church steeples, running away to the horizon in a flatland of suburbs, and fronted on the river bank by the grotesque and mighty Parliament. Six bridges connect the two halves of Budapest, and the whole city suggests to me a figure of lapidary pride, commemorating always the sieges, battles, rebellions, and miscellaneous splendours of its history. By and large modern Hungarians may look about as ordinary as the rest of us, but in my romantic way I like to fancy in them

the spirit of the Magyar horsemen who ride in sculpted bronze about the national memorial in Heroes' Square: haughty magnificent noblemen, ineffably proud on their caparisoned horses as they ride at a leisurely pace into the city, their kingly leader looking majestically in front of him, his companions glaring this way and that from beneath their feathered helmets like presidential security men.

And in 1956, as it happened, my fancy proved to be true: the people of Budapest, ancients to schoolchildren, rose in fury against their oppressors as the Magyar manner born. How I would love to have been there!

JAN MORRIS, *THE WRONG STORY* IN *FIFTY YEARS OF EUROPE: AN ALBUM*
Published by Penguin Books, 1997

Sir Cecil Beaton (1904–80), English scenery and costume designer, photographer, writer and painter, also wrote and illustrated many books. In his autobiographical The Wandering Years, Diaries 1922–39, *he describes his experiences of Budapest by night.*

By the time we staggered to our beds at dawn, we felt as though we'd already spent a week sightseeing and living in Budapest. Many impressions had been gathered. A letter of introduction provided us with a willing escort, who promptly guided two eager foreigners and showed them every aspect of night life. We ate Hungarian food in enormous quantities including a kind of salmon-trout from Lake Balaton. Gypsy orchestras serenaded us. In the huge inferno-nightclub *Arizona*, spectacle vyed with spectacle. There were revolving dance floors and cabaret that went on from ten o'clock until three in the morning. The walls had breathing shells; balconies suddenly shot ceilingwards on the trunk of a palm tree; stars flashed and chorus girls, suspended by their teeth, twirled at the ends of ropes. To Miss Arizona, once a beauty and now the singer-wife of the proprietor, were allotted the big 'production numbers'. Her entrances were spectacular accompanied by every variety of dog, or riding an elephant.

SIR CECIL BEATON, *A NIGHT OUT IN BUDAPEST, 1936*
in *The Wandering Years, Diaries 1922–39,* 1961

József Gvadányi (1725–1801), was a poet in close contact with the writers of his age, and he embarked on a literary career with occasional verses. His long narrative poem, A Village Notary's Journey to Buda, *which appeared anonymously in 1790, contrasted a naive provincial hero and the urban sophistication of the Hungarian capital. His hero sets out for Buda in order to study the public policies of Emperor Joseph II. Part one depicts the vicissitudes of the notary on his trip. It is always the simple people who rescue him from trouble. In part two, however, he becomes the mouth-piece of Gvadányi himself and passes judgment on contemporary morality. He finds the chief source of trouble not in the political oppression of the day but in the people's tendency to ape foreign customs.*

He was praised for his attempts at purifying the language and for his ability to strike a chord of popular sentiment. His language is simple and expressive, and his earthy humor won him many devoted readers. In the 19th century this story was adapted for the stage by József Gaál (1811–66).

I thought to view the comeliness
of freely chosen Magyar dress,
of scarlet velvets without flaw
and sables from Siberia.

I looked for capes, for cloaks of fur,
for trousers fine from belt to spur,
new girdles gay with golden threads
and sable calpacks on their heads.

Red riding-boots should grace their shins,
their backs be hung with leopard skins,
their caps be plumed, while greet the ears
their jingling jewelled bandoliers.

I thought: their long hair graceful flies,
while sabre-scabbards smite their thighs:
with battle-axe or mace they play
or dress in armour for the fray.

József Gvadányi, *On The Dress Of The Hungarians*
(excerpt from *A Village Notary's Journey to Buda*),
translated by Watson Kirkconnell in *In Quest of the 'Miracle Stag': The Poetry of Hungary,* Adam Makkai (ed.), Atlantis-Centaur Inc., Chicago; M. Szivarvany, Budapest; Corvina, Budapest, 1996

Claudio Magris, scholar and critic specializing in the field of German literature and culture, was born in Trieste in 1939. After graduating from the university of Turin, he lectured there in German Language and Literature from 1970 to 1978. He is the author of novels, plays and works of literary criticism and has translated Ibsen, Kleist and Schnitzler. In his book, Danube, *from which the following excerpts are taken, Magris embarks on a journey through the history and culture of the Danube lands. His observations here are of Budapest.*

The day is generous with undulating lines and sensual pleasure. At 9 Fortuna utca it even offers us the compliant breasts of the goddess Fortuna, carved by the not very famous Ferenc Medgyessy in 1921: they are tender models of the curvature of the earth. At No. 4 in the same street there was once the Fortuna Inn, which now houses the Hungarian Museum of Commerce and Catering. Clearly inspired by this name, Amedeo, who, like Monsieur Teste, goes through life classifying, begins to expound a theory concerning the connection between erotica and the art of travelling. He subdivides it into a number of sections: eros and coaches, eros and post-houses, adventures in trains, licentious cruises, the customs of ports and of inland cities, the differences between capital cities and provincial towns, the aeroplane and sexual inactivity (imputed chiefly, but not solely, to the brevity of air trips and the constant interruption to which one is subjected).

The *Musée de l'Hôtellerie* appeals to gluttony rather than to lasciviousness. It displays posters for historic pastries such as Joseph Naisz's creation which promised maraschino from Zara, Curaçao, Anisette and Tamarind: it shows majestic cakes like towering temples, reproduces sweetmeats of illustrious memory, figures once fashioned of chocolate and cream, Gâteau d'ananas à la Zichy, Fruits entiers à la Duchesse Gisèle. Gluttony ogles other pleasures in the Pain de Framboises à la Leda, a pyramid of temptations, a dish supporting a naked woman in a shell, who appears to be offering herself to a swan: the bird, who looks equally delicious, is stretching out his neck to her. These dainties end up by making one feel slighty sick, like every kind of affectation. But in the reconstruction of an older-days pastry-shop, the knobs on the drawers are exactly the same as those in use in Fiume and Trieste forty years ago: the tiniest indications of a domestic Mitteleuropa, mysterious treasures of childhood, the distant feel of home.

We stop at Margaret Island where, according to the proverb, love begins and ends. This transience of the heart and senses was made much of in the Hungarian novels of the 1930s, that production line of books entitled *The Most Beautiful Woman in Budapest* or *Meeting at Margaret Island*, which seemed to match the caressing, stereotyped aura of these burgeoning flower-beds, parks, hotels and *belle époque* pavilions, with fountains playing among the roses. But even this allurement touches the soul, like some tired old waltz, and is a little promise of happiness; it induces the melancholy associated with any meditation on joy. And that love can end is always a thought that wrings the heart, even if expressed in the banal refrain of a popular song. That evening, at the *Matthias*, a gypsy fiddler plays the *Pacsirta*, the skylark. All this is still "décor" of the beginning of the century, the style of the superannuated gentry who liked Hungarian gypsy music, which was really neither Hungarian nor gypsy. But the *Pacsirta* is a lovely song, the violinist plays it in a masterly style and, at least for this evening, love is not over. Even on an ordinary evening it can happen that one finds real life in something false.

[...] The buildings of Budapest are eclectic, given to historical posturing, weighty in themselves and often adorned with heavy decorations; their non-style occasionally appears as some bizarre face of the future, the sort of backward-looking yet futuristic townscape of the cities posited in science-fiction films such as *Blade Runner:* a future that is post-historical and without style, peopled by chaotic, composite masses, in national and ethnic qualities indistinguishable, Malay-Redskin Levantines who live in shacks and skyscrapers, twelfth-generation computers and rusty bicycles fished up from the past, rubble from the Fourth World War and superhuman robots. The architectural townscape of this metropolitan future is archaic-futuristic, with skyscrapers kilometres in height and temples in the *kolossal* style like Milan Station or Grand Central. The eclecticism of Budapest, its mixture of styles, evokes, like every Babel of today, a possible future swarming with the survivors of some catastrophe. Every heir of the Hapsburg era is a true man of the future, because he learnt, earlier than most others, to live without a future, in the absence of any historical continuity; and that is, not to live but to survive. But along these splendid boulevards, in a world as lively and elegant as this, a world which does not display the melancholy of the Eastern Bloc countries, even survival is charming and seductive, magnanimous and maybe, at times, almost happy.

CLAUDIO MAGRIS, *DANUBE*
Published by the Harvill Press, 1999

Sir Georg Solti (1912–97) was one of the leading conductors of the 20th century. His musical education began in his native Budapest, and he went on to serve as musical director with orchestras in Munich, Frankfurt, London, and Chicago, and performed all over the world. He made 250 records and CDs, including more than forty operas. His memoirs tell us about an unparalleled musical life. Here he recounts some of his experiences whilst attending the Liszt Academy.

[...] When I was fifteen or sixteen, Professor Székely caught pneumonia, and we pupils were told that during his absence his lessons would be given by Professor Bartók. Although Béla Bartók was a fine pianist and needed to teach in order to earn a living, the obvious question remains: Why was he teaching piano instead of composition? The answer is he believed that composition cannot be taught. He was absolutely right. One does have to learn the elements of composition, such as harmony, counterpoint, and form, but one can't be taught how to to compose anything worth hearing; one either does or does not have a talent for composing music.

Bartók presented an austere, forbidding front to the world, and even in those years, when he was still in his mid-forties, his reputation was daunting. Until Székely became ill, I had seen Bartók only in the Liszt Academy's corridors, and I had never exchanged a word with him. I can say with absolute honesty, and without leaning on hindsight, that although he had received little official recognition and was

widely regarded as a raving radical, we music students knew exactly how important he was, and we revered him. We were fully aware that there was an authentic genius teaching at our academy.

When I learned that I would have to play for him, I felt terribly fearful. Bartók kept our class separate from his own; we spent several hours with him twice a week throughout the six weeks of Szekély's illness. Seventy years have elapsed since then and I do not remember much about those sessions, but I do recall that at every lesson each pupil played parts of *The Well-Tempered Clavier* for Bartók. I also played some Debussy preludes for him. During one of the first lessons, I made a terrible faux pas: I sat down to play his *Allegro barbaro*, for piano solo. When he saw me set the music on the stand he became quite upset. "No, no, not that!" he said. "I don't want to hear that!" It was stupid of me to have thought that he might have enjoyed hearing an immature pupil play one of his compositions, but my intentions had been good: I had wanted to show my love and respect for him.

After I left Bartók's class, I never again had significant personal contact with him. There was an occasional "Good morning, Professor," when I passed him in a corridor, but that was all. I attended many of his recitals, at which he played Scarlatti and Liszt (I particularly remember some of the less freqently performed pieces from the *Années de pèlerinage*), Haydn, Mozart, Schubert, Debussy, and even Schoenberg, whose music was as much disliked in Hungary as elsewhere in those years. I never heard him play Beethoven or Brahms, but I did hear him perform many of the pieces from his own *Mikrokosmos,* for which he favored a crisp, staccato articulation. Bartók was a marvelous pianist who took practicing seriously, but his playing was somewhat dry, not at all Romantic. He opted for a rather hard but extraordinarily clear sound, and he used less pedal than most pianists – very little even in Debussy.

Horthy and his supporters eventually forgave Kodály his Communist sympathies, but they never forgave Bartók, who had a much more uncompromising character. And yet, however isolated he may have been within the Hungarian musical milieu, his situation became even more difficult when he emigrated. The story of his departure at the beginning of World War II, and of his struggle for survival in the United States, where he died in 1945, is well known. Since his death, he has been recognised as one of the great composers of the century. In Hungary, he posthumously became a national hero: Most cities and towns have streets or squares named after him, and what used to be called the Franz Lizst Academy is now the Franz Liszt-Béla Bartók Academy.

I don't remember the name of my first teacher of musical theory at the Liszt Academy, but when, at the age of thirteen or fourteen, I won a prize in a piano competition promoted by a Budapest politician, one of the pieces I played was my own. My mother, convinced that I was a second Mozart, persuaded the politician to write a letter of recommendation on my behalf to the academy's best-known composition teacher, Zoltán Kodály.

Kodály, then in his mid-forties, was a brilliant man who went through some very bad years, on the verge of madness. There was something of the fanatic in him, and back then his youthful, ascetic face and Lenin-style beard gave him a somewhat Christ-like appearance. He believed in an almost messianic form of communism, and he became a disciple of an extremist "healthy life" cult that called for a severe form of vegetarianism, cold-water cures, and going barefoot. There was a period when he even came to the academy shoeless. His wife, Emma Sándor, the sister of a wealthy liberal member of parliament, was no beauty, but she was highly intelligent, and gifted as a composer, pianist, poet, and translator. Her wealth allowed Kodály to spend time composing and carrying out his research into folk music, which he wouldn't have been able to do so freely if he had had to teach full time.

I don't know how my mother had the courage to take me to a man of such prestige as Kodály, but there we were one day in his studio at the academy. Such was her naivete in political matters that she didn't realize that the politician who had written the letter she handed him was right-wing; Kodály was left-wing. "My son composes and has brought along some little pieces that he has written," she said. "Would you like to listen to them?"

I am sure that the pieces were terrible, but Kodály listened patiently. "The boy certainly has talent," he told my mother, "but he must finish his education. Bring him back to me when he is eighteen, and we'll discuss the matter again." This was a fair remark, but my mother was deeply offended: How had Kodály dared to turn down her little Mozart? Instead of following his advice, she took me immediately to Albert Siklós, the other principal composition professor at the academy; he listened to my pieces and accepted me as a pupil.

[...] Composition exams were held twice a year; we were given blank music paper early in the morning and had to produce a certain type of composition by noon. Together, Siklós and Kodály looked at each student's work and graded it. On those occasions – and there were at least eight such tests over a four-year period – Kodály never gave the slightest indication that he recognized me. He always graded my work fairly, but he never said a word to me. I finished the course successfully and wrote a string quartet as a graduation piece, thereby ending my career as a composer. Kodály handed me my diploma, but not even then did he say a word to me.

One evening, a few years after my graduation, when I was a coach at the State Opera, I was sitting in my usual place in the opera house's restaurant before a performance of Kodály's *The Transylvanian Spinning Room*. The director came in with Kodály and asked me to show the composer the way to his box. As we walked, Kodály turned to me and said, "You see, you didn't need that letter of recommendation. You've made your way without it."

"Professor, do you remember that?"

"Oh yes," he said softly.

I didn't see him again for about thirty years. At Salzburg in 1964, after a performance of Mahler's First Symphony that I had conducted, an usher came to my dressing room and said that Professor Kodály wanted to see me. Kodály entered with his new, young wife – his first wife had died – and made the following astonishing remark: "I must apologize to you for the time I was so unfriendly to your mother," he said, "but, you see, the man who had written that letter of recommendation was my political enemy."

SIR GEORG SOLTI, *MEMOIRS*
Published by Alfred A. Knopf, 1997

Patrick Leigh Fermor (b. 1915) is one of the finest travel writers of his generation. In December 1933, he set out to walk from Rotterdam to Constantinople and his book, A Time of Gifts, *from which the following excerpt is taken, is the account of his journey as far as Hungary.*

[...] There was a lull in the air. Holy Saturday, with its lamps out and shrines empty and the distant tolling over the fields, cast a spell of catalepsy and suspense. It was a time of sealed tombs and sleeping sentries with the Protagonist of the week's drama deep underground harrowing Hell... There was not a fisherman on the river, not a peasant in the fields, nothing but those little volecatchers and skimming wagtails, the waterbirds and the massed larks and the frogs, whose steady diurnal croak, though universal, seemed milder than the full-moon brekekekexing the night before. A thrown stick could silence an acre for several seconds. The flecks of dust on the current and the spinning fluff suggested midsummer. I ate my bread and cheese on the shady side of a rick and fell asleep. (Hay-ricks are conical hereabouts, cleverly stacked round a centre pole and when most of the hay has been sliced away for fodder, the sun catches the shorn planes as if lopsided obelisks had been erected in the fields.) I awoke later than I had intended. The woods, full of rooks and wood-pigeons, were sending long shadows over the grass. I drank at a brook, sloshed some water on my face and tidied up. Civilization lay ahead.

Far away on the other bank I could see my destination: it had been growing steadily in size since my first glimpse that morning. A cliff loomed over a long sweep of the river and on this ledge was perched a white fane that resembled St.Peter's in Rome. A light circle of pillars lifted a gleaming dome into the sky. It was dramatic, mysterious, as improbable as a mirage and unmistakable as a landmark for many miles across the desert of liquid and solid. The Basilica of Esztergom, I knew, was the Metropolitan Cathedral of all Hungary, the largest religious building in the Kingdom and the archiepiscopal See of the Cardinal-Prince-Archbishop: the Hungarian equivalent, that is, of Rheims, Canterbury, Toledo, Armagh, and old Cracow. The Basilica, though spectacular and splendid, is not old: little in that part of Hungary was spared the ravages of the Tartars and the Turks; after the Reconquest everything had to begin again. But the town – the Latin Strigonium and the German Gran – is one of the oldest in the country. Ever since the first Apostolic King of Christian Hungary – the conquering Árpads' descendant, St Stephen himself – was born and crowned in Esztergom, history has been accumulating here and entwining itself with myth. From my footpath, the Basilica was the only building in sight. The monasteries, the churches, the palaces and the libraries that encrust the steep little town were all in baulk. The great pile, with its twin cupola-topped belfries, its ring of pillars and its great nacreous dome, hovered above water and timber and fen as though upheld, like a celestial city in a painting, by a flurry of untiring wings.

PATRICK LEIGH FERMOR, *A TIME OF GIFTS*
First published by John Murray, 1977

In and around Budapest

▲ White Cross Inn (now the *Casanova* night club)

▲ Statue Park ◆ *266*

▼ City Park and Heroes' Square ● *76* ▲ *150*

▲ Vajdahunyad Castle (City Park) ▲ *161*

▼ Ibusz building (Ferenciek tere) ▲ *121*

▲ Mosaic by Miksa Róth with Hungarian motifs ▼ Academy of Music ▲ *145-6*

▲ Calvinist Church (Városligeti fasor) ● *83* ▼ Former Post Office Savings Bank ● *80* ▲ *136*

▲ Museum of Applied Arts ▲ *171, 172* ▼ Institute for the Blind (60 Mexikói út) ● *82*

Pest

Anthony Krause

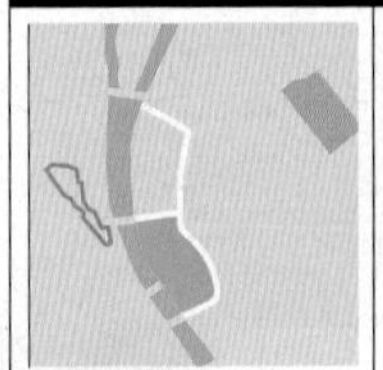

'Vörösmarty tér is Pest's best known, friendliest and most pleasant square. Here you'll find the Hungaroton record store and the Luxus fashion boutique, where the staircase has Art Nouveau handrails and painted mirrors. Talking of staircases, you must try the elevators found in most buildings at least once. They are a sort of service lift that never stops and which you have to jump into and out of while it's moving...'

Dominique Fernandez

When Budapest was unified, in 1873, it was the lower town of Pest that gave it its air of a fully fledged active, modern, cosmopolitan city. From then on, it was on a par with Prague and Vienna. It was unusual in that it was a city where architectural eclecticism and pastiche flourished (in the 1870s it acquired a neo-Gothic Parliament building and a medieval City Park); but it was also a late 19th-century city that welcomed new European architectural styles, and it was further embellished by the dazzling Hungarian Secessionist style ● *80*, *82*. Pest can easily be divided into clearly defined districts: the old historic center; the elegant Andrássy út and the City Park; the grand boulevards of the commercial district; and the working-class districts of eastern Pest.

The city's landmarks are also easily distinguishable. Many of them bear the stamp of the 19th-century imperialism and classicism that still marks the central districts of Pest.

Most of the districts are named after the Habsburg emperors and empresses: Terézváros (Maria Theresa), Józsefvarós (Joseph), Lipótvarós (Leopold). Of all the cities of Central Europe, probably to an even greater degree than Vienna, the Hungarian capital is characterized by a sense of calm and reverie – evoked by the gentle harmony of the Danube plain, the secret magic of its passages (*gang*) and courtyards, the treasures of its old Jewish quarter, and its shady parks and beautiful cemeteries.

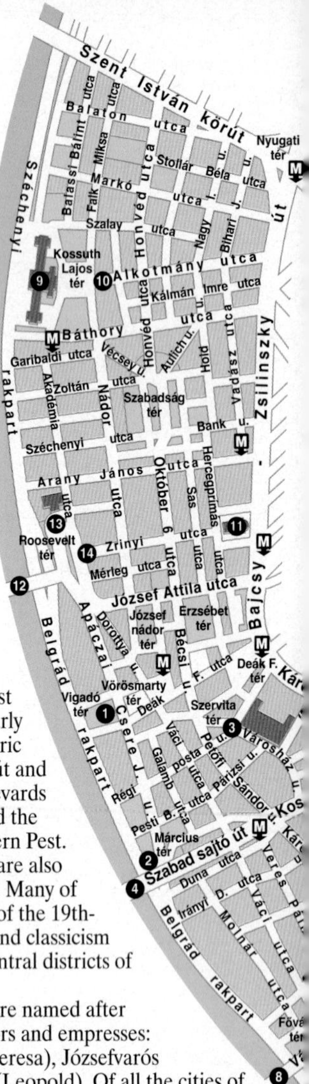

ART NOUVEAU FOUNTAIN (end of Deák Ferenc utca)
Don't leave the square before you've seen the atlantes supporting the domes at no. 3, designed by Korb and Gierg1 (1911) in typically Art Nouveau style.

VÖRÖSMARTY TÉR, THE HEART OF BELVÁROS

The Belváros ('inner city') district corresponds to the site of the old medieval town before its walls were demolished to make way for the 19th-century urban development program ● *29*, *34*. Nowadays the line of these walls is represented by Deák Ferenc utca to the north, the boulevards of Károly körút and Múzeum körút to the east, and Vámház körút to the south. Today the historic heart of Pest, which lies within the arc of the Kiskörút (Little Boulevard) ▲ *123*, is still the busiest part of the city. It is centered on Vörösmarty tér and the famous Váci utca pedestrian precinct ▲ *235*, and bisected by Kossuth Lajos utca. This is a district of cafés, restaurants, banks, businesses, boutiques and stores (including bookstores and souvenir shops). Its narrow pedestrianized streets and unrivaled views of the Buda Hills provide an ideal setting for city walks. For most of them Vörösmarty tér, the large square named after the 19th-century Romantic poet Mihály Vörösmarty, makes a convenient starting and finishing point.

Gerbeaud The Gerbeaud Cukrászda is Budapest's most famous patisserie ● *56*. It was founded in 1858, and in 1884 was bought by the Swiss patissier Émile Gerbeaud. The Viennese-style tearooms, with their luxurious Baroque decor and green velvet drapery, are one of the capital's most prestigious meeting places. Visitors from Vienna and Milan come here to soak up its early-20th-century atmosphere. Here customers, served by white-booted waitresses, can sample the famous *pogácsa* (savory cakes made with bacon and cumin), *kifli* (croissants which can be filled with poppy seeds and nuts) and *Dobos torta* (thin layers of cake with mocha cream between them, sprinkled with nuts and coated with a brittle caramel glaze).

Gerbeaud tearooms
Next door to Gerbeaud's tearooms (on the corner) you can buy cakes at the patisserie's annex, the Kis Gerbeaud.

The 'yellow metro' In front of the patisserie is the entrance to Budapest's most popular subway (*metro*) line. The yellow (no. 1) line, known locally as the Kis Metro ('little subway'), was opened in 1896, four years before the Paris Metro. It runs the length of Andrássy út ▲ *140* to the Széchenyi Baths ● *62*, ▲ *160*.

Luxus Housed in an elegant building dating from 1911 is a time-honored institution, the fashion boutique Luxus, which in the period before 1989, during the Kádár regime , was the showcase of Western fashion and symbol of Hungary's opening up to the free market economy. The enormous structure which stood opposite was demolished in 2005, making way for large outlets selling international brands.

Vörösmarty (then Gizella) tér around 1890, including the building that houses the Gerbeaud patisserie.

PESTI VIGADÓ ● *79*
The original Vigadó (1859–65), designed by Frigyes Feszl in Romantic style, was a prestigious concert hall where Liszt ● *48*, Brahms, Debussy and Bartók ● *51, 52* performed. It was rebuilt after World War Two and is today a major venue for concerts, shows and other cultural events.

GREEK ORTHODOX CHURCH (Görögkeleti templom)
The city once had a flourishing Greek community. Pest's Greek Orthodox Church has a beautiful painted wood iconostasis (1797) by the Serbian sculptor Miklós Jankovitch.

VIGADÓ TÉR

Deák Ferenc utca runs from Vörösmarty tér, past the splendid BANK PALACE (built in 1915), which now houses the Budapest Stock Exchange (right), to the VIGADÓ CONCERT HALL. Vigadó tér opens onto the DANUBE CORSO (Duna korzó), the magnificent pedestrianized embankment that runs alongside the Danube between Chain Bridge ▲ *183* and Elizabeth Bridge ▲ *181*. In summer there is a continuous stream of people strolling along the quays, eating in the restaurants and sitting at the café terraces. In the evening the Corso offers an enchanting view of the Royal Palace and the illuminated Buda Hills. It is bordered by a number of luxury hotels, including the BUDAPEST MARRIOTT HOTEL (the 10th-floor Bellevue tearooms and terrace are well worth a visit). Today floating casinos and restaurants are moored beside the quays for the benefit of tourists. This is also the departure point for cruises to the Danube Bend (Dunakanyar) ▲ *230*.

PETŐFI TÉR

Continue southward to PETŐFI TÉR, with its statue of Sándor Petőfi (1823–49), the poet-hero of the 1848 uprising. Petőfi is seen here (opposite) reciting his *Nemzeti Dal* ('National Song'), with its famous line 'Rise up Hungarians!' Each year on March 15, the date that marked the beginning of the uprising against Austrian (Habsburg) rule, the statue is covered with flowers and flags. On October 23, 1956 thousands of people gathered here, at the instigation of the Petőfi Circle ● *36*, to demonstrate against the Soviet occupation. To the left of Petőfi 's statue is the late-18th-century GREEK ORTHODOX CHURCH (Görögkeleti templom). Its Rococo façade was redesigned by Miklós Ybl ● *76* in 1872.

The Petőfi Museum of Literature is situated at no. 16 Károlyi Mihály utca.

'Europe is calm, calm once again.
Its revolutions have swept by like a whirlwind.'
Sándor Petőfi, early 1849

Anyone who was there in 1956 will never forget how in the days following March 15 the ground around the statue was littered with tiny burnt paper flags, soaked by the rain and tattered by the wind. March 15 had become an official day of remembrance, when young people (even children) were allowed to file past the statue of Sándor Petőfi, each holding a paper flag. In 1956 the unofficial demonstrations that had taken place there year after year developed into a protest against the totalitarian regime.

THE POET
Petőfi 's first poem was published in 1842. His humor and powerful imagery created a new language that elevated the ordinary to the realm of poetry. He was an epic poet who presented popular tales in the form of lyrical ballads.

ACTOR, SOLDIER, STUDENT Petőfi 's father was a butcher and café owner named Petrovics, and his mother a servant. He was expelled from school, after receiving a bad report, and became an extra at the Hungarian National Theater. After roaming the countries of the Hungarian Empire as a volunteer soldier, he became a traveling player and a student.

THE POET ACCLAIMED, THE MAN DESTROYED
In July 1849 General Josef Bem made Petőfi his aide-de-camp. Austria, then a world power, was unable to defeat Hungary and called upon another great power, Russia, to help. The soldier-poet was killed during the Battle of Segesvár, on July 31.

'RISE UP HUNGARIANS!'
When they learned of the Viennese uprising in 1848, the leaders of the youthful rebellion met in the Café Pilvax in Pest ● *58*. On March 15, Hungary, too, rebelled. Petőfi 's *Nemzeti Dal* ('National Song') and the proclamation of the writer Mór Jókai were circulated in the universities and on the streets of Pest. Today Hungarians still know Petőfi 's poem by heart. The twin parapets of the steps of the Hungarian National Museum (in the gardens a few hundred yards from Petőfi 's statue) have remained a place of national remembrance.

INNER CITY PARISH CHURCH (Belvárosi plébániatemplom) The Inner City Parish Church is a large composite building. Built in Romanesque style in the 12th century, it was refurbished in Gothic style (choir and north entrance) in the 14th century and in Renaissance style in the 16th century (the beautiful tabernacle in the chapel to the right of the choir dates from 1507). After being converted into a mosque by the Turks (as evidenced by the *mihrab* or prayer niche in the eastern wall, facing Mecca), it was partly destroyed by fire in 1723, then rebuilt in brilliant Austrian Baroque style (nave and façade) by the architect János György Paur in the late 18th century.

MÁRCIUS 15. TÉR

By continuing toward Elizabeth Bridge (Erzsébet híd) you come to Március 15 tér (March 15 Square), which commemorates the date of the 1848 uprising. To the east of the square lie the ruined 3rd-century Roman fortress of Contra-Aquincum and the Inner City Parish Church (Belvárosi plébániatemplom). The church is adjacent to Elizabeth Bridge, which until 1920 was the longest suspension bridge in the world. Destroyed during World War Two, it was rebuilt in 1964 by the Hungarian architect Pál Sávoly ▲ *181*.

Fresco in the Inner City Parish Church.

VÁCI UTCA

A pedestrianized shopping and tourist street, Váci utca (which leads from Vörösmarty tér) is a fine example of the changes that have occurred since 1989. Nevertheless, the narrow streets that run across it are much more interesting, especially Régiposta utca, Kigyó utca and Párizsi utca. Here you can see the beautiful Baroque PÉTERFY MANSION (1755) at no. 2 Pesti Barnabás utca ● *70*, and the LORAND EÖTVÖS UNIVERSITY ARTS FACULTY at no. 1. By leaving the beaten tourist track and crossing Petőfi Sándor utca, you come to the attractive town-hall district that lies parallel to Váci utca. It is centered on KAMERMAYER KAROLY TÉR (named after the first mayor of the unified city) and SZERVITA TÉR.

SZERVITA TÉR The square is named after the Baroque SERVITE CHURCH (Szervita templom) built in 1732. Also of interest is the former TURKISH BANK (Török Bankház) ● *81*, at no. 3, which has an Art Nouveau façade (1906) incorporating a huge mosaic of Hungaria, the symbolic representation of Hungary. The TOWN HALL (Polgármesteri Hivatal), an impressive and beautifully proportioned Baroque building located at nos. 9–11 Városház utca, was built in the early 18th century by Anton Martinelli to house soldiers wounded in the war against the Turks. SEMMELWEIS UTCA, which lies just behind the town hall, was named after Dr Ignác Semmelweis, who discovered the cure for puerperal fever (blood poisoning contracted during childbirth). At no. 6, PEST COUNTY HALL (Pest Megyei Önkormányzati Hivatal) ● *75* is open to the public (the main entrance is at no. 7 Városház utca). It is a fine neoclassical building, with two magnificent interior courtyards. At the far end of Petőfi Sándor utca is the JÓZSEF KATONA THEATER (Katona József Színház) ● *43*, which spearheaded avant-garde theater in the 1970s and is still one of the city's best theaters.

FRANCISCANS' SQUARE (Ferenciek tere) Just beyond the József Katona Theater lies the FERENCIEK TERE dominated by a beautiful building (1909) designed by Henrik Schmahl, in eclectic style ● *76*, as the Inner City Savings Bank. Its most interesting feature is the PARIZSI UDVAR, a shopping arcade based on the ones fashionable in early 20th-century Paris, which combines Moorish and Venetian architectural styles. The square is named after its 18th-century FRANCISCAN CHURCH (Franciskánus templom), in Italian Baroque style. In the center stands the NEREIDS FOUNTAIN (originally called the WELL OF THE NAIADS).

VÁCI UTCA PEDESTRIAN PRECINCT
With its fashionable boutiques, bookstores souvenir shops, and cafés, the Váci utca has a cosmopolitan atmosphere. The street also has a number of unusual architectural features, such as the original Art Nouveau interior of the PHILANTHIA FLORIST'S at no. 9, the Art Nouveau sculptural decorations and balcony of no. 8, and the THONET HOUSE (1889) at no. 11A, a masterpiece of Hungarian Secessionist architecture by Ödön Lechner ● *80*, ▲ *171*.

THE FRANCISCAN CHURCH AND THE PARIZSI UDVAR
A relief on the wall of the church overlooking Kossuth Lajos utca recalls the Great Flood of 1838 ▲ *179*. It shows Baron Miklós Wesselényi using a boat to rescue people stranded by the flooding.

SERBIAN ORTHODOX CHURCH
The church (below), built by the Serbs in the 17th century, has a beautiful iconostasis.

'ANTIKVÁRUM'
Budapest's many *antikvárum* are well worth a visit. These secondhand bookstores are popular with specialists and students, and some are truly amazing. KŐZPONTI ANTIKVÁRUM, at no. 15 Múzeum körút (opposite the National Museum), is full of treasures – both old books and old maps and prints. Next door, at no. 17, ZENEI ANTIKVÁRUM is a music lover's paradise: it is entirely devoted to old scores, books about music and rare recordings.

THE KLOTILD PALACES These two buildings (nos. 5 and 6 Szabadsajtó út) were built in 1902, by Floris Korb and Kálmán Giergl, in eclectic style. Ferenciek tere and Kossuth Lajos utca represent a natural boundary within Belváros. On the other (southern) side lies part of the delightful university district. The multicolored dome of the UNIVERSITY LIBRARY (EGYETEMI KÖNYVTÁR), at no. 10 Ferenciek tere, provides a good starting point for this part of the walk.

EGYETEM TÉR

Strangely, this lively student quarter is not particularly popular with tourists. However, its cafés, theaters, university buildings and narrow streets make it one of the most attractive districts of Belváros.

THE UNIVERSITY CHURCH (Egyetemi templom)
As you turn down the Károlyi Mihály utca, you come to the Egyetemi tér (University Square). In 1785 the university moved from Buda to Pest. Today it is popularly known as ELTE (Lóránd Eötvös University) and its various departments are scattered throughout the city. As well as the Law Faculty, the square also has the city's most beautiful Baroque church: the University Church, built in 1725 and 1742. Its treasures include a copy of the *Black Madonna* of Czestochowa, a richly decorated pulpit and a beautiful portal carved by the Pauline monks.

PETŐFI MUSEUM OF LITERATURE The Petőfi Irodalmi Múzeum, at no. 16 Károlyi Mihály utca, houses a collection of objects that once belonged to Hungarian poets and writers (Sándor Petőfi ▲ *119*, Endre Ady and Attila József) and an archive center used by researchers. Kecskeméti utca (which leads to Kálvin tér) is a pleasant university street, with cafés and restaurants.

SERBIAN ORTHODOX CHURCH (Szerb orthodox templom)
As you turn southward, you come to a quiet,

'We are now in Pest, the eastern half of the city, which is younger and less beautiful than Buda. Even so, it was the dynamism of Pest that made the reputation of Budapest, and in 1900 it housed 83 percent of the city's inhabitants.'

John Lukacs

shady district. At the intersection of Szerb utca and Veres Pálné utca stands the Serbian Orthodox Church. A little further on, the remains Pest's old medieval wall (1¼ miles long) can still be seen at the corner of Bástya utca and Veres Pálné utca.

KISKÖRÚT

The Kiskörút (Little Boulevard) describes an arc between Deák Ferenc tér and Freedom Bridge (Szabadság híd ▲ *180*). This main thoroughfare, which consists of three roads – Károly körút, Múzeum körút and Vámház körút – in succession, follows the line of the old walls of the medieval city. At the end of the 19th century an outer ring road, the Nagykörút (Great Boulevard) ▲ *164*, was built running parallel to it.

DEÁK FERENC TÉR This square is the departure point and terminus for most of the city's bus and subway lines. Its name is often shortened to Deák tér. Its subway (*metro*) station includes the amazing Underground Railway Museum (Földalatti Vasút Múzeum). To the south of the square is a neoclassical early 19th-century Lutheran Church ● *75*. The presbytery (at nos. 4–5 Deák Ferenc tér) – now the National Lutheran Museum – was formerly a school, which was attended by the young Sándor Petőfi.

HOTEL ASTORIA Built between 1912 and 1914, according to plans by Emil Ágoston and Arthur Hikisch, the Hotel Astoria stands at the intersection of Károly körút and Kossuth Lajos utca. The hotel's beautiful entrance hall has the charm of an early-20th-century mansion, while the adjoining tearooms offer comfortable surrounding in which to meet people or enjoy a quiet read.

HUNGARIAN NATIONAL MUSEUM (Magyar Nemzeti Múzeum) ▲ *124* A little further along Károly körút is the Hungarian National Museum. Enjoy a walk in the museum gardens before continuing along Múzeum utca, bordered by beautiful private residences.

KÁLVIN TÉR. The square is dominated by a large Calvinist Church (Református templom), founded between 1816 and 1830 by József Hofrichter. The porch was designed by József Hild.

CENTRAL MARKET HALL (Központi Vásárcsarnok). From Kálvin tér, take the Vámház körút toward Freedom Bridge (Szabadság Híd). On the left, next to the Budapest University of Economics, is the Central Market Hall. This vast brick-and-steel covered market, designed in 1896 by Samu Pecz, was restored in 1996.

Ferenc Deák (1803–76), the 'nation's sage'.

The Hungarian National Museum ● *74*, ▲ *124* This large neoclassical building was designed by Mihály Pollack. Its construction (1837–47) marked an important step toward Hungary's national renaissance. Commemorative shows to celebrate the 15 March holiday take place on the steps of the museum.

Central Market Hall (main entrance).

▲ The Hungarian National Museum (Magyar Nemzeti Múzeum)

Superb *fondo d'oro* (4th century AD), sealed in glass, bearing the inscription *'Semper gaudeatis in nomine Dei'.*

In 1786 Count Ferenc Széchenyi, a rich and erudite art lover, began to build up his library and his collection of prints, maps, manuscripts, coats of arms, coins and archeology, to such an extent that he created a rich source of reference relating to the nation's history. In 1802, with the approval of Francis II (king of Hungary 1792–1830), he donated some 20,000 pieces to serve as the basis of the Hungarian National Museum (Magyar Nemzeti Múzeum), which was initially housed in the former Pauline Convent. The imposing neoclassical building designed by Mihály Pollack ● *74* has housed the museum since 1847.

Head of Hygeia (2nd century AD) This small marble head is a copy of a Hellenistic original. It was found in the Danube, in front of the Parliament building, in the late 19th century.

The museum's departments The museum has departments devoted to archeology, the Middle Ages, modern history, medals and historical paintings, plus an archeological library and archives that contain documentation relating to excavations carried out in Hungary and photographic records of items in the museum's collections.

Cylindrical-stemmed vase (first half of 3rd millennium BC) The archeological collection is divided into three sections, covering the prehistoric and Roman periods and the 'great invasions'. The characteristic shape of this vase was developed by the peoples living on the banks of the Tisza. Vases of this kind were often decorated with engraved or etched motifs.

Crown of Constantine IX Monomachus (1042–55)

This gold diadem, composed of seven sections, is a masterpiece of Byzantine *cloisonné* enamel. The Byzantine Emperor Constantine IX, his wife Zoë and sister-in-law Theodora are represented on the three central sections.

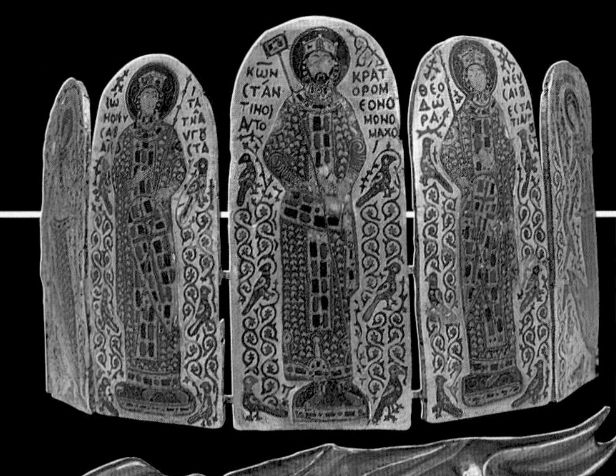

Scythian deer

Gold *repoussé* deer (6th century BC) from Zöldhalompuszta. The remains of a pale-blue *pâte-de-verre* inlay were found in the eye socket and the ear. Beneath the ear is the head of a bird of prey.

Deer with coral antlers (table decoration)

The goldsmith Sebestyén Hann (1644–1713) worked mainly in Transylvania. This is one of several pieces by him in the museum.

Crown of the Hungarian kings (12th century)

The gold crown is divided into two parts. The lower part is known as the 'Greek crown' because it bears images of the saints inscribed with Greek characters, while the upper part, or 'Latin crown', has images of the Evangelists with Latin inscriptions.

Fifty-ducat piece (bearing the image of the Transylvanian prince Mihály Apafi, 1677)

During the reign of Leopold I the gold forint began to be known as the ducat. The coin shown here was a royal gift and had no commercial value.

PARLIAMENT (Országház)
The Parliament building stretches for more 290 yards along the banks of the Danube. The tip of the dome is over 300 feet from the ground.

KOSSUTH LAJOS TÉR
Known as the 'standard bearer of independence', Lajos Kossuth (1802–94) was one of the principal instigators of the 1848 uprising. His statue (right) stands on the north side of the square.

Lipótváros (the 'town of Leopold'), named after Leopold II (1747–99), one of he Habsburg kings of Hungary and son of Maria Theresa, lies between the Danube and the Kiskörút (Little Boulevard). It is a district of offices, banks, ministries and large apartment blocks; a number of publications and political parties are based here. Lipótváros is very busy during the day – especially at lunch time, when the restaurants in Mérleg utca (next to Gresham Palace ▲ *138*) are packed – but in the evening it is extremely quiet and almost deserted.

KOSSUTH LAJOS TÉR

Situated between the Parliament building and the Ethnographical Museum ▲ *134*, Kossuth Lajos tér provides an ideal setting for the seat of the Hungarian government. The statues of Hungary's great historical and political figures dotted around the square add a touch of majesty to this broad esplanade, the venue for public demonstrations such as the 1956 uprising and its anniversaries, and the declaration of the Hungarian Republic on October 23, 1989.
Notable statues include LAJOS KOSSUTH on the north side of the square, FERENC RÁKÓCZI (the prince of Transylvania who in 1704–11 opposed the Habsburg presence in Hungary after the Turkish withdrawal; at the south end of the square); MIHÁLY KÁROLY (president of the short-lived Republic founded after World War One; to the north of the Parliament building); and IMRE NAGY (prime minister and martyr of the 1956 uprising ● *30*, ▲ *150*, in the southeast corner.)

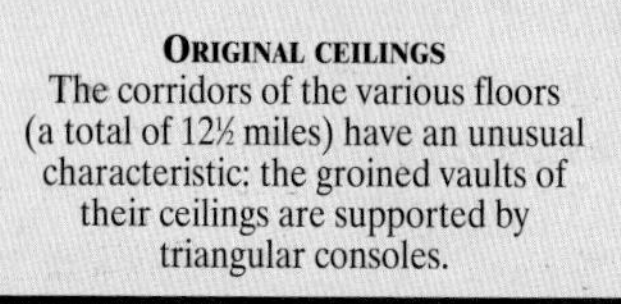

ORIGINAL CEILINGS
The corridors of the various floors (a total of 12½ miles) have an unusual characteristic: the groined vaults of their ceilings are supported by triangular consoles.

'In a building designed [to last] for centuries, I could not use ephemeral details...which is why I have made every effort to express the national and individual spirit of Hungary.'

Imre Steindl

AN ECLECTIC MASTERPIECE...
The Parliament is a fine example of eclectic architecture. The overall style is neo-Gothic, while the dome and general layout are neo-Renaissance, and the design of the various wings reflects the Baroque influence.

AND A MODEL OF SYMMETRY
The building observes the characteristic symmetry of Renaissance architecture. In the center a huge dome rises above the central hall. On either side of the dome, two identical wings contain the Chamber of Deputies (south wing) and the chamber of the former Upper House (north wing), which is now a conference hall. There are eighteen interior courtyards of varying sizes.

FAÇADES
The pediments of the façades have niches decorated with sculptures. The pediment of the main façade (right), overlooking the Danube, is decorated with arcades and surmounted by a balcony. The coats of arms of historic Hungarian towns are represented below the cornice.

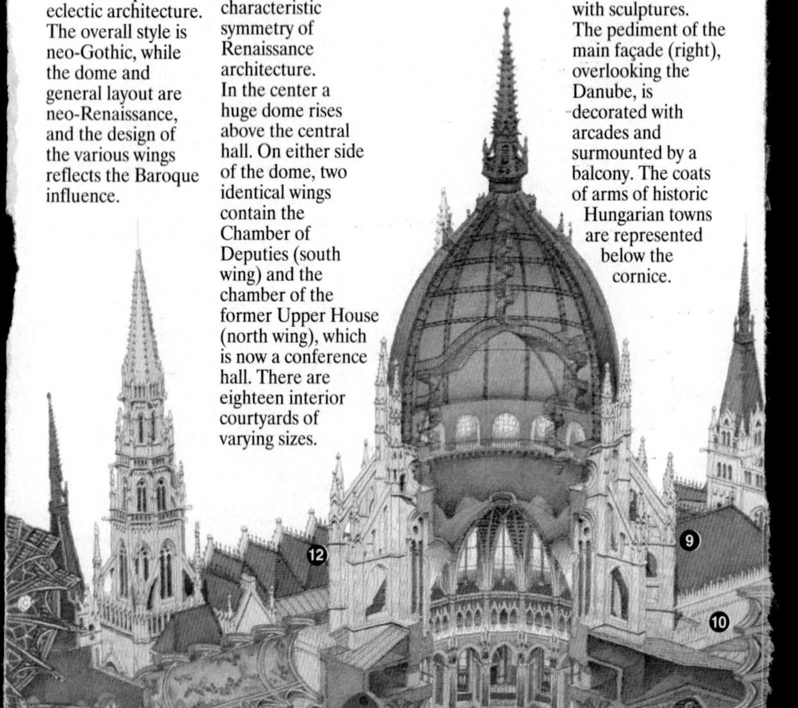

12 9 10 5 6 4

Equestrian statue of Ferenc Rákóczi (János Pásztor, 1927).

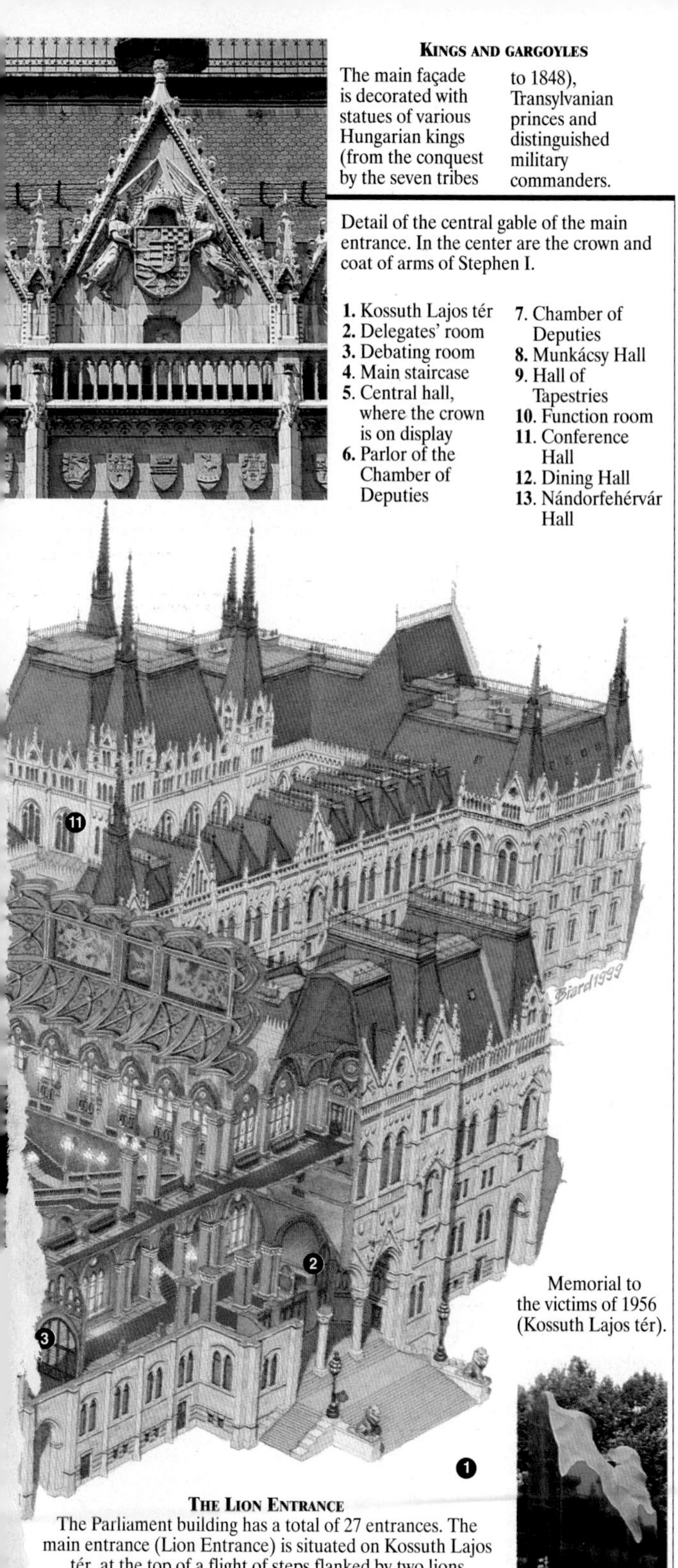

Kings and gargoyles

The main façade is decorated with statues of various Hungarian kings (from the conquest by the seven tribes to 1848), Transylvanian princes and distinguished military commanders.

Detail of the central gable of the main entrance. In the center are the crown and coat of arms of Stephen I.

1. Kossuth Lajos tér
2. Delegates' room
3. Debating room
4. Main staircase
5. Central hall, where the crown is on display
6. Parlor of the Chamber of Deputies
7. Chamber of Deputies
8. Munkácsy Hall
9. Hall of Tapestries
10. Function room
11. Conference Hall
12. Dining Hall
13. Nándorfehérvár Hall

Memorial to the victims of 1956 (Kossuth Lajos tér).

The Lion Entrance

The Parliament building has a total of 27 entrances. The main entrance (Lion Entrance) is situated on Kossuth Lajos tér, at the top of a flight of steps flanked by two lions designed by Béla Markup. It opens onto the grand staircase, leading to the central hall beneath the dome.

▲ THE PARLIAMENT (Országház)

The main halls and chambers are on the ground and first floors. The splendor of the interior decor (which combines Gothic, Renaissance and Byzantine styles), with its profusion of frescos, stained glass, sculptures and oak, mahogany and walnut ceilings, contributes to the solemnity of the building.

THE CHAMBER OF DEPUTIES (right) It is in the form of a horseshoe. Like the conference hall and the various ante-rooms rooms and reception rooms, it is richly decorated in neo-Byzantine style. Left: detail of the ceiling.

PAINTINGS IN THE PARLIAMENT BUILDING
Among the numerous art treasures in the Parliament building are a mural by Körösfői-Kriesch depicting Attila and Buda hunting bison (in the Hall of the Hunt) and a monumental fresco of the conquest of Árpád (in the Munkácsy Hall). The audience chamber contains oil paintings by Lotz.

A METICULOUSLY DESIGNED CHAMBER
The various levels of the Chamber of Deputies are punctuated by a series of boxes and balconies to improve the acoustics. The chamber is lit by twelve huge chandeliers.

SYMBOLIC IMAGERY
The decoration of the Parliament building glorifies the virtues and victories of Hungary. It has a wealth of allegorical sculptures and historical paintings by Vajda, Körösfői-Kriesch, Lotz, Duditis and Munkácsy.

One of the pillars supporting the dome.

▲ THE PARLIAMENT (Országház)

The Parliament building (Országház) is both the seat of Hungary's principal political institutions and the symbol of national independence. Its 691 rooms include the presidency of the Hungarian Republic, the apartments of the president and the leader of the Chamber of Deputies, the National Assembly, the prime minister's office, and the UN-designated Library of Parliament with its collection of over 400,000 books on history, law and political science.

IMRE STEINDL (1839–1902)
Steindl studied at the Viennese School of Fine Arts, under Friedrich Schmidt, and was particularly interested in Gothic architecture. In 1883 he won the competition for the best design for the Hungarian Parliament building. Out of the nineteen competing architects, he was the only one to choose the neo-Gothic style, inspired by the British Houses of Parliament. Work began in 1885, and the interior was completed in 1904.

AN IMPOSING BUT FRAGILE BUILDING
The extremely porous limestone used in the construction of the Parliament has been badly affected by pollution, and since 1925 the building has had to be repeatedly restored.

8

7

13

KINGS AND SAINTS
The dome presents a summary of Hungarian history. Its sixteen marble pillars support statues of Hungarian kings and saints since the time of Árpád, flanked by statues of pages.
These statues represent (in a clockwise direction): Árpád, Stephen I (Saint Stephen), László I (Saint László), Kálmán the Possessor of Books, András II, Béla IV, Louis the Great, János Hunyadi, Matthias Corvinus, István Báthory, István Bocskay, Gábor Bethlen, György I Rákóczi, Charles III, Maria Theresa and Leopold II.

'By its perfect beauty and its elegant lines, this remarkable medieval style creates a bridge between the material and spiritual world...'

Imre Steindl, architect of the Parliament building

THE DOME

The main staircase leads to the central hall beneath the star-shaped dome that forms the impressively proportioned heart of the Hungarian Parliament (almost 90 feet high and 65 feet in diameter). Its double framework is decorated with marble from Hungary and other countries. There are no figurative paintings: the sculptures and structural outline are highlighted with gold leaf and form a single, unified decor. The ribs of the vault are decorated with a variety of reliefs and the coats of arms of the kings of Hungary.

THE CONFERENCE HALL

While the layout of the conference hall, in the north wing, is like that of the Chamber of Deputies, its decor is slightly different. The arches of the boxes are crowned with ornamental foliage. Behind the chairperson's seat are the coats of arms of the Houses of Anjou, Hunyadi, Jagiellon, Szapolyai and Habsburg. On either side of it are paintings by Jantyik: on the right, András II announcing the Golden Bull of 1222; and on the left, the three estates offering their support to Maria Theresa at Pozsony in 1741. At second-floor level are sculptures symbolizing Glory, Wisdom, Unity, Rhetoric, War and Peace.

THE MAIN STAIRCASE

The staircase combines Baroque, Gothic and Byzantine styles. Its polychrome marble, the reddish-brown Swedish granite of its columns, the gold leaf of the Gothic arches and the multi-colored stained-glass windows by Miksa Róth all contribute to its lavish splendor. The grandiose frescos by Károly Lotz depict Hungaria, the symbolic representation of Hungary.

THE ETHNOGRAPHICAL MUSEUM ★
The huge central hall, designed in neo-Renaissance style by Károly Lotz.

ETHNOGRAPHICAL MUSEUM (Néprajzi Múzeum) Opposite the Hungarian Parliament, at no. 12 Kossuth Lajos tér, the Ethnographical Museum occupies the former Palace of Justice designed by Alajos Hauszmann. In best thnographical tradition, the museum houses major collections of costumes, model peasant houses, and objects associated with weaving, pottery and embroidery. The items representing rural life (such as the gaily painted peasant furniture) are fine examples of a fascinating form of decorative art, while the collections of weaving illustrate the different regional variations. Also on display are examples of traditional costume (*nép viselet*), such as the long shepherd's cloaks with shoulder cape and the black-and-red headscarves. With its marble columns and allegorical fresco of Justice, the museum's huge hall has a monumental splendor.

Below: part of the Hungarian television building.

STATUE OF IMRE NAGY The MINISTRY OF AGRICULTURE (Földművelésügyi Minisztérum) occupies the large eclectic building (1886) at no. 11 Kossuth Lajos tér. Near the side of the building looking onto Vértanúk tere stands the statue ▲ *126* of Imre Nagy (1896–1958), the Hungarian prime minister who was arrested in 1956 and executed in 1958 ● *31, 36* ▲ *151*.

SZABADSÁG TÉR

From Kossuth Lajos tér, Nádor utca leads to another of Budapest's main squares, FREEDOM SQUARE (Szabadság tér), which lies at the center of a district renovated in the 1900s. It was here that the Emperor Joseph II built the prison-barracks known as the Újépület ('new building') that became a symbol of Habsburg

'... a mixture of giantism and exuberance, which corresponds to the hybrid alliance between the Hungarian capital and the Hapsburg eagle, and is also betrayed by the eclectic quality of the architecture.'

Claudio Magris

Ethnographical Museum (central hall).

oppression in Hungary. The square was subsequently renamed Freedom Square in an attempt to break with its oppressive past. On one side of the square stands the US EMBASSY, where Cardinal József Mindszenty (1892–1975) sought refuge after the 1956 uprising and remained in 'internal exile' until 1971. Bishop of Veszprém, then Archbishop of Esztergom (1945–73) and, as such, Hungary's Catholic Primate, Mindszenty became a cardinal in 1946. Having refused to secularize Roman Catholic schools when the Communist regime was established in Hungary, he was arrested (1948), tortured and condemned to hard labor for life. He was freed in 1955 and played a key role in the 1956 uprising, opposing Soviet intervention in the same way he had opposed the Kádár regime. He left the US Embassy in 1971 and he went to Vienna, from where he continued to criticize the regime. Behind Freedom Square (on the corner of Báthory utca and Aulich utca) another square, the tiny BATHORY TÉR, also holds poignant memories. A small bronze oil lamp honors the memory of Count Lajos Batthyány (1806–49) ▲ *207*, head of the first Hungarian national government during the 1848 uprising, who was executed on October 6, 1849, in front of the barracks that have now disappeared.

Relief on the National Bank of Hungary.

Detail of the Bedő building, at no. 3 Honvéd utca.

MAGYAR NEMZETI BANK AND MAGYAR TELEVÍSIÓ Two famous buildings, the National Bank of Hungary and what is now the headquarters of Hungarian Television, stand opposite each other at nos. 8 and 9 Szabadság tér. Both were built at the start of the 20th century by Ignác Alpár (who also built Vajdahunyad Castle ▲ *111, 161*). The National Bank (1901) reflects a strong Art Nouveau influence, while the Hungarian Television building is a fine example of the Secessionist style that originated in Vienna.

A MASTERPIECE BY ÖDÖN LECHNER
Pest's Post Office Savings Bank was built by Ödön Lechner in 1901, before Otto Wagner built its Viennese counterpart. It is characterized by an exuberant Art Nouveau style. This is reflected in its faience decorations and magnificent multicolored roof tiles, with plant and flower motifs, from the Vilmos Zsolnay porcelain manufactory ● *66*, ▲ *147* at Pécs. The main hall is well worth a visit.

FORMER POST OFFICE SAVINGS BANK (Országos Postatakarékpénztár) ★ Head northward along Bank utca and turn down Hold utca. Here, at no. 4, you can admire Ödön Lechner's Post Office Savings Bank ● *80, 112*, now part of the National Bank of Hungary.

SZENT ISTVÁN TÉR

On the south side of Szabadság tér, Hercegprímás utca takes you to Szent István tér (ST STEPHEN'S SQUARE) and Szent István Bazilika (ST STEPHEN'S BASILICA) ● *76*. In spite of its name, the church does not have the traditional layout of a basilica. In fact it would be more accurate to refer to it as a cathedral, since the Archbishop of Esztergom ▲ *238* today bears the double title of

SZENT ISTVAN BAZILIKA
Built in the striking neo-Renaissance style favored by Miklós Ybl, St Stephen's Basilica is notable for its impressive proportions. It is 95 yards long and 60 yards wide; the tip of the dome is 315 feet from the ground.

'The greatest architect of this period was Miklós Ybl, the grand master of neo-Renaissance, whose works – the dome of St Stephen's Basilica, the Customs House and especially the Opera House – will be just as valid in the future as they are now.'

Hungary's Faces, 1938

Archbishop of Esztergom and Budapest. Inside is a statue of Saint Elizabeth (1207–31), daughter of András II and wife of the Count of Thuringia. Widowed at the age of twenty, she joined the Franciscan Third Order and devoted her life to the poor. There is also a reliquary containing the hand of Saint Stephen. A narrow staircase leads to the dome, which offers a magnificent view of the city – an absolute must for tourists, who are often disappointed by the somewhat soulless gigantism of the church's architecture. Behind the basilica, the buildings at no. 19 Bajcsy-Zsilinsky út are a fine example of 1930s architecture.

CENTRAL EUROPEAN UNIVERSITY (Közép Európai Egyetem) From the basilica, Zrínyi utca leads southward to the river, crossing Október 6 utca and Nádor utca. At no. 9 is the former Festetics building, designed by Mihály Pollack (1826), which is now the seat of the Central European University. Founded after the dismantling of the Berlin Wall, with a view to forming a new Central European academic elite, the center is largely funded by the Hungarian-American millionaire George Soros. This neoclassical building also houses the University's extensive English-language library. The entrance hall is decorated with allegorical statues.

ROOSEVELT TÉR Situated at one end of Chain Bridge (Széchenyi Lánchíd ● *74*, ▲ *183*), Roosevelt tér opens onto a promenade that runs alongside the quays of the Danube, offering a magnificent view of Buda. Overlooking the square is the HUNGARIAN ACADEMY OF SCIENCES (Magyar Tudományos Akadémia), conceived in 1825 by Count István Széchenyi and built during the 1860s, in neo-Renaissance style, to plans by the Berlin architect Friedrich August Stüler and the Hungarian Miklós Ybl ● *76*, ▲ *140*. In 1827 Széchenyi ● *35* – who made history by speaking Hungarian, instead of Latin, at the Diet of Pressburg (now Bratislava) in 1825 – donated the huge sum of 60,000 forints for the construction of the academy, with a view to helping the Magyar cause and developing the Hungarian language. Today it still has an important scientific library.

HUNGARIAN ACADEMY OF SCIENCES
The second floor is decorated with statues of great European scholars, among them Descartes, Galileo, Leibnitz, Lomonosov, Newton and the Hungarian linguist Miklós Révai.

'District V, Lipótváros, Roosevelt tér'

CONSTRUCTED IN THREE STAGES
The vast – it can hold 8,500 people – St Stephen's Basilica (Szent István Bazilika) has had a turbulent history. József Hild drew up the first plans in 1851, but died shortly afterward. He was succeeded by Miklós Ybl, whose dome unfortunately collapsed in 1868. Ybl died in 1891, and the church was finally completed fifteen years later by József Kauser.

Gresham Palace ★ The façade of this palatial Art Nouveau building, designed by Zsigmond Quittner, is particularly impressive. It is decorated with mosaic friezes that catch the last rays of the setting sun.

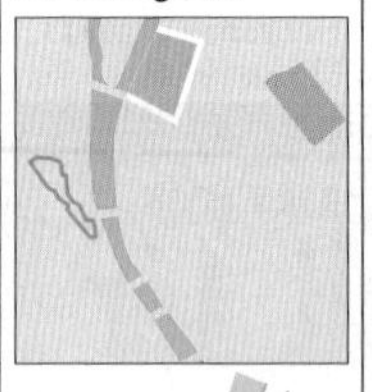

Gresham Palace ● *80*, *81* (no. 5 Roosevelt tér) owes its name to the British insurance company that commissioned this grandiose building in 1907.

Jozsef nador tér As you leave Gresham Palace and cross József Attila utca, you come to József nádor tér, from where you can return to Belváros ▲ *116*. The square is named after Palatine Archduke (*nádor*) Joseph of Habsburg ● *34*, ▲ *199* (one of the sons of Leopold II), the first Hungarian magnate (1796) and one of the leading 'architects' of Pest's development. Today this elegant, shady square provides a pleasant setting for several large companies. The Postal Bank (Postabank) at no. 1 has a beautiful interior courtyard.

Újlipótváros

The Újlipótváros district (the name means 'new town of Leopold') is bounded by Váci utca ▲ *121* and Szent István körút (St Stephen's Boulevard) ▲ *164*. Many of its buildings date from the 1930s. Before World War Two it was a wealthy middle-class residential district and, along with the VIIth district, Pest's largest Jewish quarter. Today this part of the city is much sought after for its tranquillity and the elegance of its streets, especially near the quays and Szent István Park. Jászai Mari tér, at the end of Margaret Bridge (Margit híd), is a convenient place to begin this walk.

Jaszai Mari tér On the north side of the square is the extremely elegant late-19th-century Palatinus Apartment Block. To the south, at no. 19 Széchenyi rakpart (quay), is the dull, gray modern building that Hungarians jokingly call the White House (Fehérház) ▲ *187*. It is the former Communist Party headquarters, where János Kádár, the Secretary General of the Party, had his offices until 1988. Statues of Marx and Engels have been relocated in Statue Park ▲ *110*. The building, which now houses various Party offices, is not open to the public.

Pozsonyi út This particularly beautiful street lies behind Jázai Mari tér (Pozsony is the Hungarian name for Bratislava, now capital of Slovakia). It has a number of buildings, with large interior courtyards, that offer a fine example of 1930s architecture.

Raoul Wallenberg utca On the way to Szent István Park, you cross Raoul Wallenberg utca. In July 1944 Raoul

György Konrád wrote about life in Újlipótváros in his autobiographical novel, *Ghosts from the Past.* In particular he describes Pozsonyi út, where he lived in hiding during World War Two until the Soviet troops arrived.

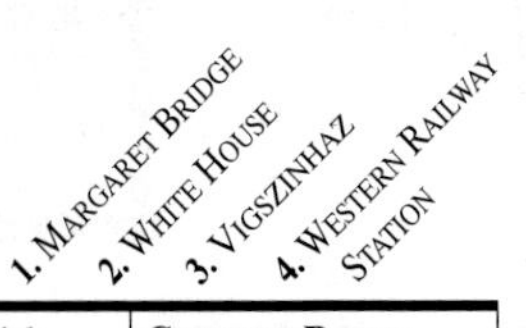

Gresham Palace, 'peacock' gate (left) Beyond the entrance passageway, with its beautiful wrought-iron "peacock" gate, is a huge glass-roofed arcade. The building is to be converted into a hotel.

Wallenberg, a young Swedish diplomat, was sent to Budapest under the aegis of US, Swedish and Jewish refugee organizations to save Hungarian Jews threatened with deportation. Between October 1944 and the winter of 1945 he saved thousands of lives by delivering visas ('Wallenberg passports') to Jewish families all over the city, or by hiding them in 'protected houses' flying the flags of Sweden and other neutral countries. He was reported missing at the end of the war, but was captured – and may have been executed – by the Soviet army, who suspected him to be a spy for the United States. The street was named after him to commemorate his courageous actions.

Szent Istvan Park This delightful little park is one of the most sought-after residential areas in the capital. Its Bauhaus-style buildings ● *85*, with balconies offering a splendid view of Margaret Island and the Buda Hills, are truly exceptional. Children play around the statue of György Lukács, who played a key role in Béla Kun's short-lived Hungarian Communist regime and, after the latter's exile to Moscow, served as Minister for Culture in Imre Nagy's government in 1956.

Lehel market (Lehel Vásárcsarnok) From the park, Victor Hugo utca (bordered by public housing units and other unprepossessing buildings from the Communist era) leads to Lehel tér (Lehel Square), where one of Budapest's oldest markets, the Lehel Vásárcsarnok, is held. The market, which moved to a modern building in 2001, offers an ideal opportunity to sample *lángos* – a savory kind of pastry made with butter, resembling pizza base, and sometimes topped with vegetables. The square is dominated by the huge St Margaret's Church (Szent Margit templom), a 1930s copy of the (now ruined) 13th-century Romanesque Collegiate Church of Zsámbék, 25 miles from Budapest. The Visegrádi utca – a working-class street crowded with small shops and *söröző* (beer bar), and teeming with life – brings you back to Szent István körút and the Nagykörút (Great Boulevard) ▲ *164*).

Art Nouveau detail (below) The Art Nouveau building at no. 152 Dózsa György út ▲ *149* (which lies to the north of Újlipótváros) was built in 1911 by the architects Lajos Schodits and Béla Eberling.

György Lukacs (1885–1971, left) In his *Geschichte und Klassenbewußtsein* (History and Class Consciousness, 1923), György (Georg) Lukács stressed the importance of the role played by the revolutionary intelligentsia in awakening the class consciousness of the working classes. He greatly influenced the mainstream of European Communist thought and regarded literature as a vehicle for the artistic representation of reality. In the 1960s the Budapest school of Marxist thought (also known as the Lukács school) became oriented toward 'critical Marxism'.

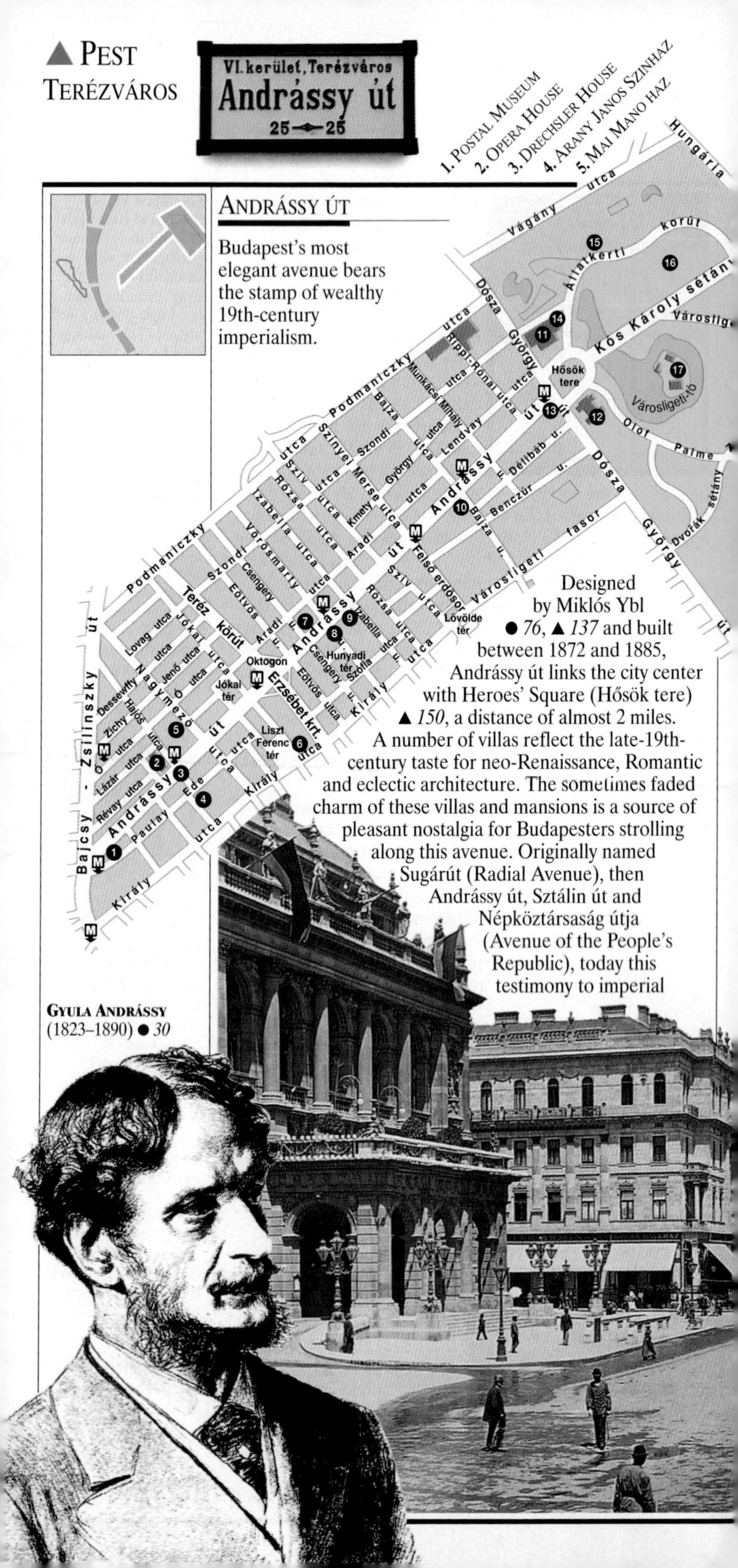

ANDRÁSSY ÚT

Budapest's most elegant avenue bears the stamp of wealthy 19th-century imperialism.

Designed by Miklós Ybl ● *76*, ▲ *137* and built between 1872 and 1885, Andrássy út links the city center with Heroes' Square (Hősök tere) ▲ *150*, a distance of almost 2 miles. A number of villas reflect the late-19th-century taste for neo-Renaissance, Romantic and eclectic architecture. The sometimes faded charm of these villas and mansions is a source of pleasant nostalgia for Budapesters strolling along this avenue. Originally named Sugárút (Radial Avenue), then Andrássy út, Sztálin út and Népköztársaság útja (Avenue of the People's Republic), today this testimony to imperial

GYULA ANDRÁSSY (1823–1890) ● *30*

6. Academy of Music
7. Horrors of War Museum
8. Franz Liszt Museum
9. Budapest Puppet Theater
10. Hungarian Press Building
11. Museum of Fine Arts
12. Palace of Arts
13. Yugoslav Embassy
14. Gundel (restaurant
15. Zoo
16. Széchenyi Baths
17. Vajdahunyad Castle
18. Petőfi Csarnok
19. Villa Balázs Sipekys
20. Transport Museum

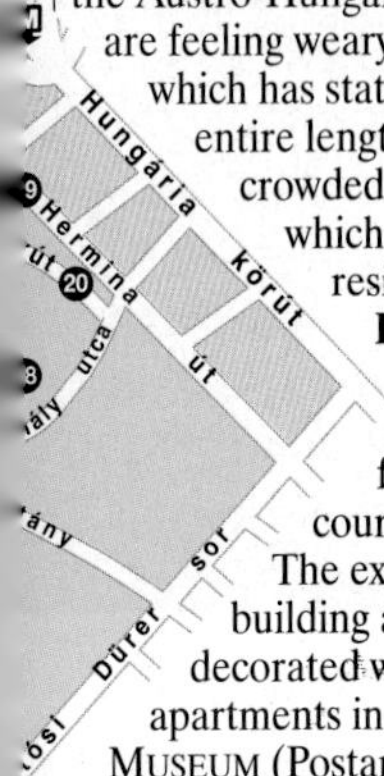

urban splendor once again bears name of the architect of the Austro-Hungarian Compromise of 1867 ● *29.* If you are feeling weary, you can always use the subway (*metro*), which has stations dotted at regular intervals along the entire length of the avenue. Andrássy út is busy and crowded as far as the Oktogon metro station, after which it becomes more sophisticated and more residential.

From Bajcsy-Zsilinzsky út to the Opera House This part of the avenue is a busy shopping street with Rococo façades that conceal beautiful interior courtyards and other unexpected features. The extremely well-preserved early-20th-century building at no. 3 is notable for its entrance, decorated with frescos by Károly Lotz. One of the apartments in this block houses the unusual Postal Museum (Postamúzeum), which traces the history of Hungary's postal services and also of the telephone, including a section on Tivadar Puskás, a colleague of Thomas Edison at the time the telephone was invented. The walls of the stairwell are decorated with splendid frescos. Other courtyards (nos. 43, 47, 79 and 83–5) are well worth a visit. The Hungarian State Opera House (Magyar Állami Operaház ● *76,* ▲ *142*), a majestic edifice built between 1873 and 1884, was designed in Italian Renaissance style by Miklós Ybl, who was strongly influenced by the Vienna Opera House. The façade has a triple-arched portico flanked by huge statues of Franz Liszt and Ferenc Erkel, the first director of the Opera House ● *49.* The first-floor niches house the muses Terpsichore (dance), Erato (love poetry), Thalia (comedy) and Melpomene (tragedy). At second-floor level there are statues of sixteen great European composers.

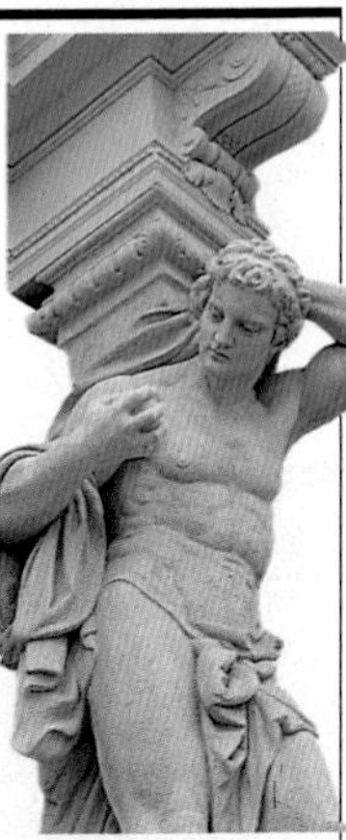

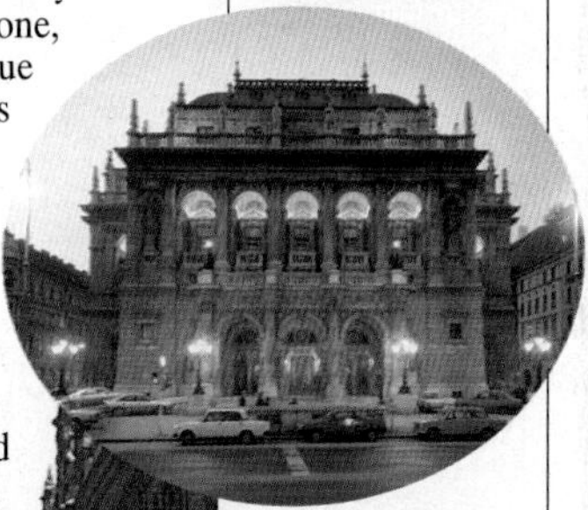

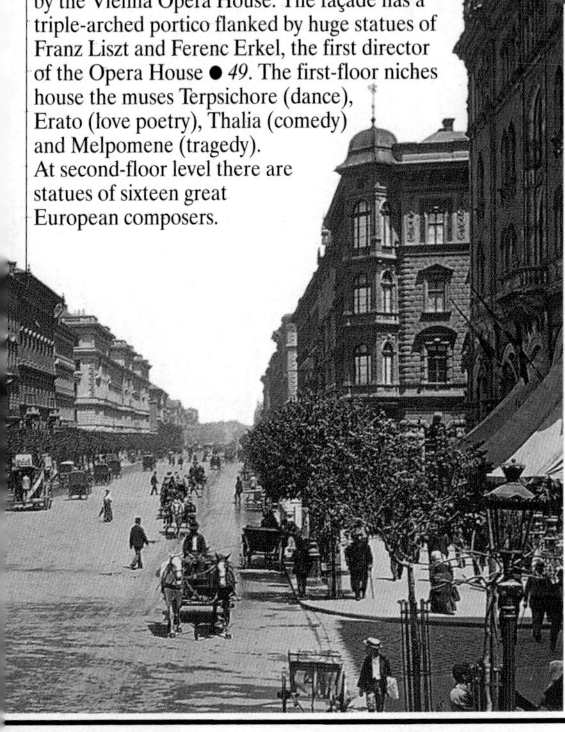

The Opera

'The grand and somewhat overly prestigious Italian-style Opera House on Andrássy út continues to reopen each season with a ritual performance of Erkel's other masterpiece *Bánk Bán* (1861).... For Erkel, torn between the desire to put an end to his country's cultural isolation and to remain faithful to a classic national style, the problem lay in trying to reconcile specifically Hungarian themes, rhythms and even instruments with European operatic forms.'

Dominique Fernandez

▲ THE HUNGARIAN STATE OPERA (Magyar Állami Operaház)

Score by Liszt ● *48*, ▲ *145* for the Hungarian State Opera.

Since the Hungarian State Opera House (Magyar Állami Operaház) opened on September 27, 1884 with a performance of *Bánk Bán* (1861) by Ferenc Erkel, it has been the home of both the Hungarian State Opera and the Hungarian Ballet Institute. A balanced program presents works by Erkel, Bartók and Kodály, as well as Mozart, Verdi and modern opera. Similarly the repertoire of the Ballet Institute includes classics such as Tchaikovsky's *The Nutcracker,* and contemporary ballet.

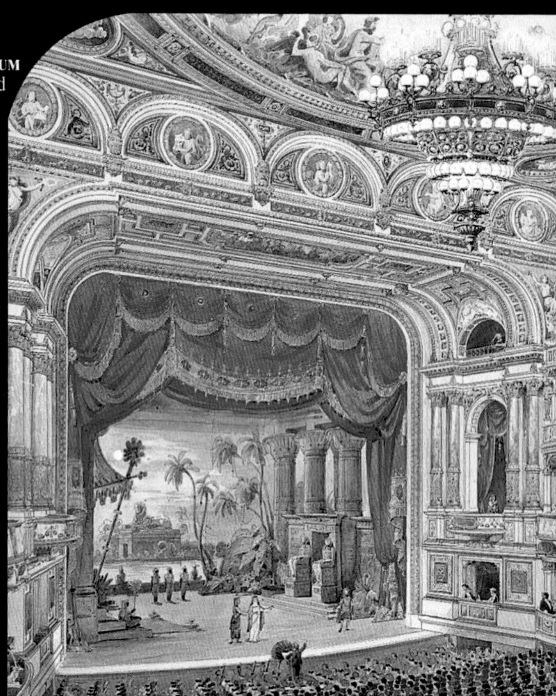

THE AUDITORIUM
The horseshoe-shaped auditorium, bedecked in gold and purple and crowned by a magnificent ceiling painted by Károly Lotz, can hold 1,285 people. Its excellent acoustics offer some consolation to members of the audience sitting in the third-floor gallery.

THE 'BÜFÉ'
In the interval you can enjoy coffee or champagne in the Büfé (bar), and at the same time meet opera lovers of all ages and from all walks of life. The decor has Bacchanalian imagery: the ceiling is decorated with three scenes by György Vastagh from the life of Dionysus, and there are eight paintings by Árpád Feszty on the walls.

THE ORCHESTRA
The Opera is proud to have one of the oldest orchestras in Hungary. Most of its members belong to the Philharmonic Society, founded in 1853 by Ferenc Erkel ● *49* and Ferenc Doppler. It is also a symphony orchestra in its own right and gives performances with well-known soloists.

MAGY. KIR. OPERAHÁZ.
Budapest, szombaton, 1884. szeptember 27-én.
A magyar királyi operaház első megnyitási előadása.
I.
BÁNK BÁN
II.
Nyitány
Hunyadi László czimü eredeti operából.

Two competitions and a festival
For several years the Budapest Opera House has regularly hosted two prestigious international (dance and operatic) competitions. In August it provides the setting for the city's summer opera festival, *Budafest*.

Operatic memories
A small first-floor museum, situated around the great marble stairway, traces the history of the Opera House through temporary exhibitions based on specific themes – posters, tickets, invitations, private and official letters, manuscripts, autographs, scores, costumes, etc.

Scene from Béla Bartók's *Duke Bluebeard's Castle* (1911) ● *51*.

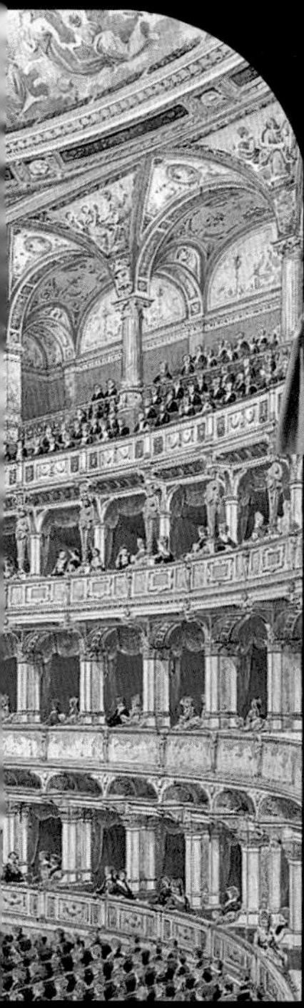

Famous directors and conductors
The Hungarian State Opera has had an impressive list of directors, including Ferenc Erkel, Gustav Mahler (right) and Arthur Nikisch. Its list of conductors is no less impressive – among them, Gustav Mahler, Arthur Nikisch, Egisto Tango, Sergio Failoni, Otto Klemperer and János Ferencsik. Each of these marked the golden age of the State Opera House with the stamp of his own individuality.

The ceiling of the auditorium.

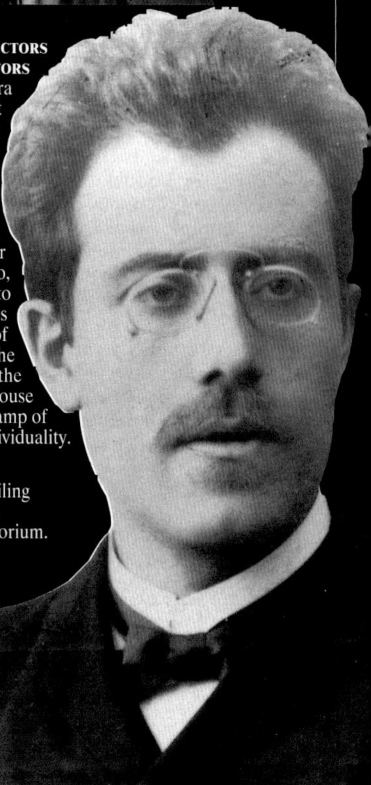

ARANY JÁNOS SZÍNHÁZ ● *84*
The theater's astonishing Secessionist façade is decorated with mosaics, geometric figures, globes and statues of monkeys.

Right, detail of the façade of the Photography Gallary (Mai Manó Haz)

Below, the Writers' Bookshop (Írók Boltja), at no. 45 Andrássy út.

FROM THE OPERA HOUSE TO THE ACADEMY OF MUSIC
Opposite the Hungarian State Opera House, at no. 29 Andrássy út, are the best tearooms in Terézváros. The CAFÉ MŰVÉSZ – which translates as 'Café of the Artists' – is an ideal place to enjoy a drink before an evening at the opera, or tea and cakes to relieve the monotony of a wet Sunday afternoon. There are a number of interesting buildings on this side of the avenue. At no. 25 the DRECHSLER HOUSE, designed by Ödön Lechner (1882), is named after the café that once occupied the ground floor. It is soon to become a luxury hotel. Behind the Drechsler House, at no. 35 Paulay Ede utca, is the János Arany Theater (Arany JÁNOS Színház), also known as the New Theater (Új Színház) János Arany (1817–82, ▲ *187)* was one of Hungary's greatest poets and a friend of Sándor Petőfi. Back on Andrássy út, at no. 39, is the DIVATCSARNOK department store, which closed in 2003; its Secessionist architecture and the first-floor frescos by Károly Lotz are a reminder that, when it was opened in 1911, this was a luxury store combined with a casino. People would ice-skate on the roof in winter.

NAGYMEZŐ UTCA This street joins Andrássy út at right angles just above the State Opera House. Budapesters refer to it as 'Broadway', but it is a pale reflection of its New York namesake. It is bordered by a few theaters – among them, the Microscope Theater (MIKROSZKÓP SZÍNPAD) and Thalia Színház – and a number of cabarets and nightclubs. It is also the home of the Fővárosi Operettszínház ● *44*, where Hungarians can indulge their passion for operetta and comic opera.

At no. 20 the PHOTOGRAPHY GALLERY MAI MANO HAZ, named after the imperial court official photographer who commissioned the building, is decorated with sculptures and glass panels. Above, detail from the façade of the building.

Back on Andrássy út, the glass-fronted WRITERS' BOOKSHOP (Írók Boltja) at no. 45 occupies the premises of the former Café Japan, at one

'The Liszt Academy is housed in a magnificent building [...]. The training I received there was difficult and at times harsh, but those who survived the experience emerged as real musicians.'

Sir Georg Solti, *Memoirs*

time a favorite meeting place for Budapest's literary set. Inside, everything is designed for the readers' comfort: armchairs, low tables and a huge tea urn. Public lectures are held here regularly. As you continue along this narrow pedestrianized street, where a number of student cafés have recently opened, you come to a quiet neighborhood that is pleasant to stroll round.

ACADEMY OF MUSIC (Zeneakadémia) ★ When you reach Liszt Ferenc tér, you cannot fail to be impressed by the strains of music drifting from the open windows of the ACADEMY OF MUSIC – which doubles as concert hall and conservatory ▲ *146* – and by the architecture of the building itself. The academy was built between 1904 and 1907 to plans by Flóris Korb and Kálmán Giergl, and was greatly influenced by the designs of Ödön Lechner ● *80.* Its eclectic style – a brilliant combination of neo-Baroque inspiration, neoclassical nostalgia and seductive Orientalism – is reflected in the luxurious entrance hall, decorated with frescos and ceramics from the Zsolnay manufactory ● *69*, ▲ *172*. On the outside is a huge bronze statue of Franz Liszt; above it are statues of Gounod and Bizet. Next to the academy (at the intersection of Nagymező utca and Király utca) there is an attractive pedestrianized square, dominated by the Baroque ST ANNE'S CHURCH (Szent Anna templom).

FROM OKTOGON TÉR TO HŐSÖK TERE Beyond Oktogon tér ▲ *166*, Andrássy út widens out into an elegant and sophisticated boulevard, with tree-lined side roads bordered with villas, mansions and flowers. Near the intersection, on the left as you walk up the avenue, was the secret-police headquarters during the Horthy era ▲ *174* and later under Rákosi's Stalinist regime. Converted in 2002, the HORRORS OF WAR MUSEUM recounts the horrors of Nazism and Communism. A little further on, you can glimpse something of Budapest's musical past by visiting the FRANZ LISZT MUSEUM (Liszt Ferenc Emlékmúzeum) – which is off to the right, at no. 35 Vörösmarty utca. The pianist and composer occupied the first floor of this building from 1879 until his death in 1886. As well as personal items belonging to Liszt (pianos, harmoniums, desks, portraits, etc.), the museum houses a small concert hall used by the students of the Academy of Music. Nearby, at no. 69, is the ACADEMY OF FINE ARTS (Képzőmüvészeti Főiskola), built in Italian neo-Renaissance style by Adolf Láng in 1877, and the STATE PUPPET THEATER (Állami Bábszínház). The theater presents puppet shows for audiences of all ages and is well worth a visit.

One of the city's most renowned coffee houses, the LUKACS KÁVÉHAZ (no. 70) – has been beautifully restored, and now shares the ground floor with a bank. Its first floor, decorated in the Baroque style, remains a favorite place for discreet meetings.

LISZT'S BÖSENDORFER PIANO

'I play with my whole body. Liszt was the first [pianist] to do this, and played with his arms, shoulders and back. He was the first to break with the tradition that limited movement to the fingers, which was the legacy of the harpsichord. Ultimately little is known about his manner of playing. Even my music teacher, who was himself a pupil of Liszt, said very little about it.'

Claudio Arrau

'Unlike Beethoven, who ignored the limitations of physiology and imposed his tyrannical will on the [pianist's] fingers, Liszt accepted them and used them for what they were...'

Camille Saint-Saëns

Metro sign. *Földalatti* literally means 'under the earth'.

▲ The Academy of Music (Zeneakadémia)

The Hungarian Academy of Music opened on November 14, 1875, at no. 4 Hal tér. Then in the fall of 1879 the academy and its president, Franz Liszt, moved to a new building, on what was then Sugár út (now Andrássy út), where Liszt lived and taught until his death in 1886. That building now houses the Franz Liszt Museum. The present academy building was opened on May 12, 1907; at the same time, the institution was renamed the Franz Liszt Academy of Music (Liszt Ferenc Zeneakadémia) in his honor.

Roth's fountain
With its gleaming bronze backdrop the mosaic fountain (right) by Miksa Róth is a reminder that the academy was built between 1903 and 1907 (during the reign of the Emperor Franz Joseph) and designed by Flóris Korb and Kálmán Giergl.

'The Fountain of Art'
The entrance hall has a delightfully eclectic decor. In 1901 Aladár Körösfői-Kriesch, who studied under Bertalan Székely and Károly Lotz, went to live in Gödöllő ▲ *240*, where, together with Sándor Nagy, he founded the 'Gödöllő School'. His wall painting *The Fountain of Art* (1907), on the first floor of the academy, reflects the influence of the English Pre-Raphaelites and is the product of a technique that sought to revive medieval artistic methods.

The main auditorium
This magnificent Secessionist masterpiece combines elegant lines and fineness of detail. Its acoustics make it the best concert hall in Hungary.

The finishing touch

Although remarkable in every respect, the decor of this temple to music has one particularly outstanding feature: the greenish-blue and yellow eosin glaze, tinged with gold, from the Zsolnay manufactory ● *69*, ▲ *172* at Pécs.

The Hubay Quartet
[Left to right: Szerémi, Popper (cello), Hubay (first violin), Kemény.] Between 1886 and 1936 Jenő Hubay taught the violin at the Academy of Music to some of Hungary's greatest musicians, among them József Szigeti, Stefi Geyer and Jelly Arányi. He was director of the academy from 1919 until his death. Hubay founded a famous quartet, and wrote operas, ballets, and symphonies inspired by Hungarian folk music. In the 1930s his school produced such world-class violinists as Zoltán Székely, Ede Zathurecky, Dénes Koromzay and Sándor Végh.

Miklós Perényi, the 'Hungarian Rostropovich' (below).

The teaching 'dynasty'

The music teaching was placed under the aegis of great masters: Ferenc Liszt ● *48* ▲ *145* (piano), Károly Huber and his son Jenő Hubay (violin), Hans Koessler (composition and organ) and David Popper (cello). They were assisted by István Thomán and Béla Bartók ● *50* (piano), Zoltán Kodály ● *50*, ▲ *148* (composition and musical notation), Leó Weiner (chamber music) and Ernő Dohnányi (piano), who at that time were less well known. Their pupils in turn became teachers at the academy.

KODÁLY CIRCUS (Kodály Körönd) A little further on, Kodály Circus is a masterpiece of architectural symmetry. Four large neo-Renaissance buildings, with beautifully structured balconies and windows, describe a circle around its edge. The rather ponderous statuary of the Circus does not detract from its elegance. The statues represent Miklós Zrínyi and György Szondy (heroes of the wars against the Turks), Vak Bottyán (one of the generals of Prince Rákóczi II ● *29, 47*) and Bálint Balassi (the great 16th-century lyric poet ● *38*). One of the houses (no. 89 Andrássy út) belonged to the composer Zoltán Kodály ● *50*, ▲ *218*. The circus is situated in a district of elegant private residences, embassies, political-party headquarters and government ministries.

DETAIL OF KODALY KÖRÖND

MANSIONS AND VILLAS It is worth taking a stroll along the smaller streets running parallel and at right angles, on either side of Andrássy út: Lendvay utca (Villa Groedel at no. 29), Délibáb utca, Bajza utca (Lederer Mansion and Sonnenberg Mansion at nos. 42 and 23) and especially the quiet and elegant Benczúr utca, which is one of the most sought-after residential streets in the capital. Throughout the district, time seems to stand still. At no. 98 Andrássy út the former Pallavicini Palace is a reminder of the dominance of the neo-Renaissance style in 19th-century Pest. In striking contrast is the beautiful Art Nouveau villa (1900) at no. 101 Andrássy út (on the corner of Bajza utca), known as the Hungarian Press Building.

FERENC HOPP MUSEUM OF EAST ASIAN ART (Hopp Ferenc Kelet-Ázsiai Művészeti Múzeum)
As you return to Andrássy út, don't miss this museum at no. 103. The fascinating collections bequeathed to the state by Ferenc Hopp in 1919 include Indonesian puppets, Indian

THE PALACE OF ARTS (Műcsarnok)
Erected in 1896, the Műcsarnok was designed by Fülöp Herzog and Albert Schickedanz ● *95* in the style of a Greek temple.
The pediment is adorned with a colored Byzantine-style fresco depicting Saint Stephen (Szent István) ● *38*, ▲ *203* flanked by Saints Gerard (Gellért) ▲ *215* and Margaret (Margit) ▲ *188*.

statues and Tibetan *tanka* (painted banners). The Chinese and Japanese collections are housed in the nearby Ráth György Múzeum, which occupies a splendid Art Nouveau villa at no. 12 Városligeti Fasor (formerly Gorky utca), one of the prettiest streets in the district.

HEROES' SQUARE (Hősök tere) ▲ *150* Andrássy út comes to an end at the impressive Hősök tere, with its famous MILLENARY MONUMENT ● *76* built in 1896 to commemorate the thousandth anniversary of the Magyar conquest of the Carpathian Basin (*honfoglalás*, the word used by the Hungarians is slightly ambiguous, meaning 'installation' or 'conquest'). In the center of the square – which to some extent symbolizes the triumph of Pest over Buda and of Hungarian history over the Habsburg influence – stands a column surmounted by a statue of the Archangel Gabriel. Around its base are equestrian statues of Árpád and the other six conquering Magyar chiefs ● *27*. In front of the column is the Heroes' Monument ▲ *150*, and behind it a colonnade surmounted by allegorical figures representing Work and Wealth (on the left), Knowledge and Glory (on the right), and War and Peace (in the center). The city's two largest museums – the MUSEUM OF FINE ARTS (Szépművészeti Múzeum) ★ ▲ *152* and the PALACE OF ARTS (Műcsarnok) – face each other across the square. The first, a fine neoclassical building, has a façade decorated with copies of the sculptures on the Temple of Zeus at Olympia (in the center is Apollo flanked by the Lapiths and Centaurs).

DOZSA GYÖRGY UT. During the Communist era, Dózsa György út – the broad avenue that runs along one side of the square – was the official venue for the May Day celebrations and military parades. The huge statue of Stalin that stood on the avenue was pulled down during the 1956 uprising. The Yugoslav Embassy stands on the corner of Andrássy út and Dózsa György út, and ironically it was in this beautiful Art Nouveau villa that Imre Nagy and György Lukács sought refuge during the last days of the 1956 uprising, before being handed over to Soviet troops and secretly deported to Romania.

THE MUSEUM OF FINE ARTS ▲ *152*
The Museum of Fine Arts was founded in 1896 to commemorate the thousandth anniversary of the foundation of the Hungarian state. Designed by Albert Schickedanz and Fülöp Herzog, it was completed in 1906.

Villa Egger, 24 Városligeti fasor (Emil Vidor, 1902).

FOURTEEN HEROES
Statues of fourteen Hungarian rulers and princes form a curved double colonnade in Heroes' Square: Stephen I, László I, Kálmán the Possessor of Books, András II, Béla IV, Charles Robert, Louis the Great, regent János Hunyadi, Matthias Corvinus ● *32*, princes István Bocskay, Gábor Bethlen, Imre Thököly and Ferenc Rákóczi II, and regent Lajos Kossuth.

Budapest's largest square was designed by Albert Schickedanz ● 95 and György Zala.

Hősök tere is one of the largest and certainly the most symbolic squares in Budapest. It lies at the end of Andrássy út and contains the nation's two most important commemorative monuments: the Millenary Monument and the Heroes' Monument (originally the Tomb of the Unknown Soldier). Since 1896 successive governments have held parades and announced changes here; and it has also been a focus for protest marches, popular demonstrations (May Day) and gatherings, and official ceremonies. But above all, Heroes' Square is a place that reflects the nation's history.

SYMBOL OF A THOUSAND-YEAR-OLD NATION

In the center of the square stands the Millenary Monument, erected in 1896 to commemorate the thousandth anniversary of the foundation of the Hungarian state. Around its base are equestrian statues of Árpád and the other six conquering Magyar chiefs ● 27. The statues of the seven chiefs surround a monumental column surmounted by the winged figure of the Archangel Gabriel, clutching an Apostolic cross in one hand and, with the other, holding the Hungarian crown above the chiefs. According to tradition, the chiefs chose Árpád as their leader, and his descendants became the first kings of Hungary. In the 1920s the Tomb of the Unknown Soldier was installed at the foot of the statue of Árpád.

SYMBOLS OF A NATION'S HISTORY

Today the square is very different from the one designed by Albert Schickedanz. The fountains and flowers have been replaced by paving decorated with geometric motifs, and the People's Democratic Government replaced the last five statues of the colonnade (five Hungarian kings) with the statues that stand there today.

The changing face of leadership

After World War Two the statues of the Habsburgs were replaced by those of the heroes of Hungarian independence: Rákóczi, Thököly and Kossuth. In the 1950s Habsburg statues were melted down so that monuments could be erected to Stalin and Mátyás Rákosi (although not in Heroes' Square). In October 1956 the crowd overturned the huge statue of Stalin ● *36*.

May Day 1919
The Habsburg statues on the colonnade of the Millenary Monument were removed during Béla Kun's short-lived Council Republic. For May Day of 1919 the colonnade, the statues of the Magyar chiefs and the column were draped in red. The sole decoration on the two great expanses of red was the famous Marxist slogan urging the working classes of Europe to unite.

Eucharistic Congress
The great Roman Catholic demonstrations organized during the interwar years reflected the close association between Catholic and Nationalist ideals.

During the International Eucharistic Congress held in 1938, the colonnade of the Millenary Monument served as a pedestal for the high altar.

National funeral
On June 16, 1989 a national funeral service was held on the square in memory of Imre Nagy and other victims of 1956. On August 20, 1991 some 200,000 people heard Pope John Paul II say mass here.

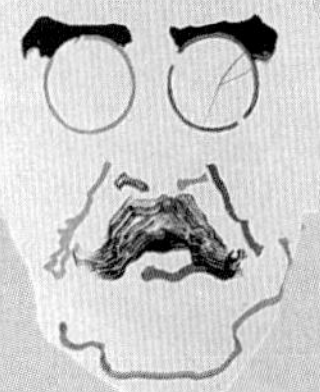

The millennial celebrations
Although work began on the square in 1894, it was not opened until 1929. The celebrations, in 1896, to mark the thousandth anniversary of the foundation of the Hungarian state were held in City Park.

The collections of the Museum of Fine Arts are derived from the Hungarian National Museum's collection of historical portraits, which became the National Art Gallery and was housed in the Academy of Sciences. Its nucleus was formed by Count Miklós Esterházy's private gallery, which he sold to the state in 1870. The National Gallery was further enriched by donations and purchases, resulting in the establishment of the Old Masters Gallery and the Prints and Drawings Room that today form the core of the Museum of Fine Arts. The Ancient Greek and Roman collection, extended since 1935, includes works from the Greek, Etruscan, Roman and Carthaginian civilizations.

The museum's collection of prints and drawings includes some 10,000 drawings and 100,000 prints. Many of the Renaissance and Baroque works are from the Esterházy collection. The works bequeathed by the artist István Delhaes are mainly 18th-century German and Austrian prints and drawings. The watercolors and drawings by French artists (Delacroix, Manet, Degas) were bought in Paris by the ministerial adviser Pál Majovszky, who donated them to the museum in 1934.

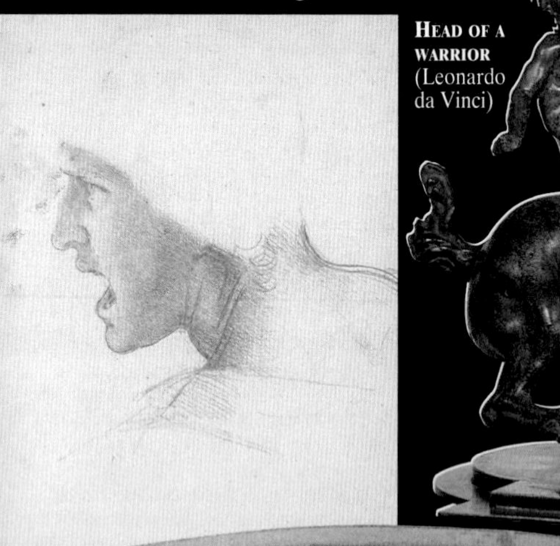

Head of a warrior (Leonardo da Vinci)

Niobid
(Greek and Roman collection)The massacre of the Niobids by Apollo and Artemis, and the grief of their mother Niobe, the legendary queen of Phrygia, provided the inspiration for a celebrated sculptural group.

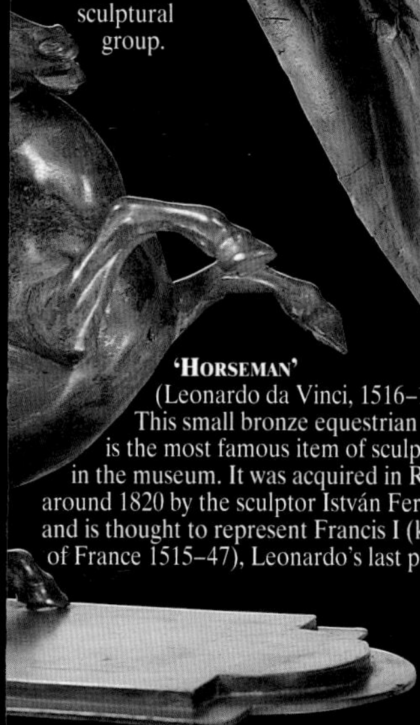

'Horseman'
(Leonardo da Vinci, 1516–19) This small bronze equestrian statue is the most famous item of sculpture in the museum. It was acquired in Rome around 1820 by the sculptor István Ferenczy and is thought to represent Francis I (king of France 1515–47), Leonardo's last patron.

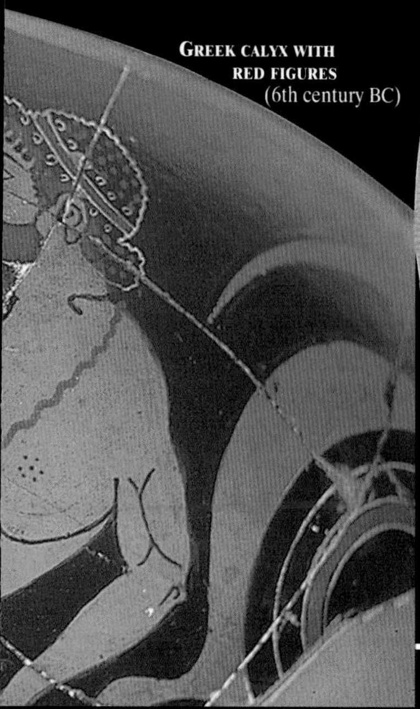

Greek calyx with red figures
(6th century BC)

Portrait of a man
(Egypt, New Kingdom, 19th Dynasty, c. 1200 BC)In 1996 the museum opened the lower-ground-floor rooms devoted to its Egyptian collection. The collection, which includes statues, funerary steles, decorated sarcophagi, statuettes of servants, amulets, scarabs, jewelry and fragments of papyri, reflects many aspects of the Ancient Egyptian civilization.

Italian and German collections

The Danube School flourished during the first thirty years of the German Renaissance (1500–30). Notable artists included Albrecht Altdorfer and Lucas Cranach the Elder, one of the school's founders.

The museum has an impressive Italian collection, which represents all the major schools from the 13th–18th centuries. The German Renaissance (Albrecht Dürer, Hans Baldung Grien) and the 'Danube School' are also represented.

THE 'ESTERHÁZY MADONNA'
(Raphaël, 1508)
Although unfinished, this painting, right, reflects the beauty and harmony achieved at the height of the Italian Renaissance. This was one of the 637 paintings in the Esterházy collection.

PORTRAIT OF A MAN
(Sebastiano del Piombo)
This portrait, below, was painted in Rome c. 1515. The enigmatic expression and the idyllic landscape in the background are reminiscent of the artist's apprenticeship in Vienna, while the sitter's stately bearing attests to the influence of Raphaël.

'ADAM' AND 'EVE'
(Hans Baldung Grien, 1484–1545)

'PORTRAIT OF A MAN'
(Albrecht Dürer, 1471–1528) (right)

'THE BETROTHAL OF SAINT CATHERINE'
(Lucas Cranach the Elder, 1516–18)
Saints Catherine, Margaret, Barbara and Dorothy are dressed as ladies at the court of the Elector Frederick the Wise of Saxony, where Cranach was employed as court painter. This painting was one of a collection sent in 1770 from the imperial collection in Vienna to decorate the royal apartments in Bratislava. From there, it was transferred to the Royal Palace in Buda, where it was 'nationalized' in 1848.

Spanish and Dutch collections

Most of the justifiably renowned Spanish collection was purchased from Lord Edmund Bourke in London between 1818 and 1821 by Pál Esterházy, on behalf of his father Count Miklós Esterházy The museum's Old Masters Gallery also has a number of 17th-century Dutch landscapes and genre paintings that are acknowledged masterpieces.

'MARY MAGDELENE IN PENITENCE'

(El Greco, 1580) The permanent collection has seven paintings by El Greco. Here the exaggerated proportions and almost unreal colors foreshadow the Mannerism that characterized the mature works of this 'most Spanish' of artists.

'Esther and Mordecai'
(Aert de Gelder, 1685)

'Peasants' Repast'
(below left)
(Diego Velázquez, c. 1617–18)
In 1908, two years after the museum was opened, the gallery acquired this youthful work by Velázquez. The simplicity of the gestures, the richly painted contrasts of light and shade, the still life on the table, and the eloquent expressions of the three people sitting round it make this a masterpiece of Spanish genre painting.

'Saint Joseph's Dream'
(above)
(Rembrandt van Rijn)

'Woman Reading a Letter'
(Pieter de Hooch, 1664)
The artist has depicted the familiar atmosphere of this Dutch middle-class interior with moving realism.

Collections of 19th-century and 20th-century art

The oldest paintings in the museum's modern collections are those by the Austrian artists of the Biedermeier period (1820–40). From 1910, the collections were complemented by a number of French Impressionist paintings and other important works.

'MARY MAGDELENE'
(Pierre Puvis de Chavannes, 1897)

'LADY WITH A FAN'
(Édouard Manet, 1871)
The lady in question is Jeanne Duval, mistress of the poet Charles Baudelaire. The painting was acquired by one of the museum's directors, Elek Petrovics, who made a number of equally discerning acquisitions.

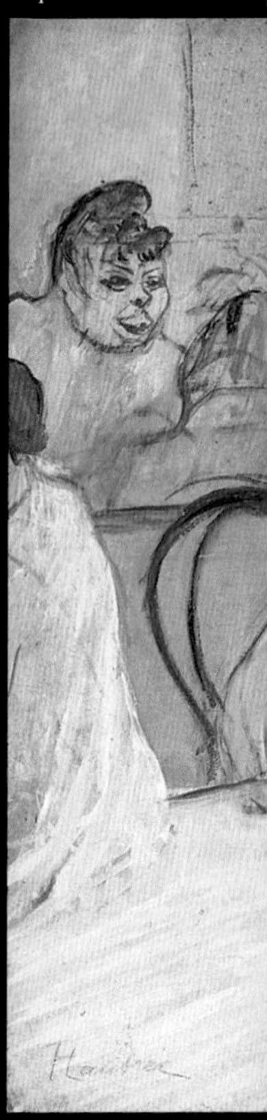

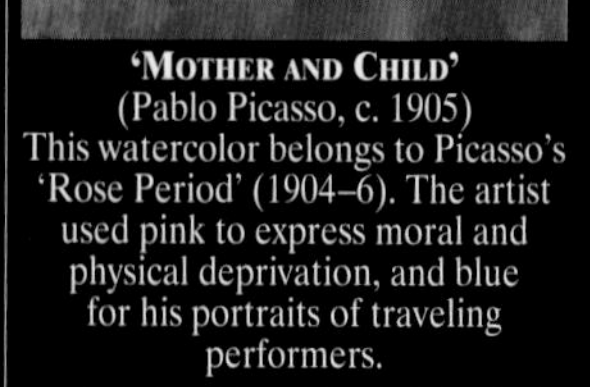

'MOTHER AND CHILD'
(Pablo Picasso, c. 1905)
This watercolor belongs to Picasso's 'Rose Period' (1904–6). The artist used pink to express moral and physical deprivation, and blue for his portraits of traveling performers.

'VERONICA'
(Oskar Kokoschka, 1911)
The artist based this expressionist work on medieval iconography showing the saint holding a veil on which the image of Christ's face had miraculously appeared.

French painters from the Romantic to the Post-Impressionist period are well represented in the museum's collection of modern art – among them, Delacroix, Corot, Courbet, Daubigny, Troyon, Manet, Pissarro, Puvis de Chavannes, Cézanne, Monet, Gauguin and Toulouse-Lautrec. Sculptors include Carpeaux, Despiau, Maillol and Rodin.

'Black Pigs'
(Paul Gauguin, 1891)
This was one of Gauguin's earliest Tahitian paintings. The museum also has one of his Impressionist works, *Jardin sous la Neige* (1879).

'Sideboard'
(Paul Cézanne)

'Blue Village'
(Marc Chagall, 1968)

'Ces dames'
(Henri de Toulouse-Lautrec, 1894)
This painting was acquired in 1913, at the same time as Gauguin's *Black Pigs*, at an exhibition held at the Ernst Museum in Budapest.

WINE AND WATER... City Park is particularly famous for two major attractions: Gundel's restaurant and the magnificent Széchenyi Baths ● *62*.

CITY PARK

Like the park on Margaret Island ▲ *187, 188*, City Park (Városliget ■ *22*) is one of the city's most popular green spaces. Designed in the late 19th century as a 'filter' for the dust from the Central Plain, this haven of peace and quiet is particularly beautiful in the fall. It is an ideal place for a Sunday walk and a great favorite with children. Conveniently situated on the edge of the city, it offers a number of recreational facilities, including a lake that serves as a boating lake in summer and an ice rink in winter. On the shores of the lake, a Rococo building houses a bar-restaurant that provides changing facilities for skaters.

ÁLLATKERTI KÖRÚT Situated behind the Museum of Fine Arts ▲ *149, 152*, at no. 3 Állatkerti körút, GUNDEL is one of the city's best restaurants. Nearby is the entrance to BUDAPEST ZOO (Állatkert); and a little further on, the MUNICIPAL CIRCUS (Fővárosi Nagycirkusz) and FUN FAIR (Vidám Park). Because of their relative age (the roller coasters are made of wood), they are reminiscent of the delightfully old-fashioned amusement parks of New York's Coney Island.

ÁLLATKERTI KÖRUT This boulevard, built in 1865 and renovated in 1907, has some delightful examples of Art Nouveau architecture – such as the Elephant House of Budapest Zoo, which is decorated with ceramic elephant heads. Above: the entrance of the Elephant House.

SZÉCHENYI BATHS (Széchenyi Gyógyfürdő) ★ Still on the Állatkerti körút, the majestic Széchenyi Baths ● *62* are an ideal place to relax for an hour or two after a long walk along Andrássy út. They are easily recognized by their huge neo-Baroque dome, flanked by equestrian statues. If you take the 'yellow metro' ▲ *117*, you can get off at the

Széchenyi fürdő subway station (in City Park), right in front of the baths. The south wing, which houses the 'medicinal baths', was built in the early 20th century and has a richly decorated interior of Art Nouveau mosaics. The north wing was built in 1927, in a more modern neo-Baroque style. This huge baths complex has swimming pools, baths and saunas. A small flight of steps leads from the indoor to the outdoor pools.

Vajdahunyad Castle (Vajdahunyad Vára) The castle stands on a little island almost at the center of City Park. It was one of the buildings designed by Ignác Alpár for the thousandth anniversary of the foundation of the Hungarian state ● *30*, ▲ *150* in 1896. In the main courtyard, the Romanesque Chapel of Ják is a copy of the 13th-century church at Ják (near Szombathely) in western Hungary, while the Gothic tower on the right was inspired by the castle at Segesvár (now Sighisoara) in Transylvania. Also on the right is the Baroque façade of the Museum of Agriculture (Mezőgazdasági Múzeum), reminiscent of the façade of the castle of the Esterházy family near Sopron. The museum's exhibits include some splendid wine presses. Opposite the entrance is the famous statue of 'Anonymus' by Miklós Ligeti (1903). An important figure in Hungarian history, the 'unknown chronicler' of the Magyars ● *38* may have been a royal clerk at the court of Béla III in the 12th century – hence the statue's inscription, which reads *Gloriosissimi Belae Regis Notarius* ('Clerk of most glorious King Béla').

Disneyland decor

The idea underlying the castle's design was to bring together in a single building the various styles employed throughout Hungary's architectural history. This gives it an extraordinarily eclectic (Gothic, Baroque, Romantic), even kitsch, appearance.
The castle was named after the one built by the Hunyadi family (the family of Matthias Corvinus ● *32*) at Vajdahunyad (now Hunedoara), in Transylvania, in the 13th century. The façade overlooking the lake is a copy of the 'real' castle's.

The outdoor pool of the Széchenyi Baths

The baths' famous outdoor pool (100° F) has a backdrop of beautiful yellow walls. In winter families and friends enjoy a dip under the watchful gaze of the snow-covered statues, while clouds of steam rise from the surface of the water. Beyond the entrance is a bar with a view of the pools.

1. PETŐFI CSARNOK
2. VILLA BALÁZS SIPEKYS
3. TRANSPORT MUSEUM
4. INSTITUTE OF GEOLOGY
5. PEOPLE'S STADIUM
6. INSTITUTE FOR THE BLIND
7. VILLA GYÖRGY ZALA
8. NO. 23 JÓZSEF-SZABÓ UTCA
9. NO. 46, THÖKÖLY ÚT

AROUND CITY PARK

On the northeast side of City Park you come to the large modern building named PETŐFI CSARNOK (Petőfi Hall), where concerts, plays and dance performances are held.

THE INSTITUTE OF GEOLOGY (Magyar Földtani Intézet) ★ As you leave the park and turn down Stefánia út, you come to the magnificent Institute of Geology at no. 14. Like the other buildings designed by Ödön Lechner ● *80*, the façade of this masterpiece of Hungarian Secessionist architecture (1897–9) combines Oriental inspiration with the Hungarian ceramic tradition. The symbol of the Institute is the globe supported by three statues that crown its pyramidal roof (opposite page, bottom right). A statue of János Böckh (1840–1909), one of the institute's directors, stands on the corner of Stefánia út and Szabó Jószef utca.

VILLA BALAZS SIPEKYS ★ This splendid Art Nouveau villa, also designed by Ödön Lechner (1905), lies slightly to the north of the Institute of Geology, at no. 47 Hermina út. Today it houses the Institute for the Blind. The beautiful pink façade has a particularly striking domed verandah.

THE PEOPLE'S STADIUM (Népstadion) ★ Those interested in the 1950s can go to the People's Stadium, along Dózsa György út. The stadium was built between 1948 and 1953, with a capacity of 100,000. It evokes the golden age of Hungarian football, when the national team (led by the famous no. 10, Ferenc Puskás) twice reached the final of the World Cup. Through Honvéd (the leading army team, based in the working-class district of Kispest ▲ *175*) and Ferencváros (Budapest's other great working-class club ▲ *174*), football served as the 'sports laboratory' of the Communist regime. The 1956 uprising put an end to this golden era: the Honvéd team found itself on the other side of the Iron Curtain when it came to European Cup matches, and many of Hungary's best players left the country. Rejuvenation work has now begun on the area around the stadium, most notably with the Sportena center, which houses a variety of events. However, Kerepesi út, which links the stadium, the Eastern Railway Station and the cemetery, remains abandoned.

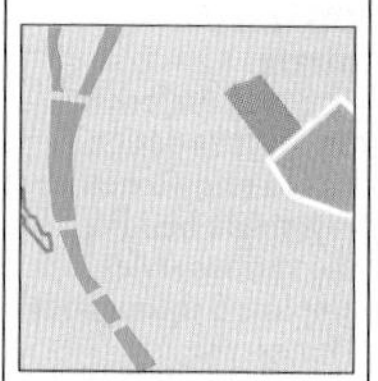

THE PEOPLE'S STADIUM
In the 1950's the Communist regime built Hungary's largest sporting facility. In the bid to 'bring sport to the people', the army formed its own football team: Honvéd.

'In the 1950s, seventy thousand spectators would crowd into the rows of seats to watch Hungary play. It is a long time since the stands echoed to the exploits of Hungarian football.'

Benoît Hopquin, 1998

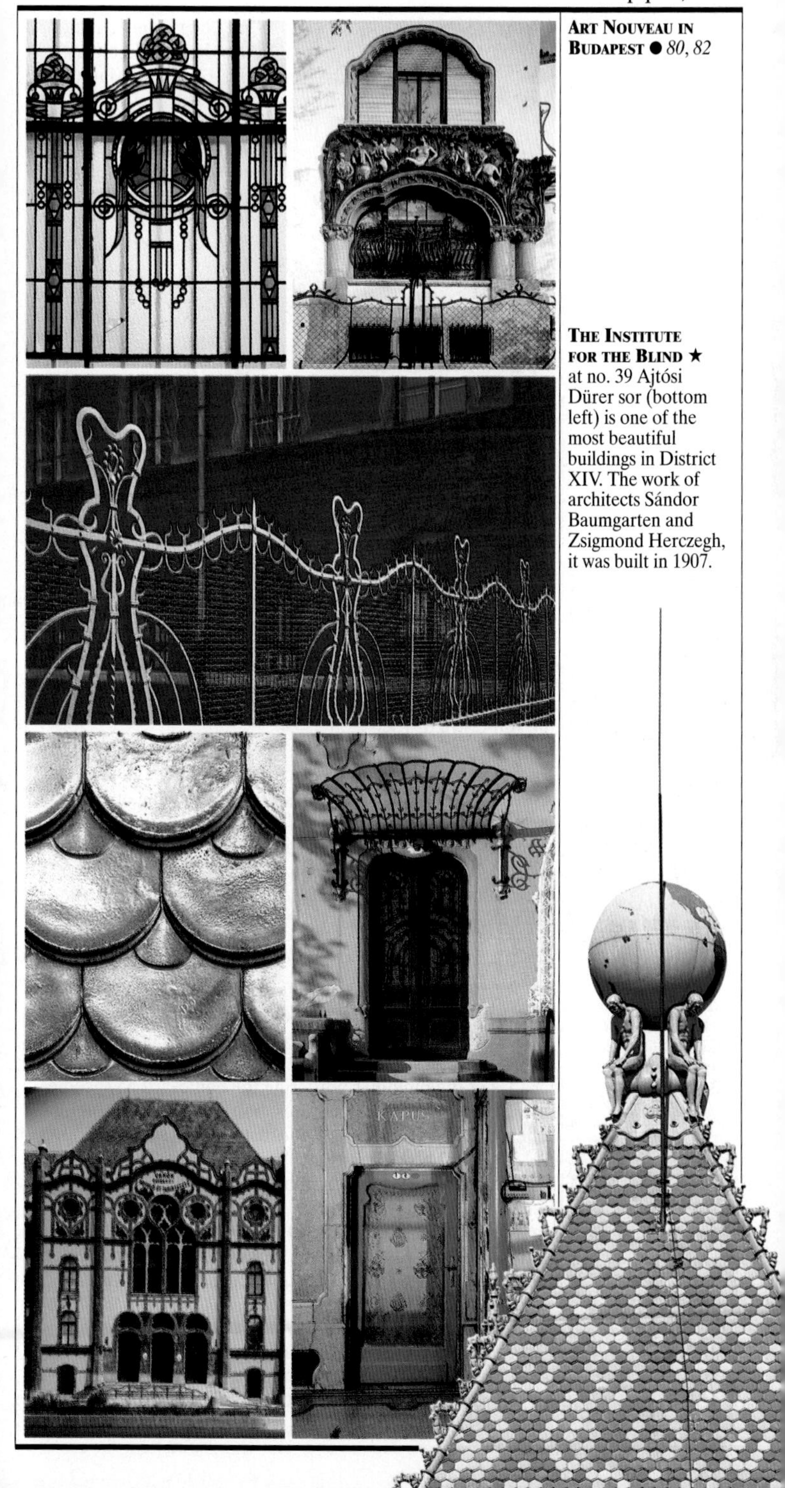

Art Nouveau in Budapest ● *80, 82*

The Institute for the Blind ★ at no. 39 Ajtósi Dürer sor (bottom left) is one of the most beautiful buildings in District XIV. The work of architects Sándor Baumgarten and Zsigmond Herczegh, it was built in 1907.

1. MARGARET ISLAND
2. HOUSE OF LIGHT
3. VÍG THEATER
4. WESTERN RAILWAY STATION
5. STROZZI PALACE
6. THE GREAT SYNAGOGUE
7. ORTHODOX SYNAGOGUE
8. ROYAL HOTEL
9. MADÁCH THEATER
10. NEW YORK PALACE

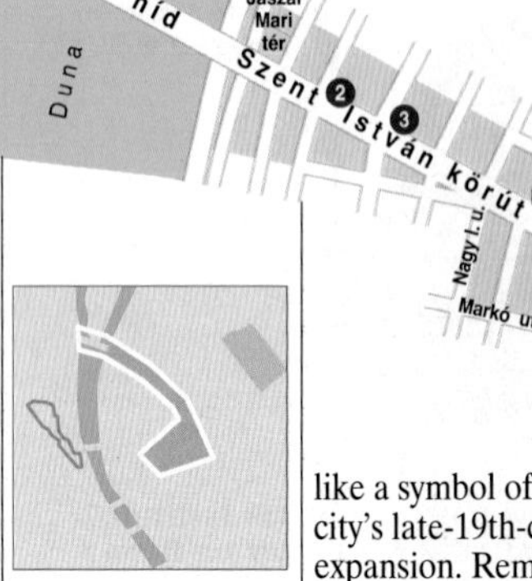

The Nagykörút (Great Boulevard) describes a huge semicircle between Margaret Bridge (Margit híd) ▲ *187* and Petőfi Bridge (Petőfi híd) ▲ *174*. It lies to the north of the Kiskörút (Little Boulevard) ▲ *123* and runs parallel to it for almost 2½ miles, like a symbol of the city's late-19th-century expansion. Reminiscent of the Ring in Vienna and the Grand Boulevards of Paris, the Nagykörút was opened in 1896 to commemorate the thousandth anniversary of the foundation of the Hungarian state ▲ *150*. It was a major project that involved the demolition of a great many buildings and the rehabilitation of the run-down districts in the vicinity of Margaret Bridge. The urban planning project gave an overall sense of structure and unity to this part of the city, linking districts that are socially very distinct. The Great Boulevard has five different names: (from north to south) Szent István körút, Teréz körút, Erzsébet körút, József körút and Ferenc körút. Much of the city's night life (theaters ● *42*, cinemas ▲ *168*, cafés ● *56*) is concentrated here .

SZENT ISTVAN KÖRUT Some of the city's best *antikvárium* ▲ *122* are to be found on Szent István körút (the one at no. 3 is famous for its prints and cards). Across the boulevard, on the right, are the antique shops of the Falk Miksa utca.

SZENT ISTVAN KÖRUT

MARGARET BRIDGE (Margit híd) Built by the French architect Ernest Gouin (1872–6), Margit híd marks the beginning of Szent István körút. Below JÁSZAI MARI TÉR the façades of the buildings bordering the boulevard have some interesting architectural features, both eclectic (atlantes and reliefs) and Art Nouveau (the former HOUSE OF LIGHT, at nos. 10–12). The VÍGSZÍNHÁZ (Víg Theater or Comedy Theater) ● *42*, at no. 14, built by the Viennese company Fellner & Helmer and opened in 1896, was for a long time the 'temple' of operetta ● *44* and comedy. Since its renovation in 1996 it has been offering a more international program, with Viennese operettas being largely replaced by (predominantly American) musicals.

NYUGATI TÉR The WESTERN RAILWAY STATION (Nyugati Pályaudvar) ★ stands on Nyugati tér. The square is also bordered by the SKÁLA METRO department stores, which introduced the consumer society to Budapest in the 1970s and 1980s. Today this is a fairly ordinary shopping district.

The Western Railway Station (Nyugati Pályaudvar) was built on the site of Pest's earliest railway station, from where the first train left for Vác on July 15, 1846. It stands on Nyugati tér and, in spite of its name, links the capital to north and east Hungary. It is, above all, renowned for its steel, brick and glass architecture. Although it has been extensively renovated, the splendid iron framework of the central concourse has been retained.

Built by Eiffel
This magnificent station was built in 1874–7 under the direction of Auguste de Serres on behalf of Gustave Eiffel's company.

The age of the railway

Between 1890 and 1914, under the Austro-Hungarian Empire, Hungary experienced a transport revolution: some 6,850 miles of railroad track (almost half the national network) were laid. The development of the railway network and shipping on the Danube were the result of the policies of Gábor Baross, minister for public works and communications (1886–9), whose name can be seen on streets and squares throughout Hungary.

'Viribus unitis'
This inscription, engraved on a marble lintel in the main concourse, marks the entrance to the former royal waiting room (now bricked up).

Fast food, high style
In the 1990s a fast-food restaurant was opened in the former railway buffet, to the right of the main entrance. It has retained the original decor – the stuccowork, frescos, old lamp fittings and huge bay windows have all been left intact.

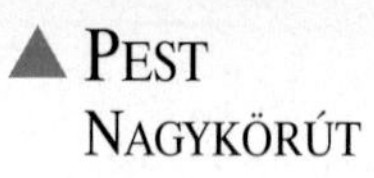

'PESTI MÜSOR' AND 'PESTI EST'
These two publications, which come out every Wednesday, provide information about Budapest's artistic and cultural events. Cinema and concert programs appear under the headings *Mozi* and *Zene* respectively.

TERÉZ KÖRUT

Beyond the railway station, Teréz körút (the section of Nagykörút named after Maria Theresa) takes you past the JÁTÉKSZÍN THEATER, at no. 48, and a fine neo-Renaissance mansion (Alajos Hauszmann, 1884), modeled on the Palazzo Strozzi in Florence, at no. 67. The building at no. 33 has a magnificent interior courtyard.

OKTOGON TÉR Oktogon tér, with its fast-food restaurants, banks, newspaper kiosks and florists' stands, lies at the intersection of Nagykörút and Andrássy út ▲ *145*. Below the square, the boulevard becomes Erzsébet körút.

ERZSÉBET KÖRUT AND THE ZSIDO NEGYED

This section of the boulevard (Erzsébet körút) is named after Queen Elizabeth ● *30*, ▲ *182*, *240*, the wife of Emperor Franz Joseph. It passes through Erzsébetváros ('Elizabeth town'), one of the city's most densely populated districts. It is also one of the busiest, with its cinemas ▲ *168*, cafés and small shops, both in the courtyards and on the upper floors of the buildings. To the south of the boulevard is the old Jewish quarter (Zsidó negyed) whose beauty and melancholy make it one of the capital's most attractive districts.

THE GREAT SYNAGOGUE (zsinagóga) ★ Europe's largest synagogue ● *78*, at nos. 2–8 Dohány utca, can hold up to 3,000 people. After a long period of work, it has now been completely restored. The three-story edifice, designed by the Viennese architect Ludwig Förster, was built between 1854 and 1859. It is characterized by a mixture of Byzantine and Moorish architectural elements, including two spectacular onion-shaped domes. Its huge capacity was justified by the size of the Jewish community, which before World War Two represented 25 percent of the city's population. Beyond the synagogue stands the HEROES' TEMPLE (Hősök temploma), designed by Ferenc Faragó and László

INTERIOR OF THE GREAT SYNAGOGUE (HOLY ARK)
The old Jewish quarter evokes a world that has almost disappeared: 70 percent of the city's Jewish community perished in the 1940s, and only twenty of the 110 synagogues that existed before World War Two have survived. Today Hungary's Jewish community (almost 300,000) is still the largest in Central Europe.

Vágó (1929–31), a memorial to Hungary's Jewish soldiers killed in World War One. Outside, a commemorative plaque indicates that Theodor Herzl (1860–1904), the founder of modern Zionism and author of *The Jewish State* (1896), was born in a house adjoining the synagogue. In the outer courtyard is a large HOLOCAUST MEMORIAL (Imre Varga, 1991), bearing the names of thousands of holocaust victims.

KIRÁLY UTCA The streets adjacent to the Great Synagogue (Király utca, Dob utca and Wesselényi utca) form the heart of the old Jewish quarter and conceal some of Budapest's most enchanting secrets: terraced courtyards planted with acacias, balconies with decorative ironwork, marvelous archways, and some truly delightful public squares. There are splendid courtyards at nos. 20, 25, 26, 27 and 28 Király utca; and no. 20 Dohány utca has an extremely elaborate courtyard and stairwell. The district also has some of the city's most intriguing passageways. For example, the GOZSDU COURTYARD – which runs between no. 16 Király utca and no. 11 Dob utca – consists of a series of interconnected courtyards and internal galleries. At no. 29 Kazinczy utca are the ORTHODOX SYNAGOGUE and the strictly kosher HANNAH restaurant (entrance at no. 35 Dob utca). Another synagogue (1872), with Moorish-style architecture, stands at no. 11 Rumbach Sebestyén utca. On the corner of Dob utca and Rumbach Sebestyén utca is a striking Secessionist mansion, designed by László and József Vágó, with colored-ceramic wall panels. KLAUZÁL TÉR, a haven of quiet in the busy city center, is a good place to pause for a rest and a snack in the family-owned canteen Kádár étkezde, or in one of the old kosher patisseries (for example, the one at no. 22 Dob utca).

ERZSÉBET KÖRUT

Erzsébet körút is bordered by many of the city's theaters and cinemas. The MADÁCH SZÍNHÁZ, at nos. 31–3, is a theater with a reputation for presenting successful musicals and reviews ● *42*.

NEW YORK PALACE A little further on (on the left, at nos. 9–11) stands the New York Palace ● *77*, built as the head-office of an American insurance company by architect Alajos Hauszmann between 1891 and 1895, in eclectic style with a neo-Renaissance façade. On the ground floor was the legendary CAFÉ NEW YORK ● *57*, a popular meeting place among the early-20th-century left-wing intelligentsia who produced the review *Nyugat* ('The West') ● *57, 97* – not only did it offer a warm refuge from cold rented rooms that they could scarcely afford but paper and ink were provided free of charge. The journalists of the literary review *2000* also held their editorial meetings here. The magnificent interior, with its twisted Rococo columns, velvet hangings and Art Deco chandeliers, occupied two floors. After many years of renovation works the New York Café reopened its doors in 2005. It now also shares the premises with a luxury hotel.

ÁRKÁD BAZÁR
(Dohány utca 22–24)
Designed by László and József Vágó, this beautiful building was built in 1908–9 in a mixture of the Secessionist and Modern styles. The nuts and bolts that, at first glance, appear to be holding together the white ceramic tiles of the east façades are in fact decorative bosses.

THE NATIONAL JEWISH MUSEUM (Országos Zsidó Múzeum)
The museum is on Wesselényi utca, just behind the Great Synagogue. Exhibits include items from Jewish religious history and photographs of the 1944 ghetto ● *30*. It has a section dedicated to the victims of the Holocaust.

▲ Budapest, capital of the Hungarian cinema

Peter Lorre in *Remorse*, by Josef von Sternberg.

Paradoxically, Hungarian cinema gained recognition through the Hungarian exiles who made a name for themselves in Hollywood, such as directors Alexander Korda and Michael Curtiz, actors Peter Lorre and Béla Lugosi. However, although among the most talented in Europe, Hungarian cinema was not fully appreciated until the 1960s. Having enjoyed its golden age in the 1960s and 1970s, Hungary – like so many other countries in Eastern Europe – is now finding it difficult to adjust to the antidotes to austerity imposed since 1989 which has meant few films produced and few international successes. However, the close relationship between Budapest and its cinemas has survived the changes. In addition, these splendid buildings continue to serve as places for a sociable or solitary drink or for a quiet read.

Örökmozgó Filmmúzeum
Many of Budapest's cinemas have a bookstore or café, or both. The Örökmozgó, linked to the Hungarian Film Institute, is a favorite with the city's film buffs. It presents carefully selected top-quality films and organizes numerous foreign-film festivals. In the evening you can go there to buy a magazine, or to enjoy a drink or read the daily papers in its studious yet relaxed atmosphere.

Corvin Cinema
When it was opened in 1923, with a seating capacity of 1,200 the Corvin ▲ *174* was the city's largest cinema. Today it has been completely renovated and is a multi-screen complex. As well as its six cinemas, it has a very pleasant café and a gallery; and you can buy videos there. The Corvin was the first of a new generation of cinemas in Budapest.

Left: publicity for Robert Capa's *Monsieur Verdoux* (1947) – 'Charlie Chaplin's latest film'.

Below: a scene from Miklós Jancsó's *The Round-Up* (1965).

Left: a scene from István Szabó's *Colonel Redl* (1985). Right: Béla Lugosi in *Dracula* (1931).

A masterpiece of Hungarian cinema

The Béla Balázs studio was founded in 1958 to provide a means of expression for a new generation of Hungarian film directors: Judit Elek, István Gaal, Pál Gábor and István Szabó. Szabó's *Mephisto* (1980) was internationally acclaimed and received an Oscar for the best foreign film.

An oppressive destiny

Miklós Jancsó's *The Round-Up* (1965) portrays rebels crushed by the oppressive machinery of power. Károly Makk's *Love* (1971) tells the poignant story of a woman and her dying mother-in-law, who are gradually destroyed as they wait for the man they love to be released from prison. Its pessimistic yet lyrical treatment of 'destiny' is typical of Hungarian cinema.

Below: Márta Mészáros *Intimate Journal* (1982), also known as *Diary for my Children.*

The post-Communist era

Sweet Emma, Dear Böbe (István Szabó, 1992)
Bolshe Vita (Ibolya Fekete, 1998)

These two films set out to express the problems of the post-Communist era. Szabó's chosen theme was the awkward metamorphosis of teachers of Russian, who 'recycled' themselves as teachers of English in an attempt to adapt to the new situation. His intimate chronicle of everyday life provides a disillusioned and deeply moving account of life in Budapest. Fekete's *Bolshe Vita* (above) adopts a more cheerful but nonetheless realistic approach to the difficult integration of Russian immigrants marooned in the city, ostensibly waiting for visas to the West.

Hungarian cinema today

More recently, numerous productions have followed the example of *Sun-Shine* (1998, István Szabó), *Hukkle* (2003, Pálfi Gyorgy), *Kontroll* (2004, Antal Nimród) or *Sorstalanság* (*Fateless* 2004, Lajos Koltai), an adaptation of the work by the same name by Nobel prize-winner, Imre Kertesz.

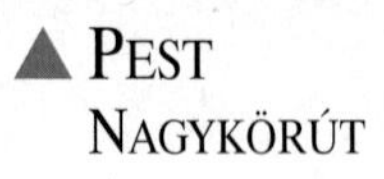

JÓZSEF KÖRÚT AND JÓZSEFVÁROS

BLAHA LUJZA TÉR This busy, noisy square is one of the city's major intersections. It is dominated by huge concrete apartment blocks built in the 1970s. The subway station below the square has become a makeshift market, with unlicensed street vendors, Peruvian musicians, and Transylvanian peasants peddling their wares.

ERKEL THEATER (Erkel Színház) As you turn down Rákóczi út toward the Eastern Railway Station, you come to the Erkel Theater at no. 30 Köztársaság tér (Square of the Republic). The former Communist Party Headquarters, at no. 26, was the scene of bloody clashes during the 1956 uprising ● *36*.

THE EASTERN RAILWAY STATION (Keleti Pályaudvar) The Keleti Pályaudar (1884) – on the north side of the square – is the terminus for all trains traveling to Budapest from the West. Since 1989 it has witnessed the arrival of large numbers of immigrants from Eastern Europe in search of a new life.

WORLDS APART
József körút bisects Józsefváros ('Joseph town') – the district named after Emperor Joseph II – both geographically and socially. While the Hungarian National Museum and Kálvin tér ▲ *123* are situated in a quiet middle-class neighborhood to the west of the boulevard, Rákóczi tér (to the east) lies in a working-class 'red-light' district, poignantly described by Giorgio and Nicolà Pressburger in their Homage to the Eighth District. The streets, some of which have dilapidated façades, provided the setting for a number of clashes during the 1956 uprising.

This photograph showing the Madách Színház and the New York Palace ▲ *167* was taken from József körút.

Kerepesi Cemetery (Kerepesi Temető) The Kerepesi Temető, to the south of the station, can be reached by tram (no. 23 or 24) along the Fiumei út. Its shady paths and carefully tended lawns make it a pleasant place in which to walk. As well as being the official burial place for such national heroes as Lajos Kossuth ● *35*, Ferenc Deák ▲ *123*, Lajos Batthyány ▲ *207*, Endre Ady and Lujza Blaha, many of the martyrs of the 1956 uprising are buried in the northwestern part of the cemetery (Division 21). Not far from the Pantheon of the Working Class Movement is the tomb of János Kádár ● *37*, the former premier of Hungary and First Secretary of the Hungarian Communist Party, whose epitaph reads: 'I lived for Communism and the people'. The Art Nouveau tombs of the Jewish Cemetery (at the eastern end of Kerepesi Temető, entrance in Salgótarjáni utca) may be more modest, but they are certainly more beautiful. As you leave the cemetery, retrace your steps to Fiumei út and make your way across Józsefváros toward the Danube and the western end of Nagykörút. This will take you to a more prosperous and well-cared-for neighborhood.

Rákóczi tér The district to the north of Rákóczi tér is typical of the working-class districts of old Budapest, with their large gypsy population. This is the preserve of gangsters and prostitutes. It is worth taking a walk down the charming old streets that run at right angles to the Déri Miksa utca, and discovering, behind Rákóczi tér, Vásár Csarnok, a picturesque covered market built in 1897. Its renovation after a serious fire has restored its colourful character. The dilapidated interior courtyards, the old borozó wine bars and the paved streets of this district give the impression that you have stepped back into the past.

Horvath Mihaly tér The square, which lies off József körút on Baross utca, is dominated by the Józsefváros Parish Church (1797–1814), a fine example of triumphant Baroque architecture. In front of the church stands the statue of Péter Pázmány (1570–1637), the Archbishop of Esztergom who led the country's Counter-Reformation.

Gutenberg tér To the west of Rákóczi tér is the beautiful Gutenberg tér. There is a splendid Art Nouveau building at no. 4, and the surrounding streets are delightful.

Mikszath Kalman tér This is another tiny square, Kálmán-Miksá tér, and the home of the legendary Tilos Az-a Bar. During the 1990s it presented performances by the cream of the Hungarian avant-garde and alternative movements. And there is the friendly atmosphere of the students bars on the nearby Krúdy utca. Further west is the more aristocratic neighborhood, with imposing residences, that surrounds the Hungarian National Museum (Magyar Nemzeti Múzeum) ▲ *124*.

Szabo Ervin Library (Szabó Ervin Könyvtár) Situated at no. 1 Szabó Ervin ter, the wonderful building housing the Szabó Ervin library has been entirely renovated and is well worth a detour. Built in 1887, it has a magnificent reading room with remarkable stuccowork and mosaics and huge chandeliers. Follow the arrows to "Palota" (palace).

The Museum of Applied Arts ★ (Iparművészeti Múzeum) ▲ *172*
This fairy-tale building, near the intersection between Ferenc körút and Üllői út, was one of the first works (1896) of the master of Hungarian Secessionism, Ödön Lechner ● *80*. As you approach it, you are immediately struck by the dazzling colored roof-tiles and decorated ceramics from the Zsolnay manufactory ● *66*, ▲ *172*. With their traditional and exotic motifs, they reflect the artists' desire to rediscover the Asiatic roots of the Magyar people and create a specifically Hungarian decorative style (*magyaros*) ● *80, 82*.

▲ THE MUSEUM OF APPLIED ARTS (Iparművészeti Múzeum)

The Museum of Applied Arts was founded in 1872. Its principal promoter was the chief conservator, Jenö Radisics, who instigated the construction of the present building. The building was opened by the Emperor Franz Joseph on October 25, 1896, as part of the celebrations to commemorate the thousandth anniversary of the foundation of the Hungarian state. The museum has five departments: metalwork (including gold and silver), furniture, textiles, ceramics and glassware, and minor collections.

SIDEBOARD
(Endre Thék cabinet makers, Budapest, 1900–6)
Among the many items of furniture on display, the Hungarian and French Art Nouveau collections deserve a special mention.

VASE
(Zsolnay manufactory, Pécs, 1899)
The Zsolnay manufactory was a family firm founded in 1853 by Vilmos Zsolnay. It became extremely successful in the early 20th century due to the collaboration of numerous artists who created its 3,000 decorations and 4,000 designs ▲ *147*.

VASES ● *66*
(Zsolnay manufactory, Pécs, 1899–1900)

Pendant (Oszkár Tarján, 1904)
For this silver-and-enamel pendant, the artist drew his inspiration from Japanese art, which was very much in vogue at the time. However, his work also reflects the influence of René Lalique.

'Ship of love' pendant
(17th century)
The museum has all sorts of metalwork, in gold and silver and other metals. The Esterházy collection includes some extremely valuable pieces, both from Hungary and other countries (especially Germany).

Tapestry
(Cassandra, Aladár Körösfői-Kriesch, 1908)
This tapestry, which can be seen in the textiles department, was influenced by the Pre-Raphaelite movement.

Composition in glass
(Zoltán Bohus, Budapest, 1980)
The department of ceramics and glassware has a wide range of works, from classical and medieval times to contemporary artists, including a remarkable international collection of Art nouveau glassware.

PETŐFI BRIDGE
An earlier bridge, built between 1933 and 1937, was designed by Pál Algyai and named after Miklós Horthy (1868–1957), Hungary's authoritarian regent from 1920 to 1944. The present Petőfi híd, named after the 19th-century poet ▲ *119*, spans the river (some 560 yards) between the southern end of the Nagykörút (Great Boulevard) and the Lágymányos district – once marshland, then the site of a small lake after embankments were built. In 1995 Lágymányos híd, the capital's most recent bridge, was opened to the south of the district. Lágymányos was hoping to host the 1996 World Fair, but the bid failed. However, a new campus for the University's Faculty of Sciences is now being built on the site.

FERENC KÖRUT AND FERENCVÁROS

To the south of Üllői út, the Ferenc Körút runs through the district of Ferencváros ('Francis town'), named after Emperor Francis II, who came to the throne in 1792. The district around Boráros tér and Angyal utca is an extension of the working-class district of Józsefváros ▲ *170*. In the 1950s Ferencváros had the city's most popular football team ▲ *162* – which symbolized the hopes of the city's working classes, especially the Vasas steelworkers. The club still exists today: its stadium is at no. 129 Üllői út.

CORVIN KÖZ This small street, near the intersection of Ferenc Körút and Üllői út, is dominated by the neo-Baroque façade of the Corvin Cinema ▲ *168*, one of Budapest's best-known cinemas.

Another aspect of the district's cultural dimension is the TRAFÓ (below) ● *43*, which opened in 1998 in a former power station at the intersection of Tüzoltó utca and Liliom utca – an echo of the regeneration of disused industrial sites in other parts of Europe. This contemporary arts center, devoted to live performances (both theater and dance), also has a large exhibition hall and a huge basement café run by the former management of the FIATAL MŰVÉSZEK KLUBJA ('Young Performers' Club'), or FMK, which inspired the avant-garde artistic movement of the 1980s.

THE MUSEUM OF APPLIED ARTS (Iparművészeti Múzeum) ★ Back on Üllöi út, the Museum of Applied Arts ▲ *172* is at nos. 33–7, near the intersection with Ferenc körút.

The working-class districts of Újpest, Rákospalota, Kispest, Pesterzsébet, Csepel, Óbuda and Budafok became part of Budapest when the city was being rebuilt in the 1950s. Since then the administratively unified capital has consisted of twenty-three districts (kerület), twelve of which form the outer suburbs. Although areas such as Csepel Island ● *14, 20* used to be heavily industrial, there are some pleasant surprises – for example, Kőbánya (literally, 'stone quarry') in District X and Kispest in District XIX.

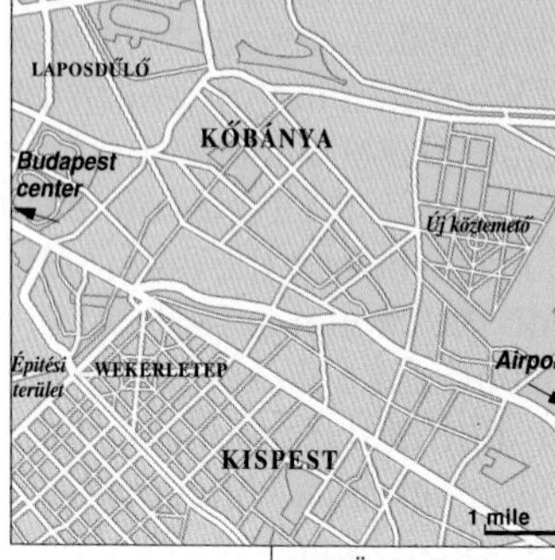

KŐBÁNYA

Actively worked from the 17th to the 19th century, to extract stone for building the city's houses, Kőbánya's underground quarrying galleries are now used for producing mushrooms and beer.

NEW MUNICIPAL CEMETERY (Új Köztemető) The no. 95 bus (from Baross tér) or the no. 28 tram (from Blaha Lujza tér) will take you to the Új Köztemető. This is where Imre Nagy ● *36, 37*, prime minister at the time of the 1956 uprising, was buried anonymously with a number of his colleagues (plots 300 and 301). After the national funeral service ● *31*, ▲ *151* held in June 1989, a memorial was erected to the martyrs of 1956. In the northeastern section of the cemetery is the JEWISH CEMETERY, which has many extremely beautiful, though neglected, tombs. It can be reached, via Kozma utca, from the no. 37 tram terminus.

'He [Ödön Lechner] used new materials, such as pyrogranite, glass, steel and ceramics, and made extensive use of the most unusual decorations.'
Dominique Fernandez

KISPEST

FLEA MARKET (Ecseri Piac) The city's main flea market (Ecseri Piac), at no. 154 Nagykőrösi út, is well worth a visit (catch a no. 54 bus from Boráros tér). It is one of the largest flea markets in Central Europe and, although less picturesque than the one at Pécs, has a wide variety of stalls. You will find absolutely everything, including beautiful Transylvanian vases and, with luck, paintings on glass (the Central European equivalent of religious icons, but with more restrained and sometimes naïve designs). In winter you can buy hot wine flavored with cinnamon, which helps produce a very friendly atmosphere.

THE WEKERLE HOUSING ESTATE (Wekerletelep) ★ ▲ *176* To reach this remarkable housing estate, situated near the flea market, take the metro to the 'Határ út' subway station and from there turn down Pannonia utca to Kós Károly tér. Conceived from the outset as a major garden-city project, the Wekerletelep was instigated by and named after Sándor Wekerle (prime minister 1892–95 and 1917–18).

ENTRANCE TO THE SCHMIDL TOMB
The crypt of the Schmidl family (near the cemetery gates on Kozma utca) is decorated with Art Nouveau ceramics and mosaics (1903), the result of a collaboration between Ödön Lechner ● *80* and Béla Lajta ● *82, 83*.

▲ THE WEKERLE HOUSING ESTATE
(Wekerletelep)

This garden city was built by architect Károly Kós in the village of Kispest, mainly between 1909 and 1929, in order to house some 20,000 manual workers and administrative employees. Today it is still a self-contained entity, despite becoming part of Budapest when the outer suburbs were officially incorporated into the capital in 1949. At first glance, the distinctive geometric layout of the Wekerletelep looks rather like a tapestry design. In spite of the simplicity of the urban planning, the architecture – the work of fifteen architects selected by means of a competition – is extremely interesting.

KÁROLY KÓS (1883–1977)

Károly Kós was born in the Bánát region (now in Romania) and was one of the first architects to develop a modern style of architecture based on Hungarian history, legends and folklore. When the Treaty of Trianon (1920) gave Transylvania to Romania, Kós left for the Transylvanian capital of Kobozsvár, now called Cluj in Romanian, where he became the tireless promoter of the 'Transylvanian School' of architecture, which sought to emphasize the region's multiculturalism. At the same time, he devoted himself to recording the cultural heritage of Transylvania (Hungarian, Romanian and Saxon village life, costume, and peasant customs and traditions), arguing that 'We should ensure that our souls are deeply rooted in the soil on which we wish to build.'

A VILLAGE WITHIN A CITY
Four Transylvanian-style porchways give access to a central square. The estate was designed to house those who had come to work in the city, and provide all the services they required for their everyday lives. The tenants were all given their own individual gardens, arranged around the apartment buildings. Today the estate still conveys the impression of a small self-contained, self-sufficient village, in a peaceful setting of trim, domesticated greenery. This theme is reflected by the statue, depicting Károly Kós taming a monster, that stands in the central square.

The Danube, banks and bridges

Miklós Mátyássy

The Zero Kilometer Stone on Clark Ádám tér ▲ *183, 206*.

Budapest's first stone bridge was built by the Romans to link the town of Aquincum with the fort of Trans-Aquincum ▲ *228*. It stood some 300 yards north of the present Árpád Bridge.

After flowing past Szentendre Island, the Danube flows through Budapest for a distance of 17 miles, during which its width varies between 400 and 600 yards. Since Roman times the river has been a main communications route, and Budapest is often regarded as its principal city. This is probably because the Danube has always dominated and molded the site of the city and, directly or indirectly, affected the lives of its inhabitants. Indeed, the collapse of the Communist regime began with protests against the series of hydroelectric dams known as the 'Dunosaur', part of which was due to be built at Nagymaros, just under 40 miles upstream from Budapest.

CROSSING THE DANUBE
Before Chain Bridge (Lánchíd) was opened in 1849, the river crossing had to be made by rowing boat, ferry or pontoon; or, in winter, across the river's frozen surface. This was how the Mongols reached Transdanubia in 1241, and how Matthias Corvinus ● *32* crossed the river for his coronation. From 1891, crossing the ice was prohibited.

'Budapest feels like a capital – it has the majestic and imposing air of a city playing a key role in history.'

Claudio Magris

Regulating the Danube

The construction of bridges made hazardous crossings unnecessary. The disastrous floods of March 1838 highlighted the need to regulate the course of the river as it flowed through the city. To prevent ice from forming, several of the islands were linked to the banks and to Margaret Island; in order to contain the river, quays were built on either side; and its width was standardized. The engineer Pál Vásárhelyi was a prominent patriot and a tireless advocate of regulation. His colleague Ferenc Retter suggested converting the backwater on the Pest side into a navigable Venetian-style canal. However, his suggestion was ignored, and in 1871 the Nagykörút (Great Boulevard) was built instead.

The ebb and flow of fortune

When World War Two reached Budapest, in 1944, the Danube provided the setting for a number of atrocities. Jews were shot right into the river; hotels and apartment blocks were bombed; and bridges (including Chain Bridge, above) destroyed by the retreating German army. The Danube and its banks were gradually rebuilt and eventually restored to their former glory. They are now classified as a UNESCO World Heritage Site.

Bathing, banks and bridges

The building work on the bridges, apartment blocks and hotels of Pest did not prevent postwar Budapesters bathing in the famous Danube Baths (Duna fürdő), a section of the river enclosed by huge nets. The banks were given paved quaysides and steps (greatly appreciated by fishermen and schoolchildren playing truant), which become submerged at high water. Finally, the two sides of the river were linked by new bridges.

Left: Chain Bridge and Margaret Bridge (Margit Híd).

▲ Freedom Bridge to Elizabeth Bridge

1. Petőfi Bridge
2. Freedom Bridge
3. Elizabeth Bridge
4. Chain Bridge
5. Margaret Bridge
6. Árpád Bridge

The 'Turuls' on the towers
Freedom Bridge (Szabadság híd), with its elaborate decorations, and four towers, reflects the spirit of 1896, the thousandth anniversary of the founding of the Hungarian state ▲*150*. This is why each tower is surmounted by a *Turul*, the mythical bird said to have guided Árpád ● *27* across the Carpathian Mountains.

Hotel Gellért and Gellért Baths

Freedom Bridge

Budapest University of Economics
(Fővám tér)
This 185-yard-long building, designed by Miklós Ybl ● *76*, ▲ *136* in neo-Renaissance style, was built in 1871–4. It is graced by colonnaded porticos, statues of Greek gods, and allegorical images of the virtues and trades. In 1948 the former Customs Office became the Karl Marx University, and that name was retained until 1990. The university still has a large statue of Karl Marx in the entrance hall.

Freedom Bridge (Szabadság híd)
This bridge was built between 1894 and 1896 by János Feketeházy and Aurél Czekelius. The decorative details were the work of Virgil Nagy, a lecturer at the nearby Technical University: his enameled blazon (below) of the kingdom of Hungary (the combined arms of Hungary and its various territories) is surmounted by the Hungarian crown. The bridge was opened on the Pest side of the Danube in the presence of the Emperor Franz Joseph. Originally known as the Franz Joseph Bridge, it retained that name for the next fifty years. Destroyed by the Germans in 1945, it was rebuilt in 1946 and renamed Freedom Bridge.

This unpretentious monastery, built in 1932, was designed by Károly Weichinger, combining Modern and Hungarian neo-Romanesque styles. Together with the Cave Church ▲ *216*, adjacent to it, it belongs to the Pauline monks. A plaque in the Polish Chapel honors the memory of the Polish refugees who sheltered there in the 1940s. In 1951 the church was boarded up and the Pauline Order (the only Hungarian order) proscribed. In 1990 the Paulines reopened the church and monastery.

RUDAS BATHS ● *62*

The Rudas Baths (Rudas Gyógyfürdő és Uszoda), which have existed since the 15th century, enjoyed their golden age under Hungary's Turkish rulers. The magnificent octagonal Turkish bath house (*hammam*), with columns supporting the central dome, was built between 1560 and 1570 by Pasha Mustapha Sokoli. The complex also has a covered swimming pool and steam baths. Today the baths are a popular meeting place and have a drinks stand and newspaper kiosk in the entrance hall.

LIBERATION MONUMENT
CITADEL
GELLÉRT HILL
RUDAS BATHS
ELIZABETH BRIDGE
STATUE OF SAINT GELLÉRT
STATUE OF THE EMPRESS ELIZABETH

BELVÁROS
INNER CITY PARISH CHURCH

The first Elizabeth Bridge (above) was built between 1897 and 1903 by the architect and one of the engineers who built the Franz Joseph Bridge (now Freedom Bridge). Its span (over 300 yards) made it the largest chain bridge in the world until 1926.

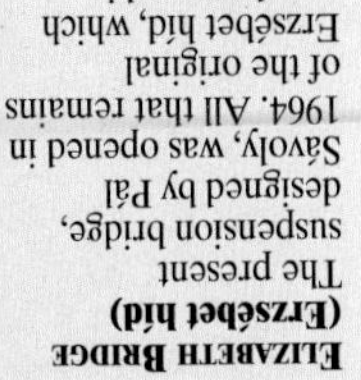

ELIZABETH BRIDGE (Erzsébet híd)

The present suspension bridge, designed by Pál Sávoly, was opened in 1964. All that remains of the original Erzsébet híd, which was destroyed in 1945, are its name (commemorating the Empress Elizabeth ▲ *182, 240*, the great protectress of the Hungarian people), its two piers and its elegance.

▲ ELIZABETH BRIDGE TO CHAIN BRIDGE

ELIZABETH, QUEEN OF HUNGARY
The statue of the Empress Elizabeth (1837–98) ● *30*, ▲ *240* by sculptor György Zala (1937) originally stood in Pest. It managed to survive World War Two, but was removed in 1947. Forty years later it reappeared in Buda, where it stands today (on tiny Döbrentei tér), surrounded by the access roads to Elizabeth Bridge.

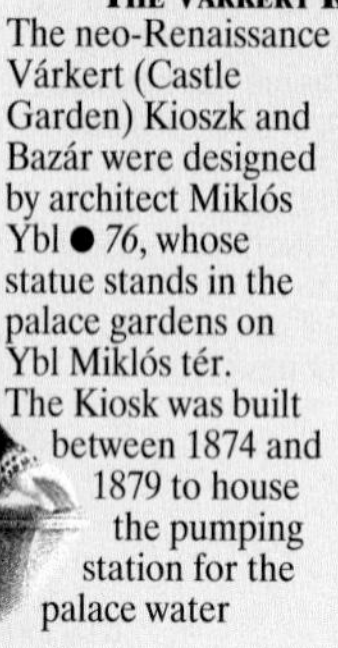

THE VÁRKERT KIOSZK AND BAZÁR
The neo-Renaissance Várkert (Castle Garden) Kioszk and Bazár were designed by architect Miklós Ybl ● *76*, whose statue stands in the palace gardens on Ybl Miklós tér. The Kiosk was built between 1874 and 1879 to house the pumping station for the palace water supply. It has since been restored (right) and is now a casino and restaurant. An arcade (the Várkert Bazár) and stairway lead to the palace gardens, laid out between 1875 and 1882 with pavilions, terraces, columns and statues. The gardens are bounded by arcades and an apartment block.

STATUE OF THE EMPRESS ELIZABETH

DÖBRENTEI TÉR

TABÁN PARISH CHURCH

CASINO

INNER CITY PARISH CHURCH

MÁRCIUS 15 TÉR

STATUE OF SÁNDOR PETŐFI

ORTHODOX CHURCH

MARRIOTT HOTEL

DANUBE CORSO ▲ *118*
Today the Duna korzó is bordered by the Marriott, Forum and Atrium Hyatt hotels, which stand on the site of their legendary predecessors – the Hungária, Bristol, Carlton and Ritz – built in the early 20th century. These vanished symbols of luxury, with their unique view of the Danube and the Royal Palace, were a favorite meeting place with the city's young smart set. The Bristol, the only one of these great luxury hotels to survive the bombing of World War Two, was demolished in the 1970s to make way for the Marriott.

Right: detail of the Pest Vigadó ● *79*, ▲ *118*.

ADAM CLARK

Chain Bridge (Széchenyi lánchíd) ● *74*, ▲ *184* is the oldest of Budapest's bridges. Designed by English engineer William Tierney Clark, it was built between 1839 and 1849 under the direction of the Scottish engineer Adam Clark (right), who was brought to Hungary by Count István Széchenyi ● *35*, ▲ *185*.

ENTRANCE TO PALACE GARDENS

ROYAL PALACE

NATIONAL GALLERY

TURUL BIRD

BUDA CASTLE FUNICULAR

CHAIN BRIDGE

ROOSEVELT TÉR

ATRIUM-HYATT HOTEL

FORUM HOTEL

PEST VIGADÓ

Chain Bridge was nearly never completed. In spring 1849, as the imperial troops retreated before the advancing Hungarian army, the Austrian commander General Hentzi would have blown it up if Adam Clark had not flooded the chambers containing the explosives. During World War Two the bridge was less fortunate: it was destroyed in 1945. Rebuilt, it reopened in 1949, a hundred years after the original inauguration.

THE GUARDIANS OF CHAIN BRIDGE ● *74*

A pair of lions stand guard at either end of Chain Bridge. It is often claimed that the sculptor, János Marschalko, depicted these fearsome creatures without tongues. In fact their tongues can only be seen from the front (which in no way not detracts from their monumental quality). In 1867 the Emperor Franz Joseph took a solemn oath at the foot of the bridge in Pest, before crossing into Buda to be crowned King of Hungary in the Castle District.

CASTLE HILL TUNNEL ● *35*, ▲ *206*. The neoclassical entrance of the Castle Hill Tunnel (Alagút), built by Adam Clark, adds the finishing touch to this harmonious complex.

'DRAWING THE DANUBE'

On the quayside, in front of a neo-Renaissance building designed by Miklós Ybl (soon to be renovated), an unusual object catches the eye. Behind the window of a cast-iron casing, a needle traces a line on paper with a scale marked on it. It is in fact a recording instrument, which monitors the water level of the Danube. Each week in the early 1990s the film director and conceptual artist Gábor Császári replaced the paper with the work of a different artist, on which the needle 'drew the Danube'.

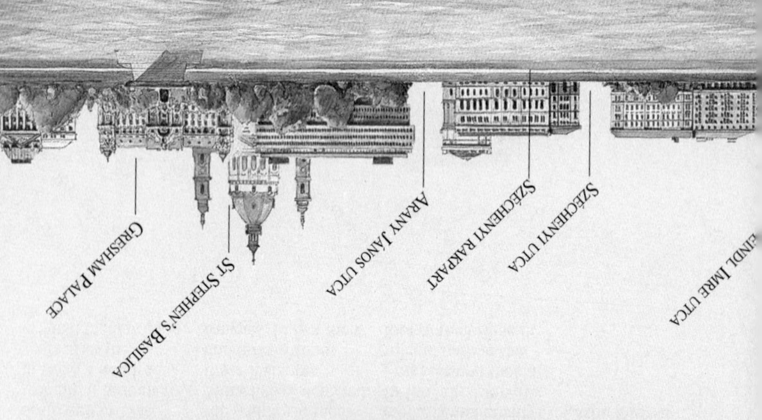

GRESHAM PALACE ● *80, 82* ▲ *138* **AND CHAIN BRIDGE** (Lánchíd)

THE PRESENCE OF THE RIVER

The Danube is very much in evidence throughout Budapest, and the names of certain districts are associated with water. For example, one of the most picturesque districts in Buda is called Víziváros (Watertown) ▲ *206*, while Vizafogó ('viza catcher') – to the north of the Újlipótváros district ▲ *138*, in Pest – is named after an impressive fish from the Black Sea, which before the regulation of the Danube was the delight of Budapest's fishermen.

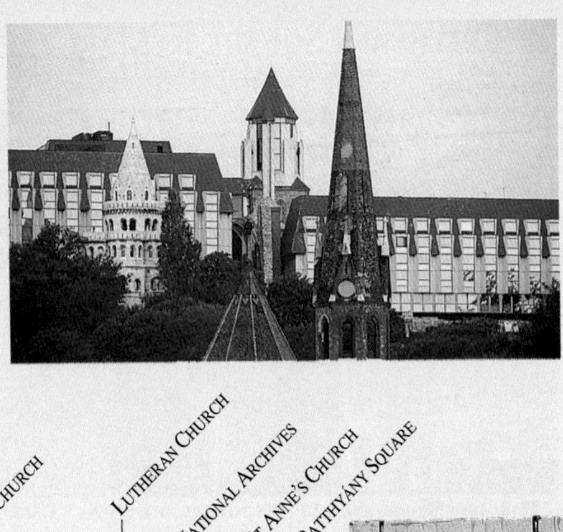

HILTON HOTEL

CALVINIST CHURCH

LUTHERAN CHURCH

NATIONAL ARCHIVES

ST ANNE'S CHURCH

BATTHYÁNY SQUARE

I. KER. BATTHYÁNY TÉR

PARLIAMENT

GARIBALDI UTCA

ZOLTÁN UTCA

RIVER TRAFFIC

The Danube still carries a great deal of river traffic – including tugs, ice-breakers, *vízibusz* ('water buses'), and the Budapest–Vienna hover link. Ukrainian and Russian river steamers dock in the city center, while seagoing vessels put in at the free port of Csepel, to the south of the city.

COUNT ISTVÁN SZÉCHENYI

(1791–1860) ● *35* ▲ *136, 213*

'Széchenyi, whose many philanthropic works included Chain Bridge, the first bridge across the Danube, shot himself in the head when the clinic for nervous illnesses, where he frantically wrote his various manifestos, threatened to send him to a lunatic asylum.'

Renaud Camus

▲ Batthyány Square to Margaret Bridge

Margaret Bridge and the twin towers of St Anne's Church ● *70*, ▲ *207* The bridge was built between 1872 and 1876 by the engineer Ernest Gouin and a French construction company.

Margaret Bridge (Margit híd)
The two sections of Margaret Bridge span the two branches of the Danube and meet at the southern tip of Margaret Island. Like the Western Railway Station ▲ *165*, the bridge was a French project.

Margaret Bridge: a victim of history
An attempt to blow up the bridge during World War Two tragically echoed the *Inauguration of the Bridge*, one of the *balladái* of the poet János Arany (1817–82), in which he described a series of suicides. The bridge had been mined by the Germans and the charges were accidentally detonated during the rush hour in November 1944, with the loss of six hundred lives. The bridge was finally destroyed by the Germans in 1945, and rebuilt after the war. Eleven years later the student protest march in October 1956 ● *36* crossed Margaret Bridge on its way from the statue of General Bem ▲ *119* to Parliament.

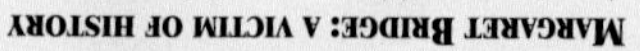

'Pest'
I was born in Pest on the banks of our beautiful river,/ I have the rich, fresh colors of the map before me,/ Its sky is broken by the clouds and hills,/ Beyond them, the sun sinks below the horizon.
János Arany

Margaret Island (Margit-sziget) ▲ 188

The Romans built fortifications and villas on Margaret Island. In the Middle Ages the Franciscans, Dominicans and Premonstratensians built churches and convents, while the Archbishop of Esztergom and the Knights of the Order of St John built fortified castles at the north and south ends of the island. After the 13th-century Mongol invasion Margit, the nine-year-old daughter of Béla IV and the Byzantine princess Maria Lascaris, was sent to the island that now bears her name to be brought up as a nun. She died there twenty years later. During the Turkish occupation the churches and convents were destroyed. The island then remained deserted until 1796, when the Palatine Archduke Joseph of Habsburg ● *34* chose the island as the site for a villa, surrounded by a vast English-style garden.

The sirens that decorate the piers of Margaret Bridge are the work of the French sculptor Thabart.

Flórián Chapel

Bem rakpart

Statue of General Bem

Przemysl Memorial

Margaret Bridge

Jászai Mari tér

The 'White House'

A health resort

In 1867 a mineral spring was discovered with medicinal properties that made it possible to build a spa complex on the island. The water was bottled as Margaret Island mineral water (Margitszigeti Ásványvíz) and became a feature of Hungarian dinner tables. In 1900 the island was linked to Margaret Bridge, which made it accessible to pedestrians and motor vehicles; and its popularity as a public park has increased since 1950, when the Árpád Bridge was opened at the north end of the island. With its Olympic-size swimming pool, boathouses, tennis courts and Palatinus Baths ▲ *188*, it is also the capital's most popular sports center.

A literary retreat

During the second half of the 19th century Margaret Island was a favorite haunt of the poet János Arany (left), who dedicated several poems to its ancient oak trees. Other writers – Gyula Krúdy, Ferenc Molnár, Sándor Bródy and Ernö Szép – also used the island as a literary retreat.

▲ Margaret Island (Margit-sziget)

In medieval times, under the Arpadian dynasty, Margaret Island was a royal hunting reserve and was known as the Island of Rabbits. At various points in its history it has also been called the Island of Our Lady, the Island of Our Lord, Danube Island and Palatine Island. Today it is one of the city's most popular green spaces. Regular open-air concerts are held there.

The Dominican church and convent were built between 1246 and 1255 by Béla IV. The king had promised that if Hungary emerged victorious from the Mongol invasion he would build a convent and have his daughter Margit (above) brought up as a nun. Margit was sent to the island at the age of nine and, having refused to marry the king of Bohemia, died in the convent in 1271 – a year after Béla, who died there in 1270. Béla was buried on the island, as were Margit and her brother Stephen V. With the arrival of the Turks in 1541, the nuns left for Pozsony (now Bratislava), taking the remains of Saint Margit with them. The ruins of the church were excavated in 1838.

Palatinus Baths Fed by the island's thermal springs, the Palatinus Baths have a number of pools and lawns. Budapesters regard them as a beach and often spend the day there. In front of the baths is a nude statue (below) by the French sculptor Émile Guillaume.

The island's features include the Centenary Monument, a sculptural group by István Kiss erected in 1973 to commemorate the thousandth anniversary of the unification of Buda, Pest and Óbuda; the Alfréd Hajós Swimming Baths, or National Sports Pool, with its exposed concrete structure and red-brick exterior; the Ramada Hotel (Miklós Ybl, 1872); and the Thermal Hotel (1979), which has a large hydrotherapy unit.

The water tower Built between 1909 and 1911, this reinforced-concrete tower, which houses the Office of Weights and Measures, doubles as an exhibition center and monument; 170 feet high, it offers an interesting view of the capital.

Buda

Péter Buza

CASTLE HILL (VÁRHEGY)

1. ROYAL PALACE
2. FUNICULAR (SIKLÓ)
3. SÁNDOR PALACE
4. CASTLE THEATER
5. MONUMENT TO THE HEROES OF 1848
6. HOLY TRINITY COLUMN
7. MATTHIAS CHURCH

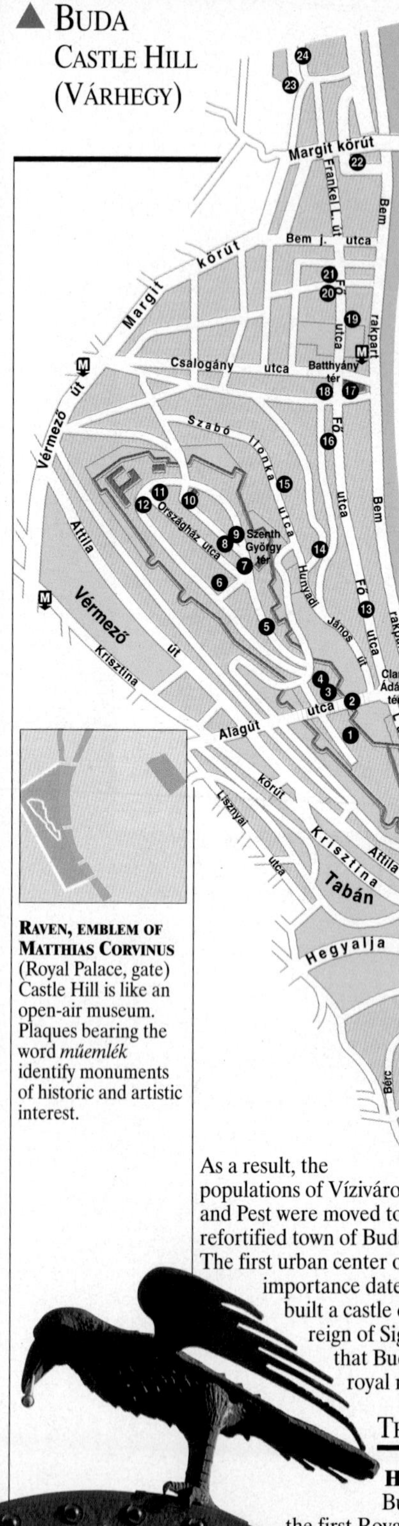

Castle Hill *(Várhegy)* is bounded by the Danube to the east, and the green Buda Hills to the north, west and south. Its unique setting explains why human settlements developed here much earlier (from prehistoric times) than on the opposite bank of the river. Buda remained the preferred site until the 19th century, when Pest's extensive areas of virgin land were claimed by industrial expansion. Castle Hill – less than a mile long and no more than a third of a mile wide – is a limestone-and-marl hill that rises to just under 1,600 feet and slopes steeply in places. Like a great land-locked galleon, it seems to drift with the river, its prow turning into the current. The first town, built in the 10th century on the southern slopes of the hill, was destroyed during the Mongol invasions (1241–2). After these invasions, it was decided to move the population to better protected sites. As a result, the populations of Víziváros and Pest were moved to the refortified town of Buda. The first urban center of any importance dates from the 13th century, when Béla IV built a castle on the hill, but it was not until the reign of Sigismund of Luxembourg (1387–1437) that Buda became the site of a permanent royal residence.

RAVEN, EMBLEM OF MATTHIAS CORVINUS
(Royal Palace, gate)
Castle Hill is like an open-air museum. Plaques bearing the word *műemlék* identify monuments of historic and artistic interest.

THE ROYAL PALACE

HISTORY OF THE PALACE ● *70*
Built at the southern end of the hilltop, the first Royal Palace (*Királyi palota*) was the residence of Louis the Great. Today nothing remains of this Gothic edifice – which was

8. Hilton Hotel
9. Fishermen's Bastion
10. Lutheran Church
11. National Archives
12. Military History Museum
13. French Institute
14. Capuchin Church
15. Buda Vigadó
16. Calvinist Church
17. St Anne's Church
18. Covered Market
19. St Elizabeth's Church
20. Király baths
21. Flórián Chapel
22. Przemysl Memorial
23. Tomb of Gül Baba
24. Lukács Baths
25. Hotel Gellért
26. Citadel

The Mongols invading Hungary.

continually modified for three hundred years, before being totally destroyed by the Christian armies when they drove the Turks out of Buda in 1686. A veritable legion of Dutch, Italian and French masters worked on the Royal Palace during the reigns of Sigismund of Luxembourg (king of Hungary and Holy Roman Emperor) ● *28* and Matthias Corvinus ● *32*, who made it a European cultural center. On the pretext of protecting the interests of János Sigismund, son of János Szapolyai (1526–40), against the pretender Ferdinand of Habsburg, the Turkish army occupied the castle and sacked the palace of King Matthias. Following the reconquest of 1686, a smaller Baroque palace was begun in 1715. But by the end of the 19th century it had almost doubled in size. Miklós Ybl and Alajos Hauszmann were the last great architects to work on the palace, which was completed in neo-Baroque style in 1904. On the point of losing World War One, the occupying German army withdrew to the palace, which became a target for the Russian artillery. Disregarding the opinion of experts who maintained that it was beyond restoration, new architects set to work on the ruined palace. They cared little for the eclecticism ● *76* of Ybl and Hauszmann, and rebuilt the Royal Palace without reference to the previous structure. Those who, at first glance, see only 'a monstrous palace next to an ancient but recently restored church' (Le Corbusier, in *Voyage d'Orient*, 1911) can take heart from the fact that the palace contains some marvelous treasures in its library and museums, which include the Castle Museum ▲ *192* (part of Budapest History Museum) and the Hungarian National Gallery ▲ *194*. Finally, archaeologists have excavated the entire fortification system surrounding the hill.

View of Pest and Chain Bridge
There are three ways for visitors to climb Castle Hill. You can take one of the many flights of steps (*lépcső*), from Hunyadi János út (to the east) or behind Vérmező Park (to the west); or walk up Várfok utca and through the Vienna Gate (*Bécsi kapu*), to the north.

▲ Budapest History Museum (Budapesti Történeti Múzeum)

The main sections of the Budapest History Museum are the Castle Museum and the Kiscell ▲ *224* and Aquincum ▲ *228* museums. The various floors of the Castle Museum present the history of the Royal Palace, together with the more general history of the city, from the Hungarian conquest to the present day. Since 1968 it has occupied Building E of the former Royal Palace.

Hooded prophet (or apostle)
(15th century)

Glass goblet
(15th century)
The goblet is decorated with the arms of Queen Beatrice, the wife of Matthias Corvinus ● *32*.

Hooded knight
(15th century)
This beautiful white-limestone head came from the Friss Mansion. Its style reflects the influence of southern-German statuary.

Dragon
(14th century)

This stove-tile fragment came from the wing of the palace built in the 14th century. By then the royal ceramic workshop had evidently achieved a high level of technical skill.

Detail from a fresco
(late 14th or early 15th century)
This fresco, showing a pair of dancers and a fool, was discovered in a house in Táncsics Mihály utca.

Saint Paul the Hermit
(15th century)
Keystone decoration showing Saint Paul, the first hermit, who lived in the Lower Thebaid in the 3rd century. On one of the trees is a raven, holding a piece of bread in its beak; the other is growing in a rocky landscape.

Apostle
(15th century)

Women's heads
(15th century) Glazed stove tile.

(Magyar Nemzeti Galéria)

The Hungarian National Gallery (Magyar Nemzeti Galéria), which occupies wings B, C and D of the Royal Palace, presents an overview of 19th-century and 20th-century Hungarian art and some six hundred works from the 11th to the 18th centuries – including Baroque art, a lapidarium devoted to medieval and Renaissance stone carvings, and some magnificent triptychs from the late-Gothic period.

SAINT STEPHEN
This statue of the first king of Hungary, almost 4 feet high, was sculpted in c. 1500–10. It originally formed part of a triptych that included Saint Ladislas – who, with Saint Stephen, was the most widely represented canonized Hungarian monarch.

HEAD OF A KING OF KALOCSA
This masterpiece of Hungarian Romanesque art was sculpted in red marble between 1200 and 1225. Its simple lines and beautiful proportions give it a monumental quality, in spite of its size (it is only 6½ inches high). Of unknown provenance, it was incorporated into a monument and may have formed part of a statue in the round.

'THE VISITATION'
depicts the visit of the Virgin Mary to her cousin Elizabeth (Luke 1:39–56). Painted on wood by the Master M.S. (1506), it adorned the high altar of the Castle of Selmecbánya. The irises, peonies and wild strawberries are all symbols of the Holy Virgin.

'The Crucifixion'
This panel (c. 1480–90) decorated the high altar of the Church of St Nicholas at Jánosrét. The scene, set against a hazy landscape, suggests a slightly Flemish influence.

'Saint Dorothy of Barka'
(c. 1410–20)
One of the finest examples of the Hungarian 'tender style'.

The Sibiu Angelus
This triptych (1510–20) combines Renaissance motifs and Gothic decoration.

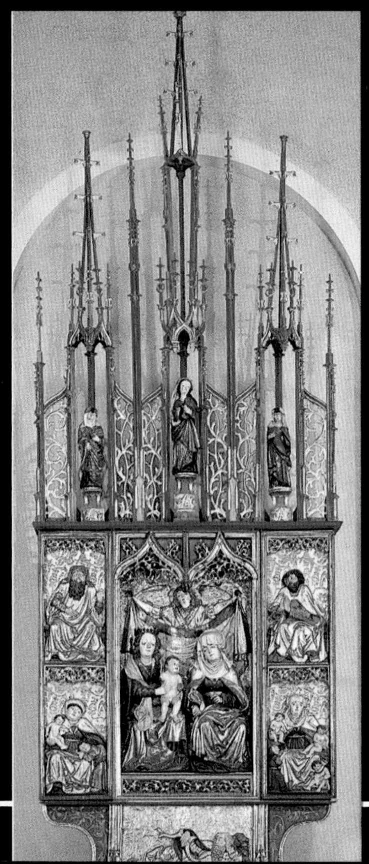

The Hungarian National Gallery has a large collection of 19th-century art, ranging from neoclassical and Romantic works to academic paintings and *plein-air* landscapes. In particular, it includes the works of Mihály Munkácsy and László Paál, to whom several rooms are devoted. The 20th-century collection reflects the major European trends between 1900 and 1945, including Art Nouveau, Cubism and avant-garde art.

'DÉJEUNER SUR L'HERBE' (1873)
(Left) Pál Szinyei Merse (1845–1920) was one of the first Hungarian Impressionists. He broke with academic tradition when he painted this extremely natural and vividly colored scene.

'PORTRAIT OF A WOMAN' (1910)
(Below) István Zádor (1882–1963) studied in France, and French influences are apparent in the composition and pastel tones of this portrait of his wife.

'OCTOBER' (1903)
Károly Ferenczy (1862–1917) was a master of *plein-air* painting – as can be seen from this view of the garden of his family home in Erdély, Transylvania, suffused by the bright sunlight bathing the countryside.

'Woman with birdcage'(1892)
(Above) This major work by József Rippl-Rónai (1861–1927) ● *96* was painted during the artist's 'black period', when he was living and working in Paris. The subject is treated extremely economically.

'Woman in white-spotted dress' (1889)
(Left) When József Rippl-Rónai painted this elegant Parisienne, he was beginning to abandon the techniques of his master, Mihály Munkácsy, and opening up to the influences of Art Nouveau, Japanese prints and French painting.

'Self-portrait'
(1896–1902)
Tivadar Csontváry (1853–1919) was a passionate man who became an artist late in life. This self-portrait, painted at the beginning of his career, reflects the influence of the Munich School.

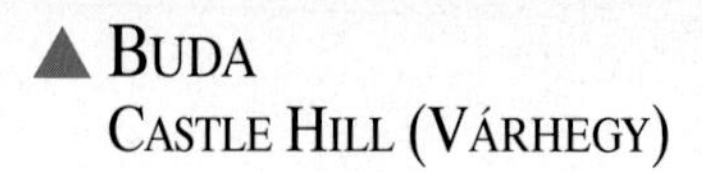

MATTHIAS FOUNTAIN
It is said that visitors who throw a coin into the fountain will return to Budapest.

THE GUARDIANS OF THE PALACE The four lion statues guarding the entrance to the Lion Court (Oroszlános udvar) are the work of János Fadrusz (1904). The first two are depicted as snarling menacingly, the other two as roaring.

EQUESTRIAN STATUE OF PRINCE EUGENE OF SAVOY A little over three hundred years ago Buda was liberated from the Turkish occupation by an alliance of European Christian armies that practically destroyed the city. One of the military commanders involved in the siege was Eugène de Savoie-Carignan (1663–1736), better known as Prince Eugene of Savoy. The great-nephew of Cardinal Mazarin, Eugene had joined the army of the Emperor Leopold I after Louis XIV had refused to give him command of a regiment. He liberated Buda in 1686, defeated the Turks at Zenta in 1697, and captured Belgrade from them in 1717. The equestrian statue of the prince – who was a man of culture, as is evident from the books and works of art that this friend of Leibnitz assembled in his Venetian mansion – stands in front of the castle's main entrance. The statue was commissioned by the town of Zenta, which was then unable to pay the artist. At the suggestion of Alajos Hauszmann, one of the architects in charge of restoring the palace, the statue was bought by Franz Joseph and erected on a spot that had been earmarked for a statue of the emperor – and which offers one of the most spectacular views of Budapest.

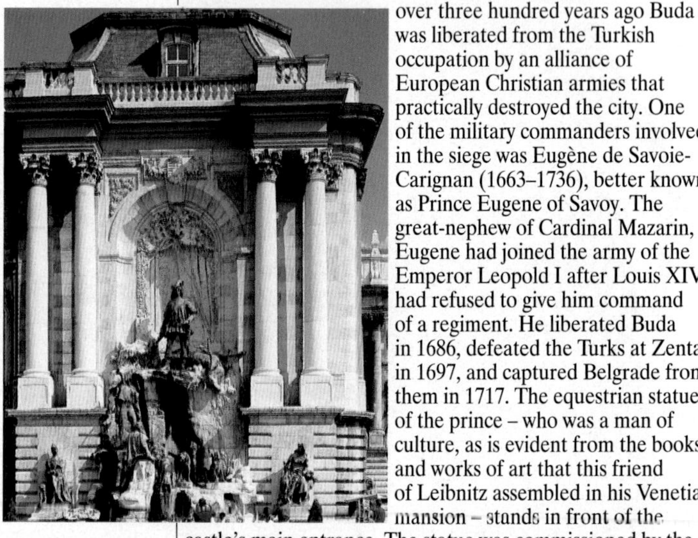

PRINCE EUGENE OF SAVOY
The bronze equestrian statue of Prince Eugene of Savoy, by József Róna (1900).

MATTHIAS FOUNTAIN (Mátyás kút) Behind the statue of Prince Eugene of Savoy, a narrow passageway leads to the northwest courtyard of the palace. On the right stands the Matthias Fountain (Mátyás kút), a bronze masterpiece by Alajos Stróbl (1904). The sculptural group, with its extremely natural detail, was inspired by a ballad written by the poet Mihály Vörösmarty ● *42*, ▲ *116*, which tells of Matthias Corvinus' encounter, while out hunting, with Szép Ilonka (Ilonka the Beautiful).

The Habsburg Crypt (Nádor kripta) The medieval Chapel of St Sigismund was rebuilt during the reign of the Empress Maria Theresa and used as a fortified church before being almost completely destroyed for the second time. The wall of the choir backs onto the artificial rocks of the Matthias Fountain. All that remains of the chapel is the Nádor kripta, the burial place of the Palatine Archduke Joseph, son of Leopold II, which was subsequently rebuilt and can be reached from the National Gallery. Under the Habsburgs the *nádor* (Palatine) was the imperial representative in Hungary, and Archduke Joseph was appointed Palatine in 1796. For the next fifty years, 'the most Hungarian of the Habsburgs' took an active part in the development of the dual city ● *34, 92,* ▲ *187*. In 1820 his daughter, who died in infancy, was buried in the crypt. Archduke Joseph, who died in 1847, is buried in a sarcophagus surmounted by a recumbent marble effigy sculpted by György Zala.

Ludwig Museum This museum, which was housed in the north wing of the castle (building A) for around ten years, has now moved to the Palace of Arts at no. 1 Komor Marcell utca.

National Széchényi Library (Országos Széchenyi Könyvtár) The National Széchényi Library was founded in 1802 by Count Ferenc Széchényi, the father of István Széchenyi ● *35*, ▲ *185*. His private collection, which he left to the state, consisted of some fifteen thousand books and two thousand manuscripts. In 1895, after being housed in several temporary locations, the library was transferred to Building F in the Royal Palace, specially refurbished for the purpose. Its reading rooms are primarily used by students and researchers. Visitors may be disappointed by the functional nature of the building, as there is no trace of the former royal apartments. However, its windows offer an unrivaled view of Budapest.

Louis the Great (14th-century manuscript)
The collections of the National Széchényi Library comprise some two million books and five million documents (posters, photographs, manuscripts, obituaries, maps, periodicals). It houses most of the publications written either in Hungarian or by Hungarians or about Hungary, known collectively as *Hungarica*.

The Royal Chapel (Budapest History Museum ▲ *192*)
Rediscovered in the 1960s, this small 14th-century Gothic chapel escaped the modifications and destruction suffered by the rest of the palace.

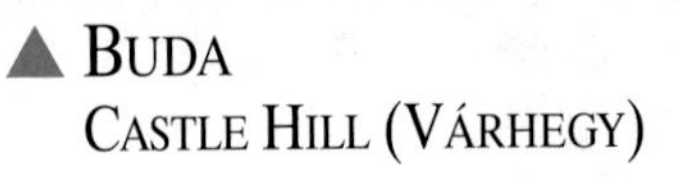

THE CASTLE DISTRICT

ÚRI UTCA
Neo-Baroque façade.

ST GEORGE'S SQUARE (Szent György tér) This square, which lies between the Royal Palace to the south and Dísz tér to the north, is named after the church that stood here in the Middle Ages. Bounded on one side by the main palace gates (surmounted by a Turul, the mythical bird of prey that supposedly led Árpád over the Carpathian Mountains), it gives access to the upper station of the BUDA CASTLE FUNICULAR (Budavári Sikló) ▲ *206*.

SÁNDOR PALACE (Sándor palota) This is a neoclassical edifice by Mihály Pollack which was built in 1806 for the counts of Sándor. It is decorated with reliefs by the Bavarian master sculptor Anton Kirchmayer. Since the second half of the 19th century, it has been the seat of the presidency of the Council of Ministers.

CASTLE THEATER (Várszínház) The Sándor Palace used to be linked to the Castle Theater by a footbridge. The theater, built in 1736 in late-Baroque style, originally housed a Carmelite chapel. Destroyed in the 1940s, it did not reopen until 1978 and was subsequently renovated in 2003. Today it is an annex of the Hungarian National Theater (Nemzeti Színház).

TÁRNOK UTCA AND ÚRI UTCA Tárnok utca begins on the north side of DÍSZ TÉR. Most of the two-story Gothic-style houses were destroyed during the confrontations between Christians and Turks in the early 18th century, and the entire district was rebuilt in Baroque style. During its reconstruction, 14th-century corbeled houses were discovered at nos. 14 and 16 Tárnok utca and no. 31 Úri utca. In places the galleries of a troglodyte settlement that run beneath these two ancient streets break through the 33-foot surface layer of Castle Hill. Used as wine cellars in peacetime, they offer shelter in time of war or unrest, since they have plenty of hiding places and their own wells. No. 9 Úri utca gives access to the caves under Castle Hill. Today the caves are occupied by the BUDA CASTLE WAXWORKS (Budavári Labyrinthus), and historical figures are displayed in a small section of a 6-mile gallery.

SZENTHÁROMSÁG UTCA This road leads from Úri utca to the very center of Castle Hill. On

CASTLE THEATER
In 1784 Joseph II, who dissolved more than one religious order, made this Carmelite chapel part of the royal estates. Six years later he gave his permission for it to be converted into a theater. The building became the first permanent theater in the city, giving performances of Hungarian and German plays alternately and also staging concerts. On May 7, 1800 virtuoso pianist Ludwig van Beethoven and horn player Giovanni Punto performed in the theater.

'The said town of Buda is a goodly commercial town and rich in all kinds of merchandise. And it produces more white wines than most, which are somewhat fiery.'

Bertrandon de la Brocquière (15th century)

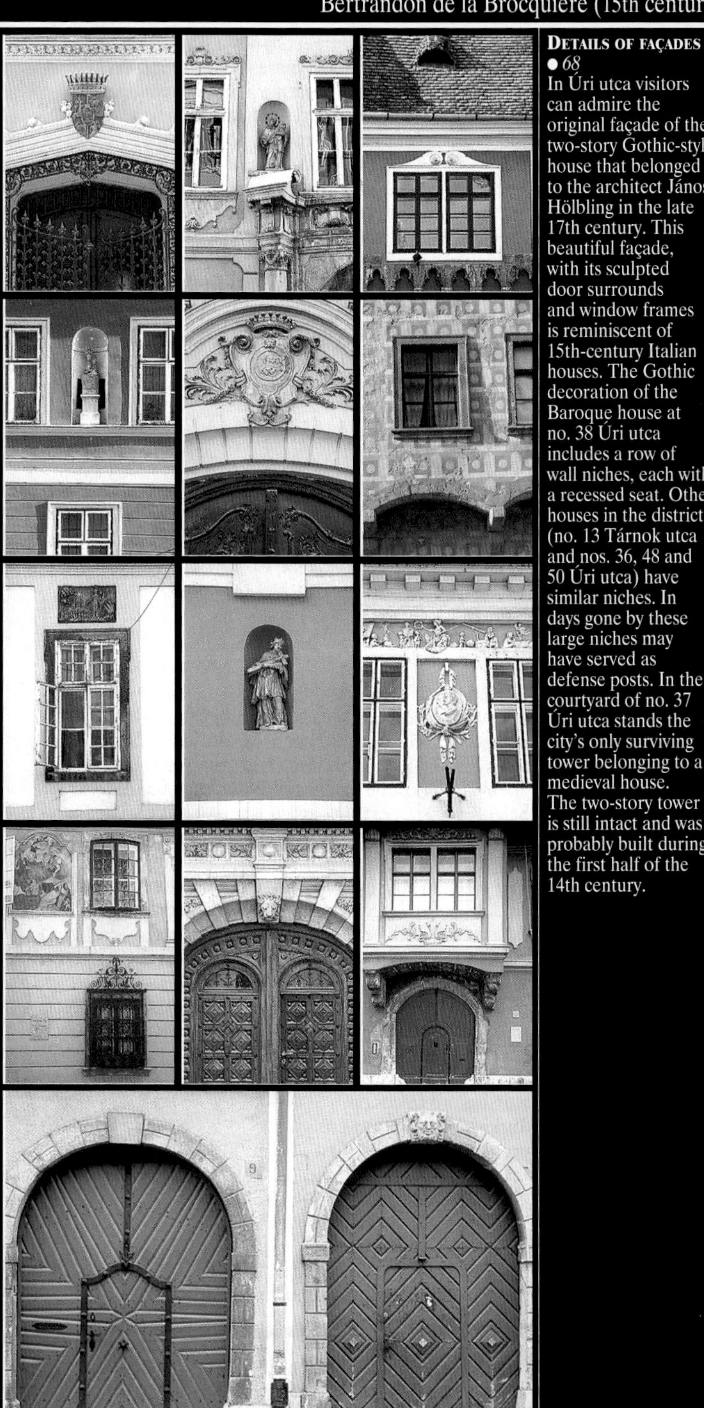

Details of façades
● *68*
In Úri utca visitors can admire the original façade of the two-story Gothic-style house that belonged to the architect János Hölbling in the late 17th century. This beautiful façade, with its sculpted door surrounds and window frames is reminiscent of 15th-century Italian houses. The Gothic decoration of the Baroque house at no. 38 Úri utca includes a row of wall niches, each with a recessed seat. Other houses in the district (no. 13 Tárnok utca and nos. 36, 48 and 50 Úri utca) have similar niches. In days gone by these large niches may have served as defense posts. In the courtyard of no. 37 Úri utca stands the city's only surviving tower belonging to a medieval house. The two-story tower is still intact and was probably built during the first half of the 14th century.

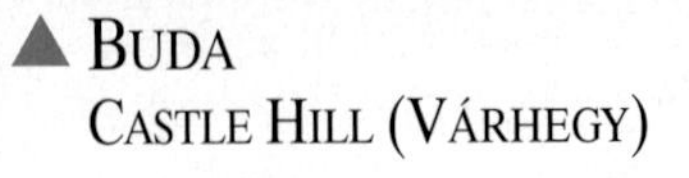

the corner of the two streets stands a statue (György Vastagh, Junior, 1937) of András Hadik (1710–90), an ordinary hussar who became a military commander and favorite of Maria Theresa of Austria. His sword, which the artist used as a model, is now in the MILITARY HISTORY MUSEUM (Hadtörténeti Múzeum), at no. 40 Tóth Árpád sétány. During his time as military governor of Buda, Hadik lived at no. 58 Szentháromság utca, built in Baroque style around 1720.

BUDA'S FORMER TOWN HALL (Régi Budai Városháza) Buda's Former Town Hall was built in the late 17th century by the Italian architect Venerio Ceresola on the ruins of Gothic buildings. The work was carried out in several stages and lasted almost seventy-five years. The elegantly proportioned building, with its beautiful interior staircase, ceased to function as a town hall in 1873, when Buda and Pest were united ● *29*. Today it houses the Collegium Budapest (Academy of Sciences).

MATTHIAS CHURCH (Mátyás templom) ★ The Matthias Church ● *77* – the popular name for the Church of Our Lady (Budavári Nagyboldogasszony templom) – is one of Budapest's architectural gems. All that remains of the original 13th-century building, and of what is generally regarded as the medieval church, are the lower section of the south bell tower and the interior pillars of the MARY PORTAL on the south façade. Although it was used by the Turks as a place of worship, all traces of Turkish occupation were eradicated during its first reconstruction (one of the architects was János Hölbling ▲ *201*). The church was almost entirely rebuilt between 1873 and 1896 under the direction of Frigyes Schulek, who drew his inspiration for the new building from the Gothic remains discovered on the site. The church's COLLECTION OF SACRED ART is one of the richest in Budapest. The

THE HOLY TRINITY COLUMN (Szentháromság oszlop) ● *71*
The Baroque Holy Trinity Column has stood in the center of Szentháromság tér since 1714. Often called the 'plague column', it was erected by Buda town council after an outbreak of plague that is evoked on one of its reliefs. Another relief depicts the construction of the column.

STATUE OF PALLAS ATHENE
Beneath the balcony of Buda's former town hall stands a statue of Pallas Athene (right). The original statue – presented to the city by the Italian stonemason Carlo Adami, who wanted to make a name for himself in Buda – has been replaced by a copy. The edifice that Athene was invoked to protect (in her capacity as goddess of wisdom, rather than of war) was Baroque Buda's first administrative building.

The arms of Hungary and King Matthias Corvinus (Matthias Church).

ROYAL FUNERARY CHAPEL (next to the St Imre Chapel) contains the double sarcophagus of King Béla III and his queen, Anne of Châtillon; its three naves are decorated in Gothic style.

STATUE OF SAINT STEPHEN Alajos Stróbl sculpted this bronze equestrian statue of Saint Stephen (1906), the first king of Hungary and founder of the Hungarian state, to suit the taste of the period.

One of the four reliefs that decorate the neo-Romanesque limestone plinth shows Frigyes Schulek, who designed the plinth, presenting a model of the Matthias Church to the king.

HILTON HOTEL Designed by Béla Pintér, the Hilton Hotel (Hilton Szálló) was opened in 1976. The statues of the monks Julianus and Gellért (1937) – not to be confused with Saint Géllert, whose statue is on Géllert Hill – which stand on the east side of Fishermen's Bastion, serve as a reminder that the hotel was built on the site of a Dominican monastery. Today the tower of the former Dominican church houses the hotel's casino; and several of the stone pillars from the nave have been reused in the Dominican Courtyard, where concerts are held. The courtyard offers a marvelous view of Pest, framed by a Gothic setting.

THE FISHERMEN'S BASTION (Halászbástya) ● *77*
The Fishermen's Bastion was built by Frigyes Schulek in 1905, in neo-Romanesque style, on a site once occupied by a fish market. It forms a balcony in front of the Matthias Church and offers a magnificent view of Pest. The bronze statue of János Hunyadi, the military commander who fought the Turks in the late 15th century, stands on Hunyadi

MATTHIAS CHURCH, DETAIL OF THE MARY PORTAL
The Matthias Church witnessed the marriage, in 1476, of Matthias Corvinus ● *32* and Beatrice of Aragon ● *33*, ▲ *192*; the coronation, in

1876, of the Emperor Franz Joseph (for which Liszt composed his *Hungarian Coronation Mass*); and, in 1916, that of the last Habsburg emperor, Charles I (Károly IV) ● *96*. It is the city's most beautiful church.

TANCSICS MIHALY UTCA
The ERDÖDY PALACE (below), at no. 7, and the ZICHY MANSION (built for Miklós Zichy) ▲ *226*, at no. 23, are well worth a visit.

ERDŐDY PALACE ● *71*
This magnificent Baroque building houses the MUSIC HISTORY MUSEUM (Zenetörténeti Múzeum), which includes an intriguing display of old musical instruments.

DETAIL OF THE FISHERMEN'S BASTION
The seven Hungarian tribes led by Árpád ● 27 are represented by seven turrets.

János út, which runs below the bastion. A little further on is a replica of St George and the Dragon by Márton and György Kolozsvári (14th century).

ORSZÁGHÁZ UTCA (Parliament Street) Beyond the palace, Országház utca runs down the broader, northern slope of Castle Hill. In the 15th century it was referred to as 'the Italian street', after the Tuscan artists and craftsmen who lived there. The houses at nos. 18, 20 and 22, which date from the 14th and 15th centuries, are the district's only surviving medieval buildings. The street's present name is a reminder that in the 1790s the Diet (Parliament) of Buda met in the large building at no. 28, known as the EGYKORI BUDAI ORSZÁGHÁZ (Old Parliament Building). Not long after, in 1806, the Diet of Buda was dissolved, at the same time as the Holy Roman Empire. Together with no. 49 Úri utca, this building – which is notable for its *copf* style (a German and Central European variety of Rococo) ▲ *231* – formed part of the Cloister of the Poor Clares. Both were built in the 1780s, under the direction of Franz Anton Hillebrandt. From the late 18th to the early 19th century, no. 28 served as the seat of the Hungarian legislature and supreme court. Its great ceremonial hall (now used by the Hungarian Academy of Sciences) and main staircase attest to the building's former splendor. During the second half of the 19th century, grand balls were held there.

FORTUNA UTCA At one time this street, which runs parallel to Országház utca, was named after its German inhabitants; previously, in the Middle Ages it was named after the French courtiers of King Sigismund. The easternmost row of houses is reached via a gateway. The late-17th-century *copf*-style ▲ *231* building at no. 4 now houses the COMMERCE AND CATERING MUSEUM (Kereskedelmi és Vendéglátóipari Múzeum). In the courtyard is a majestic

vine, planted more than two hundred years ago by the canons of Esztergom ▲ *238*, who were then responsible for recording rights of ownership.

HESS ANDRAS TÉR
The square is named after the printer András Hess, who had a workshop at no. 4. In 1473 he published the *Chronicle of Buda*, the first book printed in Hungary.
A statue of Pope Innocent IV, erected to commemorate the 250th anniversary of Hungary's liberation from Turkish rule, acts as a reminder that the Pope came to the country's assistance during the Christian reconquest.
At no. 3 is the HOUSE OF THE RED HEDGEHOG (Vörös Sün Ház), where Buda's first theatrical performances were given in the 1760s. Earlier in the 18th century several medieval houses were converted to form this building, which owes its name to the inn sign on the main façade.
The combination of neoclassical, Gothic and Baroque styles is the result of conversions carried out during the 19th century. Hess András tér is situated in the heart of an old Jewish district and at the MEDIEVAL JEWISH PRAYER HOUSE (Középkori Zsidó Imaház), which is open to the public, you can see the remains of two synagogues. The first Jewish community was already settled around Dísz tér when, after the 13th-century Mongol invasions, Béla IV (1237–70) brought Jewish, German and Italian immigrants into the city. Subsequently Louis the Great (1342–82) drove the Jews out of Hungary – and then brought them back again. The new arrivals settled on the northern slopes of Castle Hill.
Opposite the synagogue was the house of the Jewish prefect, a post created by Matthias Corvinus to provide an intermediary between himself and the Jewish community.

BÉCSI KAPU TÉR On the west side of the square there are four houses ● *71* that reflect the principal architectural styles of Castle Hill. The HUNGARIAN NATIONAL ARCHIVES (Magyar Országos Levéltár), built in 1923 according to plans by Samu Pecz, also stands on this side of the square.

STATUE OF ARTEMIS
A statue of the Greek goddess stands near to the southwest corner of the Mary Magdelene Tower.

THE MARY MAGDELENE TOWER (Mária Magdolna Torony)
The Mária Magdolna Torony (on the corner of Országház utca and Kapisztrán tér) is all that remains of a Franciscan church built between the 13th and the 15th centuries. During the Middle Ages, the church was the one where the local Hungarian population worshipped.

THE BUDA CASTLE FUNICULAR
(Budavári Sikló)
Today this hillside lift is mainly used by tourists.

VÍZIVÁROS

CLARK ÁDÁM TÉR The district of VÍZIVÁROS (Watertown) occupies the narrow strip of land – which widens out to the north – between the Danube and Castle Hill. During Roman times a road ran through the area, along the river. In the Middle Ages it was a district of craftsmen, fishermen and traders. There are several vestiges of the Turkish occupation, in particular the Király Baths ▲ *208*. The major development of Víziváros took place in the 19th century, following the construction of Chain Bridge, the first permanent bridge across the Danube ● *35*, ▲ *183*. The construction of the CASTLE HILL TUNNEL (Alagút) ▲ *184* made Clark Ádám tér a major intersection for roads from the north, south, east and west of the city. The BUDA CASTLE FUNICULAR (Budavári Sikló) was originally brought into service in 1870 for the employees of the Royal Palace. It was then operated by a steam engine. The cabins were attached to the strong metal cable of the winch, with the ascending cabin acting as a counterweight for the descending cabin. Today the funicular is run by electricity.

FŐ UTCA The main street of Víziváros runs parallel to the river. In the 1860s to 1870s the district's first mansions were built backing onto it, with their façades overlooking the Bem rakpart (Bem Quay). The side next to the river is bordered by ancient chestnut trees, and since the late 19th century Fő utca has been a very attractive street. The most interesting buildings are found near Corvin tér, where the late-18th-century houses at nos. 3, 4 and 5 are on a par with those around the Royal Palace. A little further on, at no. 20 Fő utca, the KAPISZTORY HOUSE dates from the same period, although its was originally medieval. The patisserie opened here in 1850 – and still existing today – became famous for its furnishings, commissioned by the then owner Ede Friedl. The French Institute (left) can be seen from the corner of Pala utca.

THE FRENCH INSTITUTE (Francia Intézet) The first French Institute was founded in Pest in 1940. The impressive post-Modern building which opened in 1992, at no. 17 Fő utca, looks a little out of place amid the eclecticism ● *76* of the buildings of Víziváros. The Institute has a library and café, and organizes a wide range of cultural events and activities designed to promote Franco-Hungarian relations in a cordial and convivial atmosphere. In front of the building stands the STATUE OF FRIENDSHIP by Pierre Székely Péter. The CALVINIST CHURCH ▲ *185* on Szilágyi Dezső tér was built in neo-Gothic style in the late 19th century.

THE FRENCH INSTITUTE
The plate-glass building that houses the French Institute looks like a huge ship floating in the heart of the city.

Batthyany tér Fő utca runs northward to Batthyány tér (known in the 18th century as Upper Market Square), the historic center of Víziváros. Today it is an intersection for a number of public transport links: the no. 2 (red) line of the metro, the terminus for the HÉV suburban railway (its other terminus is at Szentendre ▲ *230*), and several bus routes. The magnificent Baroque St Anne's Church ★ (Szent Anna templom, below) ● *70*, ▲ *186* was begun in 1740, under the direction of Kristóf Hamon and Mátyás Nepauer. Inside is a group showing the Virgin Mary being presented in the Temple of Jerusalem, sculpted by Károly Bebó (1770–3); the pulpit (with the exception of the reliefs) is also the work of Bebó; and the Chapel of the Holy Sepulcher has an impressive wrought-iron screen that dates from the mid 18th century.

At nos. 3 and 4 there are two magnificent old houses overlooking the river. The Hikisch Ház (1795), at no. 3, is named after the master builder ▲ *213* who lived there; the four reliefs above the ground floor are allegories of the seasons. Nearby is the delightful asymmetrical building of the White Cross Inn (Fehér Kereszt Fogadó) ▲ *110*, formed by the amalgamation of two older houses in 1770. At the end of the 18th century this famous inn presented theatrical performances. Its distinguished guests included the Emperor Joseph II and (according to local legend) Casanova. The square is bounded to the north by a former Franciscan monastery (18th–19th century), later the hospital of the Baroque Church of the St Elizabeth Nuns (mid 18th century). In front of the former monastery is a bronze statue of Ferenc Kölcsey (1790–1838), who wrote the Hungarian national anthem (Himnusz). At nos. 82 and 89 Fő utca are the Király Baths ★ ▲ *208*, probably the most beautiful Turkish baths in Budapest.

Lajos Batthyány
(1806–49)
On March 17, 1848 the Emperor Ferdinand I made Count Lajos Batthyány head of the first independent Hungarian government. Batthyány was a member of the liberal opposition and supported the Austro-Hungarian Compromise. Realizing that it was doomed to failure, he resigned his post, though he remained a member of the Diet (Parliament). When Franz Joseph succeeded Ferdinand, Austrian troops invaded Hungary, and Batthyány was tried and executed. His successor, Lajos Kossuth ● *35*, was more fortunate and managed to escape.

View of the main pool

Construction of the Király Baths (Király Gyógyfürdő) ● *62* probably commenced when Arslan, the Turkish governor of Buda from May 1565 to August 1566, started to build a wall around the city. Completed by Arslan's successor, Pasha Mustapha Sokoli, they survived the Christian reconquest of Hungary. The modernization and extensions begun in the 18th century mainly involved extending the baths and left the original Turkish structure intact.

About the baths
After the Turkish withdrawal, Leopold I gave the baths to his personal physician, Frigyes Ferdinánd Illmer. They then changed hands several times before being sold to Leonhard Aigner, who undertook the first major structural alterations. In the 18th century they were variously known as the Balneum Civitatis Inferioris, Das Baad in der Wassersdadt, Spithal-Baad (after the nearby military hospital) and finally Königs Baad, after Fere[illegible] Kön[illegible] their owner from 1796 (König being transposed into Hungarian as Király). The neoclassical extensions were completed by Mihály König.

The main pool

The foot bath and steam baths

The neoclassical wing on Fő utca
In the late 19th century the level of Fő utca was raised. As a result, the first-floor balcony was lost. Major renovation work was carried out between 1954 and 1959, when the street level was lowered again.

The regularly spaced 'bottle bottoms' in the brickwork of the vaults create a soft, diffuse light.

The wing on Ganz utca

The interior of the neoclassical wing on Ganz utca forms a cloister around which the private baths are arranged. The square on the corner of Ganz utca and Fő utca was originally occupied by the right wing of the Baroque building, which was demolished to make room for this part of the building and its domes.

Oxidation from the copper covering the four domes seeps inside and contributes to the general tonality of the building.

1. Thermal spring **2.** Main pool (97°F) **3.** Small pool (79°F) **4.** Small pool (104°F) **5.** Steam bath (113°F) **6.** Steam bath (131°F) **7.** Steam bath (149°F) **8.** Showers **9.** Main courtyard **10.** Private bath cubicles **11.** Pasha's private bath (including a large bath for four people and a sauna) **12.** Resting room **13.** Massage room **14.** Fő utca **15.** Entrance **16.** Ganz utca

The cold showers

GIRL WITH PITCHER
(Lukács Baths)

FELHÉVIZ

Budapest's many thermal springs have made it a leading spa city. Traditionally its waters are divided into two groups: the springs that rise to the north of the city center, and those which rise along the geographical fault line of the deep ravine that forms the bed of the Danube in the Budapest region. The northern springs are referred to as the Felhévíz (Upper Thermal Springs). This part of the city was built in the vicinity of what is now the Buda end of Margaret Bridge ▲ *186*. In the 13th century the bath houses of the Order of the Knights Hospitallers stood here.

LUKACS BATHS The Lukács Gyógyfürdő baths complex, at nos. 25–9 Frankel Leó út, was built in the second half of the 1880s. People come from all over the world to take the waters here and, in particular, for the mud baths. Hence, on the cornerstones in the courtyard of the complex are a number of

'FATHER OF THE ROSES'
Gül Baba utca and the Gül Baba Türbe (at no. 14 Mecset utca).
If you walk northward along Frankel Leó út, cross Margit körút and turn left into Gül Baba utca, you will come to the türbe (shrine) and Rózsadomb (Rose Hill).

votive plaques ● *63*, in a variety of languages, donated by people cured of their ailments. The most elegant ones date from the late 19th and early 20th century. The Lukacs Baths were extended and modernized in 1984.

THE EMPEROR'S BATHS (Komjádi Császár uszoda)
Entirely rebuilt in 1840 in neoclassical style, the Komjádi Császár uszoda (at no. 8 Árpád fejedelem útja) quickly became a favorite venue for the city's well-to-do society. The new complex replaced the Baths of Bey Veli, built by the Turks in the 16th century. Ten springs feed the pools and treatment rooms with 3.3 million gallons of hard sulfurous water per day, at temperatures of between 63°F and 149°F. The waters are used to treat locomotive, nervous and muscular disorders, and as postoperative therapy for road-accident victims.

'It was hard to imagine, during these explorations, the skyline – the clusters of domes, minarets and moving crescents – that Charles of Lorraine and his companions would have seen at the time of the reconquest....'

Patrick Leigh Fermor

RÓZSADOMB ★

GÜL BABA TÜRBE Situated in the south of District II, Rózsadomb (Rose Hill) is a wealthy residential district. The villas of its quiet streets are partially hidden by handsome trees. Some of these villas – nos. 14 and 16 Cserje utca, and several in Törökvész utca – are striking examples of 1930s architecture ● *84*. The first villas began to appear on these slopes (previously used for growing grapes) after the opening of Margaret Bridge in the 1870s. In the middle of the hill, near the Felhévíz baths and overlooking the Danube, stands a small domed octagonal building that dates from the 16th century. This is the Gül Baba Türbe, the funerary monument of a dervish who is still venerated by Muslims as a saint (legend has it that he planted a rose garden here – Gül Baba means 'Father of the Roses' in Turkish). The shrine was converted into a Christian chapel in the 17th century, but later restored to its original form.

Both the Szent Antal templom (above), at no. 137 Pasaréti út, and Lakóház (below), at no. 97, were designed by Gyula Rimanóczy and date from 1934.

PASARÉT

Less than a hundred years ago the fastest-flowing mountain stream in the Buda region tumbled down this valley (once known as 'the Devil's Ditch'). In the early 20th century the hillside was built on, with a dense network of streets which make this residential district in effect an extension of Rózsadomb. Pasarét (meaning 'the Pasha's pasture') is like something out of *The Arabian Nights*, as visitors who walk along the long Bimbó út will discover. In terms of architectural history, the most interesting houses such as Villa Zenta are found around Házman utca and on Napraforgó utca ★ ● *84*. Nevertheless, age apart, it is often difficult to distinguish them from the more recent houses on either side of Bimbó út – which, along with Pasaréti út, has become the district's main thoroughfare – or from those on Kapy utca, Gábor Áron utca, Orsó utca, Lepke utca and Hermann Ottó út.

VAROSMAJOR

THE PARK The district of Városmajor is situated in the northeast of District XII. The site of the present STADT MAYEROFF PARK was a hay meadow before the Turkish occupation; and again afterward, when it was used to supply the troops garrisoned in Buda Castle. In the 1780s it became a public park. The layout was conceived by a man named József Talherr, who set out to plant it with three thousand species of plants and trees. The elms that have survived from his original planting serve as a reminder of his efforts to beautify the area. In the late 18th century Városmajor became the favorite 'retreat' of the inhabitants of Buda, many of whom built villas here. The houses on Városmajor utca, which runs along the western edge of the park, are the most representative of the new residential district built in this narrow valley leading through the hills. At no. 44 is the villa of the Hungarian artist Miklós Barabás ● *92*, famous for his Romantic portraits and historical scenes.

TWO CHURCHES, A THEATER AND A RAILWAY
The small Városmajor Parish Church (VAROSMAJORI PLÉBANIATEMPLOM) stands beside the park, at no. 5 Csaba utca. Designed in 1923 by Aladár Árkay, it combines traditional Transylvanian and Finnish Romantic styles. In 1936 Aladár Árkay and his son Bertalan built another, more modern, parish church (left) next to the earlier one. A little further on, to the northwest of the church, there is an OPEN-AIR THEATER that shows films and also stages musicals. The lower terminus of the COG RAILWAY (Fogaskerekű Vasút) is at no. 16 Szilágyi Erzsébet fasor, which runs along the northwest side of the park. The railway was opened to the public in 1874. Its upper terminus is on Széchenyi Hill (Széchenyi-hegy) ▲ *218*, just over 2 miles away and 1,030 feet higher up.

KRISZTINAVAROS

This district, which is a northern extension of Városmajor, used to feature on military maps as a hay meadow for the troops garrisoned in Buda Castle. It forms a narrow – and today intermittent – green belt that stretches between Pasarét and the Tabán; in other words, from the northeastern part of District XII to the center of District I.

VÉRMEZŐ In 1795 this park witnessed the execution of the leaders of the Hungarian Jacobins, who had been convicted of disseminating the revolutionary ideas of the Enlightenment and attempting to overthrow the monarchy. The site of the executions became known locally as Vérmező ('the field of blood'), and eventually the name was officially adopted. After World War Two it was converted into a park, and a memorial stone in memory of Ignác Martinovics and his colleagues was placed on the site of the scaffold. A little further on is the SOUTH STATION (Déli Pályaudvar), which is the terminus of the no. 2 (red) line of the *metró*.

KRISZTINA TÉR Built by Kristóf Hikisch, whose house can still be seen in Víziváros ▲ *207*, Krisztinaváros Parish Church, or OUR LADY OF THE SNOWS (Havas Boldogasszony), was inaugurated in 1797. It replaced a wooden chapel that had become famous because of a holy icon (see right). As a result, it received a visit from the Empress Maria Theresa, who authorized Buda town council to name this outlying district – in those days mainly farms and vineyards – Krisztinaváros ('Christine town') after one of her daughters. Like the original chapel, the restaurant known as THE GREEN TREE became a cult center – although in a somewhat different vein, since it glorified earthly rather than heavenly pleasures. The new restaurant built on the site has little in common with its predecessor, except for its name. On February 4, 1836 the marriage of Count István Széchenyi ● *35*, ▲ *137*, *185* and Crescentia Seilern was celebrated in the church. By then the village had already achieved the proportions of a town, and even boasted a number of mansions. The church was renovated in eclectic style ● *76* in the late 19th century, and extended in the 1930s to 1940s. As a result, its furnishings are a combination of Baroque, Empire and Modern styles.

KRISZTINA KÖRUT At no. 57 is ÁLDÁSY HOUSE (Áldásy Ház), a bourgeois residence of palatial dimensions. Built in the early 19th century, it has since been renovated and today houses the Hungarian theater research institute. At the southeast corner of Krisztina tér lies HAYDN PARK (formerly Horváth Gardens), which has provided the venue for a summer theater season for several decades. The DÉRYNÉ patisserie on the corner of Krisztina körút and Roham utca is named after Madam Déry, a famous Hungarian actress and well-known gourmet.

TABÁN

This district is situated on the slopes of Gellért Hill (Gellért-hegy ▲ *215*) and Sun Hill (Nap-hegy), which lie across the valley from Castle Hill. There is evidence to suggest that the site has been inhabited since prehistoric times. Later the Romans settled in the Tabán, and in the Middle Ages a town grew up around the chapel

KRISZTINAVÁROS IN THE MID 19TH CENTURY

In 1700 a chimney-sweep named Péter Pál Francin, who had survived the plague epidemic of 1649, made a pilgrimage to the town of Re, in northern Italy, in order to give thanks to the Virgin Mary. He returned with a copy of a painting of the Holy Virgin, and built a wooden chapel to house the icon. This chapel among the trees became the center of a small village. The painting brought back by Francin is now in Krisztinaváros Parish Church.

COUNT ISTVAN SZÉCHENYI
(1791–1860)
● *35*
▲ *137*, *185*

TABÁN PARISH CHURCH IN THE SNOW
Church of St Catherine of Alexandria.

A street in the Tabán, c. 1910.

that stood where the Parish Church is now. Until the fire of 1810 the winding streets that ran along this charming valley, and the houses – many of them ancient – that clung to the northern slopes of Gellért Hill, were reminiscent of the Viennese suburb of Grinzing. With a hundred or so establishments selling wine by the bottle, the old Tabán must have been a busy district, full of temptations. This may well explain the white cross that once stood in what was then the central square and is today an area of grassy hillside. According to reliable historical sources the cross was in fact an infamous pillory, to which those judged guilty by the local court were tied.

TABÁN PARISH CHURCH (Tabáni plébániatemplom)
The Tabán Parish Church, also called the Church of St Catherine of Alexandria (on Szarvas tér, near to the Danube) was built in 1728–36, in Baroque style, by the Carinthian master builder Keresztély Obergruber. Its façade was renovated in 1880–1. In a niche below the organ the church has a copy of *The Tabán Christ* (the original is in Budapest History Museum ▲ *192*), a fragment from the carved Romanesque tympanum of the 12th-century chapel that stood here. On the same wall is a painting of the fire that destroyed much of the Tabán district in 1810. The Tabán Parish Church is one of the district's few historical remains (which can be counted on the fingers of one hand). Two of the others are worthy of mention.

STAG HOUSE The triangular building at no. 1 Szarvas tér (Stag Square) was built in the early 1700s. Originally it housed a restaurant, THE GOLDEN STAG (Arany Szarvas vendéglő). The building, which today houses a restaurant of the same name, is still graced by the splendid inn sign – a relief (opposite) of a golden stag, harassed by hounds.

SEMMELWEIS MUSEUM OF MEDICAL HISTORY (Semmelweis Orvostörténeti Múzeum) The second historical building of interest, at nos. 1–3 Apród utca, is the small but impressive manor house where the famous physician Ignác Semmelweis (1818–65) was born and is buried.

He is known as the 'savior of mothers', since his discovery of the cause of puerperal fever saved many women from dying in childbirth. A commemorative plaque honors the memory of József Antall, Hungary's first Prime Minister (1990–3) of the post-Soviet era, who was the museum's director.
If you walk around the outside of the building, you will come to a delightful old-fashioned courtyard – a fine example of the district's former charm.

GELLÉRT HILL ★

Seen from Pest, Gellért-hegy – a dolomitic hill that rises to a height of 425 feet above the quays of the Danube – looks like a veritable mountain. Its rocky slopes fall steeply to the valley floor, leaving little room for the road that runs along the river. The half-hour climb to the top of Gellért Hill is a pleasant walk and offers some splendid views of the city through the trees.
THE CITADEL (Citadella) At the top of Gellért Hill stands a circular fortress known as the Citadel , built by the Austrian army after the 1848–9 uprising ● *29*, ▲ *119*. A few strategically placed cannons made this an ideal vantage point from which to keep an eye on the city and its population. In the late 19th century the army abandoned the fortress, and it became the property of the Hungarian government. Today the Citadel, which encircles the brow of the hill like a stone crown, provides a spectacular viewpoint ★, encompassing the whole of Budapest and its environs. There is a restaurant inside the walls.

SAINT GELLÉRT
(980–1046)
Gellért Hill (Gellért-hegy) was named after the Benedictine abbot from Venice who became tutor to Prince Imre, the son of King Stephen I. Saint Gellért (Gerard), who was appointed bishop of Csanád in 1030, was killed during a pagan rebellion. According to legend, he was hurled in a barrel or wheelbarrow from the top of the hill into the Danube below. The huge bronze statue of Saint Gellért on the east side of the hill is by Gyula Jankovits (1904).

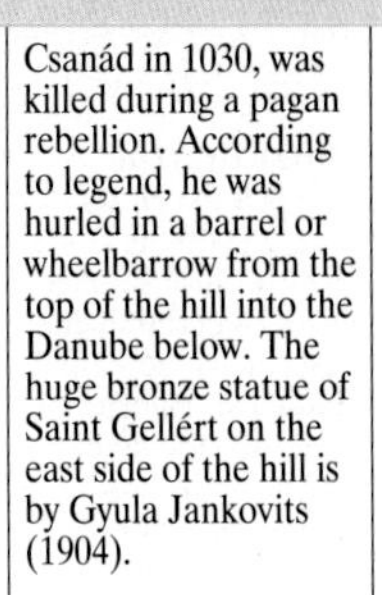

THE LIBERATION MONUMENT
This symbol of the city's liberation from the Germans can be seen from all over Budapest. Now that the Communist star on the plinth has been removed, it is possible that the

monument will be regarded as an allegory of political and economic liberalization.

LIBERATION MONUMENT (Szabadság-Szobor) Today the Liberation Monument by Zsigmond Kisfaludi Stróbl simply consists of a 45-foot-high bronze statue. It was erected in 1947 to commemorate the liberation of the city from the Germans by Soviet troops. Many people believe that it was originally commissioned as a memorial to the son of Miklós Horthy ▲ *174.* Originally a second statue, of a Soviet soldier armed with a machine gun, stood at the feet of the slender female figure holding the palm of victory. Liberty was well guarded!

THE CAVE CHURCH (Sziklakápolna) There are two ways of coming down the hill. If you climbed the steps that follow the castle walls, you might like to take the path that runs from the west wall of the Citadel (via Szirtes út, Kelenhegyi út, Rezeda utca and Verejték utca) to Szent Gellért tér, at the end of Freedom Bridge (Szabadság híd ▲ *180*). It takes you through the residential district built on the southwestern slopes of the hill in the early 20th century. Among the painters and other artists that lived in the typically Hungarian houses was Gyula Kann Kosztolányi, a master of Art Nouveau, who designed a house and studio for himself at nos. 12–14 Kelenhegyi út (now unfortunately extremely run down). On Verejték utca you can visit the CAVE CHURCH (Sziklakápolna) or CHAPEL IN THE ROCK (Sziklatemplom), which occupies a natural cave in the hillside, known for centuries as St Stephen's Cave. The church is currently used by the Pauline monks – the only Hungarian monastic order ▲ *181* – and is a major place of pilgrimage, rather like Lourdes. The Paulines have been celebrating mass in the church since 1929. The monastery, a small building with a number of towers, is built against the hillside and stands on the bank of the river.

HOTEL GELLÉRT
The palatial Hotel Gellért, with its slightly old-fashioned décor, is certainly the best-known hotel in Budapest. Since the 1910s the hotel and its baths have welcomed many of the crowned heads of Europe. The waters (115°F) of the thermal springs above which the hotel is built were already being used to cure a variety of ailments in the Middle Ages.

HOTEL GELLÉRT AND GELLÉRT BATHS (Gellért Szálló and Gellért Gyógyfürdő) ★
The square in front of the Cave Church offers a splendid view of the architectural complex of the Hotel Gellért ● *82,* probably the most glamorous showcase of this spa city, and Gellért Baths ● *63*, designed by Artúr Sebestyén, Ármin Hegedűs and Izidor Stark, and built between 1912 and 1918. Behind the hotel is an open-air 'wave pool'.

'Budapest had its orchards, the green breasts of the Buda Hills and the fields and forests beyond, stretching to the high mountains on the edge of the city.'

John Lukacs

GELLÉRT BATHS, INTERIOR AND DOMES
The decorative details of the medicinal baths, mud baths, 'champagne-bubble' pools, and other facilities are among the most beautiful examples of Art Nouveau architecture.

THE BUDA HILLS

The Buda Hills constitute a relatively wild area to the west of the city. It is not hard to imagine that its forests were once the preserve of deer, wild boars and other creatures from children's fairy tales. Today the hills are only half-an-hour from the city center, and are an ideal place for a nature walk or leisurely stroll.

SAS HILL (Sas-hegy) The bare summit of the dolomitic Sas Hill rises like a bastion to the west of Gellért Hill. The greater part of the hill consists of a 75-acre nature reserve – which can only be visited with an authorized guide, who will be able to point out the protected plant and animal species. Some of these species (such as the St Stephen's pink, the Buda centaury and the Pannonian lizard) are only found on Sas Hill. The vines that grew on the south-facing slopes from early medieval times to the end of the 19th century produced a red wine that was known and sold throughout the Austro-Hungarian Empire – until the vines were destroyed by a parasitic fungus (Peronosporales). In 1931 the school and institute of OUR LADY OF ZION (now part of Budapest's educational system) was built according to plans by Gustáv Reisch. This monumental building, the only one on the hill, has some remarkable architectural features.

THE PUBLIC CEMETERY (Farkasréti temető) Between Sas Hill and Freedom Hill (Szabadság-hegy) is a broad, flat saddle, which in 1894 was chosen as the site for Buda's Public Cemetery (Farkasréti temetö). It is the second largest cemetery in Budapest and serves as a national pantheon. This role was originally fulfilled by the Kerepesi Cemetery ▲ *171* – but when, under the Communist regime, religious burials were discouraged, those who wanted such a burial were interred here. The most famous are undoubtedly Zoltán Kodály and Béla Bartók ● *50*, ▲ *142*, *147*

ST IMRE OF THE CISTERCIANS
(nos. 23–5 Villányi út) The majestic neoclassical façade (1938) overlooks the Feneketlen tó (Feneketlen Lake, or 'Bottomless Lake'). Once part of the Tabán, this area now belongs to the Lágymányos district ▲ *174*, which was developed in the early 20th century.

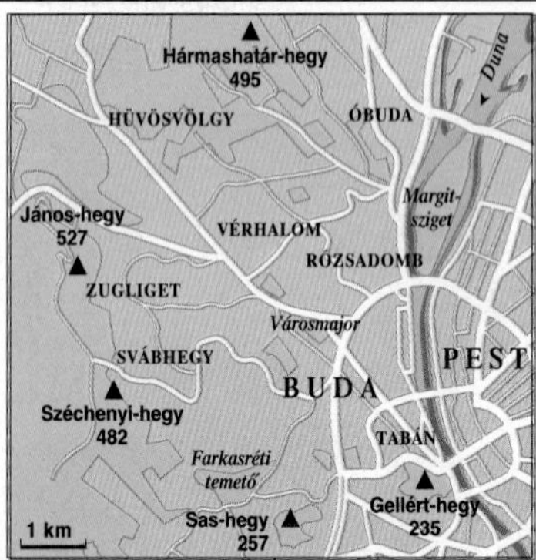

and Georg Solti ● *53*, whose tombs can be found in the artists' section of the cemetery. Many of the funeral monuments are in themselves works of art – Kodály's is signed by Pál Pátzay, and Bartók's was sculpted by Miklós Borsos.

SVAB HILL (Sváb-hegy) The hill can be reached by the Cog Railway, which leaves from Szilágyi Erzsébet fasor ▲ *212*. In the early 19th century Sváb Hill, was a favorite place for excursions and holidays among Budapesters. In the 1850s private villas and chalets began to be built on the hill, for use during the summer months. Gradually small communities were formed, with schools and local administration. The most charming area is probably the double valley basin that forms part of the hills of Zugliget, another residential and holiday district. Walkers will particularly appreciate the DISZNÓFŐ FORRÁS ('Pig's Head Spring'), which is said to have flowed across the hunting reserve of King Matthias Corvinus ● *32*. Today wild boars still inhabit the area – a fact that has not gone unnoticed by the local restaurant, which serves roast boar and boar stew.

HŰVÖSVÖLGY A little further north is Hűvösvölgy ('Cool Valley'), which lies at the end of another series of hills: the Hármashatár-hegy ('Three Frontiers Hill'). This has been a popular place to walk for almost two hundred years, but in the 19th century it also became a popular site for holiday villas. From here the CHILDREN'S RAILWAY (Gyermek Vasút) – formerly the Pioneers' Railway (Úttörők Vasút) – runs to SZÉCHENYI HILL (Széchenyi-hegy), its stations marking many of the places for walks and excursions in the Buda Hills. Another way to enjoy the hills is to take the chairlift (left) that runs from the corner of Zugliget utca and Csiga utca to the top of JÁNOS HILL (János-hegy). The nos. 190 and 21 buses also run up János Hill, offering an opportunity to drink in the beauty of the Buda Hills, especially from Istenhegyi út and Eötvös utca.

JANOS HILL CHAIRLIFT
Sváb Hill is in fact a series of hills, the highest of which is János Hill at 1,730 feet. The last half-mile is covered by chairlift (*libegő*). The stone ERZSÉBET LOOKOUT TOWER (Erzsébet kilátó), which offers one of the best views of the Buda Hills, was designed by Frigyes Schulek ▲ *203*. Built in 1910, it was named after the Empress Elizabeth ● *30*, ▲ *182*, *240*, who liked and helped the Hungarian people (something that was fairly rare among the Habsburgs).

Old photograph of the Cog Railway (right).

Óbuda

József Vinkó

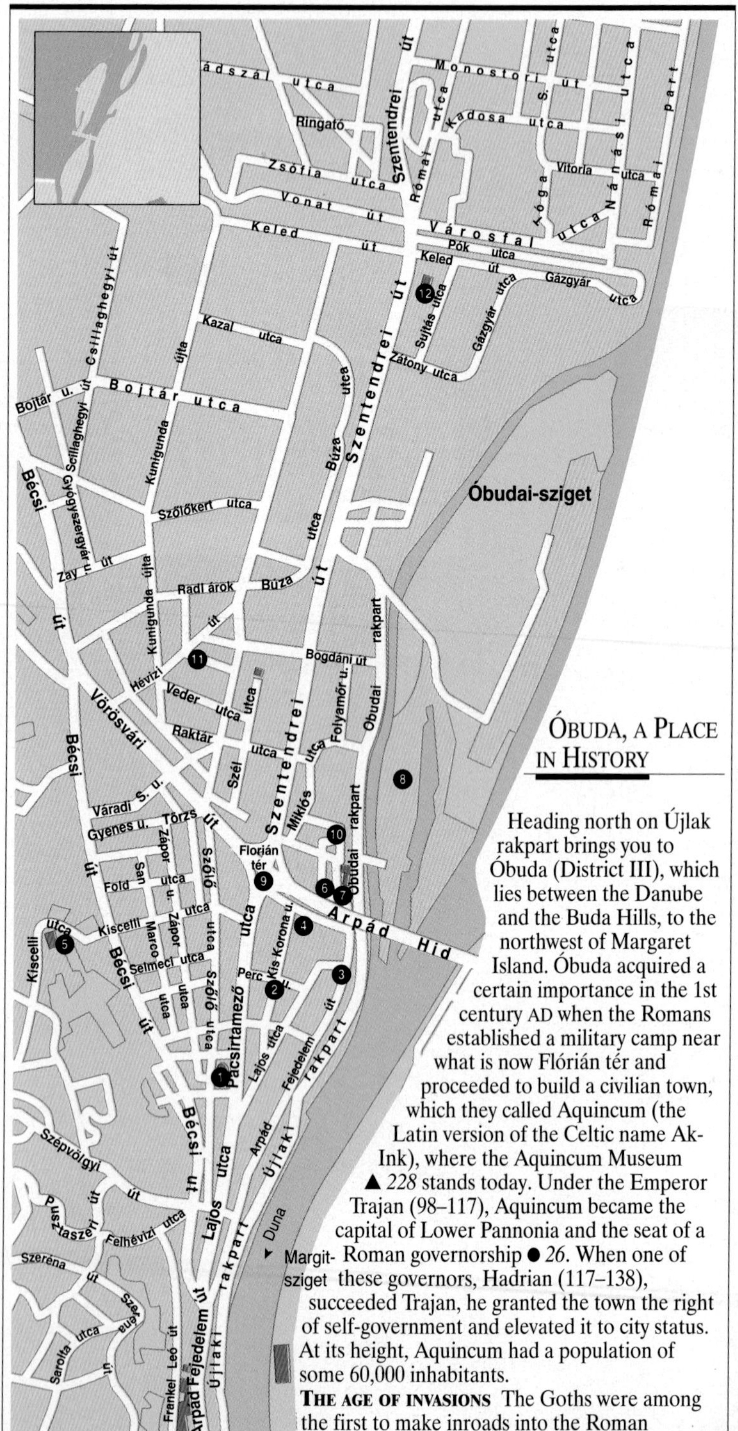

ÓBUDA, A PLACE IN HISTORY

Heading north on Újlak rakpart brings you to Óbuda (District III), which lies between the Danube and the Buda Hills, to the northwest of Margaret Island. Óbuda acquired a certain importance in the 1st century AD when the Romans established a military camp near what is now Flórián tér and proceeded to build a civilian town, which they called Aquincum (the Latin version of the Celtic name Ak-Ink), where the Aquincum Museum ▲ *228* stands today. Under the Emperor Trajan (98–117), Aquincum became the capital of Lower Pannonia and the seat of a Roman governorship ● *26*. When one of these governors, Hadrian (117–138), succeeded Trajan, he granted the town the right of self-government and elevated it to city status. At its height, Aquincum had a population of some 60,000 inhabitants.

THE AGE OF INVASIONS The Goths were among the first to make inroads into the Roman

1. Military Town Amphitheater
2. Cloister of the Poor Clares
3. Former Óbuda Synagogue
4. Óbuda Parish Church
5. Kiscell Museum
6. Zichy Mansion
7. Zsigmond-Kun Folk Art Collection
8. Hajógyár Island
9. Military Town Baths
10. Imre-Varga Gallery
11. Hercules Villa
12. Aquincum Museum

Empire, and are thought to have been responsible for the destruction of the Roman military camp (in 250 and 270) and the town of Aquincum (in 376). Then in the early 4th century the Huns conquered the Carpathian Basin. The military exploits of their leader Attila are recounted in the *Nibelungenlied* (Song of the Nibelungs), where he appears under the name Etzel. The suggestion that his castle, Etzelburg, was built on the ruins of the military camp of Aquincum is supported by the chronicle of the Emperor Frederick Barbarossa (12th century), which talks about 'the town of Attila'. After Attila's death, in 453, his vast empire disintegrated. The capture of the site by Hungarian tribes in the 9th century is described by Anonymus ● *38*, ▲ *161* in his *Gesta Hungarorum*, which tells how they crossed the Danube and reached the town of Attila under the leadership of Árpád ● *27*, ▲ *150*, *180*. The dynasty founded by Árpád renamed the town Buda (a common first name at that time). According to legend Árpád, was buried there.

The Middle Ages In 1241 a powerful Mongol army led by Batu Khan, the grandson of Genghis Khan, defeated the Hungarians at the Battle of Muhi. But because of the death of the Great Khan (Genghis' son, Ogedei), the conquering army withdrew, despite having reached the gates of Vienna. That same year Bishop Rogerius presided over the Easter festivities celebrated by Béla IV in the old town of Buda – which Rogerius described as the geographical and administrative center of the country, but which now lay in ruins. In view of its destruction, Béla IV decided to take up residence on a more secure hill. The new seat of the royal court became known as Buda, and (as recorded in an official document dating from 1261) the former seat of the royal residence was renamed Vetus Buda or Óbuda (Old Buda).

The modern age After the division of the country into three parts (1541), Buda and its environs (including Óbuda) were annexed by the Ottoman Empire for the next 145 years. Óbuda lost all administrative importance, and many Hungarian peasants fled the occupied territory. A captain from Esztergom, Miklós Pálffy, decided to help the Hungarians leave Óbuda (they are said to have escaped in a single night) and settle in Esztergom. For more than ten years

'On the evening of my arrival in the camp, the Danube was a vast roadway of red – then blue – ice, furrowed by currents that left ruts as deep as chariots tracks.'
Marguerite Yourcenar, *Memoirs of Hadrian*

Military Town Amphitheater
(2nd century AD)
The amphitheater (its ruins can be seen at the intersection of Pacsirtamező utca and Nagyszombat utca) had a seating capacity of fifteen thousand. The French writer Marguerite Yourcenar describes its atmosphere through the eyes of Hadrian: 'These Danubian legions functioned with the precision of a freshly oiled war machine; they had nothing in common with the sleepy garrisons I had encountered in Spain... Along these borders, where skillful strategy would have been, at least temporarily, crucial in winning the favor of certain nomadic chieftains, the soldier completely eclipsed the statesman...'
Memoirs of Hadrian

GYULA KRÚDY
(1878-1933)
An aristocrat and the epitome of a bohemian writer, Gyula Krúdy was a philanderer, gourmet and gambler, who loved to live it up. Yet his output was phenomenal – over 80 novels and 2,000 novellas, nostalgic tales full of vivid, and very Hungarian characters, which he wrote partly because he enjoyed writing, but also out of necessity as he was always short of money. He died at 55, exhausted and penniless.

Óbuda was uninhabited, until the liberation of Buda in 1686. In the 18th century Óbuda became a small Baroque town under the aegis of the rich Zichy family ▲ *226*. During the 19th century it enjoyed a certain level of industrial and commercial development, due in particular to the Óbuda shipyards (Óbudai Hajógyár) ▲ *226* and the Goldberger printed-textiles factory. With the urban development of the 1970s, Óbuda lost much of its old character and acquired a more modern appearance.

ÓBUDA THROUGH THE AGES

CLOISTER OF THE POOR CLARES The Cloister of the Poor Clares was built in Óbuda in the 14th century, at the intersection of what are today Kis Korona utca, Perc utca and Mókus utca, near the Franciscan monastery. An earlier cloister of the Poor Clares had been built at Nagyszombat in 1238. Some 215 feet long by 65 feet wide, the Óbuda cloister became the mother house of the order's convents throughout Hungary and a center of education for the daughters of the nobility. Medieval documents attest to its remarkable beauty. Its founder was Elizabeth of Poland, wife of Charles I (1308–42) and mother of Louis the Great of Anjou (1342–82). The charter of foundation (1344) records that she had the cloister, church, cemetery and storehouses built to ensure her own and her parents' salvation. Elizabeth also arranged that she would be buried here, though her ashes were eventually taken to Pozsony (now Bratislava), before the region was devastated by the Turks. The church and the load-bearing walls of the wings have been rebuilt, and can be seen at no. 3 Mókus utca (next to the primary school).

A VANISHED WORLD Old Óbuda, where Germans and Jews lived and worked together in an atmosphere of mutual respect, no longer exists. The houses of these thousands of industrious craftsmen have long since disappeared, as have their trade signs ▲ *224*. Mókus utca is one of the few streets that has preserved the atmosphere of this past age – including the pleasant Kéhli

THE NEOCLASSICAL FAÇADE OF THE FORMER ÓBUDA SYNAGOGUE
"The population of Old Buda had scarcely increased during the 19th century. There was a big shipyard, the city's oldest synagogue (although there were not many Jews in Óbuda around 1900) and a number of inexpensive taverns, several of which were renowned for their Danube fish dishes."
John Lukacs, *Budapest 1900*

'...beneath the plane trees of the baths, in the porch of the house opposite, by night in small stations, in a boat on the Danube, at Normafa and beneath the kiosks of Buda – he was still waiting for a woman...'

Gyula Krúdy

Porch of the Kiscell Museum
Kiscelli utca runs steeply up to the museum from Bécsi út. The museum ★ ▲ *224* occupies a former Trinitarian monastery (the church was completed in 1760, the cloister in 1784). The top of Kiscell Hill (Kiscelli-hegy) offers a view of the modern district – a concrete jungle of public housing units, built from the 1960s onward.

restaurant, where Gyula Krúdy (*see left*) used to have lunch. Krúdy's novels are imbued with the atmosphere, scents and colors of old Óbuda, and populated by the beautiful women who formed part of its intrinsic charm.

The former Óbuda Synagogue In the 18th century a Jewish community settled in Óbuda. This settlement was encouraged by the Zichy counts, since the community's commercial activity relaunched the city's trade, while the taxes collected greatly increased their income. The former Óbuda Synagogue (which was predated by other synagogues) stands at no. 163 Lajos utca. The large neoclassical building was built in the early 1820s by the architect András Landherer. After World War Two the diminished Jewish Community could not afford to rebuild the synagogue and it was taken over by the national-heritage

Óbuda Parish Church
The church was built in Baroque style (1744–9) by János György Paur. The carved Rococo pulpit and the statues of Saint Flórián and Saint John of Nepomuk (1753–4) that stand on the square in front of the church are the work of Károly Bebó. On the plinths of the statues are the coats of arms of Count Miklós Zichy ▲ *226* and his wife.

▲ THE KISCELL MUSEUM (Kiscelli Múzeum)

The Kiscelli Múzeum houses the modern-history department of Budapest History Museum, and a museum of modern art. The church and cloister were originally occupied by the Trinitarian Order, then used as barracks and, later, as a military hospital. In 1912 Miksa Schmidt, an antique dealer and maker of Viennese furniture, bought the monastery buildings which he bequeathed to the city in 1935. They were converted into a museum, in accordance with his wishes.

AN UNUSUAL BALLOT BOX (19th century)
This unusual object relates to the introduction, in 1765, of secret ballots for the election of members of the municipal council. Balls were placed in the brass dishes, and the results posted on plaques suspended between the columns.

INSTALLATION BY THE ARTIST RÓBERT SWIERKIEWITS (1994)

STATUES FROM THE HOLY TRINITY COLUMN
The museum has many relics from the past that bring the history of Buda and Pest to life. The Baroque statues of the Holy Trinity Column ● *71*, ▲ *202*, erected during an outbreak of plague in the city, are particularly intriguing.

SIGN OF A LOCKSMITH AND WROUGHT-IRON CRAFTSMAN
The museum's splendid collection of craftsmen's signs gives an idea of what a 19th-century street would have looked like when metal signs replaced painted wooden boards.

The hill on which the museum stands was named after a copy of the statue of the Virgin of Mariazell (in Austria) placed there in the 18th century. 'Klein Mariazell' became Kiscell. The cells of the former cloister have been converted into small exhibition rooms re-creating 18th-century interiors. The furniture of the Steindl studio is a marvelous example of the Hungarian Biedermeier style.

MODERN AND CONTEMPORARY ART
Budapest's Municipal Art Gallery was founded in 1933. Twenty years later, in 1953, its collections were transferred to the recently opened Hungarian National Gallery ▲ *194*, except for the paintings that remained the property of the municipality. These are now housed in the Kiscell Museum. In the 1960s a collection of contemporary art was opened, and in 1988 the former church hosted its first exhibition. Today it is a prime venue for Hungarian and international contemporary art. It is also an ideal venue for concerts and other performances. Reproduced here are *Encounter in a Cemetery* (above) by István Farkas; *At the Theater* (far left) by Pál C. Molnár; and *Girl Icon* (left) by Lajos Vajda ▲ *233*.

FŐ TÉR
The Zichy Mansion (above left) is at no. 1 Fő tér, and the town hall of District III (above right) at no. 3.

department. Since 1986 it has been used as television studios. The tympanum above the portico is still crowned by the twin tablets of the Ten Commandments.

ZICHY MANSION The beautiful and imposing Zichy Mansion stands at no. 1 Fő tér. It was built for Miklós Zichy between 1746 and 1757 in a Rococo style derived from German Baroque ● *70* and was designed by a master stone mason from Buda, Henrik János Jäger. It was carefully restored after being damaged in World War Two and has a particularly beautiful carved staircase. Today the mansion and its outbuildings house four museums: the PINCE GALLERY, the KASSÁK MEMORIAL MUSEUM (devoted to the work of Lajos Kassák, a key figure in Hungarian Constructivism but also a writer, a poet, and activist), the ÓBUDA LOCAL-HISTORY MUSEUM and the VASARELY MUSEUM.

ZSIGMOND KUN FOLK ART COLLECTION This collection is housed on the top floor of an 18th-century apartment block, opposite the Zichy Mansion, on Fő tér. In 1976 Zsigmond Kun and his wife donated their collection to District III. This small museum of folk art has collections of Hungarian ceramics, textiles, sculpture and furniture.

ÓBUDA ISLAND (Óbudai-sziget) The Óbuda shipyards were developed at the southern end of Óbuda Island, from 1834 onward, on the narrow branch of the Danube. At the time they were the country's most important industrial complex. The huge shipyard founded around 1867 by an Austrian steam-navigation company covered an area of some 30 acres. Most of its installations were built on the Hajógyár peninsula (Hajógyári-sziget), to the west of the winter port, which is joined to Óbuda Island by a narrow strip of land. Today, the island is a venue for rock concerts. Each summer, the Sziget festival, known as Europe's 'Woodstock', attracts thousands of visitors.

VICTOR VASARELY
Victor Vasarely was born Győző Vásárhelyi, in Pécs, in 1908. He served his apprenticeship in Budapest, where he was influenced by the Bauhaus tradition, and in 1931 went to live and work in Paris. He developed his artistic concepts and philosophy through a form of geometric abstraction that became known as kinetic art or Op Art. He donated hundreds of his works to Hungary.

MILITARY TOWN BATHS The remains of the Thermae Majores (Military Town Baths) can be seen in the ROMAN BATHS MUSEUM (Fürdö Múzeum), located in the Flórián tér underpass. They were discovered in 1778 by workmen digging a lime pit. From then on they were excavated on a regular basis by István Schönvisner, professor of Latin at Pest University. The news of this archeological discovery caused a sensation in Vienna, and the Empress Maria Theresa financed the excavations. In 1849 workmen laying pipes beneath Szentendrei út discovered a Roman inscription which

'Of all the districts in Budapest, [Óbuda] was the most provincial, to the point that you felt you were in an olden-day village on the Danube, with its single-story houses, winding streets and rural-Baroque churches.'

John Lukacs

confirmed Schönvisner's theory that the baths had been built for the permanent garrison (Legio II Adjutrix) of Aquincum. The excavations were finally completed in 1984. It has now been established that, like many Roman baths of this period, the Flórián tér complex had changing rooms, a tepid bath, a hot bath, a steam bath, a cold bath, a cool room and an open-air swimming pool. The water for the baths came from two main sources: aqueducts carried water from the thermal springs (still in use today) of Római Fürdő, while a system of pipes running beneath the Vörösvári Valley brought water from the hills to the west of the military town.
The soldiers exercised in a huge gymnasium (260 feet by 100 feet). The nymphaeum, a large central room surrounded by altars dedicated to the health-giving powers of the nymphs, probably served as a place for meetings and public business.

IMRE VARGA GALLERY (Varga Imre Gyűteménye) The Varga Imre Gyűteménye, at no. 7 Laktanya utca, has a permanent exhibition of the works of the sculptor Imre Varga. His public commissions (depicting, among others, Miklós Radnóti, Zoltán Kodály, Béla Bartók, Mihály Károlyi, Attila József and Franz Liszt) can be seen throughout Hungary. His Prometheus in Chains – a piece of ruthless realism – hit the headlines in 1965. This contemporary visual artist (born in 1923) is one of the greatest and most prolific Hungarian sculptors of the 20th century.

HERCULES VILLA This Roman villa (2nd–3rd century AD) is situated at nos. 19–21 Meggyfa utca, on the northern edge of the Roman military town. Its name comes from the scenes depicted on its mosaic floors. These show Hercules shooting an arrow at the centaur Nessus, who is carrying off Deianeira ● *26*; and Hercules drinking with the satyrs. In the garden of the villa are sarcophagi (3rd–4th century AD), the villa's baths, the watchman's quarters and the underfloor central heating system. More mosaics can be seen in the nearby buildings erected in the 1960s to protect the remains of the paving.

KASSAK MEMORIAL MUSEUM
(no. 1 Fö tér)
The museum presents the very varied artistic and literary works of Lajos Kassák (1916–67).

THE AQUINCUM MUSEUM ▲ *228*
The museum occupies a building (a copy of a Greek temple) erected in 1894 on the site of Roman Aquincum, which was systematically excavated in the late 19th century. It is surrounded by the excavated remains of the Roman civilian town.

▲ The Aquincum Museum (Aquincumi Múzeum)

Hydra, (water organ).

The five rooms of the Aquincumi Múzeum house the religious, functional and decorative objects discovered during the excavation of the Roman civilian town. A sculpture of Mithras ● *26* killing the life-giving cosmic bull attests to the importance of his cult in Aquincum. The cult of this Persian god of light spread to the ports and garrisons of the Western Roman Empire, in particular along the banks of the Danube and Rhine, during the 2nd century AD.

Detail from a fresco.

Nemesis (2nd century AD) The Greek goddess Nemesis was the personification of divine vengeance. She is depicted here with a torch in her right hand and a globe in her left. At her side is a griffin, resting one of its paws on a wheel.

An unusual musical instrument

In 1930 a portable water organ (hydra) was discovered among the ruins of a building in the civilian town. An inscription on a small bronze plaque revealed that Gaius Julius Viatorinus presented this organ to the firefighters of Aquincum in 228. Visitors to the museum can see a working reconstruction (top of page).

Below: marble sculptural group.

AROUND BUDAPEST

Miklós Mátyássy

Between Esztergom and Budapest the Danube makes a sharp turn and flows between the Visegrád and Pilis Hills on the right bank and the Cserhát and Börzsöny Hills on the left, before entering the Great Plain. The Danube Bend (Dunakanyar) ■ *18*, ▲ *118*, is one of the most beautiful and most visited regions in Hungary. Traversed by the Romans, Magyars, Turks, Serbs, Germans and Slovaks, it is particularly rich in history. The right bank is notable for the former royal seats of Esztergom ▲ *238* and Visegrád ▲ *235* and the 'Mediterranean' town of Szentendre, while the left bank has a series of picturesque villages, nestling at the foot of the Börzsöny Hills, and the Baroque episcopal town of Vác ▲ *234*. The primarily agricultural Szentendre Island is renowned for its strawberries.

Right: detail of a Roman tombstone (Lapidarium, Szentendre).

THE DANUBE BEND, FAMED FOR ITS NATURAL BEAUTY
The caves, gorges and broad-leaved forests make this mountainous section of the Danube one of the most visited beauty spots in Hungary. The region is also rich in game (wild boar, deer) and was one of the favorite hunting grounds of the kings of Hungary.

SZENTENDRE

In contrast to Vác, which is steeped in Catholic tradition, Szentendre is characterized by its simplicity, intimacy and harmony. Unfortunately the hordes of tourists, cheap restaurants and stores selling souvenirs and knickknacks mar the overall effect. But you only have to wander away from the main square and stop in front of a window grille, doorway or flight of steps, or pause to enjoy a hilltop view of tiled roofs with the Danube and Szentendre Island in the background, to understand what attracted so many artists to the town.

HISTORY Illyrians, Celts, Romans (their camp was called Ulcisia Castra), Huns, Lombards and then the Magyars inhabited this site, which from 1146 was known as Sanct Andreas. The town's present-day appearance, so reminiscent of Mediterranean Balkan towns, is due to southern

> ‘In the late afternoon, opposite the end of the island where I had spent the day, I reached Szentendre, a small rural Baroque town, with its pathways, paved streets, tiled roofs and onion-shaped domes.’
>
> Patrick Leigh Fermor

Slavonic influences. In 1690 some 40,000 Serbs, under the leadership of their patriarch Arzenje Cernojevic, fled from the Turks and sought refuge in Hungary. Around 6,000 of these refugees settled in Szentendre, which had become depopulated during the Turkish occupation. In the space of only a few decades the town was transformed into a thriving center of Serbian culture, with seven Orthodox churches, a bishop’s palace, a teachers’ training college and a high school. This period of prosperity came to an end in the 19th century, when the town suffered a series of fires, floods and epidemics, plus an outbreak of phylloxera, which devastated the town’s traditional red-wine production.

FŐ TÉR. In the center of the main square (Fő tér) is a commemorative cross erected by the merchants’ guild. The square has two museums and an art gallery, and a number of other interesting buildings. The Nikolics House (Nikolics Ház), built in 1800, is richly decorated in copf style (or Zopfstil), a German and Central-European variation of Rococo characterized by the use of strapwork moldings. Other Rococo buildings include the former Korona Restaurant (1770), adorned with stucco vine branches, and the Blagoveštenska Church ▲ *232* or Church of the Annunciation (on the corner of Görög utca, which leads down to the quayside). Built in 1752 by the Greek merchants of Szentendre, who lived on Görög utca (Greek Street), it was designed by András Mayerhoffer ● *70*, ▲ *240*. Outside, on one of the side walls, are the tombstone of a Greek merchant and a fresco depicting Saint Helen and Saint Constantine (the Roman emperor Constantine the Great). The icons of the richly carved Rococo iconostasis, dedicated to the Annunciation, are the work of the artist Mihály Zsivkovics. On the corner of Bogdányi utca (which takes you to Preobraženska Church) stands the delightfully named Nostalgia House, a Baroque building now devoted to tourism. From 1812 to 1816 the copf-style ▲ *231* building at no. 6 Fő tér was a Serbian teachers’ training college. Today it houses the Ferenczy

The narrow streets of Szentendre, its hills, houses, churches and Orthodox crosses give the feeling of a town on a human scale.

SZENTENDRE AND THE ARTS

In the late 19th century artists helped to put Szentendre (which now has sixteen museums) back on the map. To such an extent that by 1928 the local Society of Painters was able to attract well-known Post-Impressionist and Constructivist artists. A few years later Lajos Vajda founded the Szentendre School, which became increasingly oriented toward Surrealist and avant-garde art. The town’s first ‘artists’ colony’ was built in the 1930s, and a second colony was established in the 1970s. In the early 1980s a new generation of Hungarian avant-garde artists used to meet in the Vajda Lajos Stúdió.

Sign of the Kovács Margit Múzeum.

ARCHITECTURE
Visitors to Szentendre tend to be impressed not so much by individual monuments (although some are remarkable in their own right) as by the overall impression of the town. Its Baroque and Rococo mansions and churches, and its simple houses have a balance and harmony reminiscent of certain Italian towns.

CROSS OF THE MERCHANTS' GUILD AND BLAGOVESTENSKA CHURCH
The Rococo cross, decorated with icons, was erected in 1763 by Serbian merchants to thank God for protecting the town against the plague.

Múzeum. Károly Ferenczy (1862–1917), the founding father of modern Hungarian painting and the Nagybánya colony of Impressionists, lived and worked in Szentendre during the early part of his career. The museum offers an excellent overview of Ferenczy's own paintings, together with the work of his wife, Olga Fialka, and their twin son and daughter – Béni, a sculptor, and Noémi, a tapestry designer – who were born in Szentendre in 1890.

MARGIT KOVÁCS MUSEUM The seemingly naïve colored figurines and reliefs for which the controversial sculptor and ceramist Margit Kovács (1902–77) is known were inspired by Romanesque and Hungarian folk art. A delightful collection of her work, donated to the town by the artist, is housed in an early-18th-century Baroque building (no. 1 Vastagh György utca, near Fő tér) that has at various times served as salt warehouse, post office, parish office and merchant's premises.

ČIPROVAČKA CHURCH Built between 1750 and 1794 by refugees from Čiprovač (a town in the Srem region of Eastern Slavonia), this church is the largest in Szentendre. It is dedicated to Saint Peter and Saint Paul and has been a Roman Catholic church since 1918.

BARCSAY MUSEUM The artist Jenö Barcsay (1900–88), who developed a highly individual Constructivist style, taught at the Academy of Fine Arts in Budapest. He donated the entire

'Szentendre is a sort of Danubian Montmartre, where the colors of the houses and the paintings exhibited in the streets blend with the colors of the river, and where those who have time to linger are enveloped by a light-hearted, fluid gaiety...'

Claudio Magris

contents of his studio (paintings, mosaics and various projects for mural compositions in Szentendre) to the town, where he had lived and worked since 1929. The collection is housed in what was originally two buildings, one Baroque and the other neoclassical.

TOWN HALL Although its façade had become the symbol of Szentendre, it was renovated in its present neo-Baroque style in 1929. The rest of the building dates from the 18th century.

OPOVAČKA CHURCH The church was built by refugees from Opovac in 1746, in massively proportioned Baroque style. It was taken over by the Calvinists in 1913, and its iconostasis transferred to Hercegszántó in southern Hungary.

CATHOLIC PARISH CHURCH This church was built in the early 14th century, using the walls of an earlier 13th century church, and renovated in the 15th and 18th centuries. Its restoration in the 1950s revealed many Romanesque and Gothic elements, including a sundial on top of a buttress. The frescos in the choir date from the 1930s.

BÉLA CZOBEL MUSEUM Béla Czóbel (1883–1976) was a Hungarian Fauvist and representative of the Paris School. From 1945 until his death, he was president of the Szentendre Society of Painters. The museum (at no. 1 Templom tér) presents his own characteristically colorful work and that of his wife, Mária Mondok (1896–1971).

POŽEREVAČKA CHURCH Built by refugees from Pozerevac in 1759, this church is dedicated to the Archangel Michael. It stands on the site of an earlier wooden church (1690), from which it has retained the iconostasis (1740). The main entrance is of later construction, as is the church tower (1794).

LAJOS VAJDA MUSEUM A leading 20th-century Hungarian artist and a key figure in the second generation of Hungarian avant-garde art, Lajos Vajda (1908–41) ▲ *225, 231* spent much of his short life in the town. His drawings, collages and paintings are imbued with motifs both from Szentendre and from the rural architecture of the surrounding area – which he studied methodically, together with his friend and colleague Dezső Korniss, with a view to creating a new Central-European art form. Several works by Korniss can be seen at the museum.

RAB RABY TÉR RÁBY HÁZ (*see above right*) is situated in the old Catholic Dalmatian district and is one of a pair of houses that used to belong to a local winegrower. The date of their construction (1768) can be seen above the Baroque entrance, where the two façades meet.

CHURCH OF THE TRANSFIGURATION (Preobraženska Church) This church (at no. 40 Bogdányi út) was built between 1741 and 1746 by Serbian tanners from Bosnia. The decorative elements of the façade were added later. The raised iconostasis, with its gilt Corinthian columns, is reminiscent of Russian and Ukrainian iconostases and was the first of its kind in Hungary. On a hill not far from the church stands the BOSNIAN TANNERS' CROSS, erected by the tanners' guild in the

LITERARY HISTORY
The Ráby House is named after Mátyás Ráby, the steward of Joseph II who denounced the abuses and fraudulent practices of the town's municipal employees. He was thrown into prison and later exiled. Mátyás Ráby became the hero of Mór Jókai's novel *Rab Ráby.*

COMMEMORATIVE CROSSES
These crosses are an important feature of Szentendre. The Tsar Lázár Cross stands on the Danube embankment. In 1690 the remains of this Serbian prince, executed after the Battle of Kosovo (1389), were temporarily housed in a church in Szentendre before being taken back to Serbia. The Serbs erected a Corinthian column surmounted by a wrought-iron cross on the site of the church.

INTERIOR OF THE BELGRADE CHURCH
The icons of the richly carved iconostasis were painted by Vazul Osztojics, an artist from Újvidék (now Novi Sad, in Serbia).

CHURCHES AND CROSSES
When the Serbs arrived in Szentendre they settled in seven districts, according to their region of origin. Each community built its own wooden church, facing east in accordance with Orthodox tradition. In the 18th century these wooden churches were replaced by stone buildings in Baroque or Rococo style. The Catholic Dalmatians shared Szentendre's parish church with the Hungarians and Germans. As the Serb population gradually left the town during the 19th century, Catholics and Protestants took over some of the Serbian Orthodox churches.

18th century, in a peaceful little square that offers a splendid view of the Danube.

THE IMRE ÁMOS AND MARGIT ANNA MUSEUM The Surrealist painter Imre Ámos (1907–44) died a victim of hard labor in a prison camp. His was a dreamlike, mystical world in which even the simplest of objects assumed symbolic meaning, the world of a Humanist at odds with his age. His wife – Margit Anna (1913–77), cofounder of the postwar European School, which brought together the proponents of abstract and Surrealist art – derived inspiration for her work from primitive art.

THE SERBIAN ORTHODOX CATHEDRAL On entering the gardens of the USPENIJE CHURCH (CHURCH OF THE ASSUMPTION), surrounded by trees and bounded by tombstones, you are immediately aware of a sense of calm, intimacy and simplicity. This Serbian Orthodox Cathedral, built in Rococo style in 1756–64, is also known as the BELGRADE CHURCH, since it was erected by the descendants of refugees from Belgrade. The SERBIAN ORTHODOX MUSEUM situated in the grounds, near the bishop's palace, houses some outstanding treasures of Serbian and Hungarian church art.

VAC

The geographical situation of Vác (below) was ideally suited to human settlement and was inhabited from the end of the Bronze Age. During the Middle Ages the town, whose name appears in official records for the first time in 1075, enjoyed a period of prosperity. It was one of the ten sees founded by Stephen I ● *27*, ▲ *239*, and during the reign of Matthias Corvinus ● *32* Bishop Miklós Báthory transformed it into a cultural center. Between 1544 and 1686 Vác changed hands several times, though it was mostly under Ottoman control, and entered a period of decline. In the 18th century the extensive building program carried out by bishops Althan, Esterházy and, in particular, Kristóf Migazzi gave the town its

‘We heard as much German as Hungarian on the awakening quayside of Visegrád; it was spoken by the Swabians that Géza had told me about.’

Patrick Leigh Fermor

present blend of late-Baroque and neoclassical architecture.

RELIGIOUS BUILDINGS Between 1761 and 1777 the cathedral was built on what is now Konstantin tér (Constantine Square) under the aegis of Bishop Migazzi. The cathedral’s French architect, Isidore Canevale, who resided in Vienna, was inspired by the work of Jacques-Germain Soufflot and Giovanni Nicolo Servandoni, the architects of the Church of St-Sulpice in Paris. The frescos of the dome and high altar were the work of Franz Anton Maulbertsch, one of the most brilliant Baroque fresco painters in Central Europe. The other important religious buildings centered around the cathedral are the BISHOP’S PALACE; the SEMINARY; the PIARIST CHURCH, SCHOOL AND MONASTERY; and the former FRANCISCAN CHURCH (on Géza Király tér). The DOMINICAN CHURCH (which has a Rococo interior), the former SERBIAN ORTHODOX CHURCH, the PROVOST’S PALACE, the TOWN HALL and the INSTITUTE FOR THE DEAF AND DUMB constitute another group of Baroque buildings, around Március 15 tér.

TRIUMPHAL ARCH This structure, the only one of its kind in Hungary, was the work of Isidore Canevale (the architect of the cathedral). Bishop Migazzi had it erected in 1764, on the occasion of a visit by the Empress Maria Theresa. Since 1855 the THERESIANUM has been a prison; originally it was an academy for young aristocrats, founded by the empress. Among the many political prisoners incarcerated within its walls after the 1956 uprising ● *36* were the historian István Bibó and Árpád Göncz, the former President of Hungary.

VISEGRÁD

Visegrád is one of the jewels of the Danube Bend. The abundant natural resources of this region rich in water and forests have been exploited since the Stone Age. They were strategically exploited by the Romans who founded the town of Pone Navata, which the Slavs renamed Vise Grad (‘high fortress’). The early Hungarian kings built a fortress, church and monastery here. Visegrád enjoyed two golden ages: the first during the reign (1308–42) of Charles Robert of Anjou (Charles I) ● *28*, when Visegrád was the capital of the kingdom of Hungary, and the second during the reign of Matthias Corvinus (1458–90) ● *32*.

CHURCH OF ST ANDREW (Izbég)
Once a self-contained Serbian village, Izbég is now part of Szentendre.
The CHURCH OF ST ANDREW (Szent András templom), built by the Serbs in 1738, has been a Roman Catholic church since 1948. The double commemorative cross of the Serbian calvary is mounted on a Doric column and surrounded by wrought ironwork.

SKANZEN OR OPEN-AIR VILLAGE MUSEUM (Szabadtéri Néprajzi Múzeum)
Founded in 1967, this museum presents an overview of the vernacular architectural of ten Hungarian regions. Extending over nearly 115 acres, it will comprise more than 300 re-erected buildings: houses, workshops, mills, churches and other buildings associated with Hungarian village life.

THE RUINED PALACE OF KING MATTHIAS
The capture of Visegrád by the Turks marked the beginning of the decline of the palace. It was completely destroyed in the 18th century, when Serbian immigrants used it as a 'quarry' to build their houses. In 1934 János Schulek discovered the remains of the palace. About a third of it has now been excavated.

SOLOMON'S TOWER Built around 1250 in late-Gothic style, this tower was originally the keep of the lower fortress. The King Solomon after whom the tower is named never saw it: he was in fact imprisoned from 1081 to 1083 in another tower in Visegrád by King László I. The tower did, however, have a royal occupant: Vlad Tepes (Vlad the Impaler, better known as Count Dracula), Prince of Wallachia, who was imprisoned there until l476. Apart from its defensive functions, the tower was used to accommodate the royal court, the guests and, of course, the royal guard. The tower has been restored and extended, and now houses the KING MATTHIAS MUSEUM (Mátyás Múzeum). As well as tracing the history of the reconstruction work at Visegrád, the museum includes such items as a fountain from the Angevin period and marbles from the reign of King Matthias ● *32* – among them the Hercules Fountain (on which the demigod is depicted fighting the Hydra) and the Visegrád Madonna.

THE HISTORY OF THE ROYAL PALACE In 1316 Charles Robert of Anjou ● *28*, ▲ *235* took up residence in Visegrád. He built a royal palace, one of the most beautiful of its time, between the lower fortress and the town. In 1335 the palace hosted the Visegrád Congress, when the kings of Hungary, Bohemia and Poland and the leaders of the Teutonic Order agreed to ensure the free passage of Hungarian merchandise to the west and north. Under Louis the Great of Anjou (1342–82) the edifice became a tripartite structure – with the Royal Palace to the north, the queen's palace to the south, and the chapel in between. Sigismund of Luxembourg (1387–1437) extended the complex toward the Danube. Further construction was carried out between 1474 and 1486, during the reign of Matthias Corvinus. It was begun by Saxon craftsmen from Transylvania in late-Gothic style, and completed in Renaissance style under the direction of the Italian architect Chimenti Camicia.

Detail of the Lion Fountain According to historical records, during royal receptions the two lion's-head gargoyles spewed forth wine (one red, the other white), instead of water.

The palace today The palace was built on several levels, on a series of terraces. The first level is occupied by the main courtyard and steps. On the second are the remains of a Gothic Ambulatory surrounding the courtyard (where the red-marble Hercules Fountain, by the Italian sculptor Tommaso Fiamberti, was discovered). On the third level are the remains of the Royal Apartments, of which a balustrade and balcony can still be seen. Also on this level was the Chapel, to which King Matthias added a sculpted ceiling, alabaster altars and, above the entrance, the relief known as the Visegrád Madonna. The royal baths and the king's private garden – with its Lion Fountain, a masterpiece of Hungarian Renaissance sculpture – occupy the fourth level.

The Citadel (Fellegvár) The Citadel was built between 1245 and 1255 by Maria Lascaris, wife of Béla IV, to protect nuns and orphans in the event of renewed Mongol attacks. Charles Robert of Anjou lived there from 1323 until the completion of his palace in 1330, and constructed a number of buildings within the walls. It subsequently became a royal treasury, where the Hungarian royal insignia and, under Louis the Great, the Polish crown were housed. In 1440 Elizabeth of Luxembourg (daughter of King Sigismund) had her governess steal the Hungarian crown from the treasury, so that she could crown her son, László V. Matthias Corvinus had further work carried out on the citadel, then in 1543 it was occupied by the Turks. During the course of the next hundred years it changed hands several times. Finally, in 1702 the Emperor Leopold I, fearing an initiative on the part of Ferenc Rákóczi's independence movement, had it dismantled.

The Lion Fountain Each of the fountain's five hexagonal columns rests on a prostrate lion. The ceiling is decorated with the coat of arms of the Hunyadi dynasty and inscribed with the year (incomplete) of the fountain's construction (probably 1473). The frieze around the canopy is decorated with the arms of the territories conquered by Matthias Corvinus.

Nagymaros and Zebegény

Nagymaros, at the foot of the Börzsöny Hills, is an extremely popular resort with a splendid view of Visegrád. Zebegény occupies an elevated position on the left bank of the Danube, overlooking a bend in the river, and also offers some truly magnificent views. A row of Slovakian peasant houses in the center of the village acts as a reminder of the immigrants who founded the present community in the 18th century. In 1920 the great landscape painter István Szőnyi (1894–1960) came to live in the village.

The Visegrad Group On February 15, 1991 – 656 years after the alliance signed by Charles Robert at the Visegrád Congress – the presidents of Czechoslovakia (Václav Havel), Poland (Lech Walesa) and Hungary (Árpád Göncz) met in Visegrád at the instigation of the Hungarian prime minister, József Antall ▲ *215*. His aim was to create a strong Central-European alliance and coordinate the steps leading to the three countries joining the European Union. This tripartite alliance, known as the Visegrád Group, was recognized by Brussels.

THE BASILICA OF ESZTERGOM
The Cathedral of the Assumption was built in 1822–69 in neoclassical style, according to plans by

the architects Pál Kühne, János Packh and József Hild. It stands inside the walls of the old fortress and is the largest church in Hungary.

Chapel of the Royal Palace in Esztergom.

A large part of Szőnyi's work was devoted to views of the Danube. His house has now been transformed into a museum (the garden still contains the 'Zebegény bench', immortalized in one of the artist's best-known paintings). The village becomes particularly animated in the summer, when open workshops introduce would-be artists of all ages to various branches of the arts. The interior and exterior of the CATHOLIC CHURCH are a fine example of Hungarian Secessionist architecture. It was built in 1908–9 by Károly Kós ▲ *176* and Béla Jánsky, who were inspired by the work of Transylvanian architects. The NAVIGATION MUSEUM in the VINCE FARKAS HOUSE, named after a former river pilot, traces the history of navigation on the Danube.

ESZTERGOM

Situated about 40 miles north of Budapest, the town of Esztergom was the cradle of the Hungarian state and for the last thousand years has been the seat of the Roman Catholic Church in Hungary. The Magyar leader Prince Géza, grandson of Árpád ● *27*, transferred his residence to the town in 972. Previously it had been the site of Solva, an important military camp on the fortified boundary (limes) of the Roman Empire and, several centuries later, of Österringen, the easternmost fortress of the empire of Charlemagne. Géza's son Vajk was born in Esztergom, where he was later baptized and given the name Stephen. And it was in Esztergom, on January 1, 1001, that he became the first king of Hungary.

'Esztergom appeared, a strange silhouette: a cube and a dome supported by many columns.'

Le Corbusier

His coronation was a key event in the nation's history since it marked Hungary's incorporation into Western Europe and the creation of the Hungarian state. With the consent of Rome, the future Saint Stephen divided the country into ten sees. The Archbishop of Esztergom was made primate of Hungary, with the status of a prince, and throughout kingdom's history was responsible for crowning the kings of Hungary.

THE ROYAL PALACE The construction of Hungary's oldest royal residence – which later became the archbishop's palace – was begun by Prince Géza in the late 10th century. Its remains include the former cathedral and its Porta Speciosa; the study (the Chamber of Virtues) of the Humanist primate János Vitéz; and an 11th-century chapel with frescos, depicting lions and the Tree of Life, that reflect the influence of Byzantine art.

BASILICA The monumental interior contains some memorable treasures. The BAKÓCZ CHAPEL, built in 1506–11 by Archbishop Tamás Bakócz to commemorate his own glory, is a masterpiece of Hungarian Renaissance architecture. The ALTAR was sculpted in Carrara marble by the Florentine artist Andrea Ferrucci (1465–1526). The CHAPEL is the only part of the 11th-century Cathedral of St Adalbert to have survived intact, and was dismantled and reinstalled in the new basilica. The CATHEDRAL TREASURY contains crosses, chalices, calvaries, bishops' crooks, and other religious objects, many of them crafted in gold or silver, ranging from the Middle Ages to the 17th century. Particularly worthy of note are the richly decorated Portable Calvary of King Matthias, the Cross of Canon Böjthe, decorated with diamonds and enamel animals, and remarkable embroidered chasubles. The CRYPT contains the tombs of the bishops of Esztergom. In 1991, sixteen years after his death, the remains of Cardinal Mindszenty ● *37*, ▲ *135* were interred in the crypt.

MUSEUM OF CHRISTIAN ART (Keresztény Múzeum) ★
This is one of Hungary's most splendid museums. It was founded in the 19th century by two devoted collectors, Archbishop János Simor and Bishop Arnold Ipolyi. As well as Hungarian art from the 15th and 16th centuries (including polyptychs by Tamás Kolozsvári and Master M. S. ▲ *194*) and the extraordinary Holy Tomb of Garamszentbenedek (from a Benedictine Monastery in what is now Slovakia), it has a rich collection of about a hundred Italian paintings from the 13th and 14th centuries, including works by Duccio and his school and a beautiful Lady with Unicorn tapestry. The Austrian, German, Spanish and Flemish sections (the latter has a painting of Christ on the Cross attributed to Hans Memling) are also of great interest.

UPS AND DOWNS OF A RELIGIOUS CITY
For over two hundred years Esztergom was the capital of the kingdom of Hungary. In 1242, after the Mongol invasion, Béla IV transferred the royal residence to Buda. However, that did not prevent religious colleges and institutions from flourishing in this seat of Hungarian Catholicism and cradle of the Renaissance. In 1543 the Turkish occupation brought this golden age to an end, and the archiepiscopal see was not reinstated until 1820. The Communist regime conducted an unremitting campaign against Esztergom, its priests and, above all, its archbishop, Cardinal József Mindszenty, who became a national martyr.

Above: Víziváros Parish Church, Esztergom (18th century).

The statue of the Empress Elizabeth ● *30*, ▲ *182* still stands at the center of the park that bears her name.

VISITING GÖDÖLLŐ
The domes and shaped pediment, the grand staircase and the high windows of the great hall make the Royal Palace at Gödöllő one of the finest country residences in Hungary ● *71*. Since 1985 it has been rebuilt and the apartments refurbished in their original style. It now houses the ROYAL PALACE MUSEUM.

GÖDÖLLŐ PALACE

In 1733 Count Antal Grassalkovich (1694–1771), president of the Chamber of Deputies and confidant of the Empress Maria Theresa, embarked on an ambitious project in the village of Gödöllő, about 19 miles from Pest. Between 1744 and 1749 a Baroque country residence was built according to plans by the great architect András Mayerhoffer. The empress herself stayed there in 1751. During the second phase of construction undertaken by Count Grassalkovich – which was continued by his son Antal II and grandson Antal III (1771–1841) – the mansion assumed the form of a double 'U'. When the male line of the family ended with Antal III, the estate passed to the female line and, in 1850, was sold to Baron György Sina. It was then bought by the Hungarian state, in 1867, and modified by Miklós Ybl ● *76* before being presented the palace to the Emperor Franz Joseph and Empress Elizabeth as a coronation gift. The new queen of Hungary was particularly fond of the palace, which became the summer residence of the imperial family, and took every opportunity to stay there. The Emperor Charles I (King Károly IV) ● *96* stayed at the palace just before the collapse of the Austro-Hungarian monarchy. Two years later it became the summer residence of Miklós Horthy (regent of Hungary 1920–44). From 1945 to 1990 the Russian Army used Gödöllő as a military base and totally devastated the estate.

Practical information

Time difference
GMT + 1 (+ 2 from March to Oct)

USEFUL ADDRESSES

→ UNITED KINGDOM

■ **CONSULAR SECTION OF THE REPUBLIC OF HUNGARY**
35B Eaton Place, London SW1X 8BY
Tel. 020 7235 2664 (open 2–5pm)
Visa information: Tel. 09065 508 936 (£1 a minute)
Office open Mon-Fri 9am–noon
www.huemblon.org.uk

■ **Hungarian Cultural Centre**
10 Maiden Lane, London WC2E 7NA
Tel. 020 7240 8448
www.hungary.org.uk

■ **Hungarian Tourist Office**
46 Eaton Place London SW1X 8AL
Tel. 020 7823 1032
www.gotohungary.com

→ CANADA

■ **CONSULATE SECTIONS**
– 299 Waverley St, Ottawa, Ontario K2P 0V9
Tel. (613) 230 2717
– 121 Bloor St East Toronto, Ontario M4W 3M5
Tel. (416) 923 8981
www.docuweb.ca/Hungary

→ UNITED STATES

■ **CONSULAR SECTIONS**
– 3910 Shoemaker St, N.W. Washington D.C. 20008
Visa information: Tel. (202) 362 6730 (ext. 225)
Open Mon, Wed, Fri 10am–1pm
www.huembwas.org
– 223 East 52nd St, New York, NY 10022
Tel. (212) 752 0669
www.kum.hu/newyork
– 11766 Wilshire Bld, Suite 410, Los Angeles, CA 90025
Tel. (310) 473 9344

■ **Hungarian Cultural Center**
Tel. (212) 750 4450
www.hungariancc.org

■ **Hungarian Tourist Office**
150 East 58th St, New York, NY 10155
Tel. (212) 355 0240
www.gotohungary.com

■ **New York Hungarian House**
213 East 82nd St, New York, NY 10028
Tel. (212) 249 9360
www.hungarianhouse.org
(for information on events and activities)

→ INTERNET
www.budapest.com
www.hungaria.org
Vista Visitor Center
www.vista.hu
Budapest tourist office
www.budapestinfo.hu
Tourinform
www.tourinform.hu
www.hungarytourism.hu

MONEY

■ **MONETARY UNIT**
The forint (ft).

■ **EXCHANGE RATE**
£1 = 362 ft;
US$1 = 212 ft;
1 Euro = 245 ft.

■ **WHERE TO CHANGE MONEY**
Banks, bureaux de change, some post offices, travel agencies, hotels, department stores, automatic machines.

■ **PAYMENTS**
They are generally made in cash or with an international bankers' card.

■ **CARDS ACCEPTED**
Visa, Eurocard, American Express, Diners Club.

■ **TRAVELERS' CHECKS**
Are accepted by some hotels and stores.

CLIMATE

Moderate continental. The coldest months are December, January and February (average temperature 35°F); the warmest are July and August (72°F).

FORMALITIES

→ PASSPORT
No visa required for British passport holders for visits up to six months. Canadian and US passport holders do not need a visa for visits up to 90 days. (For an update on visa requirements, call the Hungarian consulate.)

→ CUSTOMS

■ **ON ENTERING HUNGARY**
The tax-free limit of goods is 28,200 ft per person.

■ **ON LEAVING HUNGARY**
You must obtain authorization for gold items, works of art and any items of an archeological or historical nature, whether they were items purchased or received as a gifts.
Note:
Keep all receipts.

■ **INFORMATION**
At Tourinform, in Budapest, see ◆ *243*.

PUBLIC HOLIDAYS

Jan 1; March 15; Easter Monday; May 1; Whit Monday; Aug 20; Oct 23; Dec 25–26.

LANGUAGE

Hungarian. German and English spoken.

TELEPHONE

FROM THE UK/US TO BUDAPEST

■ **LANDLINES**
From the US dial 011 (00 from the UK) 36 (Hungary) 1 (Budapest) followed by the 7-digit number.

■ **CELLPHONES**
Dial 011 36 (from US) or 00 36 (from UK) followed by the 9-digit number.

TRAVEL

→ BY AIR FROM THE UK
Now that Hungary is part of the EU, many low-cost airlines have become interested in the destination and are slashing airfares.

■ **MALÉV (HUNGARIAN AIRLINE)**
Tel. 0870 90 90 577
www.malev.hu

■ **BRITISH AIRWAYS**
Tel. 0870 850 9 850
www.ba.com

■ **LOW-COST AIRLINES**
www.skyeurope.com
www.easyjet.co.uk
www.wizzair.com

→ BY AIR FROM NORTH AMERICA

■ **MALÉV (US)**
Tel. 1 800 223 6884 or (212) 566 9944
www.malev.hu

■ **MALÉV (CANADA)**
Tel. 800 665 6363 or (416) 944 0095
www.malev.hu

■ **CHEAP FLIGHTS**
www.travelocity.com
www.Orbitz.com
www.cheapflights.com

→ BY TRAIN FROM THE UK
By Eurostar from London-Waterloo Station to Paris-Gare du Nord, then from Paris-Gare de l'Est to Vienna with the Orient-Express. Change in Vienna for Budapest. Journey time about 18 hrs.

■ **EUROSTAR**
Tel. 08705 186 186
www.eurostar.com

■ **FRENCH RAILWAYS**
www.sncf.fr

■ **RAIL EUROPE**
Tel. 08705 848 848
www.raileurope.co.uk

→ VIENNA–BUDAPEST ON THE DANUBE
From April to end October an Austro-Hungarian hydrofoil service operates between Vienna, Bratislava and Budapest: journey time: four hours Vienna–Budapest, five hours Budapest–Vienna.

■ **Mahart Tours**
Budapest
Tel. (36 1) 484 40 00
Vienna
Tel. (43 1) 729 21 61
www.mahartours.com
www.mahartpassnave.hu

US$1 = 212 ft; £1 = 362 ft
1,000 ft = US$4.72 or £2.62

CONTENTS

ADDRESSES AND TOURIST INFORMATION

→ EMBASSIES

■ **AMERICAN EMBASSY**
Szabadság tér 12,
1054 Budapest
Tel. 475 4400
or 475 4703 / 4924
(afterhours)
www.usis.hu

■ **BRITISH EMBASSY**
Harmincad u. 6,
1051 Budapest
Tel. 266 2888
www.britishembassy.hu
Mon-Fri 9am–5pm.

■ **CANADIAN EMBASSY**
Zugligeti út 51–53,
1121 Budapest
Tel. 392 3360
or 0680 012 167
(emergencies)
Tel. 613 996 8885
(collect calls accepted on this number for emergencies).

→ TOURIST OFFICES
Tel. 06 80 630 800
Open 24 hours a day.

■ **TOURINFORM**
Tourist information for Budapest and Hungary.
www.tourinform.hu

Vigadó u. 6, V
Tel. 317 98 00
Open 24 hours.

Sütő u. 2, V
(Deák tér)
Tel. 317 87 18
Daily 9am–8pm.

Western station
(Nyugati Pályaudvar)
Nyugati tér, XIII
Station main hall
Tel. 302 85 80
Open daily mid June–mid Sep: 9am–7pm (5pm Sat-Sun); mid Sep–mid June: 9am–6pm (3pm Sat).

Liszt Ferenc tér 11, VI
Tel. 322 40 98
Open mid June–mid Sep: daily 9am–7pm (6pm Sat-Sun); mid Sep–mid June: Mon-Sat 9am–6pm (4pm Sat).

Buda Castle, I
Pl. Szentháromság
Tel. 488 04 75
Fax 488 04 74
Open daily mid June–mid Sep: 9am–8pm; mid Sep–mid June: 10am–7pm (4pm Sat-Sun in Nov-March).

■ **WEST BUDAPEST**
Budaörs (Agip complex, freeway M1 and M7)
Tel. (06) 23 417 518
budaors@budapest info.hu
Open mid June–mid Sep: daily 9am–7pm (6pm Sat-Sun); mid Sep–mid June: Mon-Sat 9am–5pm (3pm Sat).

■ **INFORMATION TOUCH-SCREENS**
Throughout the city.

■ **FERIHEGY AIRPORT**
Terminals 1 and 2.

■ **SOUTHERN STATION**
(Déli pályaudvar)

■ **ASTORIA SUBWAY**
Line 2 (red)

■ **CENTRAL MARKET HALL**
(Nagycsarnok)
Fővám tér 1-3, IX

AIRPORT

→ FERIHEGY 2
Fifteen miles southeast of the city center.
www.bud-airport.hu

■ **TERMINALS**
A for MALEV,
B for all other airlines.

■ **INFORMATION**
Departures
Tel. 296 70 00
Arrivals
Tel. 296 80 00
Switchboard 24/7
Tel. 296 96 96

→ FROM THE AIRPORT TO THE CITY CENTER

■ **AIRPORT MINIBUSZ**
In the Arrival Hall. This communal taxi drops passengers where they want outside the city or in the center.
Fare: 2,100 ft per person or 3,600 ft for a return ticket.
Reservations:
Tel. 296 85 55
Daily 6am–midnight.

■ **Taxis**
Set rates are displayed per zone at the taxi rank outside the airport.
Reservations:
Tel. 341 00 00

■ **RAIL-BUS**
See under 'Stations and Termini' ◆ *244.*

■ **OTHERS**
A free shuttle service is usually provided by luxury hotels to their guests.

AIRLINES

■ **AIR FRANCE**
Váci utca 19-21, V
9th floor
Tel. 483 88 00
Mon-Fri 9am–5pm.

■ **BRITISH AIRWAYS**
Rakoczi ut 1-3
East-West Business Center,
1088 Budapest
Tel. 411 55 55
Mon-Fri 9am–5pm.

■ **MALÉV**
Váci út 26, XIII
Tel. 06 40 212 121
or 235 32 22
Mon-Fri 8.30am–7pm; Sat-Sun 10am–6pm.
Ticket reservation, flight information:
Tel. 235 3888
Apáczai Csere János u. 19, V
Tel. 235 35 75
Mon-Fri 10am–5pm (6pm Thu);
Sat 10am–2pm.
Dorottya u. 2, V
Tel. 235 35 65
Mon-Fri 8.30am–5.30pm (6pm Thu).

■ **SKY EUROPE**
Tel. 777 70 00
www.skyeurope.com

■ **WIZZ AIR**
Tel. 470 94 99
www.wizzair.com

CITY TRANSPORTATION

Budapest's efficient transportation system is run by BKV (Budapesti Kozlekedési Vállalat). Services run between 4.30am and 11pm.
www.bvk.hu

→ TICKETS
Available from subway stations, tobacconists, travel agents, hotels and newsagents.
Warning
Tickets can't be bought on board buses and tramways.

→ BUDAPEST KÁRTYA
Recommended.
It is on sale in tourist offices, travel agencies, most hotels, museums and subway stations, and gives access to most of the city's public transportation system.

■ **ADVANTAGES**
They are numerous: free admission to about 60 museums and other public places of interest; reduced prices for guided tours, car rental, shuttle to the airport, entry to thermal baths and some sports centers; savings in certain stores and restaurants, etc.

The Roman numeral within an address refers to one of the 23 Prague districts.

■ **PRICE**
4,700 ft (two days)
5,900 ft (three days).

→ SUBWAY
There are three lines distinguished by a number and a color (no. 1, yellow; it is also known as the 'Little Subway', and is the oldest metro line in Europe; no. 2, red; no. 3, blue). All three lines intersect at Deák tér station ◆ *249*.
A fourth line, which will be entirely underground, is now under construction, and will link Buda (Móricz Zsigmond Körtér, XI) to Pest (Bosnyák tér, XIV). Good quality maps are available at some ticket offices. They show all bus, tram, metro and HÉV lines plus general information on the system.

■ **FARES**
Beware, prices vary according to the complexity and length of your journey – which is why the Budapest card or a day pass are recommended.
– Single ticket (with no transfer): 115 ft. Valid for a 30-minute journey on the same line and for a maximum of three consecutive stops.
– Single ticket with one transfer 175 ft. Valid for a one-hour journey with one change and for a maximum of five consecutive stops.
– Single ticket with multiple changes 275 ft. Valid for a one-hour journey on several lines (journey with changes).
– HÉV: 90-520 ft according to the journey.

→ BUS, TRAMWAY, TROLLEY
Same tickets for all of these, and for the regional HÉV (suburban railway trains) if within the urban sector.
Warning
Validate your ticket on entering the vehicle.

■ Single tickets: 160 ft.
■ Book of 10 single tickets: 1,375 ft.
■ Book of 20 single tickets: 2,650 ft.
■ Single ticket with transfer: 275 ft.
■ One-day ticket: 1, 275 ft.
■ Three-day tourist pass: 2,550 ft.
■ Seven-day tourist pass: 3,000 ft.
■ Weekend family pass (2 adults and 1 to 5 children under 14): 1,920 ft.
■ Two-week pass (photograph required): 3,850 ft
■ Thirty-day pass (photograph required): 5,950 ft
■ Children under 6 travel for free
■ Recommended journeys: tramways no. 2 (along the Danube) and nos. 4 and 6 (on the Grand-Boulevard around the center of Pest).

→ NIGHT SERVICE
Fifteen buses and two tramways, marked with 'É', cover the most popular routes.
www.bkv.hu

→ BIKE RENTAL
Podmani Czky u. 19, VI
Tel. 0670 625 8501
www.bikebase.hu

→ TOURIST TRANSPORTATION
■ **BATEAUX-MOUCHES**
May-August, daily 9am–5pm.
From Boráros tér to Rómaifürdő.
You can board at any stop.
■ **FUNICULAR**
(*sikló*)
Clark Ádám tér, Castle District (I).
Daily (except Mon on alternate weeks): 7.30am–10.30pm.
The old-fashioned wagons (1870) climb up from the end of the Chain Bridge, which is the zero kilometer marker for all Hungary.
Journey time: a few minutes only.
Horse-drawn carriages round the old city start from the Funicular exit.
To get there:
buses no. 4 (red), 105, 86 and 16 or tramway no. 19.
■ **CHAIR-LIFT**
(*libegő*)
From Zugliget to Mount János, suspended 8 m (26 ft) above the ground over a rise of 262 m (860 ft); journey time: 15 minutes.
April-Sep: daily 9am–5pm; Oct-March daily (except Mon on alternate weeks): 9am–4.30pm.
To get there:
bus no.158 from Moszkva tér.
■ **COG-WHEEL RAILWAY**
(*fogaskerekü vasút*)
Lower terminus: Budapest Hotel (Szilágyi Erzsébet fasor 47).
Upper terminus: Mont Széchenyi (427m high, 1,400 ft).
To get there: tramways no. 18, 41, 56, 67 et 355.
Daily 5am–11pm.
Inauguré en 1874.
Opened in 1874, this is the third cog-driven railroad to be built in Europe.
■ **BOAT TOURS AROUND THE CITY**
From Gellért tér, Batthyány tér and Petőfi tér.
Daily 9am–8pm furing the tourist season.

→ LOST PROPERTY
(*talált tárgyak*)
Akácfa u. 18, 1072 Budapest
Tel. 267 52 99
Open Mon-Fri 8am–5pm (6pm Wed).

CHILDREN

→ THE CHILDREN'S RAILROAD
Úttörő Vasút or Gyermek vasút.
Daily 9am–5pm (closed on Mon out of season).
Known as the "Pioneers' Railroad", this was built in 1948. Its 7 miles of narrow-gauge track runs through the wooded hills. All the staff (except for the driver) are children aged from 10 to 14.
■ **TICKETS**
Adults: 600 ft (return); children between 6 and 14: 200 ft (return); children under 6 travel for free.
■ **TERMINI**
– Hűvösvölgy
Tel. 397 53 94
– Széchenyi-hegy
Tel. 395 54 20
www.gyermekvasut.com

DRIVING

→ SAFETY
■ Seat bells are obligatory in front seats.
■ Speed limits are: 50 km/h in towns, 80 km/h on departmental roads, 100 km/h on national roads and 120 km/h on freeways.
■ Driving is expressly forbidden if there is the slightest trace of alcohol in the blood.
■ Dipped headlights must be switched on (even in daytime) outside built-up areas.

→ PARKING
■ **COVERED PARKING LOTS**
– Szervita tér, V
– Aranykéz u. 4-6, V
– Nyár u. 20, VIII
– Mester utca, IX
■ **PARKING METERS**
You can park in the city center for a maximum of two hours, 8am–6pm (8am–noon on Sat). 120-400 ft/h.

US$1 = 212 ft; £1 = 362 ft
1,000 ft = US$4.72 or £2.62

→ TOWING
Felugyelet Kerékkilincs Ügyelet
Parking meters often display the phone number for wheel clamping release.
– Akadémia 1, V
Tel. 302 86 31
– Kisfuvarosi 6, VIII
Tel. 313 08 10

→ GAS STATIONS
You will find the MOL Hungarian chain and most international companies.
Warning
Not all gas stations accept credit cards.
■ **HUNGARIAN AUTOMOBILE CLUB**
Tel. 345 18 00
Fax 212 38 90
Breakdown services
Tel. 345 17 44
or 345 17 55
www.autoklub.hu
■ **YELLOW ANGELS**
Tel. 188

→ PEDESTRIAN ZONES
Castle District, Margaret Island, Váci utca, and Városliget at the weekend.

EXCURSIONS OUTSIDE BUDAPEST

Gödöllő, Lake Balaton, Nagymaros and the Danube Bend (Visegrád, Esztergom, Szentendre). By minibus, coach, boat, or nostalgia train.
■ **IBUSZ**
Tel. 485 27 00
■ **CITYRAMA**
Tel. 302 43 82
■ **MAHART**
Tel. 318 18 80
■ **MÁV NOSTALGIA**
Tel. 269 52 42
■ **HÉV**
(suburban trains network)
For Gödöllő, take the train from subway terminal no. 2, Örs vezér tere.
For Szentendre take the train at the Batthyány tér station.

FOOD

→ SMALL GLOSSARY
– *napi ajánlat*: dish of the day
– *levesek*: soup
– *előételek*: appetizers, first course
– *köretek*: garnishing
– *saláták*: pickled vegetables
– *édességek*: dessert
– *tészták*: pasta
– *készételek* or *főételek*: dishes
– *frissensültek*: roasted or grilled meats
– *különlegességek*: specialties
– *bor*: wine
– *sör*: beer
– *kenyér*: bread.

→ SPECIALTIES AND TYPICAL PRODUCTS
■ **BEEF, BUDAPEST STYLE**
Recent dish, created especially for the 1958 Universal Exhibition. Beef in a stew-like sauce made from red paprika from Szeged, onion, served with white mushrooms, sweet peppers, smoked bacon and goose liver.
■ **FOGAS**
Type of pikeperch, with a delicate flavor and a silver-white color.
■ **GALUSKA**
Dumplings (● *64*).
■ **GULASH**
Paprika and onion soup in which potatos and pasta (*csipetke*) are cooked. There are many variations on the theme.
■ **LECSÓ**
Mixture of potatos and sweet peppers.
■ **PAPRIKÁ**
Typical Hungarian spice, used in powdered form since 1748. It comes from the sweet pepper grown in Hungary since the end of the 17th century. There are two types of sweet pepper: the yellow or green pepper, used fresh in salads and in most Hungarian dishes; and the pepper used for making papriká. Once ripe, the red peppers are dried and ground into a powder. Their quality depends on the type of pepper used and on the proportion of crushed seeds with the pulp.
Flavors
– *Csemege*: extra sweet
– *Félédes*: semi-sweet
– *Édes nemes*: superfine
– *Rózsa*: pink
– *Erős*: strong
– *Pfefferoni*: very strong
■ **PAPRIKÁS**
Sophisticated variation of the *pörkölt* (below), with white meats, sour and fresh creams, onions and papriká.
■ **PÖRKÖLT**
Meat stew in a rich sauce, with plenty of chopped onions.
■ **SOUR CREAM**
Obtained from skimmed milk and curds.
■ **STRUDEL**
Made with apples, poppy seeds, white cheese, black cherries and pumpkin, strudel (*rétes*) is served warm with icing sugar.

→ WINES
Hungarian wines come from the following regions: Badacsony, Eger, Sopron, Villány (red), Balaton, Mecsek, Szekszárd (red), Tokaj. Seventy percent of the wine production is white.

FINDING YOUR WAY AROUND THE CITY

→ ABBREVIATIONS
u. (*utca*): street
út: avenue
krt (*körút*): boulevard
tér: place, square
sétány: alley
Lépcő: stairs
Köz: dead-end street.

→ DANUBE (DUNA)
This runs through the city from north to south, dividing it into two unequal parts: on the right bank is Buda with Óbuda to the northwest, while on the other bank is Pest, which makes up two thirds of the urban area of left-bank Budapest.

→ MOUNT JÁNOS
The city's highest point (1,686 ft).

→ HOUSE NUMBERING
Starts alongside the Danube, with streets fanning out from the river.

→ THE 23 DISTRICTS
■ The second and third digits in the postal code indicate the district, thus '1051 Budapest' means Budapest, district V.
Roman numerals are used on street signs.
■ The main places of touristic interest are located in districts I, V and VI.

GUIDED TOURS OF THE CITY

The following tours can be booked directly from the companies or at most major hotels.

→ HOT AIR BALLOON
Behing the Nyugati Station, VI.
Magnificent views of the city from a height of 456 ft.

→ RIVERBOATS
A fantastic way to take in the beauty of the Hungarian capital. Many of the city's grand sights can be seen from the river.
■ One operator is the experienced Legenda company
Tel. 266 41 90

www.legenda.hu
Duna Bella
Departures 2.30pm and 3.30pm.
One- or two-hour cruises. Commentary available in 30 languages.
Duna Legenda
One-hour son-et-lumière show, every night.
In 30 languages.
May-June and Sep: 8.15pm and 9pm.
July-August: 11am, 12.15pm, 1.30pm-6.30pm (every hour), 8.15pm, 9pm, 10pm.
Departures from the quay at Vigadó tér, V; exit nos. 6 and 7.

■ **MAHART**
Belgrád rakpart
Tel. 484 40 00
www.mahartpasshave.hu
– Daily boats to Esztergom (7.30am), Visegrád (9am), Szentendre (10.30am and 2pm).
– With meal on board from mid May-mid Sep: daily at noon (arriving 1.30pm), and 7.30pm (arriving 9.30pm).

■ **TGV TOURS**
Tel. 354 07 55
www.tgvtours.hu
For various excursions.

■ **MINIMAX KÖLYÖHAJÓ**
Tel. 266 64 03
www.kdyokhajo.hu
Departures from Vigadó tér: Sun 10am and noon. Children's boats (3-12 years) with cartoons and programs in Hungarian.

→ COACH TOURS

■ **IBUSZ**
Tel. 485 27 00
Departures from the Kempinsky Hotel, Erzsébet tér 7-8.
Three-hour guided tour in English and German, several times a day.

■ **CITY TOURS**
Tel. 374 70 70
Hourly departures from Andrássy út 2, in July-Aug 9.30am-5.30pm.
Two-hour guided tour several times a day in 16 languages.

■ **QUEENYBUS**
Tel. 247 71 59
Departures in front of St Stephen's Basilica.
Three-hour guided tour in English, French, German, Italian, Russian and Spanish, twice a day.

■ **CITYRAMA**
Tel. 302 43 82
Departures from the Chain Bridge, Széchenyi, Pest side.
Three-hour guided tour in English, French, German, Italian and Spanish, three times a day from April to October, and twice a day from November to March.

HEALTH

→ EMERGENCY PHONE NUMBERS

■ **AMBULANCES**
(mentők)
Tel. 104
Alarm centrum
Tel. 350 69 37
In French, English and German.

■ **POLICE**
(rendőrség)
Tel. 107

■ **FIRE BRIGADE**
(tűzoltók)
Tel. 105

→ DENTISTS
(fogorvosok)

■ **PROFIDENT**
Károly krt 1, VII
Tel. 342 69 72
Open Mon-Sat 8am–9pm.

■ **SOS DENTAL SERVICE**
Király u. 14, VI
Tel. 267 96 02
Open 24 hours a day.

→ HOSPITALS
(kórházak)

■ **SZENT ISTVÁN KÓRHÁZ**
Nagyvárad tér 1, VIII
Tel. 455 57 00

■ **SZENT JÁNOS KÓRHÁZ ÉS INTÉZMÉNYEI**
Diósárok köz, XII
Tel. 458 45 00

→ DOCTORS
(orvosok)
A list of doctors speaking foreign languages is available from your embassy (see Useful Addresses).

■ **EMERGENCY DOCTORS**
Falck sos Hungary
Kapy u. 49/b, IIe
Tel. 200 01 00
Daily, 24 hours.

→ PHARMACIES
(gyógyszertárak)
Open 24 hours a day, but ring the bell after.
■ Széna tér 1, I
Tel. 202 15 82 and 202 18 16
■ Frankel Leó út 22, II
■ Vörösvári út 86, III
Tel. 386 64 30
■ Pozsonyi út 19, IV
Tel. 379 30 08
■ Teréz krt 41, VI
Tel. 311 44 39
■ Rákóczi út 86, VIII
Tel. 322 96 13
Tel. 212 43 11
■ Alkotás u. 1/b, XII
Tel. 355 46 91
■ Béke tér 11, XIII
Tel. 320 80 06

INTERNET

There are Internet kiosks in shopping malls, in the Libri boosktores and throughout the city center.

INTERPRETERS

(tolmácsok)
Euroguide
Madách I. út 11, VII
Tel. 342 35 49

MAIL

→ POST OFFICES

■ **MAIN POST OFFICE**
Petőfi Sándor u.17, V
Tel. 485 90 10
Mon-Fri 8am–8pm; Sat 8am–2pm.

■ **EASTERN STATION (KELETI)**
Tel. 322 14 96
Mon-Fri 7am–9pm; Sat 8am–2pm.

■ **WESTERN STATION (NYUGATI)**
Tel. 312 04 36
Mon-Sat 7am–9pm; Sun 10am–noon.

→ STAMPS
(bélyegek)
180 ft for a postcard.

→ INTERNATIONAL MESSENGERS

■ **DHL INTERNATIONAL**
Szabadsag tér 7
Bank Center
1054 Budapest
Tel. 382 32 22

■ **TNT EXPRESS WORLDWIDE**
Icsiri u. 14-16, IX
Tel. 431 31 31

MARKETS

■ **CENTRAL MARKET HALL**
(Nagycsarnok)
Fővám tér 1-3, IX
Tue-Fri 6am–6pm; Sat 6am–2pm; Mon 6am–5pm
To get there: Kálvin tér métro station; tram nos. 2, 47, 49; trolleybus no. 83.
This vast brick-and-steel structure, designed in 1896 and restored in 1996, houses the largest and most beautiful covered market in Budapest. All the ingredients for Hungarian cuisine can be found here.

■ **LEHEL**
(Lehel vásárcsarnok)
Lehel tér, XIII
Open Sun morning.
To get there: subway line 3, alight at Lehel tér station; buses nos. 133, 153, 15; trolleybus no. 73.
One of the oldest neighborhood markets in the city, revamped in 2001.

■ **ECSERI FLEAMARKET**
See under Shopping (Antiques).

MEDIA

→ THE PRESS

■ **OFFICIAL LISTINGS OF CULTURAL EVENTS**
Flyerz, Exit, *Pesti Műsor* (free, www.pestimusor.hu) and *Pesti Est*, the equivalents of *Time Out*, appear every Wednesday. Also check the weeklies *Budapest Sun* (www.budapestsun.com) and *Budapest Business Journal* (www.bbj.hu)

US$1 = 212 ft; £1 = 362 ft
1,000 ft = US$4.72 or £2.62

■ **Tourist press**
Free, available at the airport, in hotels and from tourist offices.
– Monthlies: *Visitor's Guide, Budapest Panorama* (in English, German, Italian and Russian), *Programs in Hungary* (in English and German), *Where Budapest* (in English);
– Quarterlies: *Downtown, Budapest Pocket Guide* (in English).

→ RADIO FM

■ **BARTÓK 105,3**
Classical music and jazz.
■ **SLÁGER 100,8**
Very popular, specializes in chart hits of the 1970s–1980s.
■ **PETőFI 102,7** and **KOSSUTH 107,8**
The town's most popular national stations for news and music.
■ **RADIO C 88,8**
Gipsy radio.
■ **TILOS RADIO 90,3**
The hippest.
■ **RFI 92,1**
Radio France (in Hungarian, English, French and German).

→ TELEVISION

Two national channels. Many hotels are fitted with a dish to receive international channels, Euronews and TV5 in particular.

MONEY

→ BANKS

They are usually open Mon-Thu 8am–4pm; Fri 8am–3pm.
Banks are the best place to change money. Beware of the bureaux de change in the tourist area, which charge a high exchange rate that they try to sweeten with the words 'No commission'.
■ **BNP**
Honvéd u. 20
Tel. 374 63 00
■ **CIB BANK**
Medve u. 4-14
Tel. 212 13 30
■ **CITYBANK**
Hegyalja út 7-13
Tel. 489 76 60
■ **ERSTE BANK**
Madách tér 13-15
Tel. 235 51 00
■ **HVB BANK**
Nagymező u. 44
Tel. 301 51 00
■ **INTER EUROPA BANK**
Szabadság tér 15
Tel. 373 60 00
■ **OTP BANK**
Nádor u. 16
Tel. 353 14 44
■ **POSTABANK**
Váci u. 48
Tel. 268 40 00

→ LOST OR STOLEN

To report lost or stolen credit cards call the following numbers:
■ **VISA**
Tel. 06 800 11272
■ **AMERICAN EXPRESS**
In case of emergency call:
Tel. 484 26 62 (in Budapest)
Tel. 336 393 1111 (to US, collect)

NIGHTLIFE

→ BARS AND CAFÉS

■ The unmissable pedestrianized street **Liszt Ferenc tér** (VI) has a modern and youthful feel: *Menza, Incognito, Buena Vista, Vian, Pesti Est, Mediterrán, Miro Grande, Le Roy*...are all found here.
■ Near Liberty Bridge (IX) and the Central Market Hall, **Ráday utca** is a lively street, bordered with numerous cafés and restaurants such as *Costes, Soul, Vörös Posta Kocsi, Paris Texas, Time Café, Casztro Bisztro*...
■ **Hajos utca** (VI), behind the Opera House, is semi pedestrianized.
■ **St Stephen's Square**, entirely renovated, has a variety of good cafés.
■ The Ukranian freighter, **A38**, moored at the foot of Petőfi bridge on the Buda bank, is an absolute must for the best in Buda nightlife.
Tel. 464 39 40
Daily 11am–4am.
■ **DOKK BISTRO**
Hajógyári Sziget 122, III
Mon-Sat noon–midnight (5am Fri).
Good DJs.
■ **FONÓ**
Sztregova u. 3, XI
Tel. 206 53 00
World music.
■ **JAZZ GARDEN**
Veres Pálné u. 44/a
Tel. 266 73 64
Daily 6pm–1am.
For fans of good-quality jazz bands.
■ **TRAFÓ**
Liliom u. 41, IX
Tel. 456 20 40
Tue-Sun from 8pm.
Experimental music.
■ **WALL STREET CLUB**
Andrássy út 19, VI
Daily 11am–midnight (2am at the weekend)
■ **CAFÉ MIRÓ**
Úri u. 30, I
Tel. 201 55 73
Daily 9am–midnight.
■ In summer, you must try the "Kert", informal, hip cafés-bar in open-air courtyards like the **Zöld Pardon** or **Szimpla Kis Kert** Goldmann György tér, on the Buda bank in District XI, open until 6am.
www.szimpla.hu

→ CASINOS

■ **VÁRKERT**
Miklós tér 9-11, I
Tel. 202 42 44
www.varkert.com
Daily 2pm–5am.
Beautiful, grand, casino designed by Miklós Ybl (architect of the State Opera House).
■ **LAS VEGAS CASINO**
Atrium Hyatt Hotel
Roosevelt tér 2, V
Tel. 317 60 22
www.lasvegascasino.hu
Daily, 24 hours.
■ **TROPICANA CASINO**
Vigadó u. 2 V
Tel. 266 30 62
Daily 11am–6am.

→ NIGHTCLUBS

■ **ALCATRAZ**
Nyar u. 1, VII
Tel. 478 60 10
Open daily 4pm–2am (closed in summer)
'New Orleans' atmosphere with a jail decor!
■ **FAT MO'S**
Nyary Pál u. 11, V
Tel. 267 31 99
Open daily
In the style of the 1920s and Prohibition.
■ **BAHNHOF**
Nyugati tér, VI (behind the station)
Tel. 302 47 51
Open Wed-Sat 9pm–4am
10,000 square feet of youth.
■ **BANK DANCE HALL**
Teréz krt 55, VI
Thu-Sat 11pm–5am.
House music.
■ **CAPELLA**
Belgrád Rakpart 23, V
Tel. 318 62 31
Wed-Thu 10pm–4am (5am Fri-Sat).
A classic for drag queens, kitsch and good times! Shows at midnight and 2am.
■ **VÍZIMOZI RUDAS BATHS**
Döbrentei tér 9, I
www.cinetrip.hu
Acquatic nightclub held monthly. Old films are projected onto screens to a trip hop, Asian vibes or drum & bass soundtrack.
■ **CLUB SEVEN**
Akacfa u. 7, VII
Tel. 478 90 30
Daily noon–4am.

OPENING TIMES

■ **BANKS**
See uunder "Money".
■ **OFFICES**
Mon-Fri 8am–5pm.
■ **POST OFFICES**
(*postahivatal*)
Mon-Fri 8am–7pm; Sat 8am–1pm.
■ **DEPARTMENT STORES**
Mon-Fri 10am–6pm (8pm Thu); Sat 9am–1pm.
■ **FOODSTORES**
(*áruház, bolt*)
Mon-Fri 7am–7pm;

Sat 7am–2pm.
■ **FLORISTS, PÂTISSERIES AND TOBACCONISTS**
Mon-Fri 10am–6pm; Sat am and usually Sun.
■ **SUPERMARKETS**
Mon-Sat 10am–8pm; Sun 10am–6pm.
■ **MUSEUMS**
(*múzeum*)
Tue-Sun 10am–6pm.

SHOPPING

→ ANTIQUES

■ **ANTIK UDVAR**
Szent István krt 1, V
■ **FALK MIKSA UTCA, V**
The street of antique shops.
■ **NAGYHÁZI**
Balaton u. 8, V
Kálmán Imre u. 15, V
Open 10am–6pm.
Gallery and auction House.
■ **BÁV**
Szent István krt 3, V
Lónyai u. 30-32, IX
The equivalent of a pawnbroker.
■ **ANTIKVITÁS**
Váci u. 53, V
■ **HOUSE OF ANTIQUES**
Corner of Dévai and Kassak Lajos, XIII.
A huge store of 40,000 square feet.
■ **ECSERI FLEAMARKET**
Nagykőrösi út 156, XIX.
Open daily but the most interesting day to go is Saturday as early as 6am. This market is heaven if you like to browse or if you're simply looking for something to bring home.
■ **HEREND PORCELAIN**
Kígyío u. 4-5, V
Ceramics from Zsolnay and cristal from Ajka.

→ BOOKSTORES

■ **HELIKON BOOKSTORE**
Bajcsy Zsilinszky út 37, VI
■ **BESTSELLERS**
Oktober 6 ut 11, V
Tel. 312 12 95
French and English books.
■ **ÍRÓK BOLTJA**
Andrássy út 45, VI
Tel. 322 16 45
A 1960s bookstore, where there was a famous literary café – the Japan.
■ **KÖZPONTI ANTIKVÁRIUM**
Múzeum krt 15, V
Tel. 317 35 14
Old books, maps and translations of Hungarian literary works.
■ **LITEA**
Hess András tér 4, I (Castle District)
Tel. 375 69 87
Bookstore and tearoom.
■ **ALEXANDRA KÖNYVESHÁZ**
Nyugati tér 7, V
Tel. 428 70 70
Spread over five stories, open from 10am until midnight.
■ **LIBRI**
(Hungarian chain)
Rákóczi út 12, VII
Tel. 267 48 44
■ **VINCE**
Dózsa György út 37, XIV
In the art gallery.

→ CRAFTS

■ **FOLART CENTRUM**
Major folk stores
Váci u. 14, V
■ **NÉPI IPARMŰVÉSZET BEMUTATOTÉREM**
Corner of Fő utca and Szilágyidezső tér, I.
Opened in 1953.

→ WINE

■ **HOUSE OF HUNGARIAN WINES**
Szentháromság tér 6
Tel. 212 10 31
Daily noon–8pm.
www.magyarborokhaza.hu
For a token fee you can spend hours here sampling wines; knowledgeable and helpful staff.
■ **BUDAPEST WINE SOCIETY**
Batthyány u. 59, I
Tel. 212 25 69
Mon-Sat 10am–8pm (6pm Sat).
■ **FEHÉR GYŰRŰ**
Balassi B. u. 27, V
Tel. 312 18 63
Daily 3pm–1am.
■ **BOR LA BOR**
Veres Pálné u. 7, V
Daily noon–midnight.

→ MUSIC

■ **MCD**
Deak u. 19, V
Tel. 318 66 91
■ **RÓZSAVÖLGYI MUSIC STORE**
Szervita tér 5, V
Tel. 318 33 12
Probably the best music store in town.
■ **ZENEI ANTIKVÁRIUM KODÁLY ZOLTÁN**
Múzeum krt 17
(music scores, books on music, etc.).
■ **WAVE**
Révay u. 4, VI
■ **UNDERGROUND RECORDS**
Király u. 54, VI

→ OPEN 24 HOURS

(*éjjel-nappali*)
■ **FOOD STORES**
– Nonstop ABC
Hegedűs Gyula u. 20/A, XIII
– Budai nonstop
Margit krt 62
– Supermarkets
Tesco Váci ut, Fogarasi and Budaörs
■ **PHOTO PROCESSING**
Sooter's Deák Ferenc krt 23, IX
■ **FLOWERS**
Virágbolt Jászai Mari tér, V (terminal of tramway no. 2).

→ SHOPPING MALLS

■ **CAMPONA**
Nagytétényi út 37-43, XXII
■ **DUNA PLAZA**
Váci út 178, XIII
■ **MAMUT**
Lövőház u. 2-6, II
■ **MOM PARK**
Alkotás út 53, XII
■ **WESTEND CITY CENTER**
Váci út 1-3, VI
400 stores.

SHOWS, OPERA, THEATER

→ RESERVATION CENTERS

■ **TICKET EXPRESS**
– Andrássy út 18, VI
– Jokai u. 40, VI
– Deák Ferenc u. 19, V
Tel. 312 00 00
www.ticketexpress.hu
Daily 9.30am–6.30pm.
■ **PUBLIKA**
Károly krt 9, VII
Tel. 322 20 10
www.publika.hu
■ **VIGADÓ**
Vigadó tér 1, V
Tel. 327 43 22

STATIONS AND TERMINI

→ RAILWAY STATIONS

■ **KELETI PÁLYAUDVAR (EASTERN STATION)**
Baross tér, VIII
Tel. 413 46 10
Trains from western Europe.
■ **NYUGATI PÁLYAUDVAR (WESTERN STATION)**
Nyugati tér, XIII
Tel. 349 85 03
Tourist office on the main concourse.
■ **DÉLI PÁLYAUDVAR (SOUTHERN STATION)**
Krisztina körút 37/a, I
Tel. 375 65 93
To Croatia, Vienna and Lake Balaton.

→ TRAIN INFORMATION

www.elvira.hu
■ **NATIONAL**
Tel. 461 54 00
(24 hours)
■ **INTERNATIONAL**
Tel. 461 55 00
(24 hours)

→ RAIL-BUS

A shuttle bus (12-seater minibus) links the stations to the airport. It also stops to drop passengers wherever they want.
■ **RESERVATIONS**
At railway stations and with the ticket inspector on the train.
■ **INFORMATION**
Tel. 353 27 22

→ COACH TERMINI

■ **NÉPLIGET**
Népliget, IX
Tel. 382 08 88
At the Népliget stop of the red metro line.
■ **EUROLINES-VOLÁNBUSZ CO**
Tel. 485 21 00
Daily 6am–10pm.

TAXIS

→ TARIFS

Basic charge
300 ft (10pm–

US$1 = 212 ft; £1 = 362 ft
1,000 ft = US$4.72 or £2.62

6am: 420 ft).
Price per km
240 ft (10pm–6am: 336 ft).
Waiting
60 ft (10pm–6am: 84 ft).

→ COMPANIES
Avoid cars that do not belong to any taxi company. Use one of the following:
City Taxi
Tel. 211 11 11
Fő TAXI
Tel. 222 22 22
www.fotaxi.hu
Buda Taxi
Tel. 233 33 33
Taxi 4
Tel. 444 44 44
Tele 5
Tel. 355 55 55
6x6 Taxi
Tel. 266 66 66

TELEPHONE

→ DIALING CODES
■ **CALLS WITHIN BUDAPEST**
Dial the 7-digit number.
■ **CALLS FROM BUDAPEST TO THE UK AND US**
Dial 00, wait for the tone, then dial 44 for the UK or 1 for the US then the number (minus the initial 0 for UK numbers).
Barangoló cards
It will be cheaper calling abroad using one of these international calling cards (on sale for 5,000 ft newsagents, from newsstands, post offices etc.).
■ **CALLS TO ANOTHER HUNGARIAN TOWN FROM BUDAPEST**
Dial 06 – wait for the tone – dial the city code and then the number.
■ **Calls to Hungarian cellphones**
– From a public or private home telephone, dial the 11-digit number starting with 06.
– From a foreign network, dial 00 36 and a 9-digit number, omitting the initial 06.

→ DIRECTORY ENQUIRIES
Tel. 199 (international)
Tel. 198 (national)

→ PUBLIC TELEPHONES
Coin-operated (10, 20, 50 and 100 ft) or with phonecards (500 ft and 5,000 ft) available from post offices, hotels, travel agencies, gas stations, newsstands, and newsagents.

THERMAL BATHS

Budapest has no less than thirty thermal baths, fed by hot springs which surface here and there. Around ten of them are remedial centers recommended for the prevention and treatment of certain disorders. If the water sometimes appears cloudy (it is constantly renewed), this is due to its high mineral content.
Warning
To simply bathe, make sure you obtain the right ticket: csak fürdő (bathing only), and arrive at least one hour before closing time.

→ CORINTHIA THERMAL-HOTEL AQUINCUM
Árpád fejedelem útja 94,
1036 Budapest
Tel. 436 41 30
www.corinthiahotels.com
To get there: bus no. 106; tramway no.1; suburban train (HÉV) to Szentendre.
■ **THERMAL FACILITIES**
Daily 7am–10pm.
■ **BAINS**
Three thermal pools, one gaseous thermal pool.
■ **TREATMENTS**
Spine complaints, therapy following locomotor system surgery.
■ **SERVICES**
Sauna, hot and cold showers, hammam, hydromassage, inhalation, natural medicine, water therapy, electrotherapy, hairdresser, beautician.

→ DAGÁLY GYÓGYFÜRDŐ, USZODA, STRANDFÜRDŐ
Népfürdő u. 34-36,
1138 Budapest
Tel. 452 45 00
To get there: bus no.133; tramway no. 1.
■ May-Sep 6am–7pm; Oct-April Mon-Fri 6am–7pm; Sat-Sun 6am–5pm.
■ **BATHS**
Covered bathing pool, two thermal baths at 33°C (91°F) and 36°C (96°F) and a children's pool.
■ **TREATMENTS**
Articulatory, rheumatic and arthritic disorders, and related injuries.
■ **SERVICES**
Hydromassage, massage, swimming, sauna, games area, beautician, solarium, chiropody.

→ DANDÁR GYÓGYFÜRDő
Dandár u. 5-7
1095 Budapest
Tel. 215 70 84
To get there: buses no. 23, 54; tramway no. 1.
■ Mon-Fri 6am–7pm.
■ **BATHS**
Three thermal baths at 20°C (68°F), 36°C (96°F) and 38°C (100°F).
■ **TREATMENTS**
Articulatory, rheumatic and arthritic disorders, slipped disc, neuralgia.
■ **SERVICES**
Hydromassage, massage, swimming, sauna, chiropody.

→ DANUBIUS HOTEL HELIA
Kárpát u. 62-64
1133 Budapest
Tel. 889 58 00
www.danubiushotels.com/helia
To get there: buses no. 7, 7/A, 86; tramways no. 18, 19, 47, 49.
■ Daily 7am–10pm.
■ **BATHS**
Four pools.
■ **TREATMENTS**
Locomotor system disorders, treatment of fractures, sporting injuries, therapy following orthopedic surgery, articulatory deterioration.
■ **SERVICES**
Orthopedic and cardiovascular investigation, hydromassage, massage, mud baths, physiotherapy, electrotherapy, inhalation, chiropody, manucure, solarium, sauna, gaseous thermal baths, steam baths, solarium, beautician, fitness room, tennis, sun-tanning.

→ DANUBIUS THERMAL MARGIT-SZIGET & DANUBIUS GRAND MARGIT-SZIGET
Margit-sziget (Margaret Island)
1138 Budapest
Tel. 452 64 04 or 889 47 00
www.danubiushotels.com/grandhotel
To get there: bus no. 26.
■ Daily 6.30am–9pm.
■ **BATHS**
Swimming pool, four thermal pools.
■ **TREATMENTS**
Rheumatic and arthritic disorders, Locomotor system disorders, disgestive and nervous system complaints.
■ **SERVICES**
Medical center, dental clinic, sauna, solarium, fitness room, beauticians, hairdressers.

→ GELLÉRT GYÓGYFÜRDŐ
Kelenhegyi út 4-6,
1111 Budapest
Tel. 466 61 66
www.danubiushotels.com/gellert

To get there: buses no. 7, 7/A, 86; tramways no. 18, 19, 47, 49.
■ Daily 6am–7pm.
■ **BATHS**
Gaseous thermal pool, pool with wave machine, four thermal pools at 26°C (78°F), 35°C 95°F), 36°C (96°F), 38°C (100°F), and a children's pool.
■ **TREATMENTS**
Degenerative arthritic disorders, joint inflammation, slipped disc, neuralgia, cardiovascular problems.
■ **SERVICES**
Hydromassage, massage, inhalation, seated baths, physiotherapy, dry and humid steam rooms, sauna, naturist suntan area, hairdresser, beautician, chiropody.

→ KIRÁLY GYÓGYFÜRDŐ
Fő u. 82-84, Batthyány tér, 1027 Budapest
Tel. 202 36 88
To get there: buses no. 60, 86; tramway no. 2.
■ Women: Mon, Wed and Fri 7am– 6pm. Men: Tue, Thu and Sat 9am–8pm.
■ **BATHS**
Four pools at 26° (79°F), 32° (90°F), 36° (96°F) and 40° (104°F).
■ **TREATMENTS**
Rheumatic and arthritic disorders, spine distorsion, slipped disc, neuralgia, decalcification, related injuries.
■ **SERVICES**
Hydromassage, massage, dry and humid steam rooms, hairdressers, chiropody.

→ LUKÁCS GYÓGYFÜRDŐ ÉS USZODA
Frankel Leó út 25-29, 1027 Budapest
Tel. 326 1695
To get there: buses no. 6, 60, 86; tramways no. 4, 6, 17; suburban train (HÉV) to Szentendre.
■ Daily 6am–7pm.
■ **BATHS**
Two swimming pools, four thermal pools at 24°C (75°F), 32°C (90°F), 36°C (96°F) and 40°C (104°F), mud bath, foot bath.
■ **TREATMENTS**
Rheumatic and arthritic disorders, spine distorsion, slipped disc, decalcification, neuralgia, related injuries, digestive and respiratory disorders.
■ **SERVICES**
Hydromassage, massage, dry and humid steam rooms, mud baths, physiotherapy, Finnish sauna, sun-tanning, swimming lessons, beauticians, hairdressers, chiropody.

→ PESTSZENTERZSÉBET JÓDOS-SÓS GYÓGYFÜRDŐ, STRANDFÜRDŐ
Vízisport út 2
1203 Budapest
Tel. 283 0874
To get there: buses no. 48, 51, 59; suburban train (HÉV) to Soroksár.
■ Mon-Fri 7am–4pm (3pm Sat). Renovated in 2005.
■ **THERMAL FACILITIES**
Men: Tue, Thu and Sat. Women: Mon, Wed and Fri.
■ **BATHS**
Three thermal pools at 28 (82°F), 36° (96°F) and 39 °C (100°F); pool with wave machine, children's pool.
■ **TREATMENTS**
Rheumatic and arthritic disorders, slipped disc, neuralgia.
■ **SERVICES**
Hydromassage, massage, dry and humid steam rooms, beach volleyball.

→ RUDAS GYÓGYFÜRDŐ, ÉS USZODA
Döbrentei tér 9
1013 Budapest
Tel. 356 13 22
To get there: buses no. 7, 7/A, 86 ; tramways no. 18, 19
■ Daily 6am–7pm (1pm Sat-Sun).
■ **THERMAL FACILITIES**
Men only: Mon-Fri 6am–7pm; men and women: Sat-Sun 6am–1pm.
■ **BAINS**
Swimming pool, six thermal pools at 16°C (60°F), 28°C (82°F), 30°C (86°F), 33°C (91°F), 36°C (96°F) and 42°C (107°F).
■ **TREATMENTS**
Rheumatic and arthritic disorders, slipped disc, decalcification, digestive and respiratory complaints.
■ **SERVICES**
Hydromassage, massage, thermal water therapy, physiotherapy, dry and humid steam rooms, swimming lessons, sun-tanning, chiropody.

→ SZÉCHENYI GYÓGYFÜRDŐ
Állatkerti krt 11
1146 Budapest
Tel. 363 32 10
To get there: trolleybus no. 72; subway yellow line 1.
■ Mixed bathing and thermal pool: daily 6am–10pm (7pm thermal facilities).
■ **BATHS**
Swimming pool, five mixed thermal pools at 20°C (68°F), 34°C (93°F), 35°C (95°F), 36°C (96°F) and 37°C (98°F); four thermal pools for women at 30°C (86°F), 34°C (93°F), 36°C (96°F) and 38°C (100°F); three thermal pools for men at 25°C (77°F), 34°C (93°F) and 38°C (100°F).
■ **TREATMENTS**
Arthritic and rheumatic disorders, related injuries, digestive complaints.
■ **SERVICES**
Hydromassage, massage, thermal water therapy, physiotherapy, natural medicine, underwater gym, dry and humid steam rooms, sauna, swimming lessons, naturist sun-tanning, chiropody.

→ ÚJPESTI GYÓGYFÜRDŐ ÉS USZODA
Árpád út 114-120
1042 Budapest
Tel. 369 31 94
To get there: buses no. 20, 25/A, 96, 104, 120.
■ Pool: Mon-Fri 6am–7pm (1pm Sat-Sun). Mixed steam rooms: Mon, Wed and Fri 6.30am–7pm (1pm Sat-Sun).
■ **BATHS**
Pool, children's pool in summer, three thermal pool at 20°C (68°F), 34°C (93°F) and 38°C (100°F).
■ **TREATMENTS**
Rheumatic and arthritic disorders.
■ **SERVICES**
Hydromassage, massage, dry and humid steam rooms, swimming lessons, sun-tanning, chiropody.

→ SUMMER BATHS BEACHES
(Strand Fürdő)
■ **PALATINUS BEACH**
(Margit-sziget)
Margit-sziget, XIII
Tel. 340 45 05
Open May-Aug 8am–7pm.
■ **PÜNKOSDFÜRDŐ**
Királyok útja 272
Open July-Aug 9am–7pm.

TIPPING

■ **RESTAURANTS, CAFÉS AND TAXIS**
Around 10 percent of the bill.
■ **HOTELS**
Quite generous tipping is usual for luggage and room service.

VOLTAGE

220 volts; 2-pin plugs.

US$1 = 212 ft; £1 = 362 ft
1,000 ft = US$4.72 or £2.62

Hotel prices are not included here since they vary from one season to another. Additionally, in a fast-developing country such as Hungary, prices can alter radically in the wake of improvement schemes and the restructuring of tax systems. In general, a double room with bath in a 3- to 5-star hotel will cost from 22,000 (US$104) to 50,000 ft (US$260). (Note: booking over the Internet can offer substantial discounts).
As for restaurants, the price given here is that of a standard menu for one person, including soup, a main dish and dessert, but excluding drinks. (Note: these dishes are usually selected from the à la carte menu.).
You are advised to study the prices on display at hotels, and to ask for them if they are not given.

FLAT RENTAL

Esprit immo
Magyar utca 22, 1053 Budapest
Tel. 441 16 16
Fax 411 16 17
www.centralapparts.com
A pleasant, original and economical base for exploring the city of Budapest. The company, Esprit Immo, located in the city center, have about 30 charming apartments to let in the historic center of Pest – all furnished and fully equipped. Reservations can be made in person at the office. Minimum stay of two nights. Possibility of private parking (small extra cost).

DISTRICT I

HOTEL

Art'otel **** AC4
Bem Rakpart 16-19
Tel. 487 94 87
www.artotel.de
Restaurant open daily.
À la carte: 7,000 ft.
Designer hotels were the travel industry's bright idea of the 1990s and Budapest, as a modern touristic European city in the making, got its own in 2000. Standing by the Danube, in the heart of Budapest, the Art'otel is a stylish place to stay. As befits such a location, most rooms afford magnificent views of the river and city. The hotel, made up of one new building and four restored Baroque houses (the prettiest part of the hotel), dates back to the 18th century and serves as a gallery for 600 or so works by American artist Donald Sultan. Rooms are spacious and comfortable, with contemporary furnishings and all the modern amenities you'd expect. The hotel's restaurant, The Chelsea, is renowned.
165 rooms.

Hilton Budapest ***** AB4
Hess András tér 1-2
Tel. 889 60 00
Fax 889 66 44
info.budapest@hilton.com
www.hilton.com
Restaurant open daily noon–3pm, 6–11pm.
On the heights of Buda, the modern and elegant Hilton overlooks Pest, the Parliament and the majestic sweep of the Danube. It blends in perfectly with its historical setting, and shares one of its walls with a Jesuit cloister next door. Its panoramic restaurant, Le Dominicain, offers a gastronomic feast at affordable prices. The dining room is huge, with large and elegant tables – choose one near the window if you can, the best spot to enjoy the view. The service is first class and the food excellent (the combination of braised foie gras with a glass of Tokaj Aszu n° 3 is wonderful).
322 rooms

RESTAURANTS

Alabárdos AB4
Országház u. 2
Tel. 356 08 51
Mon-Sat noon–4pm, 7–11pm.
Menu: 5,000 ft.
Close to the Matthias Church, set in an ancient cellar of old Buda. Alarbardos specializes in Hungarian and Transylvanian cuisine: stewed venison with galuska, potatoes or pasta, and excellent wild boar. Live guitar music.

Aranykaviár AA3
Ostrom u. 19
Tel. 201 67 37
Daily noon–midnight.
Menu: 5,000 ft.
A corner of old Russia, where you can try all different kinds of caviar complemented by shots of assorted vodkas. Zakuski, borsch, shashlik, vareniki *and other Russian specialties, with the authentic flavor of the motherland. Live music; very friendly atmosphere.*

Café Pierrot AB4
Fortuna utca 14
Tel. 375 69 71
Daily 11am–midnight.
Menu: 2,000 ft.
Pleasant stopping place for a light lunch or dinner (a salad, a sandwich, or foie gras with a glass of Tokay) in the Castle district. Live piano music in the evening. Somewhat pricey as the district attracts a lot of tourists.

Le Jardin de Paris AC4
Fö utca 20
Tel. 201 00 47
Daily noon–midnight.
Menu: 5,000 ft.
Twentieth-century paintings adorn the walls of this restaurant owned by a French lover of Hungarian art. The Franco-Hungarian menu is based on local produce. With its large, attractive garden, it is the most beautiful outdoor restaurant in the city. Particularly pleasant in the summer when food and drinks are served under the scented linden trees. Small jazz band some evenings from 8pm until 11pm.

DISTRICT II

RESTAURANTS

Margitkert AC1
Margit u. 15
Tel. 326 08 60
Daily noon–midnight
Menu: 4,000–4,500 ft
This centuries-old inn is one of the most ancient in Budapest. Here you can sample authentic dishes from the Puszta, known as the Great Hungarian Plain, and other great classic dishes of the country: cabbage stuffed with meat and rice, mushrooms with sheep's cheese, etc. The garden and dining rooms echo

Addresses are listed in alphabetical order according to districts.
A A1 are the coordinates of the maps found at the front of the guide (**A**), and at the back (**B**).
A list of logos can be found on p. 241.

the sound of gypsy music. Make sure to book, and gentlemen should wear a tie (except for outside in the garden during summer).

Náncsi Néni BA3
Ördögárok u. 80
Tel. 397 27 42
Daily noon–11pm
Menu: 4,000–4,500 ft
*Delicious and unpretentious traditional food: bean soup (*bableves*), game, fromage blanc (*túrógombóc*), superb goulash straight from the pot and excellent beer. There is a wonderful terrace in summer, when reservations are recommended.*

Remiz Kávéház és Étterem BB4
Budakeszi út 5
Tel. 275 13 96
Fax 394 18 96
Daily 9am–1am
Menu: 5,000 ft
The word remiz means warehouse or depot, and the owners have installed some yellow ironwork from a 1930s tramway to add to the atmosphere. The extensive menu includes many regional specialties, such as goulash with palacsintas*. Delicious desserts. The clientele is a mix of artists, diplomats and businessmen. Reservations recommended.*

DISTRICT III

HOTEL

Corinthia Thermal-Hotel Aquincum ***** BD3
Árpád fejedelem útja 94
Tel. 436 41 00
Fax 436 41 56
reservation@aqu.hu
www.corinthiahotels.com
Located on the way out of Budapest on the right bank of the Danube opposite Margaret Island, on the site of a Roman settlement. Excellent service and amenities, and a very good thermal spa (see also ◆ 249 under Thermal Baths).
312 rooms; 12 suites

RESTAURANTS

Kéhli Vendéglő BC3
Mókus u. 22
Tel. 250 42 41
Open daily noon–midnight.
Menu: 5,000 ft
Kéhli is one of the oldest restaurants in Óbuda, once a favorite haunt of the writer and gourmet Gyula Krúdy. The place could be the setting for a late 19th-century romantic novel, enhanced by the evocative photos and prints on the wall. Each dish is dedicated to Krúdy's hero Szindbád. Traditional homely cuisine in an atmosphere of great charm.

Kisbuda Gyöngye BC3
Kenyeres u. 34
Tel. 368 64 02
Mon-Sat noon–midnight.
Menu: 6,000 ft.
This is a fine restaurant with a rustic, comfortable interior, and violin or piano music adding to the charm of the place. Hungarian specialties can be followed by somloi galuska, *an irresistible cake made of biscuit, chocolate, vanilla and crème Chantilly.*

Vadrózsa AA1
Pentelei Molnár u. 15
Tel. 326 58 17
Daily noon–3pm, 7pm–midnight.
Menu: 7,000 ft.
'The Wild Rose' is housed in a beautiful baroque villa in the residential quarter of Buda. The luxurious interior boasts elegant fabrics and hangings, Louis XV chairs and crystal chandeliers. The cuisine, too, is sumptuous, with specialties such as foie gras, and breast of goose stuffed with truffles and cheese. The extensive and select wine list includes some splendid Rieslings, Tokays, Sauvignons Chardonnays and Cabernets. Live piano music every evening.

DISTRICT III

HOTELS

Astoria **** AF6
Kossuth Lajos u. 19-21
Tel. 889 60 00
www.danubiushotels.com/astoria
This hotel has stood at the center of several historical and political storms! It opened in 1914 and it was here that the country's first democratic government was formed, following the collapse of the Austro-Hungarian Empire in 1918. In 1944 the Gestapo set up its headquarters here, detaining prisoners in the basement, and, during the 1956 Revolution, it was the turn of the Red Army to set up camp in the palace. It is also a gem of Hungarian art nouveau, standing out from the faceless modern buildings that surround it. Sit back in one of the bar's comfortable club armchairs and enjoy what you see: the window opens onto a panorama of the modern city, with lifts gliding up and down the futuristic high-rise buildings. The interior features granite columns with mahogany panels picked out in brass and copper. The Empire-style rooms have recently been refurbished to cater for an increasingly international clientele. Close to the city center, with parking (payable) nearby.
126 rooms; 5 suites

Erzsébet Hotel *** AF6
Károlyi Mihály u. 11
Tel. 328 57 00
Fax 328 57 63
www.danubiushotels.com/erzsebet
Near the traffic-free pedestrian center of Budapest, this is the second Erzsébet (the first opened in 1873 but was pulled down in 1985). It is modern and functional and the restaurant, Janos Pince, specializes in regional dishes.
123 rooms

Kempinski Hotel Corvinus Budapest ***** AF5
Erzsébet tér 7-8
Tel. and fax 429 37 77
www.kempinski-budapest.com
This was Hungary's only five-star hotel when it opened in 1992 and its modern design, giant windows and lobby flooded with light made it one of the city's new curiosities. The Kempinski is still probably the most luxurious hotel in Budapest. It is true that from outside the nine-storey building lacks the charm of the surrounding Art

US$1 = 212 ft; £1 = 362 ft
1,000 ft = US$4.72 or £2.62

Nouveau town houses, but inside it is a world of elegance and style. Perfect service, of course.
369 rooms

Mercure Korona Hotel **** AG7
Kecskeméti u. 14
Tel. 486 88 00
h1765@accor-hotels.com
www.mercure-korona.hu
Its central location, between the Covered Market and the pedestrian precinct, has confirmed this hotel's popularity. Its two buildings on either side of the street are linked by a footbridge. Bureau de change, hotel taxis, babysitting, restaurant and bar.
433 rooms

Le Méridien ***** AF5
Erzsébet tér 9-10
Tel. 429 55 00
Fax 429 55 55
www.lemeridien.com
Menu: 7,000 ft
The Meridian, housed in a stylish palace that, under Communism, was once the police headquarters, is a sophisticated and stylish hotel. Its restaurant, The Bourbon, has a wonderful glass dome and serves a magnificent brunch on Sundays.

Sofitel Atrium Budapest ***** AE5
Roosevelt tér 2
Tel. 266 12 34
Fax 266 91 01
www.accorhotels.com
Early in the 1980s the left bank of the Danube became the home of huge new hotels, boasting more than 1000 first-class rooms to cater for the international clientele. This establishment (ex Hyatt Regency Budapest) belongs firmly to the new class of hotels. Every detail that can enhance a visitor's stay here has been carefully thought out: there is a café with a south-facing terrace, two restaurants, two bars, a nightclub, a casino, a swimming pool and a fitness center.
351 rooms

Taverna Hotel **** AE6
Váci u. 20
Tel. 485 31 00
Fax 485 31 11
www.hoteltaverna.hu
The most central of city center hotels. Access is via the pedestrian Váci utca and Petőfi utca. Behind the façade of columns decorated with sculptures are well-appointed rooms, thoughtfully arranged around the complex. The architects and interior designers have exercised their imagination to optimum effect to ensure the Taverna's practicality and comfort. The hotel's gastronomic restaurant, Gambrinus, is one of the best addresses in the city. The hotel also has a small bowling alley, a coffee lounge, a bar, a brasserie, and a café, the Zsolnay, which serves tea in porcelain of the same make.
227 rooms

Gresham Palace Four Seasons AE5
Roosevelt tér 5-6
Tel. 268 60 00
Fax 268 50 00
www.fourseasons.com/budapest
Menu: 6,000 ft.
The Four Seasons is found in one of the most beautiful Art Nouveau buildings in the heart of the city and affords magnificent views plunging down to the Széchenyi Bridge. The hotel opened in July 2004 after five years of spectacular work. Everything is a study in perfection. Wonderful atmosphere in the Gresham café, where the French pastry chef's work is nearly always exceptional.

RESTAURANTS

Admiral AE7
Belgrád rakpart 30
Tel. 318 07 23
Daily 11am–midnight.
Menu: 3,000 ft.
With its wood-paneled walls, the interior of this restaurant on the left bank of the Danube resembles an old-fashioned schooner. The menu consists of Hungarian and international (notably Chinese) dishes. In summer ask to dine outside on the terrace planted with flowers.

Baraka AF6
Magyar utca 12-14
Tel. 483 13 55
Open Mon-Sat 6–11pm.
Menu: 6,000 ft.
Close to one of the prettiest squares in Budapest, Károlyi Kert, this prized restaurant presents international cuisine that fuses Hungarian, French and Oriental flavors deliciously, thanks to its chef, Victor Ségal. Trendy atmosphere and decor.

Café kör AE4
Sas utca 17
Tel. 311 00 53
Mon-Sat 10am–10pm.
Menu: 3,000 ft.
Close to St Stephen's Basilica, this bistro has an almost Parisian atmosphere. Excellent cuisine at reasonable prices. Various wines are served by the glass – a somewhat rare occurrence – and waiters are very friendly and efficient. Rather busy between 1 and 2pm when local workers come here for lunch, so choose a less popular time (food is served all day), or go for dinner (reserve in advance).

Cyrano AE6
Kristóf tér 7-8
Tel. 266 30 96
Daily 11am–5pm, 6pm–midnight.
Menu: 6,000 ft.
Easy to spot, with its huge flag fluttering in the breeze, Cyrano is right in the heart of Pest, in a pedestrian street. It owes its name to having lent its chandelier for use in the motion picture Cyrano de Bergerac, *starring Gérard Depardieu. The house also has a very modern and attractive decor, little balconies and a large terrace. Delicious, mostly seasonal, cuisine: veal with paprika and gnocchi, fillet of pike-perch, etc..*

Kárpátia AF6
Ferenciek tere 7-8
Tel. 317 35 96
Ouvert tlj. 11 h-23 h
Menu : 7 000 ft
The Kárpátia is richly decorated in Gothic style with painted vaulting and attractive tables. The menu is traditional Hungarian – try

dishes such as the crispy leg of duck with prune-cabbage, or the stuffed cabbage Kolozsvár style: a mixture of minced pork, rice and spices, accompanied by sauerkraut and smoked meat in a sour cream sauce. The finished dish is then sprinkled with dill. The regional wine list is outstanding. Live gypsy violin music.

Képíró AF6
Képíró utca 3
Tel. 266 04 30
Fax 266 04 25
www.kepirorestaurant.com
Open Mon-Fri noon–3pm, 6pm–midnight; Sat 6pm–midnight.
Menu: 5,000-6,000 ft.
Three years after being voted the city's "best new restaurant", Képíró remains fashionable. Contemporary decor and seasonal dishes which are elaborate and still exciting. Good selection of Hungarian wines. Terrace in summer on the small street.

Légrádi Antique AF5
Bárczy István u. 3-5
Tel. 266 49 93
Open Mon-Sat noon–3pm, 7pm–midnight.
Menu: 7,000 ft.
This fashionable yet discreet candlelit restaurant is tucked away at the back of an antique shop, and is filled wih beautiful old furniture. Specialties include dishes from the north of Hungary, such as goose offal with Heves rice, served with crackling from the bird, carrots, baby turnips, celeriac and mushrooms. Reservations are recommended.

Lou Lou AD4
Vigyázó Ferenc u. 4
Tel. 312 45 05
Open Mon-Fri noon–3pm, 7pm–midnight; Sat 7pm–midnight.
Menu: 4,500 ft.
The menu is mostly Italian but the decor in this bistro is traditional French. There are prints of old Paris on the walls, and in the small dining room Napoleon looks proudly down on its eight tables. Reservations are essential since Lou Lou's high quality cooking is no longer a secret.

Pilsner Urquell Sörforrás AE6
Váci u. 15
Tel. 318 38 14
Daily noon–midnight.
Menu: 2,400 ft.
A popular rendezvous which serves a range of dishes in generous portions, accompanied by Pilsner beer. The national dish, chicken with paprika, is prepared here in a simple and authentic fashion, while most gourmet establishments seem to exclude the dish from their menus. Gypsy music every night and operettas twice weekly.

Spoon Café & Lounge AD5
Vigadó tér 3, Kikötő
Tel. 411 09 33
Fax 411 09 46
www.spooncafe.hu
Open daily noon–2am.
Menu: 4,000 ft.
Coming here is about more than experiencing fusion food, since Spoon is a large three-decker riverboat which has been moored at the foot of Szechenyi Bridge, across from the Buda Castle, since 2003. Sophisticated, contemporary and hip, it comprises a restaurant, several bars and a magnificent ope terrace. Dishes at the modern, beautiful Spoon Café include garlic octopus with basil olives, goose liver terrine with fig mellowed in Tokaj wine, Thai shrimp soup with coconut, lemon grass and glass noodles, sushi and more.

Tom George AE4
Október 6 utca 8
Tel. 266 35 25
Daily noon–midnight.
Carte: 5,000 ft.
Without question one of the most fashionable restaurants around – where politicians and artists come to see and be seen against a laid-back 1970s background decor. The international menu (Indian, Mediterranean and Hungarian) is exceptional, as is the sushi bar presided over by a Japanese chef.

TEAROOM

Gerbeaud Cukrászda AE5
Vörösmarty tér 7
Tel. 429 90 00
Daily 9am–9pm.
Gerbeaud's sign has been on the wall here since 1884, when a Swiss industrialist called Emil Gerbeaud bought the place from businessman Henrik Kugler. It is one of the most famous coffee-houses in Budapest, and is decorated in the 1920s style typical of central Europe. Mouthwatering cakes are invitingly displayed in the window, tempting passers-by to self-indulgent acts of gluttony! Try pogácsa, *a savory brioche, and* dobos torta, *a rich caramel and chocolate cake with cream filling!*

DISTRICT VI

HOTELS

Hotel Pest *** AF4
Paulay Ede utca 31
Tel. 343 11 98
www.hotelpest.hu
Opened in 2004 in a beautiful 18th-century building, the Pest is a very good value-for-money three-star establishment close to the Hungarian State Opera.

K+K Hôtel Opéra **** AF4
Révay u. 24
Tel. 269 02 22
www.kkhotels.hu
A quiet hotel, located between the State Opera and St Stephen's Basilica. The decor is unassuming, but its rooms are very comfortable. The usual services: bureau de change, hotel taxis, baby-sitting, bar, etc.
205 rooms

Radisson SAS Béke Hotel Budapest **** AH5
Teréz krt 43
Tel. 889 39 00
Fax 889 39 15
http://budapest.radissonsas.com
The imposing façade of the Radisson overlooks the ring boulevard of the city. High-quality accommodation and attentive service. The Shakespeare restaurant is dominated by a large mural illustrating the

US$1 = 212 ft; £1 = 362 ft
1,000 ft = US$4.72 or £2.62

playwright's works, and offers a good selection of national dishes, together with excellent wines from the region. The Zsolnay Café (not the same as the Zsolnay Café of the Hotel Taverna) is decorated with mirrors and chandeliers – a beautiful place to relax and listen to the pianist. Bureau de change, hotel taxis, babysitting.
247 rooms

RESTAURANTS

Articsóka AF4
Zichy Jenő u.17
Tel. 302 77 57
Daily noon–midnight.
Menu: 4,000 ft.
A good place to sit outside on the terrace, and sample the flavor of fine papriká, *which is typical of the cuisine of Southern Hungary (an elaborate stew of white meats with a rich sauce made of onions, sour and fresh creams and papriká).*

Belcanto Étterem AF4
Dalszínház u. 8
Tel. 269 27 86
www.belcanto.hu
Open daily noon–3pm, 5pm–2am.
Menu: 8.000 ft.
The arias you can hear are not coming from the Opera house opposite, but are the voices of the waiters singing Bellini as they go about their work in this handsome restaurant. Naturally enough, the cuisine is Italian too: such delights as seafood risotto, spaghetti with anchovies and Venetian ratatouille are accompanied by a good range of Italian wines.

DISTRICT VII

HOTEL

Best Western Grand Hotel Hungaria **** AH5
Rákóczi út 90
Tel. 889 44 00
Fax 889 44 11
www.danubiushotels.com/grandhotel-hungaria
A mere ten-minute walk from the city cente, this luxury establishment has light, spacious and quiet rooms. Restaurant, taxis, bar.
511 rooms

Marco Polo AH5
Nyar utca 6
Tel. 413 25 40
www.marcopolo.com
A youth hostel in the heart of the city, renovated in 2005. There are 47 rooms for one or two people. Friendly atmosphere.

Queen Mary *** AG4
Kertesz utca 34
Tel. 413 35 10
www.hotelqueenmary.hu
A small, friendly hotel which opened in 2003, a few minutes from Franz Liszt square, in a district which has undergone rejuvenation work. There are 26 rooms arranged over five floors. Possible parking on site (extra cost).

RESTAURANTS

Fausto's Ristorante AG6
Dohány u. 5
Tel. 269 68 06
Mon-Sat noon–3pm, 7–11pm.
Menu: 6,000–15,000 ft.
One of the landmarks of Budapest, with a cheerful but slightly kitsch Venetian decor. Northern Italian cooking with a Hungarian twist: lasagne with boar and cabbage in Taleggio cheese sauce, pasta filled with venison, apple and in a clove and cabernet sauce, salmon filet with beetroots and black mussels. Excellent specialties from Tuscany too.

Fészek Művészklub AG4
Kertész u. 36
Tel. 322 60 43
Daily noon–midnight.
Menu: 3,000 ft.
It takes a while to read the entire menu here – it is virtually an encyclopedia of Hungarian cuisine, including most of the country's typical dishes. The place is a local haunt for actors and artists, who love to sit in the shady courtyard in summer, and in winter crowd the medieval-style dining room. As the restaurant is located inside a theater, booking is recommended.

Kadar Étkezde AG5
Klauzál tér 9
Tel. 344 49 79
Open Tue-Sat.
Menu: 800 ft.
For an authentic Hungarian experience try this local canteen serving homemade, rustic dishes at prices which beat all the competition – a fact which explains the regular clientele. You pay on your way out, and don't forget to mention glasses of water and bread. Warning, credit cards are not accepted.

DISTRICT VIII

HOTEL

Mercure Budapest Nemzeti *** AH5
Jozsef Krt. 4
Tel. 477 53 00
Fax 477 53 53
H1686@accor.com
www.mercure-nemzeti.hu
Located near Blaha L. Tér métro station. Behind its attractive 'Transylvanian blue' façade are quiet, comfortable bedrooms. The old-fashioned dining room is a masterpiece of gilding, glasswork and art deco furnishing. Restaurant, bar, bureau de change.
76 rooms; 1 suite

RESTAURANT

Múzeum AG6
Múzeum krt 12
Tel. 267 03 75
Open Mon-Sat noon–midnight.
Menu: 7,000 ft.
This elegant, high-ceilinged restaurant dates back to 1885, and still has the original murals painted by Károly Lotz. It is also a brasserie and restaurant, renowned among Budapest gourmets. The menu is a skillful blend of traditional dishes and more modern cuisine. The wine list is outstanding. A good place to eat after a visit to the adjacent Hungarian National Museum.

DISTRICT IX

HOTEL

Ibis Budapest Centrum *** AG7
Ráday u. 6
Tel. 456 41 00
h2078@accor.com
Comfortable, modern hotel with a plain

Addresses are listed in alphabetical order according to districts.
A A1 are the coordinates of the maps found at the front of the guide (**A**), and at the back (**B**).
A list of logos can be found on p. 241.

decor, but recently renovated rooms. Located in a popular street. Restaurant.
126 chambres

DISTRICT XI

HOTELS

Danubius Hotel Gellért **** AE8
Szent Gellért tér 1
Tel. 889 55 00
Fax 889 55 05
www.danubiusgroup.com/gellert
A temple of Art Nouveau, frequented by those coming to take treatments at the extravagant adjoining thermal baths complex (free entry if you stay at the hotel). Built after World War One at the foot of the Gellért Hill, the hotel shows its age here and there, but it remains an establishment of great, if a little overrated, charm. At the back is an outdoor swimming pool with wave-machine. Solarium, bar, and a very good restaurant. (See also ◆ 248 under Thermal Baths.)
221 rooms; 13 suites

Hotel Charles *** AC7
Hegyalja út 23
Tel. 212 91 69
Fax 202 29 84
www.hotelcharles.hu
The Charles comprises 70 spacious, clean studios, each with its own kitchenette, where in the morning you can cook your own breakfast if you don't feel like going to the buffet on the ground floor. Business Center (ie three computers allowing you Internet access); restaurant. The modern building lacks charm but the location is central and the staff very helpful. Very good value for money.

RESTAURANT

Hemingway AC10
Kosztolányi tér, 2.
Tel. 381 05 22
Open noon–2am (the kitchen closes at midnight).
Menu: 4,500 ft.
Located by the small Feneketlen tó lake, this restaurant offers over a hundred cockails and a fine selection of wines. Live Latin American concerts some evenings and a magical view over the illuminated lake from the large terrace in summer.

DISTRICT XII

HOTEL

Budapest Hotel **** BD4
Szilágyi Erzsébet fasor 47
Tel. 889 42 00
Fax 889 42 03
www.danubiusgroup.com/budapest
From the Buda hilltops rises a circular white tower, 15 storeys high, with large bay windows in the rooms to help you enjoy the superb view. There are two restaurants, a bureau de change, and hotel taxis.
280 rooms; 9 suites

DISTRICT XIII

HOTELS

Danubius Grand Hotel Margit-sziget BD3
Margitsziget
Tel. 889 47 00
Fax 889 49 88
www.danubiusgroup.com/grandhotel
The 130-year-old Danubius Grand was completely refurbished a few years ago. Rooms are large and elegantly furnished – the most sought-after are those overlooking the park. Wonderfully located on a small park on peaceful Margaret Island, the hotel is only a few minutes from the city center, and shares thermal baths and other remedial facilities with the Danubius Thermal Hotel Margit-Sziget next door (see below). Garden terrace with live gypsy-style music, and all the usual amenities and services you'd expect from a four-star hotel. (See ◆ 249 under Thermal Baths.)
154 rooms; 10 suites

Danubius Thermal Hotel Margit-sziget **** BD3
Margitsziget
Tel. 889 47 00
Fax 889 49 88
www.danubiushotels.com/thermalhotel
A modern and spacious hotel on leafy, car-free, peaceful Margaret Island. Package deals for guests wishing to take thermal treatments. Massage and fitness facilities are also available. (See ◆ 249 under Thermal Baths.)
259 rooms; 8 suites

Danubius Thermal Hotel Helia **** BD4
Kárpát u. 62-64
Tel. 889 58 00
Fax 889 58 01
www.danubiusgroup.com/helia
This luxury spa hotel specializes in various fitness and beauty programs. Its modern Scandinavian design includes chrome and leather chairs in the lounges, and attractive blond wood in the bedrooms. Buffet-restaurant serving local specialties, vegetarian café. (See ◆ 249 under Thermal Baths)
254 rooms; 8 suites

DISTRICT XIV

RESTAURANTS

Gundel Ai1
Állatkerti krt 2
Tel. 468 40 40
Fax 363 19 17
www.gundel.hu
Daily noon–4pm, 6.30pm–midnight; brunch Sun 11.30am–3pm.
Menu: 6,000–25,000 ft.
The most famous gastronomic restaurant in Hungary, and one of the best tables in Eastern Europe. The restaurant, located by the zoological gardens in City Park, has been named after the Gundel family. The entire history of the establishment has been written by the Gundel dynasty, starting with János Gundel, who was appointed President of the Association of Hoteliers-Restaurateurs in Budapest in 1894. His son Károly followed in his father's footsteps and took over the restaurant in 1910, but gave it up during the Communist years. From generation to generation, the restaurant has become the finest address in the city thanks to its original

US$1 = 212 ft; £1 = 362 ft
1,000 ft = US$4.72 or £2.62

culinary creations: pikeperch, tokány, *veal cutlets,* palacsinta *(stuffed pancakes)... "Gastronomy and music share the need for novelty and self-renewal." (Károly Gundel). Excellent brunch on Sundays (3,700 ft). It is cheaper to eat at the tables set in the cellars of the restaurant. Food served on the terrace in summer.*

Robinson
Városliget Állatkerti krt. 3
Tel. 422 02 22
Daily noon–4pm, 6pm–midnight
Menu: 4,000–6,000 ft
Robinson is by Heroes' Square, behind the Fine Arts Museum, on a small island in the lake at Városliget (City Park), a romantic setting for this fine restaurant. The predominantly light cuisine can be savored outside, in the shade of poplar and willow trees. Try the palacsinta *Robinson (a crepe filled with fresh fruit and smothered in vanilla cream), accompanied by a glass of pezsgő (a local sparkling wine). Enjoy gourmet cuisine at affordable prices or just a drink on the terrace. One of the coolest places in the city in the summer.*

AROUND BUDAPEST

ESZTERGOM

HOTEL

Hotel Esztergom Danubius Beta ***
Primás-sziget
Tel. 33/412 555
Fax 33/412 853
www.hotel-esztergom.hu
This little gem of a hotel has delightful bedrooms, and runs a program of activities such as exploring the local widlife, fishing and sailing on the Danube, and pony trekking. Restaurant, bar, bureau de change, fitness center.
36 rooms

RESTAURANTS

Prímás Pince
Szent István tér 4
Tel. 33/313 495
Fax 33/313 495
Daily 10am–10pm.
Menu: from 2,000 ft.
As its vaulting, stone columns and flagged floor suggest, this medieval building was originally the town's first cathedral. Later it became the residence of the archbishop. Now it is an elegant restaurant specializing in regional cuisine.

Szalma Csárda
Nagy Duna sétány 2
Tel. 33/315 336
Fax 33/315 336
Ouvert tlj. 11 h-22 h
Menu : 2 500 ft
Daily 11am–10pm.
Menu: 2,500 ft.
The surrounding countryside finds an echo here in the bouquets of wild flowers that decorate the tables. The emphasis here is on the rustic, with terracotta pots, old farm implements and tresses of garlic and paprika hanging from the ceiling. A large stove makes it equally welcoming in the winter. The extensive menu includes dishes of fish from the Danube. The restaurant's unique atmosphere is enhanced by a group of gypsy musicians, and the terrace enjoys a superb view of the river.

SZENTENDRE

RESTAURANTS

Aranysárkány
Alkotmány u. 1/A
Tel. 26/311 670
Fax 26/311 670
Daily noon–10pm.
Menu: 4,000 ft.
Diners come all the way from Budapest to taste the lamb stew in this friendly small restaurant. The interior is unpretentious: two rows of bistro tables, and a long polished wooden bench against the wall. The warm welcome offered by the father-and-son team that runs the place is friendly and genuine – one of the secrets of Aranykarny's continued success.

Nemzeti Bormúzeum and Labirintus
Bogdányi u. 10
Tel. 26/317 054
Fax 26/317 054
Daily 10am–10pm.
Menu: 1,300–6,900 ft.
The Museum of Wine here explains the history of winemaking in Hungary, and its different vintages in a well-laid-out series of displays, which also offer an opportunity to taste different Chardonnays, Pinots noirs and Merlots – and sparkling wines as well. Its restaurant, housed in an adjacent cellar, features many dishes prepared with Hungarian wine.

Rab Ráby
Kucsera Ferenc u. 1/a
Tel. 26/310 819
Fax 26/310 819
Daily noon–11pm.
Menu: 3,000-6,500 ft.
From its extraordinary decor, you might think you had stepped into another museum. Musical instruments, armor, clocks, oil lamps, old radios and a thousand other curiosities jostle for space on the walls and in the corners. Each table is named after a famous personality from the area. The food is fantastic: try fish soup, or leg of goose – and the desserts are out of this world.

◆PLACES TO VISIT
Addresses and opening times

Places are listed by district and in alphabetical order. ★ Not to be missed

BUDAPEST

Address	Description	Page
ADY ENDRE EMLÉKMÚZEUM Veres Pálné u. 4–6, V Tel. 337 85 63 Subway line 3 Ferenciek tere; bus 8, 15; tram 2	**ADY MEMORIAL MUSEUM** *Open Tue-Fri 10am–5.30pm; Sat-Sun 10am–3.30pm.* *Home of the poet Endre Ady.*	
ÁLLATKERT City Park, Állatkerti körút 6–12, XIV Tel. 363 37 10 www.zoobudapest.com Subway line 1 to Széchenyi fürdő; bus 4	**BUDAPEST ZOO** *Open May 1–Aug 31: daily 9am–6pm (7pm Fri-Sat & school holidays); March–April & Sep–Oct: 9am–5pm; Nov 1–Feb 28: 9am–4pm.*	▲ 160
- AQUINCUMI MÚZEUM ÉS ROMTERÜLET Szentendrei út 139, III Tel. 250 16 50a.	**AQUINCUM MUSEUM** *Open March 15–April 30 and Oct: Tue-Sun 9am–5pm; May 1–Sep 30: Tue-Sun 9am–6pm.* *Guided tours. Remains of Roman villa.*	▲ 227
- HERCULES-VILLA Meggyfa u. 19–2, III Tel. 250 16 50 Bus 42, 134; Suburban trains HÉV to Aquincum	**HERCULES VILLA** *Third-century mosaic floor, with sarcophagi from the 3rd to the 5th centuries in the gardens.*	▲ 227
ARANY SAS PATIKAMÚZEUM Tárnok u. 18, I Tel. 375 97 72 Bus 16; várbusz (Castle bus)	**GOLDEN EAGLE PHARMACY MUSEUM** *Open Tue-Sun 10.30am–5.30pm.* *History of pharmacy from the Middle Ages to the 17th century.*	
BARTÓK BÉLA EMLÉKHÁZ Csalán út 29, II Tel. 394 44 72 or 394 21 00 Bus 5, 29	**BARTÓK MEMORIAL HOUSE** *Open Tue–Sun 10am–5pm.* *The composer's house, arranged to display his life and work.*	
BELVÁROSI PLÉBÁNIA TEMPLOM ★ Március 15. tér, V Subway line 3 Ferenciek tere; tram 2	**INNER CITY PARISH CHURCH** *Splendid building completed in a whole mixture of styles (Roman, Gothic, Renaissance, Turkish and Austrian Baroque). The oldest building in Pest.*	▲ 120
BÉLYEGMÚZEUM Hársfa u. 47, VII Tel. 341 55 26 Tram 4, 6; trolleybus 74	**STAMP MUSEUM** *Open Tue-Sun 10am–6pm.*	
CONTRA AQUINCUM East of Március 15. tér, V Bus 7, 78 (Ferenciek tere), 5, 8 (Március 15. tér stop)	**AQUINCUM CAMP** *Ruins of Roman fort (late 3rd century).*	▲ 120
EGYETEMI TEMPLOM Egyetem tér, V Bus 7, 78 (Ferenciek tere stop), 5, 8 (Március 15. tér stop)	**UNIVERSITY CHURCH** *The city's most beautiful baroque church.*	▲ 122
ERNST MÚZEUM Nagymezə u. 8, VI Tel. 413 13 10 Subway line 1 (yellow) to Oktogon; trolleybus 70, 78	**ERNST MUSEUM** *Open Tue-Sun 10am–6pm.* *Temporary exhibitions of contemporary artists from Hungary and other countries.*	
EVANGÉLIKUS MÚZEUM Deák Ferenc tér 4–5, V Tel. 317 41 73 Subway lines 1, 2, 3 to Deák tér; bus 4, 9, 15, 105; tram 47, 49	**NATIONAL LUTHERAN MUSEUM** *Open Tue-Sun 10am–6pm. Guided tours in English and German.* *In the presbytery of the Lutheran church, with Martin Luther's original Bible (1542).*	▲ 123
FÖLDALATTI VASÚTI MÚZEUM Deák Ferenc téri aluljáró (underground passage) Tel. 485 53 00 Subway lines 1, 2, 3 Deák tér; bus 9, 16, 105; tram 47, 49	**UNDERGROUND RAILWAY MUSEUM** *Open Sun-Tue 10am–6pm.* *The museum contains two carriages dating from 1896, when the Budapest underground opened for the first time.*	▲ 123
GOETHE INSTITUT Andrássy út 24, VI Tel. 374 40 70 Subway line 1 Opéra	**GŒTHE INSTITUTE** *Open Mon-Fri noon–7pm; Sat noon–4pm.* *Temporary exhibitions.*	● 57

Hungarian name / address	English name / details	Page
GÖRÖKELETI TEMPLOM Petófi tér, V Bus 7, 78 (Ferenciek tere stop), 5, 8 (Március 15. tér stop)	**GREEK ORTHODOX CHURCH** *18th-century church with rococo façade.*	▲ 118
GÜL BABA TÜRBE Turbán u. 11, II Tel. 355 88 49 Bus 91	**TOMB OF GÜL BABA** *Open May 1–Sep 30: Tue-Sun 10am–6pm; Oct 1–April 30: Tue-Sun 10am–4pm.* *Today, museum and place of pilgrimage.*	
HADTÖRTÉNETI INTÉZET ÉS MÚZEUM Tóth Árpád sétány 40, I Tel. 356 95 22 Bus 16; várbusz (Castle bus)	**MILITARY HISTORY MUSEUM** *Open Tue-Sun 10am–6pm.* *Guided tours in English & German.*	▲ 202
HALÁSZBÁSTYA Szentháromság tér, I Tel. 06 20 348 18 83 Bus 16; várbusz (Castle bus)	**FISHERMEN'S BASTION** *Open daily May 1–Sep 15: 9am–11pm; Sep 16–Nov 15: 9am–9pm; March 15–April 30: 9am–7pm.* *Lookout tower; crypt of St Michael's Chapel.*	▲ 203
HOLOKAUSZT EMLÉKKÖZPONT Páva utca 39, IX Tel. 216 65 57 www.hdke.hu Subway line 3 Ferenc Körút; tram 4, 6;	**HOLOCAUST MUSEUM AND DOCUMENTATION CENTRE** *Museum opened in 2004.*	
HOPP FERENC KELET-ÁZSIAI MIVÉSZETI MÚZEUM Andrássy út 103, VI Tel. 322 84 76 Subway line 2 to Bajza u.; bus 4, 105	**FERENC HOPP MUSEUM OF EAST ASIAN ART** *Open Tue-Sun 10am–6pm.* *Ferenc Hopp's collection of Asian art (India, Tibet, Nepal, Mongolia).*	▲ 148
IPÁRMIVÉSZETI MÚZEUM H Üllői út 33–37, IX Tel. 456 51 00 Subway line 3 to Ferenc körút; tram 4, 6	**MUSEUM OF APPLIED ARTS** *Open Tue-Sun 10am–6pm.*	▲ 171
JÓZSEF ATTILA MÚZEUM Gát u. 3, IX Tel. 216 61 27 Tram 4, 6, 30	**ATTILA JÓZSEF MUSEUM** *Open Tue-Sun 10am–6pm.* *The poet's home, with a collection of his manuscripts.*	
KERESKEDELMI ÉS VENDÉGLÁTÓIPARI MÚZEUM Fortuna u. 4, I Tel. 375 62 49 Bus 16; várbusz (Castle bus)	**COMMERCE AND CATERING MUSEUM** *Open Wed-Fri 10am–5pm; Sat-Sun 10am–6pm.* *A look at hotels, restaurants and thermal baths (objets, furniture etc.) in early 20th-century Budapest.*	▲ 204
KIRÁLYI VÁR ★ Budavári palota, I Bus 5, 16, 78 ; várbusz (Castle bus); tram 18; funicular	**ROYAL PALACE** *The Castle district is forbidden to cars.*	▲ 190
– MAGYAR NEMZETI GALÉRIA Wings B, C, D of the Palace Disz tér 17 Tel. 375 79 92 / 423	**– HUNGARIAN NATIONAL GALLERY** *Open Tue–Sun 10am–6pm.* *Guided tours (English, Russian) of the Crypt of Archduke Joseph.*	▲ 193
– BUDAPESTI TÖRTÉNETI MÚZEUM Wing E of the Palace Szent György tér 2 Tel. 225 78 15	**– BUDAPEST HISTORY MUSEUM** *Open May 15–Sep 15: daily 10am–6pm; March 1–May 15 & Sep 15–Oct 31: Tue-Sun 10am–6pm; Nov 1–Feb 28: Tue-Sun 10am–4pm.*	▲ 192
– NÁDOR KRIPTA Access via the National Gallery	**– THE HABSBURG ROYAL CRYPT**	▲ 199
– ORSZÁGOS SZÉCHÉNYI LEVÉLTÁR Wing F of the Palace Tel. 224 37 00	**– NATIONAL SZÉCHÉNYI LIBRARY (NATIONAL ARCHIVES)** *Open Mon-Fri 9am–5.30pm; Sat 10am–8pm.* *Free admission. Medieval manuscripts*	▲ 199
KISCELLI MÚZEUM ★ Kiscelli u. 108, III Tel. 388 78 17 www.btmfk.uf.hu Bus 60, 165; tram 17	**KISCELL MUSEUM** *Open Tue-Sun 10am–6pm.* *Collection of works representing Budapest and contemporary Hungarian art collection.*	▲ 223

Name / Address	Description	Page
KODÁLY ZOLTÁN MÚZEUM Kodály körönd 1, VI Tel. 342 84 48 Subway line 1 (yellow) to Kodály körönd; bus 4, 105	**ZOLTÁN KODÁLY MUSEUM** *Open Wed 10am–4pm; Thu-Sat 10am–6pm, Sun 10am–2pm.* *The composer's home; popular works collection.*	
KOGART HÁZ Andrássy út 112, VI Tel. 354 38 29 www.kogart.hu Subway line 1 (yellow) to Hősöktere	**KOGART HOUSE** *Open daily 10am–6pm.* *Temporary exhibitions in a museum that was a former palace.*	
KÖZLEKEDÉSI MÚZEUM Városligeti körút 11, XIV Városliget Tel. 273 38 40 Tram 1; trolleybus 70, 72, 74	**TRANSPORTATION MUSEUM** *Open May 1–Sep 30: Tue-Fri 10am–5pm; Sat-Sun 10am–6pm;* *Oct 1–April 30: Tue-Fri 10am– 4pm; Sat–Sun 10am–5pm. Free on Wed.*	
KÖZLEKEDÉSI MÚZEUM Zichy Mihály u. 14 (City Park), XIV Tel. 363 08 09 Subway line 1 to Széchenyi fürdő; trolleybus 70, 72, 74	**AVIATION MUSEUM** *Open May 15–Sep 30: Tue-Fri 10am–5pm; Sat-Sun 10am–6pm. Free on Wed.* *Planes and gliders; model aircraft.*	
KUN ZSIGMOND GYŰJTEMÉNY Fó tér 4 (opposite Zichy Mansion), III Tel. 368 11 38 Bus 86	**ZSIGMOND KUN FOLK ART COLLECTION** *Open Tue-Sun 10am–5pm.* *Museum of folk arts & crafts on the top floor.*	▲ 226
LISZT FERENC MÚZEUM Vörösmarty u. 35, VI Tel. 322 98 04 Subway line 1 (yellow) to Vörösmarty utca	**FRANZ LISZT MUSEUM** *Mon-Fri 10am–6pm; Sat 9am–5pm.* *The composer's last home, with displays of his life and work.*	▲ 145
MAGYAR ÁLLAMI OPERAHÁZ ★ Andrássy út 22, VI Tel. 331 25 50 Subway line 1 (yellow) to Opera; bus 4	**HUNGARIAN STATE OPERA HOUSE** *Guided visits every day at 3 and 4pm (English, French, German, Italian and Spanish).*	▲ 141
MAGYAR FÖLDTANI INTÉZET Stefánia út 14, XIV Tel. 251 09 99 Subway line 2 to Népstadion; bus 7; trolleybus 75	**THE INSTITUTE OF GEOLOGY** *Open Thu-Sun 10am–3pm.* *Masterpiece of the Hungarian Secession.*	▲ 162
MAGYAR NEMZETI MÚZEUM Múzeum krt 14–16, VIII Tel. 327 77 49 Subway line 2 (red) to Astoria, line 3 (blue) to Kálvin tér, bus 9; tram 47, 49	**HUNGARIAN NATIONAL MUSEUM** *Open Tue-Sun 10am–6pm.* *History of Hungary since its founding.*	▲ 123
MAGYAR TERMÉSZETTUDOMÁNYI MÚZEUM Ludovika tér 2, VIII Tel. 333 06 55 Subway line 3 (blue) to Klinikák	**MUSEUM OF NATURAL SCIENCES** *Open Tue-Sun 10am–6pm.*	
MAGYAR TUDOMÁNYOS AKADÉMIA Roosevelt tér, V Bus 105 (József Nádor tér stop); tram 2 (Roosevelt tér stop)	**HUNGARIAN ACADEMY OF SCIENCES** *Statues of famous European scientists on the second floor.*	▲ 137
MÁRIA MAGDOLNA TORONY Kapisztrán tér 6, I Bus 16, várbusz (Castle bus)	**MARY MAGDELENE TOWER** *Open daily 10am–6pm. Medieval church tower with a peal of 24 bells (8am–9pm; every 30 mins.)*	▲ 205
MÁTYÁS TEMPLOM ★ also known as **BUDAVÁRI NAGYBOLDOGASSZONY TEMPLOM** Szentháromság tér 2, I Tel. 488 04 75 Bus 16, várbusz (Castle bus)	**MATTHIAS CHURCH** **(BUDA CHURCH OF OUR LADY)** *Contains a magnificent treasury. Concerts held.* *Open Mon-Fri 9am–5pm; Sat 9am–1pm* *Sun 1–5pm.*	▲ 202

MILLENÁRIS PARK Fény utca 20-22, II Tel. 438 53 35 www.millenaris.hu Subway line 2 to Moszkva tér	**MILLENNIUM PARK** *Open daily 10am–6pm.* *Temporary exhibitions; concerts.*	
M|CSARNOK Hősök tere 1, XIV Tel. 363 26 71 www.mucsarnok.hu Subway line 1 to Hősök tere; bus 4 (red), 20, 30, 105; trolleybus 75, 79	**THE PALACE OF ARTS** *Open Tue-Sun 10am–6pm.* *Hungary's largest modern and contemporary art gallery. Temporary exhibitions of applied and decorative arts, design and photography.*	▲ 148
MUVESZETEK PALOTÁJA Komor Marcell u. 1, IX Tel. 555 30 00 www.mupa.hu Bus 23, 54, 79, 103; tram 1, 2, 24, 30 Közvágóhíd **- LUDWIG MÚZEUM** Wing A of the Palace Tel. 375 91 75	**PALACE OF ARTS** *Opened in March 2005.* *Theater and concert hall to the national philharmonic orchestra.* **- LUDWIG MUSEUM** *Open Tue-Sun 10am–6pm.* *American Pop Art, & art of the 1980s and 1990s.*	
NAGYTÉTÉNY KASTÉLY Kastély Park utca 9-11, XXII Tel. 207 00 05	*Open Tue-Sun 10am–6pm.* *Exhibition of Gothic style furniture in the castle at Biedermeir.*	
NÉPRAJZI MÚZEUM ★ Kossuth Lajos tér 12, V Tel. 473 24 00 www.neprajz.hu Subway line 2 to Kossuth tér; bus 15; tram 2; trolleybus 70, 78	**ETHNOGRAPHICAL MUSEUM** *Open Tue–Sun 10am–6pm.* *Hungarian peasant life (customs, costumes) from the beginning of the 20th century.*	▲ 134
ORSZÁGHÁZ ★ Kossuth Lajos tér 1–3, V Tel. 441 30 00 Subway line 2 (red) to Kossuth tér; bus 15; tramway 2; trolleybus 70, 78	**PARLIAMENT** *Guided group visits available Mon-Fri 8am–6pm; Sat 8am–4pm; Sun 8am–2pm.* *Closed during special sessions.* *Entrance Door XII.*	▲ 127
PESTI VIGADÓ Vigadó tér 2, V Subway line 1 (yellow) to Vörösmarty tér, 2 (red) and 3 (blue) to Deák tér; tram 2 **- VIGADÓ ART GALLERY** (on the groundfloor)	**CONCERT HALL** *No visits, except for performances.* **- VIGADÓ ART GALLERY** *Open Tue-Sun 10am–6pm.*	▲ 118
PETÓFI IRODALMI MÚZEUM Károlyi Mihály u. 16, V Tel. 317 36 11 Subway line 2 to Astoria, line 3 to Ferenciek tere; bus 5, 8, 15, 112; tram 47, 49	**PETŐFI MUSEUM OF LITERATURE** *Open Tue-Sun 10am–6pm.* *Introduction to the great Hungarian writers.*	▲ 122
POSTAMÚZEUM Andrássy út 3 Tel. 269 68 38 Subway line 1 (yellow) to Bajcsy–Zsilinszky út, lines 2 (red) and 3 (blue) to Deák tér; bus 4, 105	**POSTAL MUSEUM** *Open April 1–Oct 31: Tue-Sun 10am–6pm; Nov 1–March 31: Tue-Sun 10am–4pm.* *Guided tours in English & German.* *Two examples of 19th-century post-offices.*	▲ 141
PRO ARTS / A.P.A! Horánszky u.5, VIII Tel. 486 23 70 www.ateliers.hu	**PRO ARTS / A.P.A! STUDIOS** *Open Mon-Fri 2–7pm; Sat 11am–6pm.* *Studios/galleries in an old factory.*	
RÁTH GYÖRGY MÚZEUM Városligeti fasor 12, VI Tel. 342 39 16 Subway line 1 (yellow) to Bajza utca; bus 4, 105; trolleybus 78, 79	**GYÖRGY RATH MUSEUM** *Open Tue-Sun 10am–6pm.* *Guided tours in English, German and Mongolian.* *Collections of Chinese and Japanese art, including Gyögy Rath's, in an art nouveau villa.*	
SEMMELWEIS ORVOSTÖRTÉNETI MÚZEUM Apród u. 1–3, I Tel. 375 35 33 Bus 5, 7, 78, 86; trams 18, 19	**SEMMELWEIS MUSEUM OF MEDICAL HISTORY** *Open Tue-Sun 10.30am–6pm.* *Guided tours in English, French and German.* *Housed in the birthplace of Ignac Semmelweis, the museum traces the history of medicine.*	▲ 214

Name / Address	Description	Page
SZABÓ ERVIN KÖNYVTÁR Szabo Ervin tér 1, VIII Tel. 411 50 01	**ERVIN SZABÓ MUNICIPAL LIBRARY** *Open Tue-Sun 10am–6pm.* *Lecture halls in the Weckheim palace.*	▲ 171
SZENT ANNA TEMPLOM ★ Batthyány tér, II Subway line 2 Batthyány tér	**ST ANNE'S CHURCH** *Baroque masterpiece.*	▲ 207
SZENT ISTVÁN TEMPLOM Szent István tér, V Tel. 317 28 59 Subway line 3 to Arany János u.	**ST STEPHEN'S BASILICA** *Houses the basilica treasury (examples of 19th-century Hungarian, Austrian and German religious art).*	▲ 136
SZÉPMŰVÉSZETI MÚZEUM ★ Dózsa György út 41 (City Park), XIV Tel. 363 26 75 www.szepmuveszeti.hu Subway line 2 to Hősök tere; bus 4, 20, 30, 105; trolleybus 75, 79	**THE MUSEUM OF FINE ARTS** *Open Tue-Sat 10am–5.30pm.* *Magnificent mixed collection, rich in Spanish old masters.*	▲ 149
SZOBORPAR Corner of Balatoni út and Szabadkai utca, XXII Tel. 227 74 46 Bus 50	**STATUE PARK** *Open daily 10am–dusk.* *Open-air exhibition of the statues that used to adorn the city streets during the Communist era.*	▲ 110
TELEFÓNIA MÚZEUM Úri u. 49, I Tel. 201 81 88 Bus 16, várbusz (Castle bus)	**TELEPHONE MUSEUM** *Open April 1–Oct 31: Tue-Sun 10am–6pm;* *Nov 1–March 31: Tue-Sun 10am–4pm.* *Guided tours in English and German.*	
TERROR HÁZ Andrássy út 60, VI Tel. 374 26 00 www.terrorhaza.hu Subway line 1 Vörösmarty u.	**HORRORS OF WAR MUSEUM** *Open Mon-Fri 10am–6pm; Sat-Sun 10am–7.30pm.*	▲ 145
TRAFÓ Liliom u. 41, IX Tel. 456 20 40 www.trafo.hu Subway line 3 Ferenc Körút; tramway 4, 6	**ARTS AND CONTEMPORARY SHOWS CENTER** *Housed in an old electrical factory.*	▲ 174
VAJDAHUNYAD VÁRA Városliget (City Park), XIV **- MEZŐGAZDASÁGI MÚZEUM** Tel. 363 50 99 Subway line 1 to Széchenyi fürdő; bus 4 (red), 20, 30, 105; trolleybus 75, 72, 75, 79	**VAJDAHUNYAD CASTLE** *Roman chapel and gothic tower in the castle's gardens.* **- MUSEUM OF AGRICULTURE** *Open Tue–Sun 10am–5pm.*	▲ 161
VÁRBARLANG (corner of Dárda u.), I Access via Úri u. 9 Tel. 489 32 80 www.labirintus.com	**CASTLE LABYRINTH (BUDAVARI LABYRINTHUS)** *Open Tue-Sun 9.30am–7.30pm. Guided tours only (in English, French and German). The Labyrinth is part of the Buda Castle Waxworks ▲ 202.*	▲ 200
VÁRFOK GALÉRIA Várfok utca 11 & 14, I Tel. 213 51 55 Subway line 2 Moszkva tér	**VÁRFOK GALLERY** *Contemporary art gallery showing Hungarian and international works.*	
VARGA IMRE GYŰJTEMÉNY Laktanya u. 7, III Tel. 250 02 74 Bus 6, 86; suburban train HÉV to Árpád híd	**IMRE VARGA GALLERY** *Open Tue-Sun 10am–6pm.* *Guided tours in German. Standing collection of the work of the sculptor Varga.*	▲ 227
VASUT TÖRTENETI PARK Tatai út 95, XIV Tel. 238 05 58 www.vasuttortenetipark.hu	**INTERACTIVE RAIL MUSEUM** *Open Tue-Sun 10am–3pm.*	
ZENETÖRTÉNETI MÚZEUM In the Erdődy Palace Táncsics Mihály u. 7, I Tel. 214 67 70 Bus 16, várbusz (Castle bus)	**MUSIC HISTORY MUSEUM** *Under renovation; due to reopen 2007.* *Collection of historical musical instruments, exhibition devoted to Béla Bartók.*	▲ 204

ZICHY PALOTA Fő tér 1, III Bus 6, 86 (red), 86, tram 1, suburban train HÉV to Árpád híd	**ZICHY MANSION**	▲ 226
- KASSÁK LAJOS EMLÉKMÚZEUM Tel. 368 70 21	**- KASSÁK MEMORIAL MUSEUM** *Open Tue-Sun 10am–6pm.*	
- ÓBUDAI HELYTÖRTÉNETI GYIJTEMÉNY Tel. 250 10 20	**- ÓBUDA LOCAL HISTORY MUSEUM** *Open Tue-Fri 2pm–6pm; Sat-Sun 10am–6pm.*	
- VASARELY MÚZEUM Tel. 250 15 40 Bus 6, 86 (red), 86; tram 1; suburban train HÉV to Árpád híd	**- VASARELY MUSEUM** *Open Tue-Sun 10am–6pm. Guided tours in English. Exhibition of more than 400 works by Victor Vasarely and works by Hungarian artists living outside Hungary.*	
ZSIDÓ MÚZEUM Dohány u. 2, VII (entrance also on Wesselényi u.) Tel. 342 89 49 Subway lines 1 (yellow), 2 (red), 3 (blue) to Deák tér; tram 47, 49; trolleybus 74	**THE NATIONAL JEWISH MUSEUM** *Open Mon-Thu 10am–3pm, Sun 10am–2pm* *Part of the Synagogue (Zsinagoga). Jewish history, Jewish mausoleum.*	▲ 167

AROUND BUDAPEST

ESZTERGOM 2000

BASILICA Szent István tér 1	**THE BASILICA OF ESTERGOM (WITH TREASURY)**	▲ 239
KERESZTÉNY MÚZEUM Tel. (33) 403 162	**MUSEUM OF CHRISTIAN ART** *Open Tue-Sun 9am–5pm.*	▲ 239
VÁRMÚZEUM Szent István tér Tel. (33) 415 986	**PALACE MUSEUM** *Open March-Oct: Tue–Sun 10am–6pm;* *Nov–Feb: Tue-Sun 9am–4pm.*	▲ 239

GÖDÖLLO 2100

GRASSALKOVICH KASTÉLY Tel. (28) 420 588 www.royalpalace-godollo.com	**ROYAL PALACE MUSEUM** *Open April 1–Oct 31: Tue-Sun 10am–5pm;* *Nov 1–March 31: Tue-Sun 10am–4pm.*	▲ 240

SZENTENDRE 2500

ANNA MARGIT-ÁMOS IMRE MÚZEUM BARCSAY MÚZEUM Bogdányi u. 10/b Tel. (26) 310 244	**ANNA-MARGIT-IMRE-AMOS MUSEUM AND BARCSAY MUSEUM** *Open Tue-Sun 10am–6pm.*	▲ 232
CZÓBEL MÚZEUM Templom tér 1 Tel. (26) 312 721	**BÉLA CZÓBEL MUSEUM** *Open Tue-Thu 10am–6pm; Fri-Sun 10am–8pm.*	▲ 233
FERENCZY KÁROLY MÚZEUM Fő tér (Main square) 6 Tel. (26) 310 244	**FERENCZY MUSEUM** *Open Tue-Sun 10am–6pm.*	▲ 232
KOVÁCS MARGIT MÚZEUM Vastagh György u. 1 Tel. (26) 500 453	**MARGIT KOVÁCS MUSEUM** *Open Mon-Thu 10am–6pm; Fri-Sun 10am–8pm.*	▲ 232
SKANZEN Sztaravodai út Tel. (26) 502 500 www.skanzen.hu Road no. 11/HÉV to Szentendre and bus terminal 7	**ECOMUSEUM OF TRADITIONAL HUNGARIAN AGRICULTURE** *Open April 1–Oct 31: Tue-Sun 9am–5pm.*	▲ 235
VAJDA LAJOS MÚZEUM Hunyadi u. 1 Tel. (26) 310 244	**LAJOS-VADJA MUSEUM** *Open Tue-Sun 10am–6pm.*	▲ 233

FESTIVALS AND EVENTS

Public holidays: January 1; March 15; Easter Monday; Whit Monday; May 1; August 20; October 24; December 25-26

PUBLIC HOLIDAYS AND FESTIVALS		
DECEMBER 31	Tel. 302 42 90 www.viparts.hu	**MASKED BALL AT THE OPERA HOUSE**
JANUARY 1	Tel. 317 50 67	**NEW YEAR'S GALA** *Operetta concert given in the Royal Palace in Pest (Pesti Vigadó), with an ensemble of 100 violins.*
FEB 19–DEC 31	Tel. 365 22 93	**CLASSICAL MUSIC CONCERTS** *Take place every year at the Matthias Church at Buda Castle.*
MARCH 15		**NEMZETI ÜNNEP** (public holiday) *Celebrates the day in 1848 when Hungary was proclaimed a republic (start of the 1848 revolution).*
MARCH 15–31	Tel. 201 87 79 Fax 201 51 28	**INTERFOLKTÁNC** *Folk dance festival.*
MARCH 14–31	Tel. 486 33 00 www.festivalcity.hu	**BUDAPEST SPRING FESTIVAL** *Hungary's largest cultural festival. Events in and around Budapest. International artists, music, theater, etc.*
JUNE		**BUDAPEST FAIR**
JUNE 21		**INTERNATIONAL MUSIC DAY**
JUNE 24	www.festivalcity.hu	**BÚCSÚ** *One of the biggest street festivals, celebrating the departure of Russian forces in 1991. Music and other events.*
MAY 1		**LABOR DAY** (*a munka ünnepe*) *Celebrations in the City Park and Tabán district.*
JUNE–AUGUST	Tel. 26 / 312 657	**SUMMER IN SZENTENDRE** *Theater festival.*
MID JUNE/MID JULY	Tel. 215 79 05 Fax 218 31 00	**FERENCVÁROS CELEBRATIONS** *In Bakáts Square: opera, classical and rock concerts.*
MID JULY	Tel. 26 / 398 255 Fax 26 / 398 163	**INTERNATIONAL CASTLE FESTIVAL AT SEGRAD** *Jousting and troubadour music.*
JULY 24	Tel. 87 / 343 255 Fax 87 / 343 457	**ANNE CELEBRATIONS** (Balatonfüred) *Celebration dating back to the Reformation: beauty contest, chamber music, etc.*
JULY/AUG		**SUMMER ON THE CHAIN BRIDGE** *Szechenyi Bridge traffic-free on Sundays.*
AUG	Tel. 372 06 50 www.sziget.hu	**SZIGET FESTIVAL** (Obuda Island) *or the Eurowoodstock. Week-long music festival since 1993, with an audience of more than 300,000 people; 600 bands; 30 stages.*
AUGUST		**BAROQUE CELEBRATIONS** (Gödöllő Castle)
AUGUST	Tel. 302 42 90 www.opera.hu	**BUDAFEST** *Summer Opera and Ballet Festival.*
AUGUST 20		**ST STEPHEN'S DAY** (Szent István ünnep) *One of the two most important national holidays. Firework displays.*
AUG/SEP	Tel. 344 54 09 www.jewishfestival.hu	**JEWISH SUMMER FESTIVAL** *Dance, music perfomances, films, exhibitions...*
SEPTEMBER 7–12	Tel. 203 85 07 www.winefestival.hu	**BUDAPEST INTERNATIONAL WINE FESTIVAL** *Auction of vintage wines, Harvest Ball, wine, music, food and dancing.*
OCT 16–NOV 1	Tel. 486 33 00 www.festivalcity.hu	**BUDAPEST AUTUMN FESTIVAL** *Contemporary Arts Festival. Competition for young composers.*
OCTOBER 23		**ANNIVERSARY OF THE REVOLUTION** (56-as forradalom évfordulója) *Commemorating the 1956 uprising.*
DECEMBER		**CHRISTMAS MARKET** *In Vörösmarty tér and other places.*
DECEMBER 6		**ST NICHOLAS' DAY** (Mikulás)
SPORTING EVENTS		
END AUGUST	Tel. 317 2811 / 266 2040 www.hungaroring.hu	**FORMULA 1 GRAND PRIX** (Mogyoród)
OCTOBER	Tel. 367 32 34 www.budapest marathon.com	**HUNGARIAN MARATHON** *For sportsmen and amateurs.*

PRONUNCIATION OF HUNGARIAN

CONSONANTS

c ts
cs ch
h h
j, ly y
ny gn
s sh
sz s
ty ty (as in 'twenty')
zs j (as in 'pleasure')

DOUBLE CONSONANT
(ll, ff, etc.): the pronunciation of these sounds is twice as long

VOWELS
Accents denote a longer vowel.

a between a and o ('cat' and 'hot')
á long a ('task')
e e ('pet')
é ay
i i ('hit')
í ee ('sleet')
o o
ó long o ('awful')
ö er
ő long er
u u ('put')
ú long u ('boot')
ü French u or German ü
ű long French u or German ü

See also "History of the Hungarian language" pages 38–40

HUNGARIAN-ENGLISH and phonetic pronunciation

Words of greetings

Bocsánat (boachanot): pardon
Bor (bore): wine
Csókolom (chokolom): good day (from a man to a woman)
Fizetek (fizzaytake): the bill, please
Igen (eegain): yes
Jó (yó): good
Jó estét (yo estate): good evening
Jó napot (yo nopote): good afternoon
Jó reggelt (yo raygailt): good morning
Kávé (cavay): coffee
Kenyér (kaynyair): bread
Köszönöm (kersernerm): thank you
Most (moast): now
Nem (name): no
Sör (ser): beer
Tea (tayo): tea
Tudja, merre van a... (tootya, merray von o...): can you tell me where there is a ...
Viszontlátásra, viszlát (vissontlatashra, visslat): goodbye

Days and hours

Délben (dailben): at midday
Éj (ayi): night
Év (ayv): year
Hét (hate): week
Holnap (hoalnop): tomorrow
Ma (maw): today
Nap (nop): day
Óra (erer): hour
Perc (pairk): minute
Reggel (raygel): in the morning
Tegnap (taignop): yesterday

Days of the week

Csütörtök (chuterterk): thursday
Hétfő (hetfer): monday
Kedd (ked): tuesday
Péntek (paintek): friday
Szerda (sairdo): wednesday
Szombat (somboht): saturday
Vasárnap (vozhanop): sunday

Urban vocabulary

Állomás, megálló (allomash, megallo): stop, station
Áruház (aruhaz): shop
(Autó)busz (outo)boos: bus
Bástya (bashtyo), or torony (toron ya): tower
Bejárat (bayarot): entrance
Bolt (bolt): boutique
Cím (tseem): address
Domb (dombe): hill
Duna (doono): Danube
Folyó (foeeo): river
Földalatti (ferldolotti): Small Metro
Fürdő (foorder): baths
Gang (gung): open landing
Ház (haz): house, building
Hegy (heddy): mount
Híd (heed): bridge
Kijárat (keearat): exit
Körút (keroot): boulevard
Lakás (lockash): apartment
Metro (metro): metro
Múzeum (muzeum): museum
Név (nayv): name
Pályaudvar (payoodvor): station
Rakpart (rokport): wharf
Repülőtér (repuletér): airport
Szálloda (sallodor): hotel
Színház (sinharz): theater
Templom (tameplom): church
Tér (tare): square
Udvar (oodvor): courtyard
Uszoda (oosoda): swimming pool
Utca (ootsa): street
Út, sugárút (oout, shugaroout): avenue
Vár (var): castle
Város (varosh): city/town
Vendéglő, étterem (vendaygler, aytterem): restaurant
Villamos (villomoash): tramway
Vonat (vonot): train
Zárva (zarvo): closed

ENGLISH-HUNGARIAN

Words of greetings

Beer: sör
The bill, please: fizetek
Bread: kenyér
Can you tell me where there is a...: Tudja, merre van a...
Coffee: kávé
Excuse me: bocsánat
Good: jó
Good afternoon: jó napot
Good bye: viszontlátásra, viszlát
Good day (from a man to a woman): csókolom
Good evening: jó estét
Good morning: jó reggelt
No: nem
Now: most
Tea: tea (tayo)
Thank you: köszönöm
yes: igen
Wine: bor

Days and hours

Day: nap
Hour: óra
In the morning: reggel
Midday: délben
Minute: perc
Night: éj
Today: ma
Tomorrow: holnap
Week: hét
Year: év
Yesterday: tegnap

Days of the week

Monday: ***hétfő***
Tuesday: ***kedd***
Wednesday: ***szerda***
Thursday: ***csütörtök***
Friday: ***péntek***
Saturday: ***szombat***
Sunday: ***vasárnap***

Urban vocabulary

Address: cím
Airport: repülőtér
Apartment: lakás
Avenue: út, sugárút
Baths: fürdő
Boulevard: körút
Boutique: bolt
Bridge: híd
Bus: busz
Castle: vár
Church: templom
City/town: város
Closed: zárva
Courtyard: udvar
Danube: Duna
Entrance: bejárat
Exit: kijárat
Hill: domb
Hotel: szálloda
House, building: ház
Metro: metro
Mount: hegy
Museum: múzeum
Name: név
Open landing: gang
Restaurant: vendéglő, étterem
River: folyó
Shop: áruház
Small Metro: földalatti
Square: tér
Station: pályaudvar
Stop, station: állomás, megálló
Street: utca
Swimming pool: uszoda
Theater: színház
Tower: bástya or torony
Train: vonat
Tramway: villamos
Wharf: rakpart

Numbers

One: ***egy*** (aydi)
Two: ***kettő*** (kaytter)
Three: ***három*** (harome)
Four: ***négy*** (naydi)
Five: ***öt*** (ert)
Six: ***hat*** (hot)
Seven: ***hét*** (hate)
Eight: ***nyolc*** (nyok)
Nine: ***kilenc*** (keelents)
Ten: ***tíz*** (teez)
Twenty: ***húsz*** (hoose)
Thirty: ***harminc*** (hormints)
Forty: ***negyven*** (naydiven)
Fifty: ***ötven*** (ertven)
Sixty: ***hatvan*** (hotvon)
Seventy: ***hetven*** (hate-ven)
Eighty: ***nyolcvan*** (nyokvon)
Ninety: ***kilencven*** (keelentsven)
One hundred: ***száz*** (saz)
One thousand: ***ezer*** (ayzare)
Zero: ***nulla*** (nolla)

◆ BIBLIOGRAPHY AND DISCOGRAPHY

HISTORY AND CULTURE

◆ BEATON (C.), *The Wandering Years, Diaries 1922–39*, Weidenfeld, 1961

◆ BROOK (S.), *The Double Eagle: Vienna, Budapest, & Prague*, Hamish Hamilton

◆ COOPER (L.R.), KENESI (A.), *Hungarians in Transition : Interviews with Citizens of the Nineties*, Mcfarland and Co., 1993

◆ DENES (M.), *Castles Burning*, Doubleday, 1997

◆ GERő (A.) (ed.), *Modern Hungarian Society in the Making*, CEU Press, 1995

◆ GERő (A.), *The Hungarian Parliament (1867–1918): A Mirage of Power,* East European Monographs, 1997

◆ GUNDEL (K.), *Gundel's Hungarian Cookbook*

◆ HOENSCH (JÖRG. K.), Traynor (K.), *A History of Modern Hungary 1867–1994*, Longman, 1995

◆ KOESTLER (A.), *Arrow in the Blue*, Collins with Hamish Hamilton Ltd 1952

◆ LÁZÁR (I.),*Hungary: A Brief History*, Corvina

◆ LEIGH FERMOR (P.), *A Time of Gifts*, Penguin Books, 1979

◆ LUKÁCS (J.), *Budapest 1900: A Historical Portrait of a City and Its Culture*, Grove Press, 1990

◆ MARAI (S.), *Memoirs of Hungary, 1944–8*

◆ POGANY BENNETT (P.) CLARK (V.R.), *The Art of Hungarian Cooking*, Hippocrene Books, 1997

◆ TAYLOR (A.J.P.), *The Habsburg Monarchy 1809–1918*, Penguin, 1964

ARTS

◆ CHALMERS (K.), *Bela Bartok (20th-Century Composers)*, Phaidon, 1995

◆ COOPER (D.), *Bartok: 'Concerto for Orchestra'*, Cambridge University Press, 1996

◆ COTIER (J.), *Nudes in Budapest*, Aktok, 1992

◆ ERNYEY (G.), *Made in Hungary: The Best of 150 Years in Industrial Design*, Rubik Innovation Foundation

◆ FODOR (I.) et al, *Baroque Splendor: The Art of the Hungarian Goldsmith*, Bard Graduate Center, 1995

◆ FRIGYESI (J.), *Béla Bartók and Turn-of-the-Century Budapest*, University of California Press, 1998

◆ GERLE (J.), *The Turn of the Century*, City Hall

◆ HEATHCOTE (E.), *Budapest: A Guide to 20-Century Architecture*, Ellipsis, 1997

◆ KOLBA (J.H.), *Hungarian Silver*, Thomas Heneage, 1998

◆ LORINC, *Budapest Ballet*, Branden Publishing, 1971

◆ LUCY (M.), EVANS (C.), *Hungarian Journeys*, M.Evans, London, 1996

◆ MAGRIS (C.), *Danube*, The Harvill Press, 1999

◆ MANSBACH (S.A), *Two Centuries of Hungarian Painters 1820–1970*, University Press of America, 1992

◆ MORRIS (J.), *Fifty Years of Europe: An Album*, Penguin, 1998

◆ SOLTI (G.), *Memoirs*, Chatto and Windus, 1997

◆ VARDY (S.B.), *Clio's Art in Hungary and Hungarian–America*, East European Monographs, 1986

LITERATURE

◆ ADY (E.), *Neighbours of the Night: Selected Short Stories*, Corvina

◆ ADY (E.), *Poems*, University Press of America, 1988

◆ BIRO (V.), *Hungarian Folk Tales*, Oxford University Press, 1992

◆ CZIGÁNY (L.), *The Oxford History of Hungarian Literature from the Earliest Times to the Present*, Oxford University Press, 1988

◆ ESTERHÁZY (P.), *A Little Hungarian Pornography*, Quartet, 1995

◆ ESTERHÁZY (P.), *She Loves Me*, Quartet,1997

◆ FISCHER (T.), *Under the Frog*, Penguin, 1993

◆ GATTO (K.), *Treasury of Hungarian Live*, Hippocrene, 1996

◆ GOMORI (G.), SZIRTES (G.), *The Colonnade of Teeth*, Bloodaxe Books, 1996

◆ GYORGYEY (C.), *A Mirror to the Cage: Three Contemporary Hungarian Plays*, University of Arkansas, 1993

◆ GONCZ (A.), et al, *Plays and Other Writings*, Garland, 1990

◆ JÓZSEF (A.), *The Iron-Blue Vault*, Bloodaxe Books, 1999

◆ KABDEBO (T.), *Life of Attila Jozsef*, Libris,1995

◆ KERTÉSZ (I.), *Fateless*, Northwestern University Press, 1992

◆ KONRÁD (G.), *The Case Worker*, Penguin

◆ KONRÁD (G.), *The Loser*, Harcourt Brace International

◆ KOSZTOLÁNYI (D.), *Anna Edes*, New Directions, 1993

◆ KOSZTOLÁNYI (D.), *Skylark*, CEU Press

◆ KRUDY (G.) SZIRTES (G.), *The Adventures of Sindbad*, Central European University Press, 1998

◆ LENGYEL (P.), *Cobblestone*, Readers International,1993

◆ LYNNE (A.), *Safe Houses*, Penguin

◆ MAKKAI (A.) (ed.), *In Quest of the 'Miracle Stag': An Anthology of Hungarian Poetry from the 13th Century to the Present*, Atlantis-Centaur/Corvina/ M. Szivarvany, 1996

◆ NADAS (P.), *A Book of Memories*, Vintage,1998

◆ NADAS (P.), GOLDSTEIN (I.), *The End of a Family Story*, Jonathan Cape, 1999

◆ NEMES-NAGY (A.) et al, *Agnes Nemes Nagy on Poetry: A Hungarian Perspective*, Edwin Mellen, 1998

◆ NEMES-NAGY (A.), *Between: Selected Poems of Agnes Nemes Nagy*, Dedalus Press

◆ ÖRKÉNY (I.), *One Minute Stories*, Corvina

◆ ÖRKÉNY (I.) et al, *The Flower Show and the Toth Family*, W.W. Norton, 1982

◆ TIBOR (D.), *The Portuguese Princess*, Calder, 1967

◆ VAJDA (M.) (ed.), *Modern Hungarian Poetry*, Columbia University Press, 1979

CLASSICAL MUSIC

Béla Bartók

◆ *Allegro Barbaro Sz 49, 3 Rondos Sz 84, 3 Hungarian Folk Tunes Sz 66, Romanian Dances Sz 56, 15 Hungarian Peasant Songs Sz 71*, Zoltán Kocsis (piano).

◆ *Cantata Profana Sz 94, Concerto for orchestra Sz 116*, József Réti (tenor), András Faragó (baritone), Budapest Choir and Symphony Orchestra, János Ferencsik (conductor).

◆ *Concerto for orchestra, Three Village Scenes, Kossuth…* Budapest Festival Orchestra, Iván Fischer (conductor).

◆ *Violin Concerto No.2 Sz 112 (+ Violin Concerto in D* by Igor Stravinsky), Viktoria Mullova (violin), Los Angeles Philharmonic Orchestra, Esa-Pekka Salonen (conductor), 1 CD Philips 456 542-2

◆ *Gyermekeknek (for Children) Vols. 1–IV*, Zoltán Kocsis (piano).

◆ *Complete works for piano and orchestra (3 concertos), Rhapsody Op.1 Sz 27, Scherzo Op.2 Sz 28)*, Zoltán

Kocsis, Budapest Festival Orchestra, Iván Fischer (conductor).
◆ *Complete works by Bartók* performed by the composer, Béla Bartók (piano).
◆ *Kossuth (Symphonic Poem DD75a), Piano Quintet DD77*, Budapest Symphony Orchestra, György Lehel (conductor), Csilla Szabó (piano), Tátrai Quartet.
◆ *Duke Bluebeard's Castle*, Walter Berry (Bluebeard), Christa Ludwig (Judith), London Symphony Orchestra, Kertesz (conductor).
◆ *The Miraculous Mandarin, Hungarian Peasant Songs, Romanian Dances*, Budapest Festival Orchestra, Iván Fischer (conductor).
◆ *The Wooden Prince (complete ballet), Dance Suite*, Iván Fischer (conductor).
◆ *Three Piano Concertos*, Géza Anda (piano), Berlin Radio Symphony Orchestra, Ferenc Fricsay (conductor).
◆ *Mikrokosmos Sz 107, Gyermekeknek (for Children)*, Dezsö Ránki (piano), Sz 42.
◆ *14 Bagatelles Op.6 Sz 38, 2 Elegies Op.8b Sz 41, 6 Romanian Dances Sz 56, Sonatina Sz 55, 3 Hungarian Folk Tunes Sz 66*, Zoltán Kocsis (piano).
◆ *Six String Quartets*, Takács Quartet.
◆ *Sonata for 2 pianos and 2 percussion Sz 110 (+ Andante and 5 Variations K.501 by Mozart; En blanc et noir by Debussy)* M. Argerich and S. Bishop Kovacevich (pianos), W. Goudswaard, M. de Roo (percussion).

Bartók and Kodály

◆ *Cantata Profana* (Bartók), *Psalmus Hungaricus* (Kodály), *Serenade for small orchestra Op.3* (Leo Weiner), Tamas Daroczi (tenor), Alexandre Agache (baritone), Hungarian Radio & Television Choir, Budapest Festival Orchestra, Georg Solti (conductor)
◆ *Háry János Suite, Dances of Galánta, Dances of Marosszék* (Kodály), *Hungarian Sketches, Romanian Dances* (Bartók), Hungarian Philharmonic Orchestra, Antál Dorati (conductor),
◆ *Sonata for unaccompanied violin* (Bartók), *Duo Op.7 for violin and cello* (Kodály), Gérard Poulet (violin), Christoph Henkel (cello),

Zoltán Kodály

◆ *Solo Cello Sonata Op.8, Sonata for cello and piano Op.4*, Miklós Perényi (cello), Jenö Jandó (piano).
◆ *Te Deum of Budavár, Missa Brevis*, Éva Andor (soprano), Márta Szirmay (contralto), József Réti (tenor), József Gregor (bass), Budapest Symphony Orchestra, János Ferencsik (conductor),

Franz (Ferenc) Liszt

◆ *Concerto No.1 in E Flat Major for piano and orchestra, Totentanz, Concerto No.2 in A Major for piano and orchestra, Hungarian Fantasia for piano and orchestra*, György Cziffra (piano), 2 CDs EMI 7 47640 2
◆ *Mephisto Waltz, Jeux d'eaux à la villa d'Este, Valse-Impromptu, Valse-Caprice No.6, St Francis of Paule Walking on the Waves, Chasse-neige, Ricordanza, Gaudeamus Igitur*, György Cziffra (piano.
◆ *Rêve d'amour No.3 in A Flat Major, La Ronde des lutins, St Francis of Assisi Preaching to the Birds, Valse oubliée in F Sharp Major*, György Cziffra.
◆ *Hungarian Rhapsody No.2 for orchestra, Fantasia on Hungarian Folk Melodies for piano and orchestra, Hungarian Rhapsody No. 4 for orchestra, Hungarian Rhapsody No.6 "Pest Carnival" for orchestra, Rákóczi March for orchestra*, Jenö Jandó (piano), Szeged Symphony Orchestra, Tamás Pál (conductor); Hungarian National Orchestra, János Ferencsick (conductor, Gyula Németh (conductor).
◆ Hungarian Rhapsodies György Cziffra (piano).

Sándor Veress

◆ *Homage to Paul Klee, Concerto for piano, strings and percussion, Six Csardas*, András Schiff (piano), Dénes Varjon (piano), Budapest Festival Orchestra, Heinz Holliger (conductor),

CONTEMPORARY MUSIC

◆ *Contemporary Romanian and Hungarian Music* (Cornel Taranu, Máté Hollós, Adrian Borza, László Dubrovay, Péter Szegö), Anonymus Ensemble, Péter Szegö (conductor).

György Ligeti

◆ *Concerto for cello and orchestra, Chamber Concerto for 13 instruments, Concerto for piano and orchestra* Miklós Perényi (cello), Ueli Wiget (piano), Ensemble Modern, Péter Eötvös.
◆ *Chamber Concerto, Ramifications, String Quartet No.2, Adventures, Lux Aeterna, Manning*, Thomas Pearson, Ensemble InterContemporain, Pierre Boulez (conductor), LaSalle Quartet, Hamburg Radio Choir, Franz (conductor).
◆ *Études for piano (1st and 2nd books, part of 3rd book), Musica Ricercata*, Pierre Laurent Aimard.
◆ *String Quartets No.1 "Métamorphoses Nocturnes" and No.2*, Arditti Quartet.
◆ *Horn Trio, Passacaglia ungherrese, Hungarian Rock, Continuum, 3 Pieces (Monument, Selbstporträt, Bewegung)*, Gawriloff, Baumann, Besch, Chojnacka, Ballista, Canino.

György Kurtág

◆ *Jaketok (Games)*, Márta and György Kurtág (piano).
◆ *Music for stringed instruments*, Keller Quartet, Miklós Perényi (cello), György Kurtág (celesta).

TRADITIONAL MUSIC

◆ Ando Drom (Gypsies of Budapest) *Phari Mamo*.
◆ Music from Transylvania *Erdélyi Népzene* (traditional music of Romania's Hungarian minorities).
◆ Muzsikás and Márta Sebestyén *Hazafelé* (traditional Hungarian music).
◆ *Muzsikás Szól a Kakas Már* (Jewish folk music from Transylvania).
◆ FELIX LAJKÓ, *Hetedik*, 2004
◆ BEÁTA PALYA, Ágról-Ágra, Orpheia 2003
◆ PARNO GRASZT, *Rávágok A Zongorára* 2002

JAZZ

◆ Akosh S. Unit *Élettér*.
◆ Seffer (Yochk'o) *Rétrospective*.
◆ Szabo (Gabor) *The Sorcerer*.

◆ LIST OF ILLUSTRATIONS

Abbreviations
KM: Kiscell Museum, Budapest; BHM: Budapest History Museum; HNM: Hungarian National Museum, Budapest; NHD: National Heritage Department; Ph: photograph.
Front cover *Entrance in the Tabán district*, Jakub Warschág © BHM, ph. Tihanyi/ Bakos **Spine** illustration Pierre-Marie Vialat. **Maps:** Édigraphie. Drawings and infomaps © Gallimard **1** Klotild Palaces and Elizabeth Bridge under construction, ph. G. Klösz © KM. **2-3** Boats at the quayside in Pest, ph. G. Klösz © KM. **4-5** Drechsler House, Andrássy út, ph. G. Klösz © id. **6-7** Leopold Bld, ph. G. Klösz © id. **8** Belváros district, ph. G. Klösz © id. **9** View of the Danube and Buda © K. Szelenyi/ Hungarian Pictures. **12** *The Tragedy of Man* © Theater Museum and Institute, Budapest. Drawing Ph. Biard. Silver-gilt fibula, 6th century © BHM. **13** Mary Magdelene Tower © S. Pitamitz. **17** Drawings Cl. Felloni, C. Lachaux. **18** Fishermen on the quayside © K. Szelenyi/Hungarian Pictures. Drawings J. Chevallier, F. Desbordes, P. Robin.**19** Drawing F. Desbordes. **20-21** Drawings J. Chevallier, F. Desbordes, Cl. Felloni **22** Margaret Island © T. Hortobagyi/Hungarian Pictures. **22-23** Drawings J. Chevallier, Cl. Felloni,F. Desbordes, C. Lachaux. **24** The Buda Caves © A. Hasz. **25** Seal of Óbuda © KM. **26** Mosaic paving, Aquincum Museum, Budapest © E. Lessing/ Magnum, Paris. Mithra © Aquincum Museum, Budapest. **27** *Prince Árpád* © National Széchenyi Library, Budapest Silver-gilt fibula, 6th century © BHM. Fragment of an angel © id. **28** Seal of the University of Óbuda, 1438 © RR. *Sigismund of Luxembourg*, Pisanello, parchment/ wood, 1430, Kunsthistorisches Museum, Vienna © Erich Lessing/ Magnum. **29** *Budapest occupied by the Turks*, Hofnagel, engraving, 1617 © J-L. Charmet, Paris. Emblem of Budapest © RR. **30** *Queen Elizabeth of Hungary*, Guyla Benczur, 1899, oil/canvas © HNM, ph. A. Dabasi. *Count Guyla Andrássy*, Guyla Benczur, oil/ canvas © HNM, ph. A. Dabasi. *A call to arms*, poster by R. Bereny, 1919 © J.-L. Charmet. **31** *Congress of Combatants for Peace and Socialism*, 1950, poster © HNM, ph. A. Dabasi. Funeral ceremony (1989) for those who died during the 1956 uprising © P. Korniss. **32** Stove tile showing King Matthias © BHM, ph. B. Tihanyi. Majolica tiles © BHM, ph. B. Tihanyi. *Buda and the Royal Palace*, Michael Wogelmut, wood-block engraving © HNM, ph. B. Képessy. **33** *King Matthias and his court*, manuscript © National Széchenyi Library, Budapest Arms of King Matthias carved in red marble © BHM, ph. B. Tihanyi. Portrait of Matthias Corvinus © J.-L. Charmet. **34** *View of Pest in 1834*, M.-P. Félix, lithograph© BHM, ph.Tihanyi/ Bakos. József Nador, C. Agoston, oil/canvas © BHM, ph.Tihanyi/ Bakos. *Lajos Kossuth in front of the National Museum*, 1847, Franz Weiss, lithograph © HNM, ph. A. Dabasi. **35** *IstvánSzéchenyi during the construction of the Chain Bridge*, K. Sterio, colored engraving © BHM, ph.Tihanyi/ Bakos. *Lajos Kossuth* © HNM, ph. B. Képessy. **36** Statue of Stalin, October 1956 © AFP, Paris. Street scene, Budapest, 1956 © RR. *Zoltán Tildy, Imre Nagy and the Minister of Defense*, November 4, 1956 © AFP, Paris. **37** *János Kadar* © Roger Viollet, Paris. Budapest 1956 © Erich Lessing/ Magnum. *France-Soir*, October 25, 1956 © Roger Viollet, Paris. Cover of *Time*, 1956 © J.-L. Charmet. **38** *King Stephen I with his son Imre* in the *Gesta Hungagorum*, János Thuroczy © J.-L. Charmet. Act of foundation for the Abbey of Tihany © K. Szelenyi/ Hungarian Pictures. Funeral oration, the first text written in Hungarian © id. **39** *Ferenc Kazinczy* © HNM, ph. B. Képessy. Certificate of trading © HNM, ph. B. Képessy. **40** Café © B. Lenormand. **41** Portrait of a gypsy, oil/ canvas © Music History Museum, Budapest, ph. L. Szelenyi. **42** *The Tragedy of Man*, Theater Museum and Institute, Budapest. Vígszínház © id. *Catsplay* © id. **43** *Ferenc Molnár* © Theater Museum and Institute. József-Katona Theater, poster © id. **44** Royal Orfeum, program © Commerce and Catering Museum, Budapest. *Ferenc Lehár* © Theater Museum and Institute. *Offenbach in Hungarian costume* © id. *The Merry Widow*, Király Színház, 1907 © id. *Imre Kálmán* © id. **45** *Róbert Ráthonyi* © Theater Museum and Institute. *Hanna Honthy* © id. **46** Flute player © Music History Museum, Budapest. Fragment of an antiphonary © A. Mudrak/ Hungarian Pictures. Violin and gardon players, © Music History Museum. **47** Pipe and bagpipes © Music History Museum. *Musicians*, Italian School, 1600, oil/canvas © Museum of Fine Arts. Budapest. Musician, stove tile, 15th century © BHM, ph. Tihanyi/Bakos. **48** Gypsy musicians, anonymous, HT/© Ethnographical Museum, Budapest. *Pipe and drum players*, Martin Engelbrecht, colored engravings © Music History Museum, ph. L. Szelenyi. **49** *Ferenc Erkel c. 1870*, Archiv für Kinst und Geschichte, Berlin © AKG, Paris. Baryton © HNM, ph. A. Dabasi. Ferenc Liszt, Miklós Barabás, oil/canvas © HNM, ph. B. Képessy. *Ferenc Liszt giving a recital at the Royal Palace in Buda*, oil/canvas © HNM, ph. B. Képessy. **50** Score for Hungarian folk music © AKG, Paris. Young Romanian recording folk songs © Ethnographical Museum, Budapest. *Zóltan Kodály* © AKG, Paris. **51** *The Székeli Spinning-Room*, opera by Zóltan Kodály © P. Korniss. *Béla Bartók* © RR. *The Miraculous Mandarin*, choreography by Maurice Béjart, 1992 ©C.Masson/Enguerrand. **52** *György and Marta Kurtág* © M. Kalter. **53** *György Cziffra* © M. Kalter. *Sir Georg Solti* © Th. Martineau. *György Ligeti* © M. Kalter. **54** Costume design for *The Wooden Prince* © RR. *The Taming of the Shrew*, choreography by László Seregi © P. Korniss. *The Miraculous Mandarin* © Operaház Fotoarchivum/B. Mezey. **55** Hungarian folk dances © P. Korniss. *Danse du Feu*, choreography by Csaba Horvath © K. Molnár. *Homage to Mary Wigman*, choreography by Yvette Bozsik © RR. **56** *Frigyes Karinthy*, caricature © RR. *At the café (January 1940)*, ph. Jenö Dulovits © courtesy of the Hungarian Museum of Photography, Kecskemét. *Meeting at the Café Pilvax in 1848* © KM. Café table decorated with portraits and signatures © Commerce and Catering Museum, Budapest. **57** Café New York © AKG, Paris. Café New York, menus © Commerce and Catering Museum, Budapest. *Waiters*, Ödön Miklóse, drawing © Commerce and Catering Museum, Budapest. *Frigyes Karinthy*, 1917 © RR. **58** *Snow in Budapest c. 1920*, ph. Rudolf Balogh © courtesy of the Hungarian Museum of Photography, Kecskemét. *Hail in Budapest*, 1928, ph. Károly Escher © id. *The Tabán District*, ph. Iván Vydarény © id. **59** *Buda Hill in the 1970s*, ph. János Reisman © id. *Spring Shower*, 1920, ph. André Kertész © French Ministry of Culture. **60** *Váci út*, 1940, ph. Robert Capa © courtesy of Cornell Capa, New York. *Holy Trinity Square*, ph. Károly Hemzö © courtesy of the Hungarian Museum of Photography, Kecskemét. *Aerial view of Parliament*, ph. Miklós Rév © id. *On Gellért Hill in the 1950s*, ph. Zoltán Zajky © id. *Ruins in Budapest*, 1945, ph. József Pécsi © id. **61** *Elizabeth Bridge*, ph. Miklós Rév © id. **62** Rác Baths, ph. G. Klösz © KM. Chess players at the Széchenyi Baths © Diaf. Király Baths © P. Korniss. **63** Gellért Baths, pool © L. Lugo Lugosi. Gellért Baths © AKG, Paris. Széchenyi Baths © NHD. Lukács Baths © K. Szelenyi/Hungarian Pictures. **64** *Street trader in front of the National Museum*, Henrik Weber, lithograph © HNM, ph. B. Képessy. **65** Recipe © E. Guillemot. **66** Herendt porcelain © K. Szelenyi/ Hungarian Pictures. Advertisement for Gerbeaud chocolate © Commerce and Catering Museum, Budapest. Specialties © Gallimard / ph. E. Guillemot. **67** Drawing Ph. Candé. **68-9** © Gallimard / ph. B. Lenormand. **70-1** Drawings A. Soro. **72-3** Drawings Fr. Brosse, Éditions La Villette. **74-5** Drawings Ch. Rivière. **76-7** Drawings J.-B. Héron, J.-F. Péneau B. Lenormand. **78-9** Drawings J.-S. Roveri. **80-1** Drawings M. Pommier. **82-3** Drawings M. Pommier. **84-5** Drawings Ph. Candé. **86-7** Drawings Cl. Quiec. OTP Bank, renovation © L. Lugo Lugosi. **89** *Entrance in the Tabán district*, Jakub Warschág, oil/canvas © BHM, ph. Tihanyi/ Bakos. **90** *Portrait of the Hun chieftain Buda*, Hungarian School, oil/canvas © HNM, ph. B. Képessy. **91** *Triumph of the Duke of Lorraine on the West Slope of the Castle of Buda*, Heinrich Faust, 1694, oil/canvas © BHM, ph. Tihanyi/Bakos. *Siege of Buda*, Frans Geffels, 1686 © HNM, ph. A. Dabasi. **92-93** *Quays on the Danube at Pest*, Miklós Barabás, watercolors © BHM, ph. Tihanyi/ Bakos. *Budapest from József-hegy*, Antal Ligeti, 1884, oil/canvas © BHM ph. Tihanyi/ Bakos.**94** *Kálvin tér*, Pest, József Molnár, oil/canvas © BHM, ph. Tihanyi/ Bakos. *Holy Trinity Square*, Albert Schickedanz, oil/canvas © BHM, ph. Tihanyi/Bakos. **95** *Ferenciek tere*, Josef Kuwasseg and Frederick Martens,

◆ LIST OF ILLUSTRATIONS

187 Margaret Bridge © KM. János Arany © RR. **188** *Saint Margaret*, Christian Museum, Esztergom © K. Szelenyi/Hungarian Pictures. Margaret Island, the lake © id. Palatinaus Baths © CNMH, ph. E. Revault. The water tower © P. Korniss. **189** The Royal Palace, Buda © S. Piamitz. **190** Buda, detail of cannon © P. Korniss.**191** *The Mongols invading Hungary* in the *Gesta Hungagorum*, János Thuroczy © J.-L. Charmet. View from the Royal Palace © NHD. **192** Hooded prophet © BHM, ph. A. Bakos. Glass goblet © BHM, ph. A. Bakos. Hooded knight © BHM,ph.Tihany/Bakos. **192-193** Fresco, detail © BHM, ph. A. Bakos. **193** Dragon, fragment of a stove tile © BHM, ph. A. Bakos. Saint Paul the Hermit © BHM, ph. A. Bakos.Apostle © BHM, ph.Tihany/Bakos. Women's heads © BHM, ph. A. Bakos. **194** *Saint Stephen*, carved wood statue © Hungarian National Gallery, ph. T. Mester. *Head of a king of Kalocsá*, red marble © id. The Visitation, the Master M.S. oil/wood © id. **195** *The Crucifixion*, anonymous, oil/wood © id. *The Sibiu Angelus*, anonymous, oil/wood © id. *Saint Dorothy of Bárka*, carved wood statue © id. **196** *Déjeuner sur l'herbe*, Pál Szinyei Merse, 1873, oil/canvas © id. *October*, Károly Ferenczy, 1903, oil/canvas © id. *Portrait of a Woman*, István Zádor, 1910, oil/canvas © id. **197** *Woman in white-spotted dress*, József Rippl-Rónai, 1889, oil/canvas © id. *Woman with birdcage*, József Rippl-Rónai, 1889, oil/canvas © id. *Self-portrait*, Tivadar Csontváry Kosztka, 1896– 1902, oil/canvas © id. **198** Matthias Fountain © Csaba/ Hungarian Pictures. Terrace of the Royal Palace © K. Szelenyi/ Hungarian Pictures.**199** *Louis the Great*, Hungarian manuscript, National Széchenyi Library © J.-L. Charmet. Royal Chapel, Budapest History Museum © P. Korniss. **200** Úri utca © T. Hortobagyi/Hungarian Pictures. St George's Square © S. Pitamitz. **201** Details of façades © P. Korniss (1, 2, 3, 6, 8, 9, 10, 11, 12); Budapest Tourist Office (4, 13); S. Pitamitz (5, 7). **202** Matthias Church, roof detail © S. Pitamitz. Holy Trinity Square, drawing Ph. Biard. Statue of Pallas Athene © K. Szelenyi/ Hungarian Pictures. **203** Coat of arms of King Matthias, Matthias Church © A. Hasz. Detail of Mary Portal, Matthias Church © P. Korniss. **204** Music History Museum © T. Hortobagyi/ Hungarian Pictures. Fishermen's Bastion © Tourist Office. Táncsics Mihály utca © NHD. **205** Drawing Ph. Biard. Mary Magdelene Tower © S. Pitamitz. **206** Buda Castle Funicular © RR. French Institute © NHD. Interior of St Anne's Church © NHD. **207** Lajos Batthyány © HNM, ph. B. Képessy. St Anne's Church © K. Szelenyi/ Hungarian Pictures. **208-209** Drawing A. Soro, photos B. Lenormand © Gallimard. **210** Lukács Baths © P. Korniss. Gül Baba utca © T. Hortobagyi/ Hungarian Pictures. Tomb of Gül Baba © C. Gabler/ Hungarian Pictures. **211** Szent Antal templom, Pasaréti út © NHD. Pasaréti út © id. **212** Városmajor Parish Church © NHD. **213** *Krisztinaváros c. 1840*, anonymous, oil/canvas © BHM, ph. Tihanyi/ Bakos. *Count István Széchenyi*, oil/canvas © K. Szelenyi/ Hungarian Pictures. **214** Tabán Parish Church © NHD. *Tabán c. 1910*, ph. Mór Erdelyi © KM. **215** Gellért Hill, drawing Ph. Biard. Inn sign, The Golden Stag restaurant © NHD. **216** Liberation Monument © RR. Hotel Gellért, drawing Ph. Biard. **217** Hotel Gellért © S. Pitamitz. Hotel Gellért © T. Hortobagyi/ Hungarian Pictures. St Imre of the Cistercians © K. Szelenyi/ Hungarian Pictures. **218** János Hill chairlift © K. Szelenyi/ Hungarian Pictures. Cog Railway, ph. G. Klösz © BHM. **219** Óbuda © T. Hortobagyi/ Hungarian Pictures. **221** Mosaic, Hercules Villa, Aquincum Museum © E. Lessing/ Magnum. Military Town Amphitheater © K. Szelenyi/Hungarian Pictures. **222** *Gyula Krúdy* © RR. Óbuda synagogue © A. Frankl. Church of SS Peter and Paul © T. Hortobagyi/ Hungarian Pictures.**223** Porch of the Kiscell Museum © T. Hortobagyi/ Hungarian Pictures. **224** 'Ballot box'. Locksmith's sign. Artist's installation © BHM, ph. Tihany/Bakos.**225** *Encounter in a Cemetery*, István Farkas, oil/canvas © id. *At the Theater*, Pál C. Molnár, drawing © id. *Girl Icon*, Lajos Vajda, oil/canvas © id. Statues from the Holy Trinity Column © id. **226** Óbuda, Fö tér © NHD. Op Art, Victor Vasarely © Vasarely Museum, Budapest. **227** Collage and photomontage, Lajos Kassák © Kassák Memorial Museum. Aquincum, baths © T. Hortobagyi/ Hungarian Pictures. **228** Fresco, detail of an archer, Aquincum Museum © BHM. Marble bas-relief © Tourist Office. Water organ, Aquincum Museum © BHM. Statue of a goddess, Aquincum Museum © P. Korniss. Statue of Nemesis, Aquincum Museum © K. Szelenyi/ Hungarian Pictures. **229** Szentendre © P. Korniss. **230** The Danube Bend © L. Köteles/ Hungarian Pictures. Roman tombstone © P. Korniss. **231** Art gallery, Szentendre © L. Lugo Lugosi. **232** Serbian cross © P. Korniss. Main square, Szentendre © L. Köteles/ Hungarian Pictures. **233** The Ráby House © P. Korniss. **234** Belgrade Church, interior © P. Korniss. Vác © Hungarian Pictures. **235** Open-air Village museum © P. Korniss. **236** The ruined palace of King Matthias, Visegrád © P. Korniss. *Visegrád*, Marko Károly the Elder, oil/canvas © Hungarian National Gallery, ph. T. Mester. **237** Lion Fountain, detail © P. Korniss. Lion Fountain © A. Mudrak/ Hungarian Pictures. **238** Esztergom © A. Mudrak/ Hungarian Pictures. The Basilica of Esztergom © P. Korniss. Chapel of the Royal Palace, Esztergom © A. Mudrak/Hungarian Pictures. **239** Víziváros Parish Church, Esztergom © A. Mudrak/Hungarian Pictures. **240** The royal family at Gödöllö Palace, lithograph © HNM. The tower, Gödöllö Palace © T. Hortobagyi/ Hungarian Pictures. Statue of Queen Elizabeth © id.

With thanks to:
Photographers: Peter Korniss, László Lugo Lugosi, Károly Szelenyi/ Hungarian Pictures, Aliona Frankl, Sergio Pitamitz. The Hungarian Museum of Photography, Kecskemét: Magdolna Kolta, Károly Kincskes. **The Kiscell Museum**: Judit Faryné Szaltatnyay, photographer. **The Budapest History Museum**: Bence Tihany, Agnès Bakos, photographers. **The Hungarian National Museum**: Bence Képessy, András Dabasi, photographers. **The Museum of Applied Arts**: Agnès Kolozs, photographer. **The National Heritage Department**: Ibolya Plank, photographic archives. **The Franz Liszt Museum and Research Center**: Maria Echardt, conservator. **The Theater Museum and Institute. The Commerce and Catering Museum. The Kassák Memorial Museum. Budapest Tourist Office**: Anita Obrofta.

Acknowledgments for the literary section:
Rupert Crew Ltd: Excerpt from *The Wandering Years*, Diaries 1922–39 by Sir Cecil Beaton (Weidenfeld, 1961). Reproduced in the UK and US by permission of The Literary Trustees of the Late Sir Cecil Beaton and Rupert Crew Limited.
Fourth Estate Ltd: Excerpt from *The Man Who Loved Only Numbers* by Paul Hoffman, copyright © Paul Hoffman, 1998. Reproduced in the UK by permission of Fourth Estate Ltd. Published in the USA by Hyperion.
Harvill Press: Excerpt from *Danube* by Claudio Magris, copyright © Garzanti editore s.p.a., 1986. Translation copyright © Harvill and Farrar, Straus & Giroux, 1989.
John Murray (Publishers) Ltd:
Excerpt from *A Time of Gifts* by Patrick Leigh Fermor, copyright © Patrick Leigh Fermor, 1977. Reprinted in the UK and US by permission of John Murray (Publishers) Ltd.
Penguin Books Ltd: Excerpt from *The Wrong Story in Fifty Years of Europe: An Album* by Jan Morris, 1998. Reproduced in the UK by permission of Penguin Books Ltd.
Peters Fraser & Dunlop: Excerpt from *Arrow in the Blue* (Vol.2), by Arthur Koestler (Collins with Hamish Hamilton, 1954). Reprinted in the UK and US by permission of Peters Fraser & Dunlop.
RANDOM HOUSE, INC./ ALFRED A KNOPF: Excerpt from *Memoirs* by Georg Solti, copyright © Music Productions, Inc., 1997. Reproduced in the US by permission of Alfred A.Knopf, a Division of Random House, Inc. Published in the UK by Chatto and Windus.

We have been unable to locate the copyright holders and authors of certain documents before going to print. We will, however, acknowledge these sources in the next editions if and when we are made aware of their identity. We do apologize for this.

◆ INDEX

◆ SUBWAY MAP

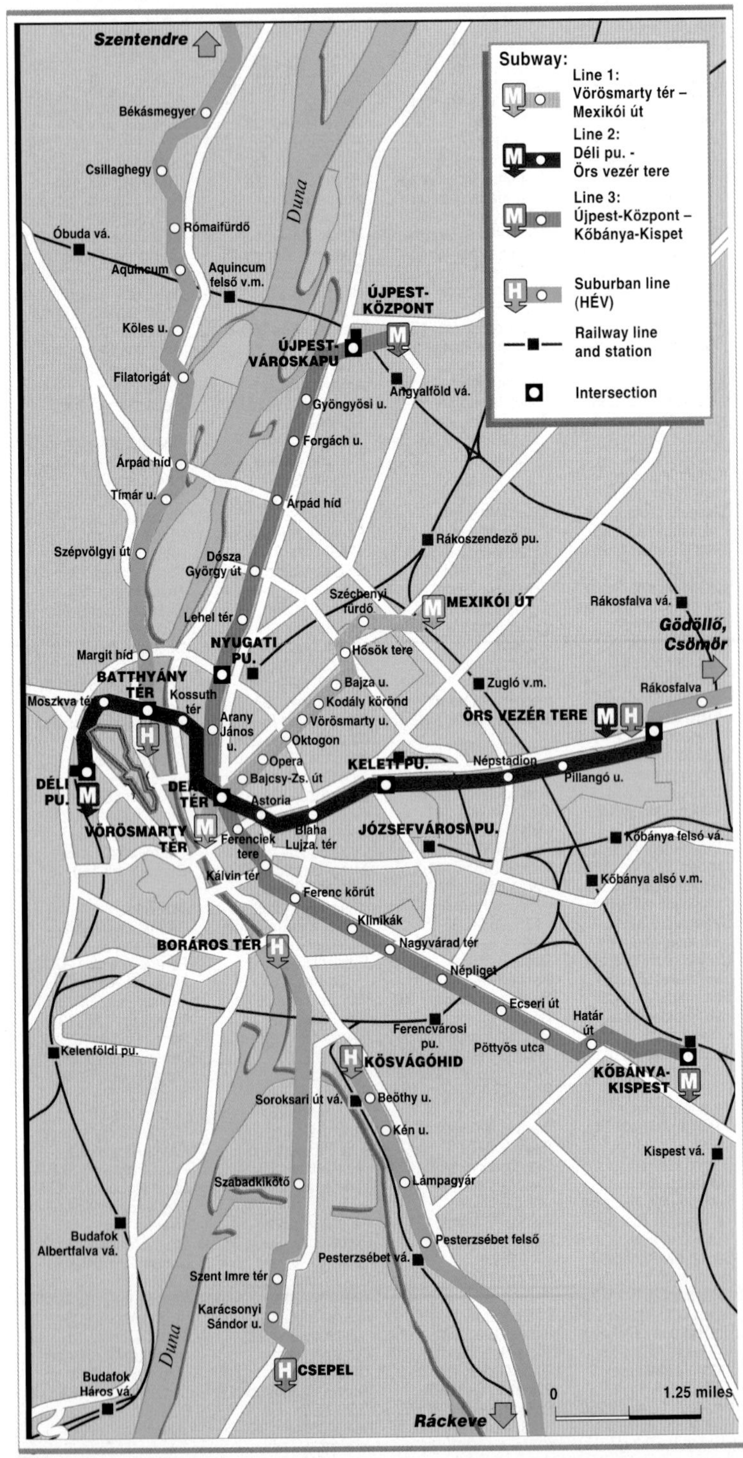
Subway:
Line 1: Vörösmarty tér – Mexikói út
Line 2: Déli pu. - Örs vezér tere
Line 3: Újpest-Központ – Kőbánya-Kispet
Suburban line (HÉV)
Railway line and station
Intersection
Szentendre
Békásmegyer
Csillaghegy
Rómaifürdő
Óbuda vá.
Aquincum
Aquincum felső v.m.
Duna
ÚJPEST-KÖZPONT
ÚJPEST-VÁROSKAPU
Köles u.
Filatorigát
Angyalföld vá.
Gyöngyösi u.
Forgách u.
Árpád híd
Tímár u.
Árpád híd
Rákoszendező pu.
Szépvölgyi út
Dósza György út
Széchenyi fürdő
MEXIKÓI ÚT
Rákosfalva vá.
Lehel tér
Gödöllő, Csömör
NYUGATI PU.
Hősök tere
Margit híd
BATTHYÁNY TÉR
Bajza u.
Zugló v.m.
Rákosfalva
Moszkva tér
Kossuth tér
Kodály körönd
Arany János u.
Vörösmarty u.
ÖRS VEZÉR TERE
Oktogon
Opera
KELETI PU.
Népstadion
DÉLI PU.
Bajcsy-Zs. út
Pillangó u.
DEÁK TÉR
Astoria
VÖRÖSMARTY TÉR
Ferenciek tere
Blaha Lujza. tér
JÓZSEFVÁROSI PU.
Kőbánya felső vá.
Kálvin tér
Kőbánya alsó v.m.
Ferenc körút
Klinikák
Nagyvárad tér
BORÁROS TÉR
Népliget
Ecseri út
Határ út
Ferencvárosi pu.
Pöttyös utca
Kelenföldi pu.
KŐSVÁGÓHID
KŐBÁNYA-KISPEST
Soroksari út vá.
Beöthy u.
Kén u.
Kispest vá.
Szabadkikötő
Lámpagyár
Budafok Albertfalva vá.
Pesterzsébet felső
Pesterzsébet vá.
Szent Imre tér
Karácsonyi Sándor u.
Duna
CSEPEL
Budafok Háros vá.
0
1.25 miles
Ráckeve

NOTES

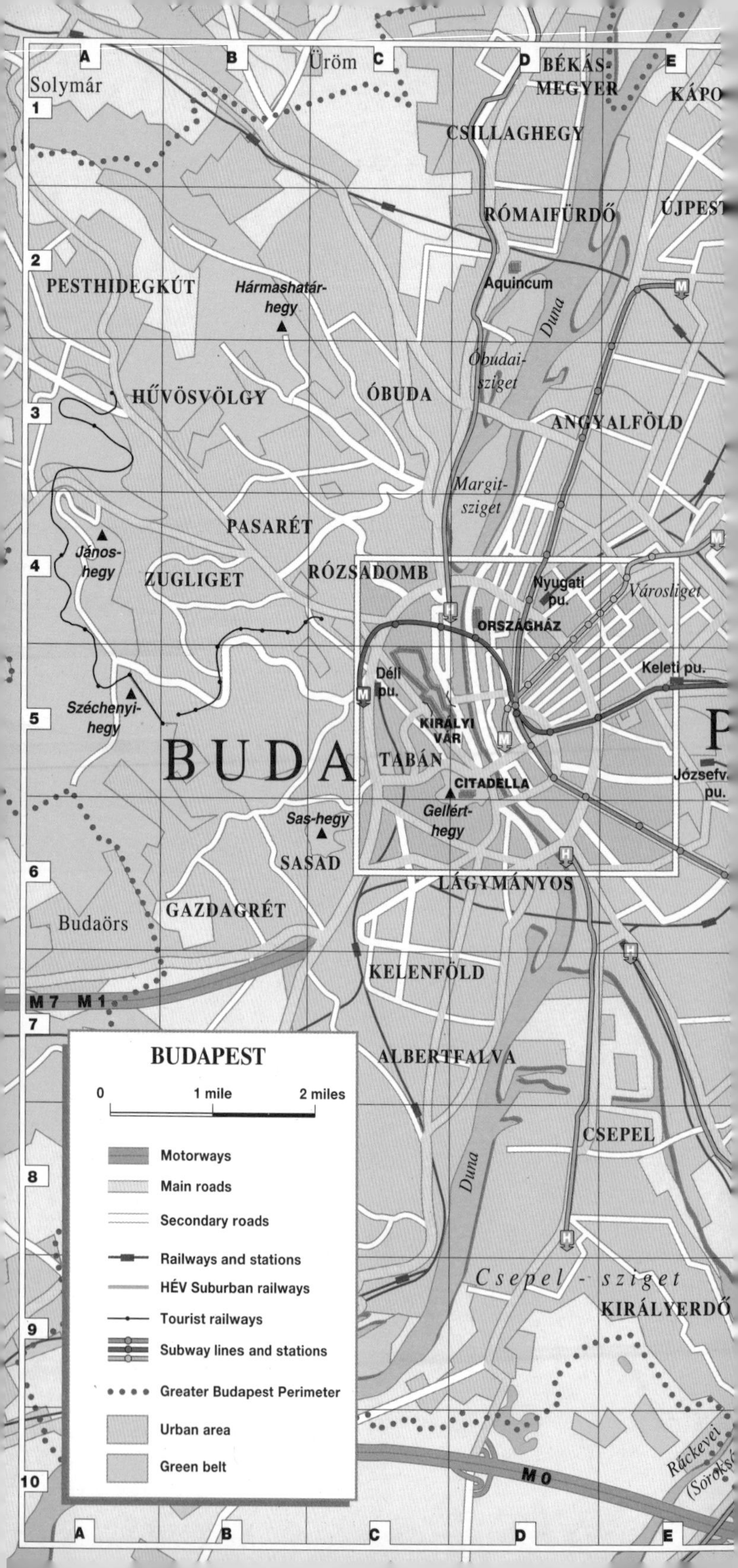

BUDAPEST
0
1 mile
2 miles
Motorways
Main roads
Secondary roads
Railways and stations
HÉV Suburban railways
Tourist railways
Subway lines and stations
Greater Budapest Perimeter
Urban area
Green belt
Solymár
Üröm
BÉKÁS-MEGYER
CSILLAGHEGY
RÓMAIFÜRDŐ
Aquincum
PESTHIDEGKÚT
Hármashatár-hegy
Óbudai-sziget
HŰVÖSVÖLGY
ÓBUDA
ANGYALFÖLD
Margit-sziget
PASARÉT
János-hegy
ZUGLIGET
RÓZSADOMB
Nyugati pu.
Városliget
ORSZÁGHÁZ
Déli pu.
Keleti pu.
Széchenyi-hegy
KIRÁLYI VÁR
BUDA
TABÁN
CITADELLA
Gellért-hegy
Sas-hegy
SASAD
LÁGYMÁNYOS
Budaörs
GAZDAGRÉT
KELENFÖLD
M7 M1
ALBERTFALVA
CSEPEL
Duna
Csepel - sziget
KIRÁLYERDŐ
M0
Ráckevei